to
Patrick Wilshere
(who does not need it!)
with best wishes
Serge Entov

Introducing Ireland

A serious visitor's guide with biographies
of over 700 leaders

by

GEORGE EATON

THE MERCIER PRESS

The Mercier Press Ltd
P.O. Box No. 5, 5 French Church Street, Cork
24 Lower Abbey Street, Dublin 1

© George Eaton FCA 1989, 1992

A CIP catalogue record for this book
is available from the British Library

ISBN 0-85342-996-0

First published 1989
Revised and enlarged edition 1992

To My Mother

Printed in Ireland by Colour Books Ltd.

Contents

Preface

In writing this second edition of *Introducing Ireland* I have again tried to provide for the needs of the serious visitor, whether coming to take up a post in diplomacy, education, industry or commerce. I have tried also to cater for residents who may be charged with introducing such visitors to our island.

Except where specifically requested to do so, private residential addresses or telephone numbers are not given for security reasons, distinguishing this work from others in a way which is, perhaps, a sad commentary on the progress of civilization.

I am indebted to all those who contributed biographical information, much of which is provided for the first time.

Although every effort has been made to keep the information up to date in a fast-changing scene, it is inevitable that some changes will have occurred after the beginning of the printing process and, alas, some information may well be received too late for inclusion.

George Eaton
Charlemont Place,
Dublin 2
13 November 1991

Acknowledgments

In the course of writing this work I received help and encouragement from a great many people in all walks of life, from many official bodies, companies and organisations, in the Republic of Ireland, and in Northern Ireland, and I sincerely thank them for it.

I am especially grateful to Eilish Quigley for her dogged attention to the detailed preparation of the text without which this book would never have gone to press.

I would also like to thank Paddy Farrell of the *Irish Independent* Photographic Department and photographers Jim O'Kelly, Tom Burke, Tom Conachy, Brian Farrell and Matt Walsh. Also to those others who supplied photographs, especially IDB, ICA, Bord na Móna, RNLI, CERT, US Chamber of Commerce, Lensmen, Derek Speirs/Report, Bord Fáilte, Independent Newspapers, Pacemaker, RTE, Aer Lingus, Waterford Glass, and Mitchelstown Co-operative Agricultural Society.

Not forgetting Patrick Doris of Belfast, John Spillane and Emer Ryan of Mercier Press, Jim Aughney of the *Irish Independent*, Lt Gen. Tadhg O'Neill, P.J. Fahy, and Michael Quinn who encouraged the work, and Captain Tom Ahern, Superintendent Denis Mullins and Inspector Paddy Murray, who enhanced the flow of information.

Chapter 1
Finding Focus

I appeal to all Irishmen to pause, to stretch out the hand of forgiveness and conciliation, to forgive and forget and to join in making for the land which they love a new era of peace, contentment and goodwill.

King George V
Belfast 1921

Take the Universe

We Irish have no problem with the Universe. We conceive it to be an area so vast as to be almost beyond comprehension — an area where there is plenty of space for the planets to move around in their own well-ordained and particular ways.

Take the World

We Irish are at peace with the world. Again, it is a vast place and as far as we know, it has room to spare for the hundreds of millions of Americans and hundreds of millions of Chinese and, indeed, hundreds of millions of other nationalities with whom we have little contact, all of these hundreds of millions of people going about their daily business without impinging too much on our national consciousness and without allowing us to impinge too much on theirs.

Take Ireland

Take this island off the North West of Europe inhabited by about one per cent of Europe's population. It is complex and divided. It seethes with passion. It is fractious. Sometimes it seems that only a great event, like the visit of a reigning Pope, can bring about a unity of purpose, and even such a visit can bring about unity in one part of the island only. Settlers have come to Ireland for more than 5,000 years, and each group of settlers has contributed something to the evolution and enrichment of Irishness. The value of these contributions was appreciated by the Young Ireland Movement of the 1840s, who had a concept of nationalism which would 'embrace Protestant, Catholic and Dissenter — Milesian and Cromwellian — the Irishman of a hundred generations and the stranger who is within our gates'.

9

It was this movement which introduced the flag, known as the Irish Tricolour, inspired by the French Tricolour of 1848. When Meagher presented it, he explained that the white in the centre defined a lasting truce between Orange and Green and trusted 'that beneath its folds the hands of the Irish Protestant and the Irish Catholic may be clasped in generous and heroic brotherhood'.

The white in the centre may signify peace. The design of the flag effectively means that the green is at one extreme and the orange at the other. To this extent the design is faulty. To suggest an even distribution of green and orange polka dots on a white background, however, would probably be considered by many to be irreverent, although it would convey the idea of the integration of the two communities so deeply desired by so many. The flag may be flown in Northern Ireland also but, as Northern Ireland is part of the United Kingdom, the official flag for that territory is the Union Jack.

The complexity of the island begins with its division into Northern Ireland and the Republic of Ireland. The name of the State is, according to the Constitution of Ireland, 'Éire or in the English language Ireland', in other words the name of the island, Ireland, is also the name of that part of the island which is not part of the United Kingdom. The Republic of Ireland Act 1948 provides that the name of the State 'shall be the Republic of Ireland'. In spite of this law being more recent by eleven years than the Constitution, the preferred usage by Government is the constitutional one.

In this way the President is known as the President of Ireland, the Government is the Government of Ireland, the Ambassadors are Ambassadors to Ireland, even though most of them are not Ambassadors to that part of Ireland which forms part of the United Kingdom! Irish and English are the official languages of the Republic but, while Irish has great cultural value, its importance in the political and economic life of the country has been in steady decline and, in fact, it could, perhaps, be said that its usage in political life is merely symbolic while its usage in economic life is virtually nil.

The purpose of this book is to introduce Ireland to the visitor and to help those charged with making such an introduction — an unenviable task, indeed.

Lady President

Her Excellency Mrs Mary Robinson (right) was elected Uachtarán na hÉireann — President of Ireland — in November 1990 for a seven-year term. The Constitution permits the maximum of two seven-year terms only. Seen with the President above is Monica Prendiville, National President of the Irish Countrywomen's Association.

IRELAND AS WE SEE OURSELVES

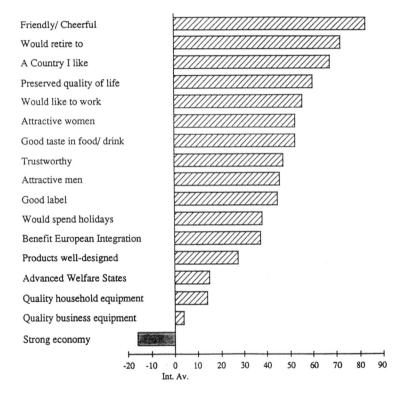

(Reproduced by permission of
Lansdowne Market Research and the *Sunday Press* .)

IRELAND AS OTHERS SEE US

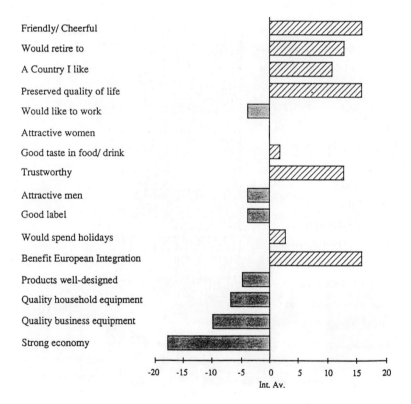

(Reproduced by permission of
Lansdowne Market Research and the *Sunday Press*.)

Man of Peace
Gordon Wilson of Enniskillen with his niece, Heather Sheane of Limerick, and the Tipperary Peace Prize which he received in March 1988.

Chapter 2
Above Politics

The condition upon which God hath given liberty to man is eternal vigilance; which condition if he break, servitude is at once the consequence of his crime, and the punishment of his guilt

John Philpot Curran

The visitor coming from afar may well presume that the Irish are rather like the English. If the visitor is Brazilian or Chinese, for example, the Irish in general will appear to be a tall fair race and this may induce the presumption of similarity.

Whenever possible, the visitor should attend a wedding, a christening or a funeral. Most people would think the wedding best for enjoyment, but there are more than a few Irish people who consider a good funeral better than a good wedding, probably because in spite of the basically sad reason for the gathering, funerals or the assemblies that follow them are less structured and, because of the short notice period, much more informal.

Preconceptions about the Irish being rather like the English should be dumped as early as possible and the dumping should be simple. It can be pointed out, for example, that the average Englishman manicures his lawn and washes his car on Sunday whereas the average Irishman has a few drinks before reading the papers and going to the football match. Or the English worship their Queen while the Irish, by and large, take their President for granted.

Unlike the English, the Irish have a written constitution adopted by Referendum in 1937. The Constitution lays down the method of election and terms of reference of the President, defines the system of courts and the system of appointment of judges. The fundamental rights of the citizen are also outlined in the Constitution and these fall into five broad headings, personal, family, educational, property and religious. The personal rights include freedom of speech, freedom from class discrimination, and freedom of religion. Family rights include the protection of the family and of the institution of marriage. Educational rights include an undertaking for the provision of free primary-level education, and there is a guarantee of the right to hold private property subject to the common good.

In this parliamentary democracy, the National Parliament, or Oireachtas, consists of the President (Uachtarán) with two Houses: the Representatives (Dáil Éireann) and the Senators (Seanad Éireann). Any citizen over the age of thirty-five can stand for election as President by direct vote of the people. The term is seven years and one re-election only is permitted. The President is Head of State and the Guardian of the Constitution. There is no Vice-President of Ireland but the President can be advised by a Council of State. Membership of the Council is defined by the Constitution and includes the Prime Minister (Taoiseach) and former prime ministers, judges and some others.

MARY ROBINSON AS PRESIDENT

DISSATISFIED
15%

UNDECIDED
11%

SATISFIED
74%

Q: Are you satisfied or dissatisfied with the way Mary Robinson is doing her job as President of the Country?

Satisfaction with new President
(Reproduced by permission of
Lansdowne Market Research and the *Sunday Press*.)

The life of the President is remarkably low-key, and she acts normally on the 'advice' of the Government. Governments are not prone to sharing limelight unnecessarily with presidents who, of course, take precedence over ministers and even prime ministers. Similarly the deliberations of the Council of State are extremely low-key and rarely, if ever, become a subject of media or popular interest. In February 1991 President Robinson's seven appointments to the Council of State were announced. They were Ms Monica Barnes TD, a front bench spokesperson on marine and urban affairs, Professor Emer Colleran, Associate Professor of Microbiology at UCG, Mr Quintin Oliver from Belfast, Director of the Northern Ireland Council for Voluntary Action, Ms Patricia O'Donovan, a Barrister and Assistant General Secretary of ICTU, Ms Rosemarie Smith, Chairperson of the Farm Family Committee of the Irish Farmers' Association, Mr Dónal Toolan, a freelance Journalist who is confined to a wheelchair and Dr T. Kenneth Whitaker a native of Co. Down who is Chancellor of the National University of Ireland. The ex-officio members of the Council are the Taoiseach Mr Haughey, the Tánaiste Mr Wilson, the Attorney General Mr Harold Whelahan, former Taoisigh Mr Liam Cosgrave, Dr Garret FitzGerald and Mr Jack Lynch, the Chief Justice Mr Thomas Finlay, the President of the High Court Mr Liam Hamilton, the former Chief Justice Mr T.F. O'Higgins, the Cathaoirleach of the Senate Mr Seán Doherty and the Ceann Comhairle of the Dáil Mr Seán Treacy.

Young people between the ages of fifteen and twenty-five who set and achieve some demanding challenge of themselves, may be presented with a *Gaisce* (feat) or President's award. The Gaisce Organisation also arranges special events for young people, such as a West of Ireland Cycling Tour. Cycling is also a part of the annual programme of Co-operation North. Their idea is an annual maracycle in which thousands of enthusiasts complete the 206 mile journey between Belfast and Dublin.

Co-operation North is an organisation truly above politics. It was formed in the late 1970s, when a group of leaders in business and academic life, in the trade unions and professional bodies and in voluntary organisations came together with a view to taking action to build mutual respect and understanding through practical co-operation in the economic, social and cultural spheres with no political strings attached.

Finance for Co-operation North was provided initially by AIB Bank, Bank of Ireland, P.J. Carroll, Northern Bank and Ulster Bank. These companies have been joined by many others since the early days and several organisations have seconded executive staff in order to augment human resources. Overseas support has also been forthcoming notably from the EC Commission, from Co-operation Ireland Inc in the United States and Co-operation Ireland in London. Since 1982 the Irish and UK Governments have made matching grants to Co-operation North to assist with its projects.

The organisation walks a political tight rope with great success and great probity. Given the inevitable suspicion that must be aroused in the minds of many Northern Irelanders towards any organisation working on North-South lines, given that half the British people are said to want their troops out of Northern Ireland and only a quarter of them want Northern Ireland to remain within the United Kingdom, and given also that three-quarters of the British people object to Northern Ireland receiving more subsidies than any other part of the United Kingdom, the great difficulties that surround their work can be appreciated.

Another organisation whose activities straddle the border is the International Fund for Ireland, a well-endowed international organisation established by the British and Irish Governments. Major grantors to the fund include the United States, Canada and New Zealand. The United States authorised grants of $120 million over a three-year period, which gives some idea of the resources available to the fund. The European Commission sanctioned donations over a three-year period which started in 1989.

The Irish Association for Cultural, Economic & Social Relations was founded in 1938. It is non-secterian and non-political and its task is to make reason and goodwill take the place of passion and prejudice in the relationship between North and South. It aims to foster through the initiative of individual members, more neighbourly relations between those Irish people who differ from each other in politics and religion.

Ireland Fund

Josephine Hart-Saatchi, Chairman of the Ireland Fund of Great Britain, presenting the Ireland Fund award to Northern Secretary Peter Brooke at the Fund's Midsummer Night's Ball in June 1991. Also in the picture is Dr A.J.F. O'Reilly, Chairman of the Ireland Fund.

Examples of the opposite sentiments to those fostered by Co-operation North are sadly common-place. The Millennium Invitation sent from Dublin to Belfast is one example. 1988, as is well known, was the year in which Dublin decided to celebrate one thousand years of its history, and was seen by fair-minded people everywhere as a fairly harmless excuse for a party which would boost business in the City. An invitation from the Lord Mayor of Dublin to the Lord Mayor of Belfast to attend a function in Dublin, at which he would receive a replica viking gold ring, was considered by the General Purposes and Finance Committee of Belfast's Council, where it was frowned upon by nine votes to one, and later considered at the monthly Council meeting where it was rejected by twenty-four votes to eighteen.

The Experiment in International Living, which functions in Ireland, has been conducting a variety of inter-cultural exchange programmes for over half a century. This organisation was built up on the premise that the best way 'to immerse oneself in a new culture is to become a member of the basic social unit of that culture — a family'. The Irish branch, with offices at Cork and Bray, provided hosting in 1990 for 166 students of the US-based Beaver College Centre for Education Abroad, as well as introducing new programmes which featured, for example, a group of seven young Irish people attending a French Lycée for three months, a young worker exchange programme with the Algarve region of Portugal, and a group of five Mexicans attending an Irish secondary school.

The Irish Peace Institute, based at the University of Limerick, and the Centre for International Co-operation based at Shannon Airport, are non-governmental associate organisations which have as their primary objectives, the promotion of peace and international co-operation. In the short number of years since they have been established, they have seen 20 students successfully complete MA courses in peace studies; 30 students successfully complete the Effective Manager course of the Open University especially designed for people working in the field of reconciliation in Ireland (North and South); five major international peace building conferences organised together with six international youth conferences under the title 'young people together'; hosted meetings in Ireland of other international peace building organisations; and fostered the formation of the Ireland-Estonia co-operation progamme.

Innocent Victims
When the mourners were attacked at a funeral in Milltown Cemetery, Belfast, in March 1988, Thomas McErlean was one of those killed. His widow, Ann, aged nineteen and mother of two, was four months pregnant at the time. Mr McErlean was buried a few hundred yards from where he was killed. His mother asked that there be no retaliation.

There is no national honours system in the Republic and one wonders if at this point in time the political leaders have enough maturity to establish such a system on a sufficiently high professional basis to prevent the honours being devalued. Difficulties encountered in connection with the National Day of Commemoration to honour the country's dead would certainly not lead to any confidence in our ability to institute a system which would honour the living. Northern Ireland is within the British honours system, and in both parts of the island, universities regularly confer honorary degrees on great achievers of Irish and other nationalities, and many other insitutions admit the meritorious to honorary membership. The British system has no fewer than 250 different honours, some of which are granted 'for political services' which in most cases means service to the Government party. Oustide the system, hereditary titles are, from time to time, sold at public auction, a practice which many foreigners find totally incomprehensible. The auctions are normally held in London, and provide the vain with the opportunity to become an Irish Lord, by cheque rather than by birth.

The National Day of Commemoration is held in mid-July at the Royal Hospital Kilmainham and is attended by the President, the Taoiseach, several members of the Cabinet, of the Council of State, members of the Diplomatic Corps, relatives of the veterans of the War of Independence, former British Service personnel, and families of Irish soldiers killed while on service with the United Nations. The Ceremony is in two parts — a civil wreath-laying and an inter-denominational religious service. Although the occasion is decidely national and not municipal, civic representation is always at the highest level (President and Taoiseach) but some religious denominations fail to send top national figures, and some of them fail even to send top municipal figures.

INTRODUCING IRELAND

SIR CHARLES E.B. BRETT
Solicitor
Belfast
Born to Charles Anthony and Elizabeth Joyce Brett (née Carter) on 30 October 1928. Educated at Rugby School and New College, Oxford. Qualified as solicitor. Married to Joyce Patricia Worley with three sons. Formerly journalist, *Radiodiffusion Française* and *Continental Daily Mail*. Member Child Welfare Council of Northern Ireland, Northern Ireland Committee and Council of National Trust and chairman Northern Ireland Labour Party, Ulster Architectural Heritage Society, Northern Ireland Housing Executive and International Fund for Ireland. At present partner L'Estrange and Brett, Solicitors, and chairman HEARTH Housing Association and Revolving Fund. Knighted 1990. Honorary member Royal Society of Ulster Architects, Royal Institute of Architects in Ireland, and honorary fellow Royal Institute of British Architects. Publications include *Buildings of Belfast 1700–1914*, *Court Houses and Market Houses of Ulster*, *Long Shadows Cast Before*, *Housing a Divided Community*, and lists and surveys for Ulster Architectural Heritage Society, National Trusts of Guernsey and Jersey and Alderney Society.

MÁIRÉAD CORRIGAN MAGUIRE
Voluntary Worker
224 Lisburn Road, Belfast BT9 6GE
663465
Aunt of the three Maguire children whose deaths, when they were struck by a gunman's getaway car, led to the formation of the Community of the Peace People. Within weeks of its foundation, more than 100,000 people, many of them women, had marched in rallies led by Máiréad, Betty Williams, and Ciarán McKeown in Belfast, Derry, London, Dublin and other places — all demanding an end to the violence. Prior to her work with the Peace People, worked as a private secretary to the managing director of a major Northern Ireland firm. Also volunteered as Belfast director of the Legion of Mary, where she began her work with prisons and prisoners. Is the co-founder of the Committee for the Administration of Justice. Recipient of numerous honours and awards, including the Norwegian People's Prize, an honorary doctorate from Yale University, and special prizes from Trinity College (DC), St. Michael's College (VT), the College of New Rochelle (NY), and several others.Was a special honouree of the UN 'Women of Achievement' programme in 1978, and of the American Academy of Achievement. In September 1981, was married to Jackie Maguire, widower of her sister Anne, who never recovered from the loss of her children and died in 1979. In addition to the remaining children from the earlier marriage — Mark, Joanne, and Mary Louise —Máiréad and Jackie are parents of John Francis, born 1982 and Luke, born 1984.

23

DR GARRET FitzGERALD

Former Taoiseach and Public Representative
Dáil Éireann, Dublin 2
(01) 680830

Born to Desmond and Mabel FitzGerald (née McConnell) at Dublin in 1926. Educated in an Irish-speaking college in Co. Waterford, at Belvedere College and UCD whence he graduated with a first class honours degree in History, French and Spanish. Later admitted to membership of the Irish Bar and Institute of Transport and awarded a PhD in Economics. Married to Joan O'Farrell with two sons and one daughter. Formerly research and schedules manager Aer Lingus, consultant to the Irish Tourist Board, managing director Economist Intelligence Unit of Ireland, consultant to Federation of Irish Industries, Construction Industry Federation, and Representative Body for Garda, director Hill Samuel Ireland, correspondent in Ireland for *Financial Times*, *Economist* and BBC, economics correspondent of *Irish Times*, lecturer in economics in UCD, member of Seanad Éireann, president and chairman Irish Council of the European Movement, member of Council of the Irish Management Institute, member of executive committee of the Institute of Public Administration, president, Electoral Reform Society of Great Britain and Ireland, president of Fine Gael, Minister for Foreign Affairs, Taoiseach and president of the European Council. At present member of Council of State, member of Dáil Éireann (since 1969), European vice chairman of the Trilateral Commission, a member of the Action Committee for Europe. Director of Guinness Peat Aviation, Trade Development Institute, Comer International, Corporate Finance Group and International Institute for Economic Affairs. Awarded honorary degrees by New York University, University of St Louis, St Mary's University Halifax Canada, University of Keele, England, Boston College, and Oxford University. Decorated by Germany, Japan, Portugal, Jordan and Tunisia. Honorary member of the Chambers of Commerce of Ireland.

PATRICK J. HILLERY

Former Head of State
Sutton, Co. Dublin

Born to Dr Michael Joseph and Ellen Hillery (née McMahon) at Miltown Malbay, Co. Clare on 2 May 1923. Educated at Miltown Malbay NS, Rockwell College, Cashel and UCD whence he graduated with BSc (hons), MB BCH BAO Hons degrees. Married to Mary Beatrice (née Finnegan) with one son, John, and one daughter, Vivienne, died 1987. Formerly medical officer and coroner, TD for Clare, Minister for Education, Industry and Commerce, Labour and Foreign Affairs and vice president of the Commission of the European Communities. Formerly President of Ireland. Has received honorary degrees from

National University of Ireland, University of Dublin, University of Melbourne, Pontifical University of Maynooth, University of Limerick. Awarded honorary fellowships by Royal College of Surgeons in Ireland, All-India Institute of Medical Sciences, Royal College of Physicians of Ireland, Royal College of General Practitioners, Pharmaceutical Society of Ireland, and honorary life membership Irish Medical Association. Decorations include Robert Schuman Gold Medal, Grand Cross of Legion of Honour, Grand Cross of the Netherlands Lion and Gran Croche of Italy. Freeman of the City of Dublin.

MICHAEL JOHN LAVER
Professor of Politics
University College Galway
(091) 24411
Born to Murray and Kathleen Laver (nee Blythe) at London on 3 August 1949. Educated at University of Essex. Married to Bríd Goretti O'Connor with one son, Conor Murray, and one daughter, Katharine Rose. Formerly lecturer in politics, Queen's University Belfast and senior lecturer in politics, University of Liverpool. At present professor of political science and sociology at UCG. Member Political Studies Association of Ireland, and Royal Irish Academy.

JACK LYNCH
Former Taoiseach
Born to Daniel and Nora Lynch (nee O'Donoghue) at Cork on 15 August 1917. Educated at North Monastery CBS, Cork and UCC and at King's Inns Dublin. Married to Máirín O'Connor. Formerly Taoiseach, Minister for Finance, for Industry and Commerce, for Education and for the Gaeltacht, and parliamentary secretary to the Government and to the Minister for Lands. TD 1948–1981. Also former president European Council, president International Labour Conference, vice president, Consultative Assembly of the Council of Europe and president of the Irish Council of the European Movement. At present member of Council of State. He has received many awards and decorations, including the Grand Cross of the Belgian Order of the Crown, the Robert Schuman Award for services to European Unity, and the gold medal, Mérite Européen. Has received honorary degrees of doctor in law from Dublin University and National University of Ireland and doctor of civil law from North Carolina and Rhode Island Universities. A Freeman of the city of Cork.

JOHN MURPHY
Executive Director
Carrisbrook House, Ballsbridge, Dublin 4
(01) 686017
Born to John and Theresa Murphy (née Sexton) at Skibbereen on 17 September 1946. Educated at Abbey NS and St Facthna's High School, Skibbereen and at UCD. Married to Mary Kelly with three sons, Niall, Kevin and Brendan. Formerly chief executive Macra na Feirme, board member Youth Employment Agency, and President Agricultural Science Association. At present executive director *Gaisce* — The President's Award, and director of Macra na Feirme Training; member of Agricultural Science Association.

TOM O'DONNELL
Politician
Shannon Airport, Co. Clare
(061) 363352
Born to Patrick and Josephine O'Donnell (née O'Connell) at Limerick on 30 August 1926. Educated at Cappamore National School, Crescent College Limerick and University College Dublin whence he obtained a BA Degree. Married to Helen O'Connor. Formerly TD for Limerick East, Minister for the Gaeltacht and member of European Parliament. At present chairman Centre for International Co-operation Shannon, chairman Irish Peace Institute, University of Limerick and council member of Co-operation North. Honorary member of European Parliament. Awarded Schuman Medal (European Christian Democrat Group) and Diplôme d'Honneur.

BRENDAN O'REGAN
Organisation President
37 Upper Fitzwilliam Street, Dublin 2
(01) 610588
Born to James and Nora O'Regan (née Ryan) at Sixmilebridge on 15 May 1917. Educated at Sixmilebridge NS and at Blackrock College Dublin. Married to Rita Barrow with two sons and three daughters. Formerly chairman Shannon Free Airport Development Company, Bord Fáilte, DEVCO and Comptroller Sales and Catering, Shannon. At present president Co-operation North, Irish Peace Institute, Centre for International Co-operation, and DEVCO. Awarded Honorary Doctorate NUI, fellow Institute of Engineers of Ireland, Tourism Endeavour Award, Travel Hall of Fame, American Society of Travel Agents.

MARY ROBINSON
Lawyer
Áras an Uachtaráin, Dublin 8
(01) 772815

Born to Dr Aubrey de Vere and Dr Tessa Bourke (née O'Donnell) at Ballina on 21 May 1944. Educated at Sacred Heart Convent Mount Anville Dublin, Trinity College whence she graduated with BA Mod. LL.B (1st class) and with MA degrees, at King's Inns, Dublin (BL 1st class) and at Harvard University Law School (LL.M. 1st class). Married to Nicholas Robinson with two sons, William and Aubrey, and one daughter, Tessa. Formerly Reid Professor of constitutional and criminal law at Trinity College Dublin and member of EC Committee on Enlargement of European Parliament and on Energy Efficiency. Formerly barrister, senior counsel, member of the English Bar (Middle Temple), lecturer in European community law TCD, member of Seanad Éireann for Dublin University Constituency, member of Oireachtas Joint Committee on EC Secondary Legislation. Formerly chairman of Legal Sub-Committee, member of Advisory Board of Common Market Law Review, member of editorial board, *Irish Current Law Statutes Annotated*, member of International Centre for the Legal Protection of Human Rights, member of National Commission of Jurists. At present Uachtarán na hÉireann (President of Ireland). Has special interest in Irish constitutional law, human rights law and European community law. Has pleaded cases before European Commission and Court of Human Rights in Strasbourg, and Court of Justice of European Communities in Luxembourg.

CHARLES V. WHELAN
Retired Ambassador
57/61 Lansdowne Road, Dublin 4
(01) 686233

Born to Charles J. and Bridget Whelan (née McCann) at Dublin on 11 March 1925. Educated at CBS Synge Street Dublin, Rockwell College Co. Tipperary, University of London and Georgetown University Washington DC. Married to Monica Quinn with three sons and one daughter. Formerly Irish Ambassador to Spain, Japan, Greece, Israel and the Soviet Union. Consul General, San Francisco and New York, minister-counsellor London Embassy and member of Irish Government delegation at Sunningdale Conference. Since June 1990 joint chairman Anglo-Irish Encounter. Member Royal Dublin Society, Hibernian United Service Club, Grange & Blainroe Golf Clubs and Fitzwilliam Lawn Tennis Club. Awarded Grand Cross of Isabella La Catolica (Spanish Royal Decoration).

WILLIAM GORDON WILSON

Retired Company Director
Enniskillen
Born to George Edward and Henrietta Wilson (née Conn) at Manorhamilton, Co. Leitrim on 25 September 1927. Educated at Masterson School Manorhamilton, and Wesley College Dublin. Married to Joan Watson with one son, Peter, and two daughters, Julie Anne and Marie (deceased). Formerly president Enniskillen Chamber of Commerce, Enniskillen Rotary Club, captain Enniskillen Golf Club, Justice of the Peace. Following the death of his twenty-year-old daughter Marie in the 1987 Remembrance Day bombing at Enniskillen, he was mentioned by name by H.M. Queen Elizabeth II in her Christmas Day message, was awarded the Tipperary Peace Prize 1987, chosen as Man of the Year 1987 by BBC Radio 'Today' programme, received the Paul Harris award from Rotary International, chosen as Britain's Man of the Year again in 1988, and was presented with the World Methodist Award in 1988. Has written with Alf McCreavy, *Marie — A Story from Enniskillen*, published by Marshall Pickering 1990.

SIR OLIVER WRIGHT

Company Director
1 Savoy Hill, London WC2
Born to Arthur and Ethel Wright at London on 6 March 1921. Educated at Solihull School, Christ's College Cambridge and the Royal College of Defence Studies. Married to Lady (Lilian) Marjory Wright with three sons. Formerly in the British Diplomatic Service, British Government Representative Northern Ireland, British Ambassador to Germany and to the United States. At present chairman Anglo Irish Encounter and director Savoy Hotel plc. Decorated GCMG, GCND and DSC. Member of Travellers' Club London.

Chapter 3
On Politics

Power tends to corrupt and absolute power corrupts absolutely.
                                                           Lord Acton

Ireland is a democratic place, and the idea of people being governed by those whom they themselves choose is implemented by
the election of 183 parliamentary representatives: 166 members of
Dáil Éireann, known as TDs or Teachtaí Dála (Deputies of Parliament) and seventeen members of Parliament at Westminster
known as MPs. Westminster also has a House of Lords with a
small number of Northern Ireland Members. The number of TDs
equates to one for every 21,000 people which contrasts sharply
with France where each Deputy represents 96,000 citizens, and
Germany where the representation is one for 106,000 citizens.
When we look at the situation in the poorer countries of the EC,
we find the ratio in Greece to be one for every 33,000, in Portugal
one for every 41,000 and in Spain one for every 110,000.

In the Republic there is a Senate with sixty members, eleven of
whom are nominated directly by the Prime Minister or Taoiseach
(Leader), six are elected by the universities and forty-three are
elected by a group consisting of the members of the Dáil, the
members of the outgoing Senate and members of county and borough councils. Citizens vote in presidential elections every seven
years (if there is a contest), in parliamentary elections every five
years, European elections every five years and in referenda on
constitutional amendments from time to time.

In Northern Ireland the two main parties favouring union
with Britain are the Democratic Unionists and the Official Unionists. The nationalist parties, who are opposed to union with
Britain, are the Social Democratic and Labour Party (SDLP) and
Sinn Féin.

In the Republic a right/left division has been emerging in
recent years with Fianna Fáil, Fine Gael and the Progressive
Democrats, being, in international terms, more of the centre than
the Labour Party and the Workers Party, who are somewhat to
the left of centre. Voter-support for the parties of the Left was

boosted by the success of the Labour Party's candidate in the 1990 Presidential Election, and by the progress made by Left candidates in the June 1991 Local Elections. The percentage of the popular vote gained by the Labour Party and the Workers Party combined had declined from the general election in 1982, the local in 1985 and again to the general election in 1987. At this stage Labour had 6.3 and Workers had 3.8 to make a total of 10.1 per cent. In the 1991 local elections the corresponding figures were 10.6 and 3.7 to make 14.3 per cent. This group has significant potential for long-term growth.

Although the percentage turnout in the Republic's local elections in 1991 was only 55 per cent, ranging from 41 per cent in South Dublin to 75 per cent in Leitrim, there is a great passion for the democratic ideal, and the temperature at a meeting in any part of the country is likely to rise considerably if a participant should make an accusation of 'undemocratic' behaviour against a fellow participant or against the chair. The late Eamon de Valera is often remembered for his claim to be able to understand the wishes of the Irish people by looking into his own heart, but he was by no means unique in this respect. The Constitution provides that any matter can be referred to the people in a referendum. This power has never been used except when it was necessary to approve amendments to the Constitution itself. This is an unhealthy state of affairs. After seventy years of independence, the people should be directly consulted much more frequently, and be allowed to make decisions on issues which affect them.

Certain individual parliamentarians have made surprising sacrifices in recent years. The decision on the part of two Progressive Democrat TDs to surrender their ministerial pensions worth £17,500 per annum as gifts to the State impressed party supporters and opponents alike. Former President Patrick Hillery surrendered his ministerial pension in 1986, and did so privately, with the result that it continued to appear in lists of pensions as an amount payable , while it was not in fact being paid out. In the North, the Leader of the Democratic Unionists, Ian Paisley, spent a very brief period in prison for non-payment of a fine imposed for taking part in an illegal demonstration. Such sacrifices contrast strangely with the story of lavish dining out by a Tory member of the European Parliament, which featured dinner for two in Strasbourg at a cost of £349 sterling! Mr Paisley is also a member of the European Parliament but is not known to have indulged in this kind of dining-out as a solace for his imprisonment!

The New Ireland Forum
The Forum was established in 1983 for the purpose of holding consultations on the manner in which a lasting peace could be achieved in a New Ireland through democratic processes. Fianna Fáil, Fine Gael, the Labour Party and the SDLP participated in the work of the Forum. They represent in terms of voter support about 75 per cent of the people of the island. The report of the Forum dealt with three possible structures for a new Ireland: the Unitary State being the preferred option, a Federal or Confederal State as an alternative and a further option under which the British and Irish Governments would share responsibility for Northern Ireland.

Northern Ireland is still part of the United Kingdom and under the terms of the Anglo-Irish Agreement, which was signed in November 1985, an Inter-Governmental Conference has been established enabling the Irish Government to put forward views and proposals on matters concerning Northern Ireland, but only in so far as these are not the responsibility of a devolved government in Northern Ireland. The thrust of the Agreement is to promote cross-border co-operation in the interest of both countries. The Secretary of State for Northern Ireland and the Minister for Foreign Affairs of the Republic jointly chair the Conference. The Agreement is a serious practical pact between two neighbouring sovereign states, and making it did not of course diminish the sovereignty of either government in any way.

Violence
A report prepared by Economic Consultants Davy Kelleher McCarthy highlighted that security costs in Northern Ireland were twice as high as those in the Republic when measured on a per capita basis. The report, which was prepared for the Bank of Ireland, estimated at 1988 prices that the violence in Northern Ireland cost the government of the Republic about £78 million

each year, while costing the British government a further £358 million. The report also highlighted the effect of the violence on tourism, estimating that the island as a whole lost £36 million annually because of it, split £23 million for Northern Ireland and £13 million for the Republic

There has been tragic violence in the Republic also, especially the Dublin and Monaghan bombings of May 1974 in which 33 people were killed and over 100 badly injured in a series of car bombings.

Forum Over
Seen at the conclusion of the meetings of the New Ireland Forum at
Dublin Castle on 30 May 1983 were, left to right, Dr Garret FitzGerald,
John Hume, Colm Ó hEocha, Charles Haughey and Dick Spring.

HENRY ABBOTT

Public Representative
Dáil Éireann, Dublin 2
(01) 766336
Born to Henry and Evelyn Abbott (née Fitpatrick) at Mullingar on 18 December 1947. Educated at Taughmon NS, St Mary's CBS, Franciscan College, Gormanston, TCD and King's Inns. Graduated with BA economics and barrister-at-law degrees. Married to Pauline Hefferan with one son and three daughters. Formerly research assistant with Confederation of Irish Industry, chairman Westmeath Co. Council, director Midland Regional Development Organisation, director Midland Regional Tourism Organisation and Fianna Fáil TD for Longford/Westmeath 1987–89. At present barrister practising on the Midland Circuit, chairman Valuation Tribunal, chairman Westmeath VEC, Midland Arts Education sub-committee and member of Westmeath Co. Council. Member Clonkill Hurling Club and Westmeath Agricultural Show Society.

GERRY ADAMS

Political Activist
147 Bóthar Bhaile Anderson, Béal Feirste
301939
Born to Gerry and Annie Adams (née Hannaway) at Belfast on 6 October 1948. Educated at St Finian's Primary School, St Mary's Grammar School. Was imprisoned in Longkesh Prison Camp and on Maidstone Prison Ship. Married to Colette McArdle with one son. At present West Belfast MP and president Sinn Féin. Author of *Falls Memories, The Politics of Irish Freedom, Pathway to Peace* and *Cage 11*.

PETER BARRY

Tea Importer and Public Representative
Kinsale Road, Cork
(021) 966644
Born to Anthony and Rita Barry (née Costelloe) at Cork on 10 August 1928. Educated at Model School and CBC Cork. Married to Margaret O'Mullane with four sons and two daughters. Formerly Minister for Transport and Power, for Education, for Environment and for Foreign Affairs. At present Fine Gael TD and spokesman on Industry and Commerce. Played major part in negotiation of the Anglo-Irish Agreement.

NIAMH BREATHNACH

Public Representative
16 Gardiner Place, Dublin 1
788411
Born to Breandán and Lena Breathnach (née Donnellan) at Dublin on 1 June 1945. Educated at Carysfort National School Blackrock, Dominican Convent Sion Hill and Froebel College Sion Hill. Married to Tom Ferris with two children. Formerly chairwoman Labour Women's National

Council. At present chairperson Labour Party, elected Councillor to Dún Laoghaire Borough Council and Dublin County Council. Member An Taisce and executive member of Women's Commemorative and Celebration Committee.

JOHN BRUTON
Public Representative
Dáil Éireann, Dublin 2
(01) 680830

Born to Matthew J. and Dorothy M. Bruton (née Delany) at Dublin on 18 May 1947. Educated at St Dominic's College, Cabra, Clongowes Wood College, UCD and at King's Inns whence he graduated with BA and BL degrees. Married to Finola Gill with one son, Matthew, and three daughters, Juliana, Emily and Mary-Elizabeth. Formerly National Secretary Fine Gael Youth Group. Parliamentary Secretary to the Minister for Education, Parliamentary Secretary to the Minister for Industry and Commerce, spokesman on Agriculture, spokesman on Finance, Leader of the House with responsibility for implementing reforms in the Dáil. Minister for Finance, Minister for the Public Service, Minister for Industry, Trade, Commerce and Tourism. Formerly deputy leader of Fine Gael, Fine Gael spokesman on Industry and Commerce, Fine Gael spokesman on Education and member of the Parliamentary Assembly of the Council of Europe. Leader of Fine Gael since 20 November 1990 and TD since 1969.

RICHARD BRUTON
Public Representative
Dáil Éireann, Dublin 2
(01) 785998

Born to Matthew J. and Dorothy M Bruton (née Delany) at Dublin on 15 March 1953. Educated at Cabra Convent, Belvedere College, Clongowes Wood College, UCD and Nuffield College Oxford. Married to Susan Meehan with two sons and one daughter. Formerly Minister of State, Dept of Industry and Commerce. At present Fine Gael spokesman on Health and Director of Policy, member Oireachtas Committee on State Sponsored Bodies and member Dublin City Council.

PATRICK M. COONEY
Solicitor and Public Representative
Northgate Street, Athlone
(0902) 72010

Born to Mark and Margaret Mooney (née Blake) at Dublin on 2 March 1931. Educated at National School, Longford, at Castleknock College and UCD. Married to Brigid McMenamin with three sons and one daughter. Formerly Minister for Justice, for Posts and Telegraphs, for Transport, Defence and Education. At present European Parliament member for Leinster, group European Peoples' Party.

MARY THERESA COUGHLAN

Public Representative
Dáil Éireann, Kildare Street, Dublin 2
(01) 789380
Born to Cathal and Marian Coughlan (née Breslin) at Donegal Town on 28 May 1965. Educated at Keellogs and Frosses National Schools, Ursuline College, Sligo, and UCD whence she graduated with a BSocSc degree. Married to David Charlton. Formerly social worker. At present Fianna Fáil TD for South West Donegal, member of Donegal County Council, member of the Joint Committee on the Irish Language and member of the Joint Services Committee. Chairperson of Donegal VEC. Secretary of the National Fianna Fáil Women's Committee.

(JOSEPH) AUSTIN CURRIE

Public Representative
Dáil Éireann, Dublin 2
(01) 610302
Born to John and Mary Currie (née O'Donnell) in Co. Tyrone on 11 October 1939. Educated at Edendork P.E.S., St Patrick's Academy Grammar Dungannon and Queen's University Belfast. Married to Annita Lynch with three daughters and two sons. Formerly leader of Northern Ireland Civil Rights Movement, founder member Social Democratic and Labour Party (SDLP), candidate for Presidency of Ireland, MP East Tyrone, member Northern Ireland Assembly, member Constitutional Assembly, advisor to European Commission and minister of Housing, Planning and Local Government. At present Fine Gael TD for Dublin West and front bench spokesperson on communications. Member Council of European Movement and Anti-Apartheid Movement.

BARRY DESMOND

Politician
43 Molesworth Street, Dublin 2
(01) 6791270
Born to Cornelius and Margaret Desmond (née O'Connor) at Cork on 15 May 1935. Educated at Model School Presentation Brothers and Coláiste Chríost Rí, Cork, School of Commerce Cork and at UCC whence he graduated with an MComm degree. Married to Stella Murphy with four sons — Ciarán, Marcus, Eoin, and Aidan. Formerly Labour Party spokesman on Social Welfare, Labour Party TD and Chief Whip, Deputy Leader Labour Party, Minister of State, Dept of Finance with special responsibility for economic planning, Minister for Health and Social Welfare, fellow Institute of Industrial Engineers and vice president Irish Council of the European Movement. At present and since 1989, Member of the European Parliament, vice chairman Socialist Group EP, member Economic Monetary Policy, and Industrial Policy Committees.

SEÁN DOHERTY

Public Representative

Seanad Éireann, Kildare Street, Dublin 2

(01) 789911

Born to James and Maureen Doherty (née Hogg) on 29 June 1944. Educated at St Michael's NS Boyle, Presentation Brothers' College Carrick-on-Shannon, UCD and King's Inns Dublin. Married to Maura Nangle with four daughters. Formerly Minister of State at the Dept of Justice and Minister for Justice. Member of Roscommon County Council and of the Western Health Board. At present Cathaoirleach of Seanad Éireann and ex officio member of the Council of State, member of Midland Regional Development Organisation, Boyle Chamber of Commerce and of Roscommon Archaeological and Historical Society.

AVRIL DOYLE

Housewife and Public Representative

Dáil Éireann, Dublin 2

(01) 681547

Born to Dick and Freda Belton (née Ryan) at Dublin in April 1949. Educated at Holy Child Convent Killiney and UCD whence she graduated with an honours degree in science. Married to Fred Doyle with three daughters. Formerly member Wexford Corporation, Mayor of Wexford 1976/7, Minister of State in Dept of Finance and Dept of the Environment, spokesperson on the Marine. At present Member Seanad Éireann, party spokesperson on Finance, and member Wexford County Council.

ALAN M. DUKES

Public Representative

Dáil Éireann, Dublin 2

(01) 766336

Born to James and Margaret Dukes (née Moran) at Dublin on 22 April, 1945. Educated at Scoil Cholmchille, Coláiste Mhuire and UCD. Married to Fionnuala Corcoran with two daughters, Louise and Gwendolyn. Formerly Minister for Agriculture, for Finance, for Justice; chief economist National Farmers' Association; director Irish Farmers' Association office, Brussels; advisor to EC Commissioner Richard Burke; Governor European Investment Bank; and leader of Fine Gael. At present TD for Kildare. Fluent in French and Irish. Appointed Minister for Agriculture on his first day in the Dáil.

JOHN V. FARRELLY

Public Representative

Dáil Éireann, Dublin 2

(01) 789911

Born to Denis and Oonagh Farrelly (née Keegan) in Drogheda. Educated at Kilmainham-Wood NS, St Finian's College Mullingar and Warrenstown Agricultural College. Married to Gwen Murphy with two daughters. Formerly chairman Meath County Committee of Agriculture. At present Fine Gael spokesperson on Tourism, chairman Meath County Council and member North Eastern Health Board.

CHARLES J. FLANAGAN
Public Representative
Leinster House, Dublin 2
(01) 610294
Born to Oliver J. and Mai Flanagan (née McWey) at Mountmellick, Laois on 1 November 1956. Educated at Mountmellick NS, Ring College Dungarvan, Knock-Beg College Carlow, UCD and Law School of Incorporated Law Society. Married to Mary McCormack with one daughter Olwyn. Formerly principal of law practice Charles J. Flanagan & Co. Solicitors Portlaoise; Fine Gael spokesman on Law Reform. At present Chief Whip Fine Gael party, Dáil Deputy Laois/Offaly, member Laois County Council, Midland Health Board and Mountmellick Town Commission. Member Rotary International.

PÁDRAIG FLYNN
Public Representative
Carrow Brinogue Lodge, Castlebar, Co. Mayo
(094) 22686
Born to Patrick and Nan Flynn (née Mulcrone) at Castlebar on 9 May 1939. Educated at St Patrick's NS and St Gerald's College, Castlebar and St Patrick's College, Drumcondra. Married to Dorothy Tynan with one son, Turlough, and three daughters, Sharon, Beverley and Audrey. Formerly national school teacher, publican, member of Mayo County Council, Minister of State at the Department of Transport, Minister for the Gaeltacht, Minister for Trade, Commerce and Tourism, and Minister for the Environment. At present Fianna Fáil TD.

MAIRE GEOGHEGAN-QUINN
Public Representative
Dáil Éireann, Dublin 2
(01) 689333
Born to the late John and Barbara Geoghegan (née Folan) at Carna, Co. Galway on 5 September 1950. Educated at Convent of Mercy Carna, Coláiste Mhuire, Tourmakeady, Co. Mayo and Carysfort Teachers' Training College, Blackrock, Co. Dublin. Married to John Quinn with two sons Rúairí and Cormac. Formerly primary school teacher and member of Galway Borough Council. Minister of State at the Dept of Education, Minister for the Gaeltacht, Parliamentary Secretary and later Minister of State at the Dept of Industry Commerce and Energy, and Minister of State at the Dept of the Taoiseach with special responsibility as Coordinator of Government Policy on European Community matters. At present Fianna Fáil TD. The first woman deputy to be appointed Cabinet Minister in the Irish Republic since the foundation of the State.

SEÁN FERGAL HAUGHEY
Public Representative
Seanad Éireann, Dublin 2
(01) 789911
Born to Charles J. and Maureen Haughey (née Lemass) at Dublin on 8 November 1961. Educated at St Paul's College Raheny and TCD whence he graduated with a BA degree in economics and politics. Married to Orla O'Brien. Fianna Fáil candidate for Dublin North East in 1987 general election. At present Senator, Alderman of Dublin City Council, director Dublin and East Regional Tourism Ltd and of Dublin Promotions Organisation Ltd. Board member Beaumont Hospital and St Vincent's Hospital Dublin.

MICHAEL D. HIGGINS
Public Representative
Dáil Éireann, Dublin 2
(01) 785456
Born to John and Alice Higgins (née Canty) at Limerick on 18 April 1941. Educated at National University of Ireland, Indiana University and Manchester University. His study and research spans the areas of economics, sociology, politics, human rights, developing countries, literature and myth. Married to Sabina (née Coyne) with three sons and one daughter. Formerly visiting professor at Southern Illinois University, vice chairman and chairman of the Labour Party, member of Galway County Council, Mayor of Galway and member of Seanad Éireann. At present statutory lecturer in political science and sociology at UCG. TD, member of Galway Corporation and spokesman for the Labour Party in the areas of foreign affairs, education, Gaeltacht and the Irish language. Member of Amnesty, the Robert White Federation of Human Rights, the committee for the Defence of Refugees and Emigrants at Basle, Switzerland, and the Irish Council against Blood Sports. Author of many studies and articles, he has been a columnist for the rock paper *Hot Press* since 1982. In 1985 he was invited to research, write and present a television film of the history of the Island of Monserrat in the Carribean, and he has also presented a poetry programme on RTE 1, which included some of his own poems. He has been a regular visitor to Central America, Turkey, North Africa and East Africa in connection with his work on human rights and overseas development.

BRENDAN HOWLIN
Public Representative
Leinster House, Dublin 2
Born to John and Mary Howlin (née Dunbar) at Wexford on 9 May 1956. Educated at St John of God NS Wexford, CBS Wexford and at St Patrick's College Dublin. Single. Formerly national teacher, Mayor of Wexford, and Labour Party spokesperson on Health. At present Labour Party chief whip and spokesperson on the Environment. Member of Dáil

Committee on Procedures and Privileges, Committee on Dáil Reform, Broadcasting Committee, and Wexford Corporation and Co. Council.

JOHN HUME
Public Representative
5 Bayview Terrace, Derry BT48 7EE
Born to Samuel Hume on 18 January 1937. Educated at St Columb's College Derry and at St Patrick's College Maynooth. Married to Patricia Hone with two sons and three daughters. Formerly member of New Ireland Forum, president Credit Union League of Ireland, MP for Foyle NI Parliament, member SDLP NI Assembly, NI Constitutional Convention, Minister of Commerce NI, Member European Parliament for Northern Ireland, Associate Fellow Centre for International Affairs Harvard and Research fellow in European Studies TCD. At present MP for Foyle and MEP for Northern Ireland. Awarded Honorary Doctorate of Letters University of Massachusetts, Catholic University of America (Washington DC) and St Joseph's University Philadelphia.

GEMMA HUSSEY
Writer
29 Temple Road, Dublin 6
(01) 971169
Born to James and Patricia Moran (née Rogan) at Dublin on 11 November, 1938. Educated at St Brigid's and Loreto Convent Bray, Sacred Heart Convent Mount Anville, and UCD whence she graduated with a degree in economics and politics. Married to Derry Hussey with one son, Andrew, and two daughters, Rachel and Ruth. Formerly advertising executive, administrative officer, founder director of the English Language Institute, Senator, Minister for Social Welfare, for Labour and for Education, spokesperson on Education. At present writer (first Cabinet Diaries in Ireland, *At the Cutting Edge*, published April 1990 by Gill & Macmillan), chairperson Opera Theatre Company and Dublin Rape Crisis Centre. Founder member and Irish Council member European Women's Foundation, board member Coombe Lying-In Hospital and St Patrick's Hospital. Founder member of the Women's Political Association and member of Bray Chamber of Commerce. Her ambition is to contribute to the achievement by Ireland of becoming a self-reliant, thriving country with socially progressive laws, and a fulfilled young population.

LIAM KAVANAGH
Public Representative
Dáil Éireann, Dublin 2
(01) 789911
Born to William and Elizabeth Kavanagh (née Olohan) at Wicklow on 9 February, 1935. Educated at Dominican Convent, De La Salle School Wicklow, and UCD. Married to Margaret Beatty with one son and one daughter. Formerly Minister for Labour, for the Public Service, for

Environment, for Tourism, Fisheries and Forestry and president and secretary Wicklow Branch of Irish Transport and General Workers' Union. Member Wicklow County Council, Wicklow Urban District Council, Wicklow Harbour Board and Wicklow Vocational Education Committee. At present Labour TD for Wicklow and member of European Parliament.

BRIAN LENIHAN

Senior Counsel and Public Representative
Leinster House, Dublin 2
(01) 680830

Born to Patrick and Ann Lenihan (née Scanlon) at Dundalk, Co. Louth, in November 1930. Educated at Marist Brothers Secondary School Athlone, at UCD and at King's Inns, Dublin. Married to Ann Devine with four sons and one daughter. Formerly Fianna Fáil TD for Roscommon, leader of the Fianna Fáil party in the Senate, and the holder of the greatest number of government ministries on record since the foundation of the State. Tánaiste and Minister for Foreign Affairs to November 1990. At present Fianna Fáil TD for Dublin West. Holds two records in Irish politics — being a member of Dáil Éireann prior to the election to Dáil Éireann of his father Patrick Lenihan TD, and, with his sister, Mary O'Rourke, the first brother and sister to have served together in cabinet.

CHARLES JOHN McCREEVY

Chartered Accountant
Hillview House, Kilcullen Road, Naas
(045) 76816

Born to Charles and Eileen McCreevy (née Mills) at Sallins, Co. Kildare on 30 September 1949. Educated at Kill NS, Naas CBS, Franciscan College, Gormanston, and UCD whence he graduated with BComm degree. Later admitted to membership of the Institute of Chartered Accountants in Ireland. Married to Kitty O'Connor (separated) with one son, Charles, and three daughters, Claire, Áine and Carol. Formerly member Kildare Co. Council. At present Fianna Fáil TD for Kildare and partner in Tynan Dillon and Company, Chartered Accountants of Naas and Dublin.

MICHAEL McDOWELL

Senior Counsel and Public Representative
Law Library, Four Courts, Dublin 7
(01) 789911

Born to Anthony and Éilis McDowell (née MacNeill) at Dublin on 29 May, 1951. Educated at Pembroke School, Gonzaga College, University College and King's Inns, Dublin. Married to Niamh (née Brennan) with one son, Hugh. Formerly chairman of Fine Gael Dublin South East Constituency. At present TD for Dublin South East and Progressive Democrat Party Chairman and spokesperson on finance.

SÉAMUS MALLON
Public Representative
2 Mill Street, Newry
(0693) 67933
Born to Francis and Jane Mallon (née O'Flaherty) at Markethill, Armagh on 17 August 1936. Educated at St James PS, Markethill, Abbey CBS Grammar School, Newry and St Joseph's College of Education, Falls. Married to Gertrude Cush with one daughter, Orla. Formerly member of Northern Ireland Assembly, Northern Ireland Convention, Seanad Éireann and New Ireland Forum 1982. At present member Armagh District Council, SDLP Member of Parliament, member of Agriculture Select Committee, and British-Irish Interparliamentary Body. Member local GAA club and Challoner Club.

GAY MITCHELL
Public Representative
Leinster House, Dublin 2
(01) 789911
Born to Peter and Eileen Mitchell (née Whelan) at Dublin on 30 December 1951. Educated at St Michael's CBS Inchicore, Emmet Road Vocational School, Rathmines College of Commerce and Queen's University Belfast. Married to Norma O'Connor with three daughters and one son. Formerly shadow minister Tourism and Transport, Fine Gael spokesperson on European Integration and on Urban Renewal, vice chairman Dáil Committee on Crime, Lawlessness and Vandalism, chairman Finance Committee Dublin City Council and College of Commerce Rathmines. At present Shadow Minister for the Public Service and front bench spokesperson on Constitutional Reform and chairman of Public Accounts Committee. Also alderman Dublin City Council and chairman City Council Protocol and Selection Committee. Member Terenure RFC and Conradh na Gaeilge Club. Associate of the Institute of Taxation in Ireland and holder of a Masters Degree in Irish Political Studies from Queen's University Belfast.

JAMES MITCHELL
Public Representative
Leinster House, Dublin 2
(01) 789911
Born to Peter and Eileen Mitchell (née Whelan) at Dublin on 19 October 1946. Educated at St Michael's CBS, St James' CBS, Emmet Road Vocational School and TCD. Married to Patricia Kenny with three daughters and two sons. Formerly Lord Mayor of Dublin, Minister for Justice, Minister for Transport, Minister for Posts and Telegraphs and Minister for Communications. At present Fine Gael TD, shadow minister for the Environment and Peace Commissioner.

JAMES HENRY MOLYNEAUX
Politician
Aldergrove, Crumlin, Co. Antrim
(08494) 22545
Born to William and Sarah Molyneaux (née Gilmore) on 28 August 1920. Educated at Aldergrove School, Co. Antrim. Single. Formerly served with RAF, member Antrim County Council, vice chairman Eastern Special Care Hospital Management Committee, chairman Antrim Branch N. Ireland Association for Mental Health, honorary secretary South Antrim Unionist Association, MP for Antrim South, vice president Ulster Unionist Council, Leader Ulster Unionist Party, House of Commons, Member N. Ireland Association, former JP. Deputy Grand Master of Orange Order and honorary past Grand Master of Canada, Sovereign Grand Master, Commonwealth Royal Black Institution. At present MP for Lagan Valley since 1983, and Leader of the Ulster Unionist Party since 1979.

JOHN A. MURPHY
Emeritus Professor and Senator
Department of History, University College, Cork
(021) 276871
Born to Timothy and Nellie Murphy (née O'Shea) at Macroom, Co. Cork, in January 1927. Educated at Macroom Boys' NS, De La Salle Secondary School and at UCC. Married to Aileen F. MacCarthy with three sons and two daughters. Formerly visiting professor to Loyola University of Chicago 1974, James Madison University of Virginia 1979, Boston College 1984, Colby College Maine 1987, lecturer in Irish history and professor of Irish history at UCC. Independent member Seanad Éireann 1977–83 and since 1987. Has published numerous books and articles on Irish history.

MICHAEL NOONAN
Public Representative
Dáil Éireann, Dublin 2
(01) 789911
Born to Timothy and Ann Noonan (née Sheehy) at Foynes on 2 May 1943. Educated at Mount Trenchard NS, St Patrick's, Glin, St Patrick's College Drumcondra, and UCD. Married to Florence Knightly with three sons and two daughters. Formerly Minister for Justice, for Industry and Commerce, and for Energy. At present TD, Fine Gael spokesperson on finance, Fine Gael Party trustee, member of the Fine Gael National Executive, and member of Limerick County Council.

JIM O'KEEFFE
Solicitor and Public Representative
Leinster House, Dublin 2
(01) 789911
Born at Skibbereen Co. Cork on 31 March 1941. Educated at St Fachtna's High School Skibbereen, UCC, UCD and Law School of the Incorporated

Law Society. Married to Maeve O'Sullivan with seven daughters and one son. Formerly principal partner in firm of Wolfe & Co, Solicitors, Skibbereen up to 1979, member of Skibbereen Urban District Council and Baltimore Harbour Commission, spokesman on Law Reform, Foreign Affairs, Security, Health, Agriculture, Social Welfare, and Justice. Chairman Dáil Consolidation Committee. Minister of State for Foreign Affairs, Minister of State for Finance and the Public Service, and member of the Council of Europe. Member of Schull Harbour Boat Club, Baltimore Sailing Club and Kinsale Yacht Club.

MICHAEL O'RIORDAN

Political Spokesman
43 East Essex Street, Dublin 2
(01) 711943
Born to Michael and Julia O'Riordan (née Creed) at Cork on 12 November 1917. Educated at North Monastery CBS Cork. Married to Cáitlín Ní Cheocháin with one son and one daughter. Formerly Cabo, International Brigade, Spanish Republican Army, Secretary Bus Workers' Section Cork No. 1 Branch Irish Transport & General Workers' Union, chairman Bus Workers' Section Cork No. 1 Branch IT&GWU, member of Dublin No. 9 Branch Committee IT&GWU, member of Dublin District Committee IT&GWU and general secretary Communist Party of Ireland. At present national chairperson Communist Party of Ireland. Author of *Connolly Column — The Story of the Irishmen who Fought for the Spanish Republic 1936–1939*, and of *Pages from History of Irish Soviet Relations*.

IAN RICHARD KYLE PAISLEY

Minister of Religion and Public Representative
256 Ravenhill Road, Belfast BT6 8GJ
58900/54255
Born to James Kyle and Isabella Paisley (née Turnbull) at Armagh on 6 April 1926. Educated at Ballymena Model and Ballymena Technical High School, South Wales Bible College and Reformed Presbyterian Theological College, Belfast. Married to Eileen Emily Cassells with two sons, Kyle and Ian Jnr, and three daughters, Sharon, Rhonda and Cherith. Formerly leader of opposition, Northern Ireland Parliament, chairman, Public Accounts' Committee, member Northern Ireland Assembly and member of Constitutional Convention. At present Moderator of Free Presbyterian Church, Leader Democratic Unionist Party, Member of House of Commons and Member European Parliament. Member Royal Geographical Society and International Cultural Society of Korea. Awarded honorary doctorate of divinity by Bob Jones University of Greenville, South Carolina. Polled over 230,000 votes in 1984 European Elections, and has since topped the Poll for the third successive election year in the 1989 European election by taking 30 per cent of the entire vote.

RÚAIRÍ QUINN

Architect and Public Representative
Enterprise Centre, Pearse Street, Dublin 2
(01) 775655

Born to Malachi and Julia Quinn (née Hoey) at Dublin on 2 April 1946. Educated at St Michael's, Ailesbury Road, Blackrock College, University College School of Architecture, Dublin, and in Greece at the Athens Centre for Ekistics. Married secondly to Liz Allman, 1990 with one son, Malachi, and one daughter, Sine from previous marriage. Formerly Alderman of Dublin City, Senator, Minister of State at the Department of the Environment, Minister for Labour, for Public Service. President European Coummunity Council of Social Affairs. At present deputy leader of the Labour Party, TD for Dublin South East and spokesman on Finance and Economic Affairs. Member Royal Institute of Architects in Ireland, Royal Institute of British Architects, Irish Planning Institute, Dublin Arts Club, An Taisce and World Society of Ekistics.

ALBERT REYNOLDS

Public Representative
Merrion Street, Dublin 2
(01) 764735

Born at Rooskey, Co. Roscommon in November 1935. Educated Summerhill College, Sligo. Married to Cathleen Coen with two sons and five daughters. Formerly member Longford Co. Council, president Longford Chamber of Commerce, opposition spokesperson for Energy, and for Industry and Employment, Minister for Industry and Energy, for Posts and Telegraphs, for Transport, for Industry and Commerce, and for Finance. At present Fianna Fáil TD for Longford/Westmeath and vice president Fianna Fáil Party. Founder C and D Petfoods Ltd

ALAN JOSEPH SHATTER

Lawyer and Public Representative
4 Upper Ely Place, Dublin 2
(01) 610317

Born to Reuben and Elaine Shatter at Dublin on 14 February 1951. Educated at High School Dublin, TCD, University of Amsterdam and Incorporated Law Society of Ireland. Married to Carol Ann Danker with two children. Formerly chairperson of FLAC (Free Legal Advice Centres) and of CARE (the Campaign for Deprived Children), Fine Gael spokesperson on Law Reform and on the Environment; member of the following committees — Oireachtas Legislation Committee, Oireachtas Committee on Marital Breakdown and Oireachtas Women's Affairs Committee. Consultant on Family Law to the Incorporated Law Society of Ireland. At present front bench spokesperson on labour, partner in firm Gallagher Shatter Solicitors, member of Dáil Éireann and of Dublin County Council. Only member of the Dáil in the last 32 years to have successfully enacted two pieces of legislation from the opposition benches — the Judicial Separation & Family Law Reform Act 1989 and the Adoption Act 1991 (provided for recognition in Ireland of foreign adoptions).

DICK SPRING
Politician and Public Representative
Dáil Éireann, Dublin 2
(01) 789911
Born to Dan and Anne Spring (née Laide) at Tralee on 29 August 1950. Educated at CBS Tralee, Mount St Joseph's College Roscrea, TCD and King's Inns, Dublin. Graduated with BA and BL degrees. Married to Kristi Hutcheson with two sons and one daughter. Formerly Tánaiste, Minister for the Environment, for Energy, and Minister of State at the Department of Justice. At present leader of the Labour Party and TD for Kerry North. Played Gaelic football for Kerry and rugby for Ireland.

EMMET STAGG
Public Representative
Leinster House, Dublin 2
(01) 789737
Born to Henry and Mary Stagg (née Vahey) in Co. Mayo on 4 October 1944. Educated at Newbrook NS, Ballinrobe CBS Co. Mayo and at Kevin Street College of Technology Dublin. Married to Mary Morris with one son and one daughter. Formerly medical technologist TCD, chairperson Kildare County Council and member Eastern Health Board. At present member Dáil Éireann, Kildare County Council & Committees, Kildare Vocational Education Committee, trustee of Labour Party and Labour spokesperson on Social Welfare. President Maynooth and Celbridge Soccer Clubs.

NOEL TREACY
Public Representative
Leinster House, Dublin 2
(01) 789911
Born to Martin and Margaret Treacy (née Lally) at Galway on 18 December 1952. Educated at Gurteen NS and at St Joseph's College, Ballinasloe. Married to Mary Cloonan with four children. Formerly Minister of State at the Department of Finance, Department of the Taoiseach and Department of Health, chairman and member of Galway County Council, chairman Western Regional Development Organisation and of Vocational Education Committee, and Minister of State at the Department of Justice. At present Fianna Fáil TD, member Pádraig Pearse's GAA Club, Ballinasloe Golf Club, Galwaymen's Association and Comhaltas Ceoltóirí Éireann. Made Freeman of Cashel in 1990 for his contribution to Heritage and Culture.

SEÁN TREACY

Public Representative
Dáil Éireann, Dublin 2
(01) 789911

Born to James and Margaret Treacy (née Kenrick) at Clonmel on 22 September 1923. Educated at St Mary's CBS, Clonmel Technical Institute and at UCC. Married to Catherine Connolly. Formerly Mayor of Clonmel, member of Tipperary South Riding Co. Council, president Clonmel Trades' and Labour Council, and Alderman of Clonmel Borough Corporation. Member of European Parliament. At present Ceann Comhairle of Dáil Éireann, member of Council of State, member of Presidential Commission, chairman of Civil Service and Local Appointments Commission and Independent TD for Tipperary South.

MARY WALLACE

Public Representative
Dáil Éireann, Dublin 2
(01) 789911

Born to Thomas and Rosemary Wallace (née Kirwan) at Dublin on 13 June 1959. Educated at Dunboyne and Ratoath NS, Loreto Convent Ballbriggan, Loreto Commercial College and Rathmines College of Commerce. Single. Formerly personnel officer at Blanchardstown Hospital, chairperson Meath County Committee of Agriculture and North Eastern Health Board. At present TD, member of Meath County Council, and Meath VEC. Interested in promoting tourism in Co. Meath, the environment and family issues.

IVAN YATES

Public Representative
Dáil Éireann, Dublin 2
(01) 717557

Born to John F. and Mary Yates (née Forbes) at Dublin on 23 October 1959. Educated at St Mary's NS Enniscorthy, St Columba's College, Dublin and Gurteen Agricultural College, Co. Tipperary. Married to Deirdre Boyd with one son, Andrew, and two daughters, Ciara Mary and Sarah Elizabeth. Formerly farmer, businessman, chairman of Joint Oireachtas Committee on Small Businesses, spokesperson Trade and Marketing. Alternate member of New Ireland Forum and spokesperson on Health. At present Fine Gael TD for Wexford, spokesperson for Transport, Roads and Shipping. Member of Wexford Co. Council and Enniscorthy Urban Council. The only member of the Church of Ireland to be a member of the twenty-fifth Dáil.

Chapter 4
Government

While the powers of the President are limited, the powers of the Taoiseach are formidable. The executive power of the State is exercised by, or on, the authority of the Government and, according to the Constitution, the Government must consist of not less than seven, or more than fifteen members. It normally consists of the full fifteen. The Taoiseach, the Tánaiste and the Minister for Finance must be members of the Dáil, but other Ministers can be either members of the Dáil or members of the Seanad, but not more than two may come from the Seanad.

Although Ministers speak, from time to time, in both Houses of the Oireachtas, Government is responsible to the Dáil only. The Government has, in fact, a collective responsibility to the Dáil for its decisions and for the state of the nation. For practical reasons, however, each member of Government is normally allotted responsibility for one or, in some cases, two Departments of State. They are assisted in this work by Ministers of State up to fifteen of whom may be appointed.

It is interesting to note that Ministers are nominated by the Taoiseach for the approval of the Dáil, but the Taoiseach assigns the Ministers to particular Departments without the approval of the Dáil. Ministers of State, on the other hand, are appointed by the Government on the nomination of the Taoiseach.

The Government of Northern Ireland is established under the terms of the Northern Ireland Act 1974, and is headed by a Secretary of State appointed by the British Government, who is responsible for all constitutional matters, law and order, security, as well as social and economic planning.

Administration is organised in six government departments: agriculture, economic development, education, environment, finance and personnel, health and social services.

The Secretary of State is assisted by a central secretariat, which organises the work of several inter-departmental committees and working groups, as well as maintaining close contact with the Northern Ireland Office in London.

Government Departments

The broad division of responsibility between government departments is indicated by the names of the departments themselves. For example, the Department of Agriculture and Food is responsible for animal health and veterinary matters, beef and dairy farming, livestock breeding and European Community negotiations in so far as they relate to agriculture. An Bord Glas (Horticulture Development Authority) is attached to the Department as is the Eradication of Animal Disease Board.

Similarly, the functions of the Office of the Attorney General are predictable and include the activities of the Chief State Solicitor's Office and the State Pathologist.

The Communications department is responsible for post, telecommunications, and radio and television broadcasting. In October 1988 the Government established the Independent Radio and Television Commission to ensure the creation, development and monitoring of independent broadcasting.

The Department of Education deals with all aspects of primary and post-primary education, school transport, sports, school buildings and school inspection. It also administers the Irish section of UNESCO, as well as the National Sports Council, the Primary Education Review Body, National Council for Curriculum and Assessment, and the Irish Terminology Committee.

As well as dealing with the supply and utilisation of energy generally, the Department of Energy is responsible for the Geological Survey of Ireland and for the Mining Board.

The Department of the Environment caters for local authorities, roads and housing, and has a large number of advisory committees such as Local Supplies, Local Government Manpower, the National Co-ordinating Committee for Mountain and Cave Rescue, and the National Roads Authority.

The most senior of all departments, the Department of Finance, is organised in five divisions: finance, public expenditure, budget, economic and EC, personnel and remuneration, and organisation, management and training. Attached to this

Department are the Central IT Service, the Civil Service Training Centre, the Review Body on Higher Remuneration in the Public Sector, the Committee on Top Level Appointments in the Civil Service, and the National Treasury Management Agency.

The enormous state property holdings and state involvement with contracts, quantity surveying and other construction industry activities are controlled by the Office of Public Works under the guidance of the Minister of State at the Department of Finance. The Minister for Finance appoints a Commissioner to control the Valuation Office, which makes valuations of properties for rating purposes.

The Department of Foreign Affairs is organised in seven divisions: economic, legal, administration, Anglo-Irish, EC, development co-operation and political, and is responsible for Irish Embassies overseas. The Department has the benefit of an Advisory Committee on Cultural Relations, an Advisory Council on Development Co-operation, the Scholarship Exchange Board, and the Refugee Agency set up in July 1991 to oversee the resettlement of refugees generally, and with particular reference to the 425 Vietnamese already resident here.

The Department of Health controls the regional health authorities and has a large number of affiliated organisations, such as the National Council for the Elderly, National Drugs Advisory Board, the Poisons Council, the Therapeutic Substances Advisory Committee and the Adoption Board.

The Department of Industry and Commerce is responsible for commercial and industrial policy, trade regulation, company and patents law and other related areas of economic activity. It is also responsible for the activities of the Companies Registration Office, the Registrar of Friendly Societies, the Fair Trade Commission, and the Director of Consumer Affairs and Fair Trade. It has the benefit of the work of the Credit Union Advisory Committee, the Motor Insurance Advisory Board and the Industrial Costs' Monitoring Group.

The Department of Justice administers the courts and prisons and is responsible for An Garda Síochána, the Land Registry and the Registry of Deeds. It also looks after the Film Censor's Office, Censorship of Films Appeal Board, Censorship of Publications Board, Censorship of Publications Appeal Board and the Commissioners for Charitable Donations and Bequests. It enjoys the fruits of the labours of the Committee on Court Practice and Procedure, the Registration of Titles Rules Committee, Superior Court Rules Committee, Circuit Court Rules Committee, District Court Rules Committee, Prison Visiting Committees, the Probation and Welfare Service and the Criminal Injuries Compensation Tribunal.

The Department of Labour keeps its watchful eyes on industrial relations and all aspects of employment, including health safety and welfare at work. It is assisted by the Levy Appeal Tribunal, Employment Appeals Tribunal, Employment Equality Agency, the National Industrial Safety Organisation, the Labour Court, the Rights Commissioners and the Employer-Labour Conference.

The Department of the Marine looks to every aspect of sea and inland fishing, aquaculture and fish processing, and controls harbours at Killybegs, Castletownbere, Rossaveal, Dún Laoghaire, Dunmore East and Howth.

The Department of Social Welfare deals, as its name implies, with all social insurance and social assistance schemes. It enjoys the assistance of the Combat Poverty Agency and the National Pensions Board.

The Department of the Taoiseach provides the Secretariat to the Government and acts as the liaison between Government and President. It is also responsible for the National Economic and Social Council, Government Information Services, National Archives, National Concert Hall, National Gallery, National Library, National Museum, National Heritage Council and the Royal Hospital Kilmainham.

The Department of Tourism and Transport looks to road, rail and air transport, international ferries, and the meteorological services, and is assisted by the National Committee for Geodesy and Geophysics.

Off-duty Prime Minister
A well earned cup of tea for Taoiseach Charles Haughey on
Corlea Bog, Kenagh, Co. Longford after he had spent an exhausting morning viewing the work on the excavations of the prehistoric roadway which was constructed in 148 BC. The
Taoiseach has spent many exhausting mornings and evenings in
the political life of the country, and many expect his retirement
now that he is over 66 years of age.

BERTIE AHERN

Accountant and Public Representative.
Department of Finance, Merrion Street, Dublin 2
(01) 767571
Born at Dublin in September 1951. Educated at St Aidan's CBS Rathmines College of Commerce and UCD. Married to Miriam Patricia Kelly with two daughters, Georgina and Cecilia. Formerly Lord Mayor of Dublin 1986/7, spokesman on Youth, Minister of State in the Dept of the Taoiseach and at the Department of Defence, Government Chief Whip and Minister for Labour. At present Minister for Finance.

VINCENT BRADY

Public Representative
Mobhi Road, Dublin 9
(01) 771881
Born at Dublin in March 1936. Educated at O'Connell School Dublin, and College of Commerce Rathmines. Married to Mary Neville with two sons and one daughter. Formerly elected member of Dublin City Council 1979–91 and of the Council of Europe 1982–84. Served on a number of Committees of both Bodies, member of Dublin County Board of the GAA 1965–75, and Minister of State at Dept of the Taoiseach (with special responsiblity as Government Chief Whip and for Heritage Affairs). At present Fianna Fáil TD and Minister for Defence, member of Oireachtas Committee on Procedure and Privileges and also chaired the Special All Party Committee on Dáil Reform and Televised Broadcasting. Member of Clontarf Golf Club and of the Whitehall Colmcille GAA club.

SÉAMUS BRENNAN

Accountant and Public Representative
Department of Tourism, Transport and Communications,
Kildare Street, Dublin 2
(01) 789522
Born at Galway on 16 February 1948. Educated at St Joseph's Secondary School and at UCG whence he graduated with BComm and BA (economics) degrees. Married to Ann O'Shaughnessy with two sons and four daughters. Formerly general secretary of the Fianna Fáil Party 1973–80, Senator 1977–81 and member Dublin County Council 1985–87. At present Minister for Tourism, Transport and Communications and TD for Dublin South. Honorary member of the Marketing Institute of Ireland.

RT HON. PETER LEONARD BROOKE

Public Representative
House of Commons, London SW1A OAA
(071) 2195041
Born to Rt Hon. Henry Brooke, Baron Brooke of Cumnor, CH, PC and Rt Hon. Barbara Brooke (née Mathews) in London on 3 March 1934. Educated at Akeley Wood/Ashfold School, Marlborough College, Balliol College Oxford and Harvard Business School USA. Married first to Joan Smith (decd) and secondly to Lindsay Allinson. Four children, one deceased. Formerly Swiss correspondent *Financial Times*, director (and later chairman) Spencer Stuart Management Consultants, Assistant Government Whip, Lord Commissioner of the Treasury, Parliamentary Secretary Dept of Education and Science, Minister of State, Treasury, Paymaster General, president of the Oxford Union and chairman of the Conservative Party. At present member of parliament, City of London and Westminster South and Secretary of State for Northern Ireland. Trustee Wordsworth Trust, trustee (and chairman) the Cusichaca Trust in the Andes, Brooks London, City Livery Club London, I Zinpani Cricket Club, Marylebone Cricket Club, St George's Hanover Square Conservative Club London. Awarded the Tipperary Peace Prize and the Ireland Fund Award. Senior Fellow Royal College of Art London and Presentation Fellow King's College London.

RAPHAEL BURKE

Public Representative
72 St Stephen's Green, Dublin 2
(01) 789711
Born to Mr and Mrs Patrick Burke TD, at Dublin in September 1943. Educated at Christian Brothers O'Connell Schools, Dublin. Married to Anne Fassbender with two daughters. Formerly chairman of Dublin County Council, Minister for the Environment, Minister for Industry and Commerce, Minister for Energy and for Communications. At present TD for Dublin North and Minister for Justice.

GERARD COLLINS

Public Representative
St Stephen's Green
(01) 780822
Born in Abbeyfeale, Co. Limerick in October 1938. Educated at St Ita's College Abbeyfeale, Patrician College Ballyfin and UCD where he obtained a BA degree. Married to Hilary Tattan. Formerly teacher and acting General Secretary of the Fianna Fáil Party. Junior Minister for Industry and Commerce and for the Gaeltacht, Minister for Telecommunications and for Justice. At present Fianna Fáil TD and Minister for Foreign Affairs.

RT HON. SIR JOHN COPE
Member of Parliament
House of Commons, London
Born in England on 13 May 1937. Married with children. Formerly held various government positions including Minister of State Northern Ireland Office and responsible for security at the Department of Finance. At present Deputy Chairman of Conservative Party and Member of Parliament for Nothern Ireland. Privy Counsellor and Knighted in Birthday Honours 1991.

BRENDAN DALY
Public Representative
Áras Mhic Dhiarmada, Dublin 1
(01) 740954
Born in Co. Clare in February 1940. Educated at Kilrush CBS. Married to Patricia Carmody with one daughter and two sons. Formerly Minister of State at the Dept of Labour, of the Taoiseach and of Finance, Fianna Fáil Spokesman on Tourism, Minister for Fisheries and Forestry, Fianna Fáil Spokesman on Fisheries and Forestry, Minister for the Marine and for Defence. At present Fianna Fáil TD and Minister for Social Welfare.

NOEL DAVERN
Public Representative
Department of Education, Marlboro St, Dublin 1
(01) 734700
Born in Cashel, Co. Tipperary in 1945. Educated at Boys' NS and CBS Cashel and at Franciscan College Gormanstown. Married to Anne Marie Carroll with two sons and one daughter. Formerly member Tipperary SR Co. Council, South Tipperary Local Health Committee, Vocational Education Committee, ACOT Committee, National Museum Advisory Committee, Oireachtas Joint Committee on Secondary Legislation of the EC 1987, and member and vice chairman Select Committee on Crime. MEP 1979–84. At present Fianna Fáil TD and Minister for Education.

PAT 'the Cope' GALLAGHER
Public Representative
Grand Canal Street, Dublin 2
(01) 764751
Born to Packie and Mary Gallagher (née Campbell) at Burtonport, Co. Donegal on 10 March 1948. Educated at Rosmine and Luinneach NS, Dungloe High School, St Enda's College Galway and UCG whence he graduated with honours BComm degree. Single. Formerly fish exporter, Minister of State at Dept of the Marine, and deputy spokesman for Fisheries and Forestry 1983–7. At present Minister of State at the Department of the Gaeltacht, and Dáil deputy since June 1981.

MARY HARNEY
Public Representative
Dáil Éireann, Dublin 2
(01) 789911
Born to Michael and Sarah Harney (née Crehan) at Galway in March 1953. Educated at Newcastle NS, Coláiste Bríde Clondalkin, and at TCD. Single. Formerly a research worker. At present Minister of State at the Department of the Environment with special responsibility for Environmental Protection, and Progressive Democrat TD. When she was nominated to Seanad Éireann by the Taoiseach in August 1977, she was the youngest ever member of the Senate. Founder member of the Progressive Democrats.

CHARLES J. HAUGHEY
Public Representative
Merrion Row, Dublin 2
(01) 689333
Born to Seán and Sarah Haughey (née McWilliams) at Castlebar on 16 September 1925. Educated at Christian Brothers Primary School, Marino and Secondary School, St Joseph's Fairview. Took first place in Dublin Corporation scholarship examination and winner of a university scholarship to UCD. Graduated with an honours BComm degree. Later admitted to membership and fellowship of the Institute of Chartered Accountants in Ireland. Married to Maureen (née Lemass) with three sons, Conor, Ciarán and Seán, and one daughter, Eimear. Formerly partner, Haughey Boland and Co, Chartered Accountants, Parliamentary Secretary to Minister for Justice, Minister for Agriculture. At present Fianna Fáil TD and Taoiseach (Prime Minister).

DENIS LYONS
Public Representative
Kildare Street, Dublin 2
(01) 789522
Born in Cork. Educated at Sunday's Well NS Cork, North Monastry CBS Cork and Crawford Municipal Technical Institute. Married to Catherine McCarthy with two sons and four daughters. Formerly sheetmetal worker, trade union officer and self-employed. At present Minister for State at Dept of Tourism and Transport and Communications; Fianna Fáil TD for Cork North Central; and member Irish Management Institute.

BRIAN STANLEY MAWHINNEY

Politician
Stormont Castle, Belfast
(0232) 763011
Born to Frederick Stanley Arnot and Coralie Jean Mawhinney (née Wilkinson) at Belfast on 26 July 1940. Educated at Inchmarlo School Belfast, Royal Belfast Academical Institution, Queen's University Belfast, University of Michigan USA and University of London. Married to Betty Louise Oja with two sons and one daughter. Formerly assistant professor Radiation Research University of Iowa USA, lecturer and senior lecturer Medical Physics Royal Free Hospital School of Medicine London, president Conservative Trade Unionists, Northern Ireland Young Conservatives, and Peterborough Association for the Blind. At present Minister of State Northern Ireland Office and MP for Peterborough. Joint author *Conflict & Christianity in Northern Ireland.*

RICHARD NEEDHAM

Public Representative
Stormont Castle, Belfast BT4 3ST
(0232) 63255
Born in 1942, the 6th Earl of Kilmorey, but has never used this title. Married with two sons and one daughter. MP for Wiltshire North since 1983. Formerly chairman of R G M Print Holdings Ltd. and personal assistant to The Rt Hon. James Prior MP, Shadow Employment Spokesman, vice chairman of the Conservative Parliamentary Employment Committee and a Member of the Public Accounts Committee, Parliamentary Private Secretary to the Secretary of State for Northern Ireland, and at the Dept of the Environment in Great Britain to The Rt Hon. Patrick Jenkins MP. Has also been chairman of the All Party Productivity Committee. At present Parliamentary Under Secretary of State at the Northern Ireland Office responsible for both the Dept of the Environment and the Dept of Economic Development, having also been responsible for the Dept of Health and Social Services, and Conservative Member of Parliament for Chippenham in 1979. Author of *Honourable Member*, a book on the work of an MP, founder member of the UK-Japan 2000 Group, and a former Governor of the British Institute of Florence.

MICHAEL JOHN NOONAN

Public Representative
Lesson Lane, Dublin 2
(01) 785444
Born to John and Hannah Noonan (née Slattery) at Bruff, Kilmallock, Co. Limerick on 4 September, 1935. Educated at Salesian College, Pallaskenry. Married to Helen Sheahan with two sons, John and Pat, and four

daughters, Marie, Ann, Catherine and Carmel. Formerly Minister for Defence, opposition spokesman on agriculture, member Limerick County Council, member RTE Authority, national president Macra na Feirme and member Muintir na Tíre. At present Fianna Fáil TD for Limerick West and Minister for State at the Department of the Marine.

DR RORY O'HANLON
Public Representative
Dáil Éireann, Dublin 2
(01) 789911
Born to Michael and Anna Mary O'Hanlon (née Fenelon) at Dublin on 7 February 1934. Educated at Mullaghbawn NS, Co. Armagh, at Blackrock College and UCD. Married to Teresa Ward with four sons, Rory, Ardal, Neale and Shane, and two daughters, Fiona and Dearbhla. Formerly general practitioner, member Monaghan County Council, member North Eastern Health Board, and Minister for Health. At present Minister for the Environment and Fianna Fáil TD for Cavan/Monaghan.

MICHAEL O'KENNEDY
Public Representative
Department of Labour, Adelaide Road, Dublin 2
(01) 765861
Born to Eamonn and Helena O'Kennedy (née Slattery) at Nenagh on 21 February 1936. Educated at St Mary's NS and CBS, Nenagh, St Flannan's College Ennis, St Patrick's College Maynooth, UCD and King's Inns Dublin. Married to Breda Heavey with one son, Brian, and two daughters, Orla and Mary. Formerly Senator, Parliamentary Secretary to Minister for Education, Minister for Transport and Power, for Foreign Affairs, for Finance, and for Agriculture and Food, EC Commissioner, president of Board of Governors European Investment Bank and president of Council of EC Ministers. At present Fianna Fáil TD and Minister for Labour. Member of numerous sport, cultural and social clubs.

MARY O'ROURKE
Public Representative
Dáil Éireann, Dublin 2
(01) 789911
Born to Patrick J. and Anne Lenihan (née Scanlon) at Athlone on 31 May 1937. Educated at St Peter NS Athlone, Loreto Convent Bray, UCD and Maynooth. Married to Enda O'Rourke with two sons, Feargal and

Aengus. Formerly secondary school teacher at Summerhill Convent, Athlone, chairman Athlone UDC, member Westmeath County Council, and Minister for Education. At present Fianna Fáil TD and Minister for Health. Member Soroptimists Club and Athlone Chamber of Commerce. With her brother, Brian Lenihan, the first brother and sister team to have served together in Cabinet.

JOE WALSH
Public Representive
Kildare Street, Dublin 2
(01) 789206
Born at Ballineen, Co. Cork in May 1943. Educated at St Finbarr's College, Farranferris, and at UCC. Married to Marie Donegan with three sons and two daughters. Formerly dairy manager, member of Cork County Council, and Senator. At present Minister of State at the Department of Agriculture and Food and Fianna Fáil TD for Cork South West. Honorary member of the Institute of Food Science and Technology of Ireland.

JOHN P. WILSON
Public Representative
Kildare Street, Dublin 2
(01) 789522
Born to John and Bridget Wilson (née Comaskey) at Callanagh, Kilcogy, Co. Cavan on 8 July 1923. Educated at St Mel's College, Longford, University of London, National University of Ireland whence he graduated with MA degree and HdipEd. Studied also in Spain at Saragossa University. Married to Ita (née Ward) with one son and four daughters. Formerly a secondary teacher, past president of Association of Secondary Teachers of Ireland, founder member and member of National Committee of European Association of Teachers, chairman and actor Letterkenny Players, council member Ulster Colleges' GAA, opposition spokesman on education and the arts, Minister for Education, for Transport, for Posts and Telegraphs, opposition spokesman on Communications and Minister for Tourism and Transport. At present Fianna Fáil TD for Cavan/Monaghan, Tánaiste and Minister for the Marine.

MICHAEL WOODS
Public Representative
Kildare Street, Dublin 2
(01) 789011
Born at Bray, Co. Wicklow on 8 December 1935. Educated at Synge Street CBS, UCD and Institute of Public Administration Dublin and at

Harvard Business School USA. Married to Margaret Maher with three sons and two daughters. Formerly Lecturer at Franciscan College of Agriculture Multyfarnham, Head of Dept and Principal Officer Agricultural Research Institute, managing director FII Produce Ltd and Associated Producer Groups Ltd. Held posts of Minister of State at Dept of the Taoiseach and of Defence, Minister for Health and Social Welfare and Minister for Social Welfare. At present Fianna Fáil TD and Minister for Agriculture and Food. Author of *Research in Ireland*, *Key to Economic and Social Development* and numerous technical and scientific papers.

Down South
In spite of all his apparent antagonism towards the Republic, Rev. Ian
Paisley visits the South when it suits his cause. One happy occasion was
his participation in a 'Saturday Live' show hosted by his daughter,
Rhonda.

Chapter 5
Public Administration

A place for everything, and everything in its place.

Samuel Smiles

The manner in which Public Administration is organised cries out for the benefit of hindsight. If only we could be born twice.

Take the location of airports for example. On our small island of only 5 million population there must surely have been a very strong argument for having just one major International Airport linked to the major centres of population by a network of superhighways. Instead, a great deal of money has been spent in the construction of a whole series of airports around the coast, in lieu of spending it on the road network.

Not much can be done about this situation as the coastal airports already exist, but something should be done about the excessive size of Dublin in relation to the Republic.

EC Comparison

The following table shows percentages of various EC Member State populations attributable to residents of the capital cities. The list is divided between countries which are economically prominent and those which are less so.

Country	Percentage	Country	Percentage
Germany	1	Belgium	9
France	4	Denmark	29
Italy	6	Greece	40
Netherlands	3	Luxembourg	27
Spain	10	Portugal	19
UK	12	R. of Ireland	26
		N. Ireland	20

It is significant that the strongest countries have the lowest percentages.

With the majority of the national daily newspapers published in Dublin, and the national broadcasting service headquartered there, it is not surprising that Dublin has become a market within a market for many goods, services and intrigues. There is some cause for concern, in fact, that goods and services which ought to be marketed nationally with the incumbent transport and warehousing costs that this entails, may be confined to the more lucrative unit supply situation within the Dublin area. The dominance of Dublin in the life of the country has not been achieved without cost. Overexpansion has led to the dereliction of the inner city, and to annual smoke emissions which are said to be comparable with those in the greater London area.

But that is not to say that Dubliners rest on their laurels — far from it. An example of this, from thousands of available examples, was the speech which the President of Dublin Chamber of Commerce made at a recent chamber annual dinner in which he called both for restraint in Government spending and Government investment in a national exhibition centre for Dublin — an anomaly which the next speaker at the dinner, the then Taoiseach was quick to point out! Dubliners regularly call for conference and exhibition centres for their city, in spite of there being many fine facilities available at venues, such as the Royal Dublin Society, the Point Depot, Eolas, the Industry Centre at UCD, the Burlington Hotel, and so on.

In 1986, several EC member states put forward the candidature of one of their cities, not necessarily their capital city, to be the location of the EC Trade Marks Office. Ireland put forward Dublin and Dublin has become a sub-region in itself for the purposes of the EC Structural Funds. In a paper circulated for consideration in relation to the national programme of community interest for the greater Dublin area, Dublin Chamber of Commerce quite rightly put forward a strong case for Dublin. Two pages of pie charts were used to highlight the plight of Dublin. Two of these showed Dublin's share of state support for industry up from 11 per cent in 1975 to 26 per cent in 1987 and this was stated by the Chamber to be 'still disproportionately low' in spite of the fact that other charts showed Dublin's share of national industrial output at 24 per cent and Dublin's share of national industrial employment down from 40 per cent in 1971 to 28 per cent in 1987 and this was stated to be 'declining rapidly'. The paper conceded that Dublin has 'an above average' share of national service sector employment, but omits mention of the vital fact that this is the sector which has been most rapidly growing.

However, there is some awareness of the problem and already sections of some government departments have been transferred to provincial locations — part of the Department of the Environment to Ballina, Education to Athlone, part of Social Welfare to Sligo and part of Defence to Galway. The long-term intention is to decentralise a total of 3,100 public servants but, even if all of these were married with large families, it can be seen that this decentralisation programme would have little effect on the basic imbalance in the country. Far more radical solutions to the problem will need to be found. Siting the 380,000sq. ft. National Sports' Centre, one of the biggest buildings ever to be constructed in Ireland, outside Dublin, would have been a step in the right direction. The decision to site it in the centre of Dublin is a lost opportunity.

As if the Dublin imbalance problem were not bad enough, Mr T.J. Maher MEP suggested in February 1988 that Cork should have its own office in Brussels to promote the interests of Cork at European level.

The Civil Service

Teachers, prison officers, soldiers, sailors, airmen and police are not generally classed as civil servants but they are, of course, part of the overall structure of public administration. The term 'civil servant' is normally applied to those who work in the administration of Government departments, in regional and in local authorities. Recruitment is by open public competition supervised by an independent national authority. The main categories are administrative (responsible for formulating policy), technical and scientific (providing specialist advice), executive (involved in implementation of decisions) and clerical (responsible for general office duties).

The Revenue Commissioners for example can claim a strong downward trend in the cost of administration as a percentage of net receipts from 1.85 per cent in 1985 to 1.45 per cent in 1990. The cost of the Civil Service is carefully watched by political and economic commentators, financial analysts and begrudgers. Apart from staffing all Government departments, the Civil Service also provides the human resources for the Central Statistics Office, Civil Service Commission, Local Appointments Commission, the office of the Comptroller and Auditor General, the office of the Director of Public Prosecutions, the office of the Ombudsman, the Revenue Commissioners, the State Laboratory and the Stationery Office.

The Education Division of the Institute of Public Administration offers a range of full time and part time educational courses and a library service, mainly to public servants. The courses offered include the School of Public Administration (founded in 1964) the Parliamentary Internship Programme run in conjunction with the Catholic University of America, Washington DC, the Bachelor of Arts in Public Administration course, and extra mural lecture courses.

Fraud

The numbers employed in the Civil Service have been reduced by the rather crude method of a ban on recruitment so that replacements are kept below resignations and retirements. It has been claimed that staff reductions in the Civil Service have led to the State being defrauded because of inadequate supervision.

There has been concern over a long period of time about the abuse of the system of social welfare, where figures as high as IR£260 million per annum have been suggested as representing the extent of fraud. But a report issued by the Minister for Social Welfare in June 1988 suggested that 98 per cent of all unemployment claims and 99 per cent of all disability claims were valid, and also pointed out that there are no nationwide estimates of the level of fraud, or abuse, available.

Ireland has an enviable reputation internationally for the integrity of its Civil Service. Cases of fraud by civil servants are extremely rare and, in recent times, the only cases to come to light dealt with minor matters, such as the case of a civil servant who accepted bribes in order to frustrate car parking fines.

State-Sponsored Bodies

The Republic has a great many state-sponsored organisations, some commercial, others non-commercial, some established as public or private companies and some established pursuant to an

Act of the Oireachtas. Some of the best known include Aer Lingus (Irish Airlines), Aer Rianta (Irish Airports), Agricultural Credit Corporation, the Arts Council, Bord Fáilte (Irish Tourist Board), Bord Iascaigh Mhara (Irish Sea Fisheries Board), Bord na Móna (Irish Peat Board), Dublin Bus, Provincial Bus, CERT (Catering and Tourism Industry Training), CBF (Irish Livestock and Meat Board), Bórd Tráchtála (Irish Trade Board), Electricity Supply Board, FÁS (National Manpower Authority), Industrial Credit Corporation, Industrial Development Authority, Irish Goods Council, Irish National Petroleum Corporation, Kilkenny Design Workshops, National Council for Educational Awards, National Development Corporation, National Economic and Social Council, National Lottery, National Rehabilitation Board, An Post, Shannon Development, Telecom Éireann and Voluntary Health Insurance Board.

The above, it must be emphasised, is merely a selection from the list of state-sponsored bodies operating in the Republic. Efforts have been made to reduce their number. The Post Office Users' Council and the Telecommunications Users' Council were abolished by Government without much ado, and the amalgamation of three safety organisations (the Irish Water Safety Association, the National Road Safety Association and the Fire Prevention Council), came in for some criticism because of the 'indecent haste' with which the amalgamation was organised. The Irish Goods Council has been merged with the Irish Trade Board, and the National Development Corporation with the Industrial Development Authority. Against this trend the Government has established some new authorities, such as the National Roads Authority and the National Software Centre.

For the businessman, the Industrial Development Authority (IDA) is one of the most important, if not the most important, state-sponsored body. Foreign investment inflow has been an extremely significant factor in the Irish economy, although it may have peaked in the early eighties. Most parts of the country have enjoyed benefits from the successful endeavours of the IDA to attract foreign-owned industry. For American or Far Eastern companies, a manufacturing base within the EC is of strategic importance, and companies from these regions have been big investors, but there has been major investment from European countries too. For Europeans the attractions include capital grants, training grants, availability of factory space and a uniquely low corporation tax rate. In addition, there is the availability of a young, dynamic, well-educated and highly-skilled workforce. In Northern Ireland, the Industrial Development Board has an overall objective — to encourage the introduction and development of internationally competitive companies in the manufacturing and traded services sectors so as to create the conditions for growth in durable employment. According to the 89/90 annual report, the number of Inward Investment jobs assisted is small at 1,977 but has been growing each year. The Board organises trade missions, participates in exhibitions, purchasing seminars, exporting seminars and grant aids Research and Development, Quality Development, and Total Quality Management.

Local Authorities

A visitor might be forgiven for expecting that there would not be more than one local authority per county but there are, in fact, on average over four elected local authorities per county. Not that the number of local authorities is of itself important (there are said to be over 35,000 authorities in France, for example) but, what is really important, is the extent to which the tasks of Central Government are transferred to democratically elected local and regional authorities. Ireland as a whole, North and South, is highly centralised.

The members of local authorities are elected for periods of five years and any person over eighteen is eligible to become a member and to vote.

The local authorities provide services in areas, such as housing and building, water supply and sanitation, environmental protection, agriculture, education, health and welfare, road transportation and safety, development incentives and controls, recreation, amenities and others.

Speaking in February 1988, the Minister for the Environment, Mr Pádraig Flynn, said that the structures of Local Government were fifty years out of date, creaked at every joint, and had Dickensian overtones, which had not been eliminated by repeated examinations, reviews and assessments. He said that in future, local authorities would have to view themselves as part of a competitive environment and that, if it should emerge that certain services could be provided more cheaply in new ways, then the new ways would have to be adopted.

Regional Development

The then Minister for Finance, Mr Ray MacSharry, announced a five-year development plan with funding of up to IR£4,000 million early in September 1988. This plan was announced as being likely to be supported to the extent of IR£3,100 million in aid from the European Fund, but this, of course, presumed that grants of 75 per cent would be available on every single project when, in fact, very few projects would attract the maximum grant level. The main difficulty for the Republic lay, not just in earning the highest possible grant support from Brussels, but in finding the non-grant finance either from the public or from the private sector.

Grave concern has been expressed over the manner in which the country was divided into sub-regions for this very plan. In EC terms, Ireland is one region, but for the purposes of this fund, seven sub-regions were delineated.

These added to the confusion, which already existed, regarding regional boundaries. Tourism, local government, industrial development, health boards and regional development organisations, all had different ambits, yet none of the configurations was acceptable for the seven new sub-regions. In opting for different frontiers, Government even managed to divide certain counties and, so, create new entities, such as North-Offaly and South-Offaly.

The suggestion that there might be a sinister purpose to this was made in a letter to the *Irish Times* by the distinguished past president of the Institute of Public Administration Mr T.J. Barrington. According to his letter:

> ... the purpose of this latest crazy exercise is thus quite clear. Abort the birth of any genuine regional consciousness, structures, or initiatives ... as we pick our way among the potholes, we gain a vivid picture of what is wrong with this so centralised country; the failure at the centre to care not only for a whole range of major public services but also for the institutional and personal potentialities of our people. This is because a tiny group

of politicians, of all persuasions, and bureaucrats are determined to control — well beyond the level of their own competence — the smallest details of our collective lives.

Which of the seven sub-regions will do best out of the scheme remains to be seen. Certainly, Dublin must be poised to get the lion's share of advantage. There are two reasons for this: it was the first sub-region to be delineated and organised, and secondly, in spite of its vast resources, it was not encumbered with responsibility for any other neighbouring county.

Industrial Promoters

IDB Chaiman, Sir Eric McDowell (right) and Herr Axel Assmus, Chief Executive of Sigro (UK) Ltd, examine a sun roof component manufactured by the company at its new Londonderry plant for General Motors range of Vauxhall cars. The £1.7 million investment is located in a purpose-built 33,000 sq. ft. factory at Londonderry's Campsie Industrial Estate and was expected to create 40 jobs by 1991.

KEVIN BONNER

Civil Servant
Davitt House, Adelaide Road, Dublin 2
(01) 765861
Born to Seán and Bríd Bonner (née Ward) on 17 December 1946. Educated at Meenbanad National School, Dungloe Secondary School, the Rosses, Co. Donegal, Graduate of UCD and of TCD. Married to Katherine Larkin with two sons Manus and Eoin. Joined Dept of Labour as Administrative Officer in 1967 and has worked in most areas of the Department at various levels as well as spending several years as Social Affairs Attaché in the Irish Representation in Brussels. At present Secretary Dept of Labour, member of the National Economic and Social Council, Sectoral Development Committee, Special Task Force on Employment and of the Council of Economic and Social Research Institute.

DR CHRISTY BOYLAN

Landscape Architect
Mt Prospect Avenue, Dublin 3
(01) 331941
Born to Hugh C. and Kathleen Boylan (née Hanratty) at Ballyjamesduff on 16 July, 1946. Educated at Ballyjamesduff NS, Kilnaleck VS, Multyfarnham Agricultural College, National Botanic Gardens, UCD and Michigan State University Married to Máiréad Anne O'Riordan with three daughters, Michelle, Yvonne and Louise. Formerly gardener, National Botanic Gardens, research assistant with Michigan State University, and parks superintendant, Dublin Corporation. At present senior executive landscape architect, Dublin Corporation and president of the Tree Council of Ireland.

JOSEPH BROSNAN

Civil Servant
72/76 St Stephen's Green, Dublin 2
(01) 789711
Born to Patrick and Catherine Brosnan (née Walsh) in Co. Kerry on 15 April 1946. Educated at Kilmurry Boys' and Castleisland Boys' National Schools, St Brendan's College Killarney, St Patrick's College Maynooth, UCD and King's Inns. Married to Mary Murray with two children. Formerly research counsellor Law Reform Commission. At present secretary Department of Justice.

PAUL BYRNE

County Manager
Council Offices, Riverside, Sligo
(071) 43221
Born to William and Margaret Byrne (née Brophy) at Longford on 16

June, 1932. Educated at Convent of Mercy, Marist Brothers Sligo, and at Summerhill College, Sligo. Later extra-mural student at UCG where he was awarded a diploma in social and economic science. Married to Nora McGee with three sons, Colman, Dermot and Finbarr (deceased), and two daughters, Emer and Aisling. Formerly clerical officer, Sligo County Council, town clerk, Kells UDC, staff officer, county accountant and county secretary with Donegal County Council, programme manager North Western Health Board and county manager, Rocommon. At present Sligo County Manager, chairman Sligo County Development Team and Hawkswell Theatre Co. Ltd, member Sligo County Enterprise Fund and of the North West Small Industries Committee of IDA. Member of County and City Managers' Association and County and City Managers' Society.

PATRICK J. CLARKE
Chief Executive
Kells, Co. Meath
(046) 40341
Born to Patrick and Margaret Clarke (née Gogarty) in Co. Meath on 9 April 1931. Married with six children. Formerly chief executive Central Fisheries Board Dublin. At present chairman National Ambulance Council and board member Institute of Public Administration, An Bord Altranais and National Council for the Elderly.

DÓNAL CONNOLLY
County Manager
Courthouse, Roscommon
(0903) 26100
Born to Daniel and Mary Connelly (née Kiely) in Co. Waterford on 27 November 1942. Member of the Chartered Institute of Secretaries, and the Institute of Public Administration and holds the Diploma in Local Administration. Married to Kathy Curran with eight children. Formerly clerical officer CIE, Cork County Council and Waterford County Council, staff officer Tipperary (NR) County Council, Waterford County Council, county accountant Tipperary (SR), county secretary Westmeath County Council, assistant county manager Tipperary (SR). At present Roscommon County Manager and chairman Arigna Enterprise Company.

JOHN CORCORAN
Public Administrator
Adelaide Road, Dublin 2
(01) 765861
Born to William and Margaret Corcoran (née Sheridan) at Dublin on 27 March, 1944. Educated at Donore Avenue CBS, Synge Street CBS, and at UCD. Single. Formerly held various positions within the Department of

Labour and Social Affairs Attaché, Irish Permanent Representation, Brussels. At present assistant secretary, Manpower Division, Department of Labour. Member Royal Dublin Society, Hermitage Golf Club, Regent and Civil Service Bridge Clubs.

SEÁN CROMIEN
Civil Servant
Upper Merrion Street, Dublin 2
(01) 767571
Born at Dublin in October 1929. Educated at North Brunswick Street CBS and at UCD whence he graduated with a degree in economics in 1950. Single. Formerly executive officer in Office of Public Works. He has spent most of his career in the Department of Finance which he joined as administrative officer in 1952. Head of Budget and Planning Division for ten years. Chairman of the Institute of Public Administration 1986/87. At present secretary of the Department of Finance, director of Central Bank of Ireland, member of the National Economic and Social Council, the Government Task Force on Employment and the Advisory Committee to the National Treasury Management Agency. He is also alternate governor for Ireland on the Board of the World Bank and the European Bank for Reconstruction and Development. Executive committee member of the Economic and Social Research Institute and council member of the Statistical and Social Inquiry Society. Past president of the Half Moon Swimming Club.

PHILIP F. CURRAN
Retired Public Administrator
Dublin Castle, Dublin 2
(01) 792777
Born to John and Eileen Curran (née Tucker) at Dublin on 6 May 1926. Educated at Synge Street CBS and at UCD whence he graduated with a first class honours BComm degree and Diploma in Public Administration. Married to Cumain (née Ní Chochlain) with five sons. Formerly with Depts of Foreign Affairs and Finance, he held a number of posts with the Revenue Commissioners before being appointed a revenue commissioner and eventually chairman of the Revenue Commissioners. Member of Dún Laoghaire Golf Club.

MICHAEL DEIGAN
County Manager
County Hall, Portlaoise
(0502) 22044
Born to William and Mary Deigan (née Kelly) at Kilkenny on 6 July 1931. Educated at St John's De La Salle Primary School Kilkenny, Kilkenny City Vocational School and University of Edinburgh. Married to Margaret Patricia Gleeson with two sons. Formerly assistant county engineer

73

Limerick County Council and Tipperary North Riding County Council, chief assistant county engineer Laois County Council and Tipperary North Riding County Council, senior engineer Dublin County Council, programme manager Mid-Western Health Board and Roscommon County Manager. At present Laois County Manager, and member Construction Industry Training Committee of FÁS and Nenagh Golf Club.

MICHAEL NOEL DILLON
County Manager
County Hall, Wexford
(053) 22211
Born to Michael and Mary Dillon (née Reidy) at Cork on 27 December 1936. Educated at CBS Cork, PBC Cork and UCC. Qualified FCIS. Married to Delia Barrett with three sons and two daughters. Formerly Limerick assistant county manager, Limerick county secretary and Limerick finance officer. At present Wexford county manager, deputy chairman Fire Services Council, director National Building Agency and chairman Irish National Heritage Park Trust. Member Rosslare Golf Club and Wexford Harbour Sailing Club. Awarded Gold Medal Public Administration, Wexford Person Award and World Life Saving — Citation.

SEÁN DORGAN
Civil Servant
Kildare Street, Dublin 2
(01) 614444
Born at Cork in 1951. Educated at St Brendan's College Killarney and UCD whence he graduated with BComm and MEconSc degrees. Married to Mary Lennan with four children. At present secretary Department of Industry and Commerce.

PATRICK DOWD
County Manager
County Hall, Cork
(021) 276891
Born to James and Kathleen Dowd (née Farrelly) in Co. Cavan on 16 April 1927. Educated at Keelagh National School, St Patrick's College Cavan and School of Accountancy Glasgow. Holds ACIS, FSCA and DLA qualifications. Married to Nora Sweeney. Formerly secretary Tipperary (SR) County Council and county manager Laois and Offaly County Council. At present Cork county manager. Member Douglas Golf Club.

PATRICK J. DOYLE
County Manager
Courthouse, Carrick-on-Shannon, Co. Leitrim
(078) 20005
Born to Dominick and Margaret Doyle (née Heavey) at Newbridge, Co.

Galway on 25 February 1931. Educated at Windfield National School Ballinasloe, Garbally Park, Ballinasloe and Institute of Public Administration. Married to Mary T. Leahy with four children. At present Leitrim County Manager, chairman County Leitrim Development Team, director Leitrim Enterprise Fund and Arigna Enterprise Fund.

FRANCIS J. FEELY
County Manager
City Hall, Dublin 2
(01) 6796111
Born to Thomas and Jane Feely (née Gogarty) at Dublin on 13 May 1931. Educated at Synge Street Christian Brothers and School of Accountancy Glasgow. Married to Ita Deegan with one son and three daughters. Formerly Dublin Housing Co-ordinator, Dublin assistant City and County manager and deputy Dublin City and County manager. At present Dublin City manager and town clerk, Dublin county manager, president Institute of Public Administration, member board of Dublin Tourist Organisation and of the Board of Dublin Promotions Organisation Ltd. First recipient Lord Mayor's Award. Fellow Chartered Association of Certified Accountants.

JOHN GALLAGHER
Director General
57/61 Lansdowne Road, Dublin 4
(01) 686233
Born to Paddy and Minnie Gallagher (née Whittle) at Ennis Co. Clare on 9 February 1943. Educated at Ennis CBS, St. Flannan's College Ennis, UCD and School of Public Administration. Married to Agnes McManus with two sons and three daughters. Formerly member of the Advisory Committee to the Public Accounts Committee, executive officer Dept of Industry and Commerce and administrative officer, assistant principal, principal and assistant secretary Dept of Finance. At present director general Institute of Public Administration on loan from the Dept of Finance. Fellow of Institute of Personnel Management, associate member of Public Relations Institute of Ireland and secretary to Consultative Group of Chief Executives of State Agencies.

DR JOHN F.A. HARBISON
State Pathologist
Trinity College, Dublin 2
(01) 772941
Born to Dr James Austin and Sheelagh Harbison (née MacSherry) at Dublin on 23 December 1935. Educated at St Gerard's School Bray, Stonyhurst College, Blackburn, and at TCD. Awarded Diploma in Medical Jurisprudence at London and admitted member and later fellow of Royal College of Pathologists. Formerly lecturer in forensic medicine,

University of Leeds, senior registrar in pathology at Westminister Hospital and at Royal Devon and Exeter Hospital, senior lecturer in forensic medicine at the London Hospital Medical College. At present State Pathologist and lecturer in medical jurisprudence at TCD, honorary medical advisor to Howth Life Boat Station and honorary medical referee, Ireland, Royal National Life Boat Institution. Member Howth Yacht Club, Irish Cruising Club, Irish Railway Records' Society, past president Medico-Legal Society of Ireland and council member British Association in Forensic Medicine.

SÉAMUS HAYES

County Manager
County Hall, Clonmel
(052) 21960
Born to Martin and Nano Hayes (née Burke) at Cappawhite Co. Tipperary on 29 March 1930. Associate member of the Corporation of Secretaries (ACCS). Married to Una Powell with four sons and two daughters. Formerly held posts as county accountant, county secretary and assistant county manager in Tipperary (SR), Longford and Kerry County Councils respectively, also County Manager with Wicklow County Council. At present County Manager Tipperary South Riding County Council, chairman Local Government Computer Services Board and member of the Industrial Development Authority Small Industries Board for the South East. Founder member Clonmel Lions Club and member Clonmel Golf Club.

JAMES C. HEHIR

Civil Servant
Phoenix House, Conyngham Road, Dublin 8
(01) 711900
Born to John and Susan Hehir (née McNamara) at Ennis on 19 December 1945. Educated at Lack NS, Ennis CBS and UCD whence he graduated with a BComm degree and a diploma in Public Administration. Married to Jean (née Reid) with four sons. Formerly assistant principal Dept of the Environment. At present managing director, Housing Finance Agency plc.

JACK HIGGINS

City Manager
Sarsfield House, Limerick
(061) 45799
Born in Cork in 1936. Educated at North Monastry CBS Cork. Obtained Gold Medal and Diploma in Local Administration from the Institute of Public Administration. Married to Philomena Coleman with three sons and three daughters. Formerly clerical officer Cork County Council, staff officer Clare County Council, county accountant Waterford County

Council, county secretary Wicklow County Council and assitant city manager Cork. At present Limerick city manager.

MICHAEL JOHN HOCTOR

General Manager
3 Pery Square, Limerick
(061) 315377
Born to Daniel and Eileen Hoctor (née O'Driscoll) at Fermoy Co. Cork on 26 August 1932. Educated at St Mary's College Rathmines, UCD and UCG. Married to Mary Flanagan with four children. Formerly president Chartered Institute of Transport in Ireland. At present general manager Limerick Harbour Commissioners and member of Review Group on Commercial Harbours and Pilotage established by the Minister of the Marine. Member and past president Limerick/Shannon Rotary Club and member Thomond Archaeological Society.

ANTHONY STROTHER HOPKINS

Chief Executive,
IDB House, 64 Chichester Street, Belfast BT1 4JX
(0232) 233233
Born to Strother Smith and Alice Roberta Hopkins on 17 July 1940. Educated at Campbell College and Queen's University Belfast where he obtained a BSc(Econ) degree. Married to Dorothy Moira McDonough with one son and two daughters. Formerly manager Thompson McLintock & Co, Chartered Accountants London, principal Department of Commerce N. Ireland and chief executive NI Development Agency. At present chief executive Industrial Development Board for N. Ireland. Member Oriental Club and Royal Belfast Golf Club.

DANIEL F. HURLEY

County Manager
Arus Brugha, Dungarvan, Waterford
(058) 42822
Born to David and Margaret Hurley (née Linehan) at Cork on 18 May 1932. Educated at North Monastery Cork, Cork School of Commerce and UCC. Married to Elizabeth Walsh with two sons. Formerly staff officer Cork Corporation, personnel officer Cork Corporation, industrial relations manager Irish Dunlop Co Ltd, personnel manager Southern Health Board, manager Special Hospitals Programme Mid Western Health Board, assistant county manager Cork County Council, county manager Westmeath County Council and chairman Local Government Computer Services Board. At present county manager Waterford County Council, director Housing Finance Agency, Tramore Fáilte Ltd, Waterford Airport Co Ltd, Tramore Holiday Villas Ltd and Tramore Properties Development Ltd.

BRIAN JOHNSTON

County Manager
Courthouse, Cavan
(049) 31799

Born to George and Catherine Johnston (née Wallace) at Co. Cavan on 18 January 1942. Educated at Ballyhaise National School, St Patrick's College Cavan and Institute of Public Administration. Married to Mary Dunne with four daughters, Catherine, Paula, Louise and Clare and three sons, Kieran, Philip and Brian. Formerly assistant manager Wicklow County Council, county secretary Wicklow County Council, town clerk Dundalk UDC, county development officer Louth and Longford, staff officer Longford County Council, town clerk Westport and Cavan UDCs, director National Development Corporation Ltd and Horizon Radio, Bray. At present county manager Cavan, chairman Cavan County Development Team, board member Cavan County Enterprise Fund, Small Industries IDA North/East Region and secretary County and City Managers Society. Honorary life member Wicklow Golf Club and member Cavan Golf Club.

MICHAEL KILLEEN

County Manager
Dublin Road, Longford
(043) 46231

Born to Michael and Anne Killeen (née Reidy) at Limerick on 4 October 1940. Educated at Sexton Street CBS Limerick and School of Commerce Limerick. Married with three sons and one daughter. Formerly finance officer Midland Health Board, hospitals manager Western Health Board and town clerk Tullamore. At present county manager Longford.

NOEL LINDSAY

Secretary
Marlborough Street, Dublin 1
(01) 734700

Born in Dublin. Educated at Synge Street CBS and at TCD. Married with two children. Particularly noted for his work in connection with development of community and comprehensive schools and Regional Technical Colleges. Extensive experience in curriculum and programme development and in examinations area of Department. As head of Building Unit was to the fore in up-dating and streamlining its operations in meeting accommodation and educational needs of a rapidly expanding school going population. Has been closely associated with third-level educational developments including development of links between educational institutions and industry. Also served as a consultant with OECD and had two periods of service with World Bank working on educational development in a number of European countries and throughout Middle East. At present secretary Department of Education.

SEÁN P. MacCARTHY
County Manager
Couthouse, Tullamore, Co. Offaly
(0506) 21419
Born at Cork in 1933. Educated at Presentation Brothers College Cork and UCC. Married to Marie Cashman with four sons and one daughter. At present Offaly County Manager.

EDWARD F.J. McCUMISKEY
Civil Servant
Áras Mhic Dhiarmada, Dublin 1
(01) 786444
Born to James G. and Emily A. McCumiskey (née Bingham) at London on 8 October 1941. Educated at O'Connell's School Dublin, UCD and King's Inns. Married to Mary Mullin with four children. Formerly director Social Welfare Services Office. At present secretary Department of Social Welfare.

CATHAL C. MacDOMHNAILL
Civil Servant
Dublin Castle, Dublin 2
(01) 6792777
Born to Tony and Ellen McDonnell (née Gleeson) at Tralee, Co. Kerry on 14 August 1933. Educated at Tralee CBS and UCD (where he obtained BComm 1st Class Hons degree) and by Commission Exams for Inspector of Taxes. Married to Róisín McGinley with three daughters. Formerly held various positions from Inspector of Taxes in Limerick, Letterkenny, Galway and Dublin to Assistant Secretary, Revenue Commisioners Dublin Castle. At present Chairman of Revenue Commissioners.

JOHN McGINLEY
County Manager
Courthouse, Nenagh, Co. Tipperary
(067) 31771
Born to John and Theresa McGinley (née Hunt) at Laytown, Co. Meath, on 6 August 1934. Educated at CBS Drogheda, College of Commerce Rathmines and Institute of Public Administration. Admitted to membership Chartered Institute of Secretaries and holds diplomas in Local Administration and in Social Studies. Married to Máiréad Ruttledge with four daughters. Formerly held positions with Bord Iascaigh Mhara, Department of Justice, town clerk Cavan, Ballina, and Drogheda, borough accountant Sligo, and county secretary Clare. At present county manager, Tipperary North Riding County Council. Member Geographical Society of Ireland, Regional Studies Association and Political Studies Association of Ireland.

KIERAN McGOWAN
Managing Director
Wilton Park House, Dublin 2
(01) 686633
Born to Dan and Molly McGowan (née Hayes) at Dublin on 17 November, 1943. Educated at Milltown NS, Synge Street CBS and UCD whence he graduated with an honours BComm degree. Married to Breda Fitzgerald with one son, Neil, and three daughters, Emer, Karen and Fiona. Formerly small business manager, London office manager and executive director with the IDA; board member of Engineering Studies, NCEA; member of Government Marketing Group for the International Financial Services Centre; member of UCD Advisory Committee on Commerce and Industry. At present managing director Industrial Development Authority, director National Lottery Company Limited, member of the executive committee and of the national council Irish Management Institute. Board member Peamount Hospital.

DESMOND PETER MAHON
County Manager
Áras an Chontae, Castlebar, Co. Mayo
(094) 24444
Born to Peter and Ellen Mahon (née Kenny) at Roscommon on 16 October 1946. Educated at CBS Roscommon and Institute of Public Administration. Married with two sons and one daughter. Formerly financial accountant Western Health Board, finance officer Clare County Council and assistant county manager Donegal County Council. At present Mayo County Manager. Member Westport and Enniscrone Golf Clubs and Westport Lions Club.

JOHN F. MAHONY
Civil Servant
51 St Stephen's Green, Dublin 2
(01) 613111
Born to Thomas and Margaret Mahony (née Keane) at Ardfert, Co. Kerry on 27 August 1942. Educated at Tralee CBS, School of Public Administration and College of Industrial Relations Married to Connie Cahill with one son and three daughters. At present chairman of Commissioners of Public Works and member of Board of Governors and Guardians National Gallery of Ireland. Member Stackstown Golf Club. Awarded Companion of the Institution of Engineers of Ireland.

DERMOT NALLY
Secretary to the Government
Merrion Street, Dublin 2
(01) 689333
Born to Mr and Mrs W.F. Nally (née Gilmartin) at Dublin on 10

December 1927. Educated at Synge Street, Belvedere, UCD and London University. Married to Joan McCarthy with four daughters and one son. Formerly director An Foras Forbatha, and member Executive Committee of Institute of Public Administration. At present Secretary to the Government, Civil Service Commissioner and Chairman Top Level Appointments Committee. Also responsible for International Affairs and N. Ireland Division in Dept of the Taoiseach. Member Milltown Golf Club and Lahinch Golf Club.

MICHAEL JOHN NUNAN
County Manager
New Road, Ennis, Co. Clare
(065) 21614
Born to David and Katherine Nunan (née Finn) at Kilfinane on 29 September 1929. Educated at Kilfinane, St Andrew's Secondary School and at the Institute of Public Administration. Married to Margaret O'Brien with three daughters. Formerly clerical officer and staff officer Limerick County Council, county accountant Leitrim, senior administrative officer Dublin, county secretary Carlow, assistant county manager Cork and county manager Roscommon. At present Clare county manager and director Craggaunowen Project.

SEÁN Ó BROSNACHÁIN
Civil Servant
Parkgate, Dublin 8
(01) 771881
Born in Co. Kerry in 1931. Educated at CBS Tralee and at TCD. Married to Kathleen Kelliher with four daughters. Formerly executive officer with the Civil Service and served in various sections of the Department of Defence. At present secretary Department of Defence.

PÁDRAIG Ó hUIGINN
Civil Servant
Government Buildings, Dublin 2
(01) 689333
Born at Cork in 1924. Educated at St Finbarr's College Cork, UCD and University of Edinburgh. Married to Pádraigín Ní Lideadha with four children. Formerly served in the Departments of the Environment, Industry and Commerce, Lands and Economic Planning and Development, as well as the Department of the Taoiseach. Has had extensive international experience at senior levels. Served as director for Regional Policy and deputy director general for Energy, Science and Technology at EC Council of Ministers in Brussels. Former Economic Affairs Officer with UN Economic Commission for Europe in Geneva and Officer-in-charge of the Housing, Building and Planning Branch at UN Headquarters, New York. At present secretary Dept of the Taoiseach,

chairman National Economic and Social Council, Central Review Committee, International Financial Services Committee and Task Force on Employment. Member of Customs House Docks Development Authority and Irish Museum of Modern Art.

DERMOT B. QUIGLEY

Revenue Commissioner
Dublin Castle, Dublin 2
(01) 6792777
Born to John and Ann Quigley (née O'Neill) at Dublin on 3 February 1942. Educated at CBS Greystones, CBS Westland Row and at UCD. Married to Elizabeth Dolores Kinsella with six children. Formerly assistant secretary in Budget and Taxation Division and in Finance Division (Borrowing and Debt Management), Department of Finance. At present Revenue Commissioner.

THOMAS P. RICE

Local Authority Manager
City Hall, Cork
(021) 966222
Born at Dublin in March 1934. Educated at Coláiste Mhuire and UCD. Holds diploma in Public Administration. Married to Mary (née Hamilton) with six children. Formerly assistant principal Department of Local Government, county secretary Tipperary (NR) County Council, assistant county manager Cork County Council, county manager Tipperary (SR) County Council and city manager and town clerk Limerick Corporation and chairman Local Government Computer Services Board. At present city manager and town clerk Cork Corporation and vice chairman County and City Managers Association. Member Cork Golf Club.

Chapter 6
Laws and Lawyers

Consider what you think justice requires, and decide accordingly. But never give your reasons; for your judgement will probably be right, but your reasons will certainly be wrong.

Lord Mansfield

That's Illegal!

No cry is more likely to raise hackles at a meeting than the suggestion that some decision or proposal is, in some way, in breach of the law. Stands are taken, precedents quoted, and hob lawyers consulted. And yet, as everybody knows, the law is an ass. A grey ass very often. A black and white zebra very seldom. Absolute legitimacy is a concept with which practising lawyers rarely have to contend. Besides, judges do not live in purdah and maybe even a supreme court judge might, from time to time, find the temptation to park his car where he should not park his car to be too strong to resist.

Laws can be ambiguous. Laws can be circumvented. Laws can be bent. In any event, as everybody knows, Irish law is based on English law and to that extent it may be subjected to the butt of ridicule with some impunity. Irish law is also based on the Constitution of 1937. Statutes passed before 1921 in the United Kingdom are enforceable in Ireland, unless, or until, they are revoked by the Irish Parliament. The Jurisdiction of Courts and Enforcement of Judgments (European Communities) Act came into force in the Republic on 1 June; it is a complicated Act, but in simple terms, it is intended that any person or company ordinarily resident in Ireland will have the option of suing in Ireland a person or a company ordinarily resident in another EC country, and having any judgment which they may obtain enforced in the other EC country, and vice versa. Similar legislation is also in force in the United Kingdom, and thus in Northern Ireland.

Lawyers in both parts of the island fall into three main categories, judges, barristers, and solicitors.

The Courts

Minor disputes and minor offences in the Republic are dealt with speedily in district courts, which are presided over by a judge without a jury. The judge is called a District Justice or, more familiarly, a 'DJ' but this appellation has tended towards disuse with the realisation that DJ has become a term of endearment for those purveyors of rhythm known as disc jockeys.

More serious disputes and offences are dealt with in circuit courts. Whereas there are twenty-four district courts, there are only eight circuit courts. As this is a higher court, it will also deal with appeals from the District Court.

Heavyweight disputes and offences are dealt with by the High Court where the judge may sit with a jury of twelve citizens. When the High Court deals with criminal matters, it is known as the Central Criminal Court. Naturally, it also deals with appeals against decisions of the Circuit Court.

Since 1972 there has also been a 'special' criminal court which is similar to the High Court but without a jury. The existence of this special court rests on successive governments being satisfied that special arrangements are needed to deal with subversive elements. A court of criminal appeal deals with appeals against decisions of the Circuit Court, the Central Criminal Court or Special Criminal Court in criminal matters. The final court of appeal is the Supreme Court which has, in recent years, become famous for its decisions on constitutional matters.

The legal advisor to the Government is known as the Attorney General. He attends cabinet meetings and represents the State in civil proceedings.

Criminal proceedings on behalf of the State are instituted by the Director of Public Prosecutions. This office is independent of Government, and carries most onerous responsibilities. It must not institute proceedings unless it is satisfied that they can succeed. Errors can bring disgrace and ruin to the prosecuted individual. Errors can also cause financial ruin as a defendant, who does not qualify for free legal aid, may, if he or she is successful in defending, be ruined financially by the costs.

While the courts have power to award costs to successful litigants, the State is never ordered to pay the costs of a citizen against whom it has wrongfully instituted proceedings.

North v. South

The 'administration of justice' is a phrase which was used so frequently with reference to Northern Ireland that it almost came to pass that one automatically expected it to be followed by the words 'in Northern Ireland'. Since the successful appeals by the Guildford Four and the Birmingham Six, British Justice generally has been seen to be hostile to Irish citizens.

No Extradition

Dermot Finucane making a fast getaway from the Four Courts in March 1990 on the back of a friend's motorbike after winning his appeal against extradition.

Concern about justice in Northern Ireland is legitimate. Indeed, concern about justice anywhere is legitimate. But concern about justice in the United Kingdom is so never-ending that the visitor might get the impression that the legal system in the Republic is beyond reproach and the legal system in the United Kingdom is most unsatisfactory.

Osgur Breatnach, Nicky Kelly and Brian McNally had been convicted in 1978 of involvement in the 1976 Sallins mail train robbery solely on the basis of confessions allegedly obtained by ill-treatment during incommunicado detention. The Court of Criminal Appeal in 1980 ruled that the confessions of Osgur Breatnach and Brian McNally had been involuntary and quashed their sentences. Nicky Kelly was released on 'humanitarian grounds' in 1984.

All three have attempted to bring civil actions for damages against the state (see Amnesty International Report 1990). Nicky Kelly was prevented from proceeding with his civil action in 1986; no decision has yet been reached on whether to allow Brian McNally's action.

Amnesty International was concerned that Osgur Breatnach and Nicky Kelly appeared to have been prevented from having their claims of police ill-treatment fully and impartially investigated. They urged the government to establish an independent inquiry into all the allegations of ill-treatment in custody made in connection with the 1976 Sallins mail train robbery, and to make the findings public.

Debt Collection and Appeals

There is widespread belief that anyone, lucky enough to be supplied with goods or services on credit, need not pay for them or, at any rate, need not pay for a very long time, if he or she so wishes. Incredible frustration is caused by the procedures to be followed in bringing a debtor before a court, by the costs of being professionally represented and by the number of legal representatives required. All of these factors contribute to a situation in which businessmen are reluctant to use the services of the courts, which is a most unhealthy situation.

Sometimes, small consumer complaints are taken up by journalists rather than by lawyers. Businesses are contacted by them with the implied threat of adverse publicity for the firm concerned. This adverse publicity may follow in press, on radio or on television, even if the claim is fully allowed. Consumers resort to the media because the legal system is too expensive and too slow. There must be a strong case for debt collection and consumer complaints being dealt with in small claims courts.

The tactic whereby funds may be lodged in court with a defence suggests to many people that a wealthy defendant has an unfair advantage over a struggling one. This is an unsavoury situation and rests uneasily with the general theory of justice being available to all.

The cheque book syndrome also manifests itself in the area of appeals because, as long as the client can afford to pay the lawyers, he or she can appeal decisions. Free legal aid is not widely available for civil disputes and so an injured party with a perfectly valid complaint may be forced to drop it if faced with an opponent who has the resources to appeal from a lower court to a higher.

Costs and Negligence

The appropriateness of the adversarial system as a means of dealing with personal injury cases is suspect. Take an injury which results in, say, the loss of one limb as an example. A simple tribunal could surely assess a situation like this and make an award within four months of receipt of claim. The present system takes far longer. The average period of time between injury and award, in cases reported in a national daily newspaper over a six-month period, was found to be four years (the shortest period being eleven months and the longest eight years).

Key witnesses, who might be available within four months, could very well not be available at the end of four years. Although the number of such cases coming before the courts may be in a minority, the administration of them gives reasons for concern.

The lack of direct access to barristers is frustrating, whether access is needed for communication or liability purposes. The situation where a barrister in court may perform well or badly, but *never* negligently, is obviously unjust but that is the situation that prevails.

If an Irish service company serves negligently, it may be brought to account for its negligence. The exemption of barristers from similar accountability raises serious questions as to the administration of justice in Ireland — both North *and* South.

On costs, it is high time for the legal profession to come to terms with the idea of telling customers in advance just how much they may expect to pay for various services. Competition in an open market is a desirable element in maintaining and improving customer service. Written professional standards should oblige all lawyers to declare, at the initial interview, the hourly charging rate or percentage of the value of the transaction upon which the final fee will be based. Alternative forms of dispute resolution have been developed in the US, adopted in the UK, and heralded for the Republic in August 1991. Mediations, synonymous with conciliation, and Executive Tribunals synonymous with 'mini-trials' are speedier than traditional litigation and arbitration, and dispense with the need for long drawn-out procedures.

Users

With the costs of litigation frequently exceeding the amounts in dispute, most people avoid going to court twice. If they are lucky, they will go through life without ever being in court. If they are unlucky, one such experience will ensure they avoid another like the plague.

As a result, the buyer of legal services is, more often than not, a complete novice, and the time, place, and cost of each consultation and court hearing will be arranged with little or no reference to the buyer, who is, in many respects, paying the piper without calling the tune.

Paying the piper and not calling the tune is a very unpleasant experience and, as a result, most litigants are unwilling to pay a second time, and are not interested in reform of a system which is so much in need of reform. If the system were consumer oriented, the client would indicate to the lawyer when and where he or she would be available for consultation, and for court or arbitration hearings. If, in addition, it were provided that legal fees could not exceed, say, 20 per cent of the amount in dispute, it would become incumbent on the lawyer to agree with his opposite number, a fast and efficient way of dealing with the case.

Legal costs frequently exceed the amounts in dispute. Fees should only be payable, of course, to the lawyer who undertakes the case. A frequent cause of complaint is the situation where the client consults on a number of occasions a particular barrister, who may, on the day of the hearing, transfer the pleading of the case to another barrister, without the full knowledge, prior consultation and consent of the client. Obviously, a barrister may, from time to time, be over-committed, or may not be available for some personal or professional reason but, in that case, not only should he forego his fee, but also the assumed and apparent right to transfer the brief.

Clients, on the other hand, who wish a change of barrister, quickly learn that they are prevented from so doing without first paying the fees claimed by the outgoing one. This is all very well in theory, since barristers are not entitled to sue for their fees, but, of course, in situations where an unsatisfactory service is provided, they should not be in a position to prevent a transfer of work simply by claiming that their fees are outstanding.

Reform

To the man in the street at any rate, the prospects for reform of the legal system appear to be very remote. So many senior politicians are members of the legal professions that a cosy relationship is widely believed to exist.

The Restrictive Practices Commission was asked in 1986 to make a study of the legal professions and its findings published in 1990 have been studied with interest.

Probably the best that users of the services of the legal professions can hope for in this decade is representation on the investigatory and disciplinary committees of the professional bodies. If lay participation were to comprise 50 per cent of the membership, and if such committees were not to be hampered by excess formality and over-emphasis on rules of evidence and procedure, it would represent a step in the right direction in the area of complaints. A green paper on reform of the UK's legal system, which would, of course, apply in Northern Ireland also, was published in January 1989 and contained a proposal for an advisory committee, with a majority of lay members, which would oversee professional conduct.

The Department of the Environment announced in March 1988 that legislation was being drafted to end solicitors' monopoly on the conveyancing of property. The Incorporated Law Society was reported as saying that consumers would see no lasting benefit from its ending. Yet, as long ago as 1976, the National Prices' Commission rejected the case for the monopoly in a report which concluded that 'Solicitors' charges and profits are higher than need be'.

Court and Constitution

It would be difficult to overstate the importance of the role played by the courts in dealing with the Constitution, especially in considering whether particular measures are repugnant to it or otherwise. The approach of the court will differ, depending on whether the measure was passed prior to the 1937 Constitution or subsequently. Naturally, there is a presumption that Acts passed by the Oireachtas subsequent to 1937 are Constitutional, but this, of course, is only a presumption. The work of the courts in this area is greatly admired and, on a number of occasions, interpretations of the Constitution by the courts have amounted to its own 'expansion'. While generally allowing Government considerable latitude in the difficult task of running the country, in the Crotty case for example, the Supreme Court held that the Government did not have the power to ratify the Single European Act without a Constitutional Amendment.

Legal Presidents
Her Excellency Mrs Mary Robinson, who was a prominent lawyer before her election as President of Ireland, with Mr Dónal Binchy, President of the Incorporated Law Society of Ireland.

MAX W. ABRAHAMSON
Lawyer
30 Upper Pembroke Street, Dublin 2
(01) 761941
Born to Leonard and Tillie Abrahamson (née Nurock) at Dublin on 29 October 1932. Educated at Sandford Park School and TCD. Married to Edna (née Walzman) with one son, Leonard, and three daughters, Gail, Lynne and Emily. Formerly lecturer in law at TCD, special examiner to the Incorporated Law Society of Ireland. Visiting lecturer in construction law to Trinity College and UCD, visiting professor, King's College London. At present a solicitor in practice, companion of the Insitute of Civil Engineers, honorary fellow of the Institution of Engineers in Ireland, fellow of the Chartered Institute of Arbitrators and first chairman of Irish branch, consultant to McCann Fitzgerald Sutton Dudley and to Baker and McKenzie internationally.

EAMONN MARY BARNES
Director of Public Prosecutions
St Stephen's Green, Dublin 2
(01) 789222
Born to John A. and Bridget Barnes (née Coleman) at Ballymote, Co. Sligo on 15 September 1934. Educated at Ballymote NS, Franciscan College Multyfarnham, St Nathy's Ballaghaderreen, UCD and King's Inns. Married to Dolores Walsh with five children. Formerly in private practice as barrister and legal assistant to Attorney General. At present director of Public Prosecutions. Member Woodbrook Golf Club and Bohemian Musical Society.

DÓNAL G. BINCHY
Solicitor
Quay House, Clonmel
(052) 21411
Born to James and Mary Binchy (née Devlin) on 4 February 1930. Educated at Clongowes Wood College, Incorporated Law Society and NUI. Married to Joan Kavanagh with two sons and two daughters. At present principal O'Brien & Binchy Solicitors, Clonmel and president Irish Law Society. Honorary member Canadian Bar Association.

ANTHONY EUGENE COLLINS
Solicitor
61 Fizwilliam Square, Dublin 2
(01) 761924
Born to Desmond J. and Hilda Collins (née Martin) on 12 April 1939. Educated at Xavier School Moorehampton, St Gerard's School Bray, Downside School Somerset, TCD and the Incorporated Law Society of Ireland. Married to Mary Deasy with four children. Formerly president Incorporated Law Society of Ireland. At present senior partner Eugene F.

Collins, council member Incorporated Law Society of Ireland, director Grafton Group plc and Dakota Group plc and chairman Automobile Association (Ireland). Honorary member Canadian Bar Association.

DECLAN COSTELLO
Judge
Four Courts, Dublin 7
(01) 725555
Born to John A. and Ida Costello (née O'Malley) at Dublin on 1 August 1926. Educated at Sacred Heart Convent Leeson Street, Xavier's School Donnybrook, UCD and King's Inns Dublin. Married to Joan Fitzsimons with five children. Formerly member of Dáil Éireann, Attorney General, member of Consultative Assembly of Council of Europe, appointed in 1979 to investigate and report on Whiddy Island disaster, chairman of Committee to advise on preparation of National Youth Policy and chairman of Committee of Enquiry into adequacy of statutory controls on fund raising for charitable purposes. At present Judge of the High Court, first chairman of National Association for the Mentally Handicapped in Ireland, president St Michael's House and Irish Legal History Society.

TIMOTHY HALPIN CROWLEY
Solicitor
69/71 St Stephen's Green, Dublin 2
(01) 780699
Born to Vincent and Eileen Crowley (née Gunning) at Dublin on 25 February 1935. Educated in Dublin at Xavier College, St Michael's Holy Ghost School, Blackrock College, St Vincent's College, Castleknock, UCD and at the Incorporated Law Society. Married to Bláthnait Duggan with two sons and one daughter. Formerly personal assistant to Arthur Cox, Solicitor. At present consultant to Gerrard Scallan and O'Brien, Solicitors. Member Stephen's Green Club and Royal St George Yacht Club.

TERRY de VALERA
Solicitor
Morgan Place, Dublin 7
(01) 725555
Born to Eamon and Sinéad de Valera at Dublin on 4 June 1922. Educated at Blackrock College and the Law School of the Incorporated Law Society of Ireland. Qualified as a solicitor in October 1945. Married to Phyllis Blake with two daughters, Síle and Jane. Formerly practising solicitor until appointed Taxing Master of the Supreme and High Courts in March 1969. At present Senior Taxing Master of the Supreme and High Courts. Writer and broadcaster on the life and works of the Irish composer John Field and also on Chopin, and Chopin's pupil Thomas Tellecsen. Author of unpublished biography of the late Frank McKelvey RHA. Has exhibited sculpture at RHA and Oireachtas art exhibitions. Also paintings. Member Old Dublin Society. Decorated with Order of

Merit by the Government of the Polish Peoples' Republic. Has also published lectures: 'Two 18th century Musical Instrument Makers', 'Sarah Curran's Musical Interests', 'Philip Cogan Irish Composer', 'J.B.S. MacIlwaine RHA', and many articles and lectures on John Field and on other subjects dealing with art in Ireland.

JOHN DOWLING
Chief Executive
Four Courts, Dublin 7
(01) 735689

Born to Jack and Betty Dowling (née Kielty) at Drogheda on 10 August 1944. Educated at national schools in Dublin, Navan and Kells, preparatory school London, Secondary Modern School Lingfield, Surrey, Agricultural College Multyfarnham and TCD whence he graduated with a BA in natural sciences. Later awarded graduate diploma in Industrial Relations by TCD. Married to Joan Collins with two daughters, Siobhán and Aoife. Formerly vocational school teacher, youth officer Foróige, training advisor AnCo, training specialist IPA, deputy general secretary Civil and Public Services Union, assistant general secretary Teachers' Unions of Ireland and general secretary Association of Higher Civil Servants. At present director of the General Council of the Bar of Ireland.

PATRICK ALOYSIUS DUFFY
Solicitor
Coalisland, Co. Tyrone

Born to Patrick Joseph and Margaret Duffy at Ardboe, Co. Tyrone on 19 July 1934. Educated at Mullinahoe Primary School, St Patrick's Academy Dungannon and Queen's University Belfast. Married to Mary Hackett with three sons. Formerly treasurer of SDLP, and member of N. Ireland Assembly and N. Ireland Convention. At present member Cookstown District Council, director of International Fund for Ireland, chairman Tyrone Crystal and vice president Law Society of Northern Ireland.

MICHAEL JOSEPH EGAN
Solicitor
Castlebar, Co. Mayo
(094) 21375

Born to Michael J. and Katie Egan (née Conway) at Castlebar on 6 February 1917. Educated at St Gerald's College, Castlebar, UCD and the Incorporated Law Society. Married to Eithne Rose Mary Moran with one son and eight daughters. Formerly president of Irish Association of Sovereign Order of Malta, Mayo Solicitors' Bar Association, Castlebar Chamber of Commerce and Castlebar Branch Gaelic League. At present principal of Egan, Daughter & Company Solicitors. Life member Royal Dublin Society, Royal Society of Antiquaries of Ireland and Military History Society. Member of County Club Galway, Royal Irish Automobile Club, Commonwealth Club London, Heraldry Society of Ireland

and English Heraldry Society. Honours include Bailiff Grand Cross of Obedience Sovereign Order of Malta, Papal Knight of St Gregory and Commander of Merit Sovereign Order of Malta.

SÉAMUS F. EGAN
Judge
Four Courts, Dublin 7
(01) 725555
Born to James S. and Grace Christina Egan (née O'Donnell) at Dublin on 1 December 1923. Educated at CBS Synge Street, Blackrock College, UCD and King's Inns. Married to Ada Leahy with two sons and five daughters. Formerly junior barrister on Western Circuit, practising senior counsel and Judge of the High Court. At present Judge of the Supreme Court. Member Milltown and Blainroe Golf Clubs, Fitzwilliam Lawn Tennis Club and Royal Dublin Society.

IAIN R. FARRELL
Solicitor
Newtown, Waterford
(051) 72934
Born to Riocard J. and Josephine Farrell (née Britton) at Dublin on 13 May 1938. Educated at Waterpark College Waterford, Glenstal Abbey, UCD and Incorporated Law Society. Married to Sheelagh Kane-Smith with four children. At present law agent Waterford Corporation and Waterford Harbour Commissioners. Honorary vice consul for Spain.

OLIVER GOLDING FRY
Solicitor and Consultant
Fitzwilton House, Wilton Place, Dublin 2
(01) 681711
Born to William Houghton and Marie Fry (née Fry) at Dublin on 3 May 1919. Educated at Avoca School Blackrock, TCD and Incorporated Law Society of Ireland. Married first to Marjorie Milligan (deceased 1982) with three sons, second to Hazel Archer. Formerly senior partner William Fry and Sons, Solicitors, chairman Royal Hospital Donnybrook, The Boots Co, various other companies and president Institute of Taxation. At present director Foundation for Fiscal Studies, Royal Hospital Donnybrook, Solicitors' Benevolent Association and other companies. Member Royal Irish Automobile Club and fellow Institute of Taxation in Ireland.

BRIAN GARRETT
Solicitor
7 Donegal Square East, Belfast BT1 5HD
(0232) 245034
Born to James Henry and Martha Garrett (née Clark) at Belfast in 1937. Educated at St Jude's Primary School, Methodist College, and Queen's

University, Belfast. Married to Kate Harvey with one son and two daughters. Formerly chairman Northern Ireland Labour Party, editor *Northern Ireland Law Society Gazette* and visiting fellow Harvard University 1977/78, president (1985–88) Irish Association for Social Cultural and Economic Affairs, member Northern Ireland Law Reform Advisory Committee, broadcaster, director of a number of companies, and Deputy Chairman (1988–91) Independent Commission for Police Complaints. At present partner Elliott Duffy Garrett, Solicitors, Belfast.

JOHN GORE-GRIMES
Solicitor
6 Cavendish Row, Dublin 1
(01) 748537
Born to Christopher and Dorothie Gore-Grimes (née Weir) at Dublin on 16 January 1942. Educated St Gerard's School, Glenstal Abbey, TCD and Incorporated Law Society of Ireland. Married to Jeanette (née Hallinan) with four daughters, Francesca, Emily, Natasha and Rachael. Formerly president Irish Association of Civil Liberties, member of Conveyancing Committee of Incorporated Law Society. At present partner Gore and Grimes Solicitors, deputy vice chairman Commissioners of Irish Lights, commodore Irish Cruising Club, council member Irish Association of Civil Liberties, lecturer on planning law and partnership law, member of Howth Branch Committee, Royal National Life Boat Institution. Life member Royal Dublin Society, member Irish Cruising Club, Howth and Royal St George Yacht Clubs, Royal Cruising Club, Cruising Club of America. Honorary life member Royal Irish Yacht Club and Skerries Sailing Club. Member Kildare Street and University Club and Ocean Cruising Club. Awarded Blue Water Medal of the Cruising Club of America (prior to joining) in 1983 for exploration in polar waters. Awarded Tilman Medal of the Royal Cruising Club for a voyage to the east coast of Greenland. Four times winner of Faulkner Cup of the Irish Cruising Club and numerous other awards of the ICC. Has had a number of books published by the Incorporated Law Society, has contributed towards law reform, IACL campaigns for the introducion of the Ombudsman (achieved) and abolition of juries in civil cases (nearly achieved).

JAMES J. HICKEY
Solicitor
1 Fitzwilliam Square, Dublin 2
(01) 614399
Born to J.G. and Dorinda Hickey (née Binchy) at Dublin on 27 March 1953. Educated at Mount Anville, Gonzaga College, TCD and Incorporated Law Society. Married to Fiona MacAnna with two children. Formerly director Project and Grapevine Arts Centres, and Film Makers Ireland. At present partner Amorys Solicitors and director Poolbeg Productions and Dublin Film Festival. Has practised as lawyer in media and entertainment business since 1980. Member Fitzwilliam Lawn Tennis Club.

JAMES J. IVERS
Consultant
Tullaghan, Co. Leitrim
(072) 41073
Born to John and Imelda Ivers (née Sheehan) at Cork on 1 October 1927. Educated at North Monastery and UCC and at UCD. Married to Nanette Grey with a large family. Formerly railway clerk, civil servant, general secretary Irish Dental Association, trading manager and joint general manager Waterford Co-Operative, chief executive officer North Western Health Board, president Opticians' Board and director general of the Incorporated Law Society of Ireland. At present Executive Director Solicitors' Mutual Defence Fund Ltd, member of the Legal Aid Board and Chairman, Commercial Dispute Resolution Ltd.

PATRICK C. KILROY
Solicitor/Company Director
69 Lower Leeson Street, Dublin 2
(01) 766184
Born to Thomas and Mary Kilroy (née Devine) at Callan, Co. Kilkenny on 12 October 1929. Educated at Christian Brothers Callan, St Kieran's College Kilkenny and UCD. Married to Dorothy Donnelly with five children. At present senior partner Kilroy & Co, Solicitors, chairman Gowan Group Ltd, Union Camp Ireland, director AGF-Irish Life Holdings plc, Banque Nationale de Paris (Ireland) Ltd, Irish Life plc, The Insurance Corporation of Ireland plc, Church & General Insurance plc and Irish Distillers Group plc. Member Milltown Golf Club and Fitzwilliam Lawn Tennis Club. Awarded Chevalier de l'ordre national du Mérite.

VIVIAN H. LAVAN
Judge
Four Courts, Dublin 7
(01) 720622
Born to Patrick and Sarah Lavan (née McCabe) at Derry on 27 June 1944. Educated at Cistercian College Roscrea, Terenure College Dublin, UCD and King's Inns, Dublin. Married to Una McCullough with two sons and two daughters. Formerly chairman of mining board, director of Legal Aid Board, treasurer of Bar Council, barrister at the Inner Temple, London, and the Inner Bar of Ireland. Fellow of International Academy of Trial Lawyers and honorary member of American Bar Association. At present Judge of the High Court. Member Fitzwilliam Lawn Tennis Club and National Yacht Club.

TERENCE KEVIN LISTON
Senior Counsel
Law Library, Four Courts, Dublin 7
(01) 720622
Born to Terence J. and Anne Liston (née Galvin) at Tralee, Co. Kerry on 3

July 1903. Educated at Christian Brothers Tralee, Clongowes Wood College, UCD and King's Inns. Married with four sons and one daughter. Formerly chairman of General Council of the Bar of Ireland, chairman Civil Service Arbitration Board, Garda Síochána Arbitration Board, Primary Teachers' Arbitration Board, Secondary Teachers' Arbitration Board, Vocational Education Teachers' Board, Curriculum Board, RTE and president Milltown Golf Club. At present senior bencher Honourable Society of King's Inns and 'father' of the Bar of Ireland. Member Milltown Golf Club, Fitzwilliam Lawn Tennis Club and St Stephen's Green Club.

JAMES GERALD LYONS
Solicitor
2 Upper Hartstonge Street, Limerick
(061) 314480
Born to Cornelius and Margaret Lyons (née Bartley) at Limerick on 27 February 1924. Educated at Crescent College Limerick, Clongowes Wood College Co. Kildare, UCD and the Law Society Dublin. Single. Formerly president Limerick Chamber of Commerce, Honorary German Consul for Limerick and Western Counties, member Planning Board/ University of Limerick and member Governing Body NIHE now University of Limerick. At present Limerick City Coroner. Member Incorporated Law Society, Limerick Bar Association and Limerick Chamber of Commerce. Was awarded German Cross of Merit.

OLIVER ANTHONY MACKLIN
Retired Judge
Athlone, Co. Roscommon
Born to Martin and Agnes Macklin (née Keane) at Kiltartan, Gort, Co. Galway on 1 September 1921. Educated at Athleague NS, De La Salle and CBS Roscommon, UCD, and Incorporated Law Society. Married to Philomena Kinlough with one son, David William Oliver, and one daughter, Ciara Mary Raphella. Formerly partner in Farrell McDonnell and Co Solicitors, Roscommon, and sole practitioner in Ballinasloe and Athlone; Judge of the District Court. President of the District Court. Chairman District Court Rules Committee and member of Committee on Court Practice and Procedure 1985–90.

JOHN LOYOLA MURRAY
Senior Counsel
Luxembourg
Born to John Cecil and Catherine Murray (née Casey) at Limerick on 27 June, 1943. Educated at Salesian NS, Crescent College, Rockwell College, UCD and King's Inns. Married to Gabrielle (née Walsh) with one son, Brian and one daughter, Catriona. Formerly Attorney General, president

Union of Students in Ireland, and member of the Council of State. At present Judge of the European Court and Bencher of the Honourable Society of the King's Inns.

S. WILLIAM RIORDAN
Solicitor
Wilton Place, Dublin 2
(01) 760631
Born to Syl and Eugenie Riordan (née Moriarty) at Dublin in July 1938. Educated at Willow Park Prep. School, Blackrock College, UCD and Incorporated Law Society. Married to Anne Frizelle with three children. Formerly legal officer Irish Shell & BP Ltd. At present managing partner Whitney Moore & Keller Solicitors, Dublin. Member Royal St George Yacht Club (commodore designate), Fitzwilliam Lawn Tennis Club, Stephen's Green Club and Foxrock Golf Club.

DÓNAL AIDAN ROCHE
Solicitor
3 Burlington Road, Dublin 4
(01) 760281
Born to Dónal and Eileen Roche (née Moore) at Dublin on 10 March 1954. Educated at Blackrock College, TCD and at the Incorporated Law Society. Married to Mary O'Flynn with three children. Formerly assistant solicitor Arthur Cox & Co. At present partner Commercial Department Matheson Ormsby Prentice. Member Killiney Golf Club, Royal St George Yacht Club and St Stephen's Green Club.

JOHN GALWEY RONAN
Solicitor
12 South Mall, Cork
(021) 272333
Born to John and Irene Margaret Ronan (née Nicholson) at Cobh on 3 August 1925. Educated at Worth Abbey, Clongowes Wood College and TCD. Admitted to membership of Incorporated Law Society of Ireland. Married to Wanda Melian (née Golden) with one son and four daughters. Formerly chairman, Cork Gas Company, and Trinity Bank Ltd and director, Calor Teo and Sedgwick Dineen. At present consultant with Ronan Daly Jermyn. Chairman Eagle Star Insurance, Shield Insurance, Shield Life Insurance and Eurostyle Ltd. Member Kildare Street and University Club.

NOEL C. RYAN
Director General
Blackhall Place, Dublin 7
(01) 710711
Born to Patrick and Mary Ryan (née Grimes) at Mullingar, Co.

Westmeath on 25 December 1942. Educated at St Mary's CBS Mullingar, UCD and King's Inns. Married to Una Ryan with six children. Formerly civil servant in the Departments of Defence, Finance, Public Service, Justice and Foreign Affairs, assistant secretary Dept of Justice and Foreign Affairs where he served on the Secretariat of the Anglo Irish Conference Belfast. At present director general Incorporated Law Society of Ireland.

BRYAN SHERIDAN
Solicitor
Bankcentre, Ballsbridge, Dublin 4
(01) 600311
Born to Charles J. and Eilish Sheridan (née Noonan) at Dún Laoghaire on 6 January 1951. Educated at De La Salle College Churchtown, UCD and Incorporated Law Society of Ireland. Married to Barbara Reade with three sons, Andrew, Mark and Matthew and one daughter, Melissa. Formerly assistant solicitor W.J. Shannon and Company, assistant solicitor Lysaght Dockrell Shields and Farrell, and partner Cawley Sheerin Wynne. At present group law agent, AIB Group, council member of the Irish Association of Civil Liberty, member Air Transport Users' Committee and Trademark Agent.

ANDREW FRANCIS SMYTH
Solicitor
1 Upper Ely Place, Dublin 2
(01) 766741
Born to William L. and Nora Smyth (née Kenny) at Tralee on 14 February 1934. Educated at Fairview NS, St Joseph's CBS Marino, St Joseph's CBC, Belvedere College, UCD and the Law Society. Married to Ann Ryan-Harvey with one child. Formerly captain and president Clontarf Golf Club and president Dublin Solicitors' Bar Association. At present practising solicitor and junior vice president Incorporated Law Society. Member Clontarf Golf Club and Hibernian United Service Club.

PETER D. SUTHERLAND
Bankcentre, Ballsbridge, Dublin 4
(01) 600311
Born to William and Barbara Sutherland (née Nealon) at Dublin on 25 April 1946. Educated at Gonzaga College, University College and King's Inns Dublin. Married to Maruja Cabria with two sons and one daughter. Formerly tutor in law at UCD, practising member of the Irish Bar, senior counsel, visiting lecturer University of St Louis School of Law, Bencher of the Honourable Society of King's Inns, and member of the Bar Council of Ireland. Former President of the Irish Bankers' Federation (1989/90), member of the Action Committee for Europe and a member of the Advisory Board of the European Community — American Trust. Served

twice as Attorney General and member of Council of State. Appointed member of the Commission of the European Communities in January 1985 with responsibility for competition, social affairs, education and training. Following accession of Spain and Portugal in January 1986, his responsibilities became related to the European Parliament and competition. At present senior counsel, chairman of AIB Group since October 1989, chairman of the Board of Governors of the European Institute of Public Administration (Maastricht). Also member of the Boards of The British Petroleum Company plc, GPA plc, James Crean plc, CRH plc, L.M. Ericsson Holdings (Ireland) Ltd, the Agricultural Trust and chairman Shannon Aerospace plc, member United Kingdom Bar, New York Bar, and licensed to practise in the Supreme Court of the United States of America. Awards include the first European law prize in Paris in 1988, the gold medal of the European Parliament and an LLD honoris causa from the University of St Louis, Missouri. Author of *1er Janvier 1993 — ce que va changer en Europe* (1988 University of Paris Press).

HERBERT WALLACE
Professor
Queen's University Belfast
(0232) 245133
Born to William and Sarah Jane Wallace (née Steenson) at Dungannon, Co. Tyrone on 5 September 1943. Educated at Drumglass Primary School Dungannon, Royal School Dungannon, Belfast Royal Academy and Queen's University Belfast. Married to Helen Margaret Maxwell with three daughters. Formerly member Land Law Working Group and consultant to DOE (NI) on Land Registration. At present Dean of Faculty of Law and director of School of Law at Queen's University Belfast. Also consultant to NIO on Land Law Reform. Member of Senate of Queen's University Belfast, and of the Council of Legal Education for Northern Ireland. Member of Society of Public Teachers of Law and of the Irish Association of Law Teachers.

HAROLD A. WHELAHAN
Attorney General
Merrion Street, Dublin 2
(01) 616944
Born to John Kevin and Maureen Whelehan (née Spollen) in Dublin on 17 February 1944. Educated at Christian Brothers Mullingar, Glenstal Abbley, UCD and King's Inns. Married to Joyce Boland with two daughters and four sons. Formerly practised at the Irish Bar. At present Attorney General. Member Royal Ocean Racing Club, Royal St George and Howth Yacht Clubs, Irish Cruising Club and Hibernian United Service Club.

Chapter 7
Accounts and Accountants

'For two days' labour, you ask two hundred guineas?'
'No, I ask it for the knowledge of a lifetime.'

Whistler

Visitors from many non English-speaking countries find the development of the accountancy profession in these islands something just short of incredible. This is especially true for visitors from countries where the accountant is seen as *guarda livros*, or literally, keeper of books.

In 1888, twelve accountants from Belfast, six from Cork and thirteen from Dublin petitioned the British Crown for a charter, which was subsequently granted to the Institute of Chartered Accountants in Ireland. At that time, there were probably only about nineteen accountants in practice in Belfast, six in Cork and about forty in Dublin. One hundred years later, the said Institute has 7,200 members and 2,200 student members. The mission of the Institute is to continue to be the professional body whose members and member firms are the premier providers of business services throughout Ireland, carried out to the highest professional and technical standards and whose particular purpose is to support, regulate and promote such members and member firms.

In considering this growth it must be borne in mind that members of other institutes of accountancy are recognised by law, and that the growth of the profession has been manifested not only in terms of numbers but also in terms of prestige and influence. The value of consultants' reports coming from respected firms of accountants is such that political decisions of all shapes and sizes are grounded on them. These may deal with anything from the installation of a telephone system in the parliament to a global review of the tourist industry.

The other institutes, whose members are authorised to act as auditors to limited companies, are the Chartered Association of Certified Accountants, the Institutes of Chartered Accountants of Scotland and in England and Wales, and the Institute of Certified Public Accountants. The jurisdictions of the two chartered institutes are, as their names imply, Scotland on the one hand and England and Wales on the other, while the certified accountants are organised as a world-wide body. The Institute of Certified Public Accountants is not to be confused with the Institute of Certified Public Accountants in the United States of America, which is the leading accountancy institute there.

Income tax was introduced to Ireland in 1853, thirty-five years before the incorporation of the Chartered Institute. Tax services have formed a significant part of the work of the Irish accountant for many years and although tax services are provided also by banks (mostly personal income tax) and by lawyers (mostly Stamp Duty and Capital Acquisition Tax), the lion's share of this important service industry is in the hands of firms of practising accountants. The Institute of Taxation in Ireland was formed in 1967 and now has over 1,500 members and over 1,400 students. It is an important publisher of books on taxation, including an annual summary, together with the Institute periodical, *Irish Tax Review*, and is also an important organiser of seminars on taxation issues, working sometimes jointly with the Institute of Chartered Accountants in Ireland.

Many accountants specialise in insolvency work and many firms have separate insolvency departments just as they have separate tax departments. The Institute of Chartered Accountants in Ireland was recognised under the British Insolvency Act 1986 and has issued licences to Irish chartered accountants to enable them to practise insolvency in the United Kingdom.

To the age-old question 'Who audits the auditors?' the eighth EC directive provides some form of answer. This essentially deals with the question of supervision of the work of auditors and in future this supervision will be detailed. In December 1987, in advance of details of how the eighth directive might be applied in the Republic, members of the Institute of Chartered Accountants (which operates on an all-Ireland basis) voted by a massive 88 per cent majority in favour of practice review. This means that the professional standards of each practising Irish chartered accountant will be reviewed by the Institute at least once in every five years. There are similar systems in Canada and in the USA, but the Irish Institute was the first to introduce practice review in Europe.

Price Waterhousehold
The winner of the Ulster Society prize in the Summer 1991 Examinations
of the Institute of Chartered Accountants was Ms Iseult O'Carra of Price
Waterhouse, seen here receiving the trophy from Mr Tom O'Higgins,
also of Price Waterhouse, and President of the Institute of Chartered
Accountants in Ireland.

Irish accounting firms have enjoyed a high level of public confidence for many decades, but it is unfortunate that so many firms become mesmerised by size. It is not unusual to find accountants who are far more concerned about the size of their practices than they are about the quality of the service that they offer to their clients. When this condition prevails, it is high time for the accountants concerned and for their clients, to ask where their firms are going.

The substantial growth in Irish industry, particularly in the 1960s and early 1970s, was sufficient to result in substantial growth in the Irish profession. In spite of this growth many firms chose to grow even more rapidly by merger, and many observers believed that accounting firms had no option but to grow by merger in order to match the growth in the scale of their clients' operations.

In sympathy with the very significant inward investment in manufacturing and other sectors of the economy, Irish accounting firms have entered into relationships with international accounting firms. This often results in periods during which the Irish firms operate under two titles. Of the well-known international firms, only Arthur Andersen established its own practice from scratch, rather than form an association with, or acquire, an Irish firm.

Many of the mergers and associations have proved to be of short duration and the reasons for the dissolution of linkages are many and varied. The large Irish firms do not dominate the Institute of Chartered Accountants partly because of a rule which precludes any one office from being represented on the Council by more than one member. The rule also precludes any one firm being represented by more than two members.

The users of accounting services benefit from the keen competition between accounting firms and between chartered accountants, certified accountants and management accountants, although audit appointments to companies quoted on the stock exchange rarely change.

Almost 50 per cent of the members of the Chartered Institute work in industry and commerce and a pilot scheme was introduced in 1983, whereby student chartered accountants, virtually all of whom undertake their training in the offices of practising accountants, could have the option of training under the guidance of members in industry and commerce.

Irish chartered accountants play an active role in the work of the International Federation of Accountants and the International Accounting Standards Committee. The Federation des Experts Comptables Européens, which was formed in 1987, has thirty-four member organisations drawn from twenty-one countries. Margaret Downes, who was the first lady chartered accountant in the British Isles to be president of an institute, was elected first President of the Federation.

FRANK W. BOWEN
Chartered Accountant
Earlsfort Terrace, Dublin 2
(01) 618311
Born to James F. and Eileen M. Bowen (née Flannery) at Dungarvan on 17 January 1941. Educated at CBC and UCC. Member Institute of Chartered Accountants in Ireland. Married to Ray Leahy with six children. Formerly held senior positions Magennis Burns Griffin & Co Chartered Accountants Cork, which became part of Touche Ross, now Deloitte & Touche. At present deputy managing partner, Deloitte & Touche. Member Douglas and Portmarnock Golf Clubs and Stephen's Green Club.

ALEXANDER KINGSMILL BURNS
Chartered Accountant
1 Stokes Place, St Stephen's Green, Dublin 2
(01) 7081000
Born to William Stewart and Margaret Elaine Patricia Burns (née Priestley) at Kilkenny on 25 July 1939. Educated at Mountmellick NS, Wesley College, NW University Chicago and Harvard. Married to Irene Mary Weir with one son and one daughter. Formerly articled clerk, senior assistant and partner Stokes Bros & Pim, chairman Leinster Society of Chartered Accountants, member Accounting Standards Committee, and council Institute of Chartered Accountants in Ireland. At present senior partner KPMG Stokes Kennedy Crowley, non-executive director Norwich Union Life Assurance Group, governor Wesley College. Member Institute of Chartered Accountants in Ireland, Leinster Society of Chartered Accountants, Insolvency Practitioners' Association, Dublin Chamber of Commerce, Kildare Street and University Club, Merrion Cricket Club, Milltown and Rathfarnham Golf Clubs, Old Wesley Rugby Club.

JOHN CONRAN
Chartered Accountant
Setanta Centre, Nassau Street, Dublin 2
(01) 6797500
Born to Dr Matthew and Irene Conran (née O'Connor) at Cobh, Co. Cork on 14 December 1946. Educated at Waterpark College Waterford, TCD and at the Institute of Chartered Accountants. Married to Sheila Kelly with two sons and two daughters. Formerly council member Institute of Chartered Accountants and member of the Board of Management of the Institute of Accounting Technicians. At present managing partner BDO Binder and member of the Irish Hungarian Economic Association.

LAURENCE GUNNING CROWLEY
Chartered Accountant
University College Dublin
(01) 2693244
Born to Vincent and Eileen Crowley (née Gunning) at Dublin on 9 March

1937. Educated at St Michael's, Belvedere and UCD. Married to Mella Boland with one son, Jonathan. Chairman the Michael Smurfit Graduate School of Business, P.J. Carroll and Company plc, and Century Communications Ltd; Director Bank of Ireland and Hamilton Osborne King Ltd. Member Portmarnock Golf Club and Royal St George Yacht Club.

NIALL CROWLEY
Chartered Accountant
46 Upper Mount Street, Dublin 2
(01) 762464
Born to Vincent and Eileen Crowley (née Gunning) at Dublin on 18 September 1926. Educated at Xavier School and Castleknock College. Married to Una Hegarty with five sons, Vincent, Niall, Maurice, Philip and Peter, and one daughter, Emma. Formerly managing partner Stokes Kennedy Crowley, chairman AIB Group and Irish Life Assurance Co. plc. At present chairman Cahill May Roberts Group plc and director Alliance and Leicester Building Society and other companies. Awarded honorary degrees D.Phil by Pontifical University of Maynooth and LL.D by NUI. Honorary member of Chambers of Commerce of Ireland.

JOHN KEVIN DEEVY
Chartered Accountant
Newtown, Waterford
(051) 74858
Born to William Anthony and Eileen Deevy (née Hand) at Waterford on 29 March 1930. Educated at Waterpark College. Member Institute of Chartered Accountants. Married to Noeleen Howlett with two sons and one daughter. Formerly chairman Munster Society of Chartered Accountants, member Waterford Junior Chamber, IMI and president Waterford Chamber of Commerce. At present partner Coopers and Lybrand Waterford, and council member Institute of Taxation in Ireland. Represents S. Eastern Chambers of Commerce on Review Committee for Community Support Framework for Regional Development Fund. Member Waterford and Tramore Golf Clubs and Waterford Harbour Sailing Club.

JOHN DONNELLY
Chartered Accountant
Mespil Road, Dublin 4
(01) 604400
Born to John Joseph and Mary Donnelly (née Mehegen) at Dublin on 28 January 1929. Educated at Belvedere College, TCD and King's Inns. Married to Aoibheann MacEllin with one son, John Paul, and three daughters, Grace, Caoimhe and Deirdre. Formerly president and honorary. treasurer Royal Victoria Eye and Ear Hospital, managing partner Deloitte Haskins & Sells. At present chairman Deloitte & Touche, Honorary Consul General of Finland. Member Royal Irish Yacht Club, Stephen's Green Club, Fitzwilliam Lawn Tennis Club, Kildare Street and University Club. Commander Order of the Lion of Finland.

MICHAEL PATRICK DONNELLY

Chartered Accountant
90 Ranelagh Road, Dublin 6
(01) 970935
Born to Dr James and Nora Donnelly (née O'Connor) at Bradford on 24 July 1938. Married to Aileen Browner with three sons. Formerly partner Oliver Freaney & Co, Lord Mayor of Dublin, chairman Dublin Corporation Finance Committee, chairman College of Commerce Rathmines, director Irish Life plc. At present partner Butler Fitzpatrick, Cavanagh Donnelly Chartered Accountants, director Dublin Theatre Festival, director Olympia Theatre, chairman Committee on Economy of Dublin.

RONALD FINLAY-MULLIGAN

Chartered Accountant
(01) 2831021
Born to Gerald and Norah Finlay-Mulligan (née Black) at Dublin on 13 August 1926. Educated at St Gerard's Bray, Blackrock College, UCD and Institute of Chartered Accountants. Married with one daughter and four sons. At present senior partner Finlay-Mulligan & Co Chartered Accountants and Secretary/Manager to Irish Seed Trade Association, The Plant Royalty Office, Federation of Jewellery Manufacturers of Ireland, Irish Craft & Gift Exhibitors and Irish Association of Seed Potato Exporters. Member Dún Laoghaire Golf Club.

DÓNAL P. FLINN

Chartered Accountant/Professional Director
Fitzwilton House, Wilton Place, Dublin 2
(01) 682222
Born to Hugo V. and Monica Flinn (née Wilson) at Rushbrooke, Co. Cork on 8 November 1923. Educated at CBC Cork, UCC and Institute of Chartered Accountants. Married with two sons, Hugo and Richard, and one daughter, Jennifer. Formerly chairman and managing partner Coopers & Lybrand, chairman Barclay's Bank Ireland Ltd and Irish Press plc, president Institute of Chartered Accountants in Ireland and US Chamber of Commerce. At present chairman De La Rue Smurfit Ltd, director Fitzwilton plc, Abbey Life Ireland Ltd, Irish Trade Board, Salomon Brothers Asset Management (Ire) Ltd and National Grid Investments (Ire) Company. Fellow Irish Management Institute. Member Portmarnock Golf Club, Fitzwilliam Lawn Tennis Club, Royal St George Yacht Club, Sotogrande Golf Club and Coral Beach and Tennis Club, Bermuda.

JOSEPH TIMOTHY GANNON

Chartered Accountant
Stephen Street, Sligo
(071) 61747
Born to Jim and Eileen Gannon (née Curran) at Sligo on 22 March 1946.

Educated at Marist Brothers Sligo and Summerhill College Sligo. Married to Sheila Nolan with three sons. Formerly senior assistant with Arthur Andersen, director Enterprise Equity and president Sligo Chamber of Commerce. At present partner Gilroy Gannon, director Brodricks Ltd and council member Institute of Chartered Accountants in Ireland. Member Co. Sligo Golf Club and Rotary Club of Sligo.

PETER GRAY
Finance Director
Finglas, Dublin 11
(01) 344500
Born to Edward Joseph and Una Gray (née Higgins) at Dublin on 20 November 1954. Educated at CBS Monkstown, Clongowes Wood College Kildare, and at Law Faculty TCD. Married to Aveen Mc Loughlin with two daughters, Rachel and Emma. Formerly financial director FKM Engineering, audit senior Stokes Kennedy Crowley, executive vice president Irish Operations and chief financial officer Elan Corporation plc, finance director Food Industries plc. At present finance director, Unidare plc.

NEIL PATRICK HOLMAN
Accountant
19 Pembroke Road, Dublin 4
(01) 606516
Born to Dennis and Betty Holman (née Keily) at London on 26 May 1949. Educated at Beaumont College and TCD. Married to Jane Robinson (separated) with one son, Nicolas, and one daughter, Clare. Formerly chairman National Board for Science and Technology, director, National Software Centre and Irish Life Assurance Company, board member, Higher Education Authority, and managing partner, Holman O'Connor and Co. Auditors and Accountants. At present managing director Stonebridge Finance Ltd. Member Kildare Street and University Club, Connemara Golf Club, Dublin Bay Sailing Club and Howth Yacht Club.

DERMOT REGINALD HUSSEY
Financial Director
Beechill, Clonskeagh, Dublin 4
(01) 694300
Born to Dudley and Doreen Hussey (née McSharry) at Dublin on 15 September 1934. Educated at St Mary's College Rathmines and UCD. Married to Gemma Moran with one son, Andrew, and two daughters, Rachel and Ruth. Admitted to membership and fellowship of the Institute of Chartered Accountants in Ireland. At present financial director, Jones Group plc. Member Royal Irish Yacht Club, Fitzwilliam Lawn Tennis Club and St Mary's Rugby Club.

ROGER HUSSEY

Institute Director
87/89 Pembroke Road, Dublin 4
(01) 680400
Born to Francis and Aileen Hussey (née Houlihan) at Dublin on 3 April 1935. Educated at Belvedere College and UCD. Married with one child. Formerly with AEG Germany, Metro Vickers UK, CIE Engineering Departments and P.A. Management Consultants. At present institute director Institute of Chartered Accountants in Ireland, board member Irish Heart Foundation, honorary treasurer/board member International Society and Federation of Cardiology. Member Fitzwilliam Lawn Tennis Club and East India Club London.

JOHN F. KEOGH

Retired Finance Director
Blackrock, Co. Dublin
Born to John J. and Alice C. Keogh (née Mullany) at Dublin on 1 June 1931. Educated at O'Connell Schools. Later admitted to fellowships of Institute of Chartered Accountants in England and Wales, Chartered Institute of Management Accountants, and Institute of Chartered Accountants in Ireland. Married to Mary Elizabeth Easley with two sons, Laurence and Matthew, and one daughter, Christina. Formerly with Brewer and Knott London, Cooper and Kenny Dublin, Trinidad Petroleum, Mercedes Benz (GB) Ltd, finance officer Arthur Guinness Park Royal, finance manager British Domestic Appliances, and consultant Spencer Stuart Ltd. Until recently group financial director, AIB Bank and president R. of Ireland division Chartered Institute of Management Accountants. Member Castle Golf Club, Clontarf Football Club, Hibernian United Service Club, Royal Dublin Society, An Taisce, London Irish Rugby Football Club, Military History Society and Old Dublin Society.

SIR DESMOND LORIMER

Chartered Accountant
Purdy's Lane, Newtownbreda, Belfast BT8 4AX
(0232) 491111
Born to Thomas Berry and Sarah Ann Lorimer (née Robinson) at Belfast on 20 October 1925. Educated at Belfast Technical High School and later admitted to membership of the Institute of Chartered Accountants in Ireland. Married to Patricia Doris Samways with two daughters, Susan Patricia and Katherine Anne. Formerly first chairman of Northern Ireland Housing Executive, first chairman of Industrial Development Board for Northern Ireland and president Institute of Chartered Accountants in Ireland. At present chairman Northern Bank Ltd, The Old Bushmills Distillery Co Ltd, Lamont Holdings plc, director Irish Distillers Group plc, and chairman 1991 Northern Ireland Electricity. Member Royal County Down and Royal Belfast Golf Clubs and the Carlton Club. Awarded honorary degree, Doctor of Science, by University of Ulster.

HARRY LORTON

Banker
Douglas, Cork
(021) 361301
Born to Edward and Catherine Lorton (née Daly) at Cork on 27 July 1951. Educated at CBC Cork, TCD and Harvard Business School. Married to Mary Crowley with one son, Rory, and one daughter, Cliona. Formerly with Bank of Ireland and financial controller Cork Savings Bank, deputy chief executive Cork & Limerick Savings Bank 1987. Served as president of the Irish Region of the Chartered Association of Certified Accountants 1989/90. At present chief executive, Cork and Limerick Savings Bank, member of executive committee of Cork Chamber of Commerce since 1988. Fellow of Institute of Bankers in Ireland. Member Sunday's Well Boating and Tennis Club and National Associations Committee of the International Savings Bank Institute, Geneva.

WILLIAM M. McCANN

Chartered Accountant
Gardner House, Wilton Place, Dublin 2
(01) 606700
Born to William and Maureen McCann (née McLellan) at Dublin on 7 April 1944. Educated at Presentation College Bray. Qualified as a Chartered Accountant in 1967. Married to Doreen Walsh with two sons. Often acted as receiver/liquidator and has carried out a large number of viability studies for companies trading under financial pressure. In March 1985 at the request of the Government, was appointed Administrator of The Insurance Corporation of Ireland, plc, one of the largest general insurance companies in Ireland. At present managing partner of Craig Gardner/Price Waterhouse since 1987, member of the Price Waterhouse World Firm General Council and member of the Electricity Supply Board. Member Stephen's Green Club, Royal St George Yacht Club and Woodbrook Golf Club.

SIR ERIC WALLACE McDOWELL

Chartered Accountant
64 Chichester Street, Belfast BT1 4JX
(0232) 233233
Born to Martin Wallace and Edith Florence McDowell (née Hillock) at Belfast on 7 June 1925. Educated at Inch Preparatory and Royal Belfast Academical Institution. Married to Helen Lilian Montgomery with one son and two daughters. Formerly partner Wilson Hennessey & Crawford Belfast, senior partner Deloitte, Haskins & Sells Belfast and president Insitute of Chartered Accountants in Ireland. At present chairman Industrial Development Board for Northern Ireland, director Capita Northern Ireland Ltd and TSB Bank Northern Ireland plc, vice chairman Relate (Marriage Guidance) Northern Ireland and honorary treasurer

Belfast Abbeyfield Society. Member Ulster Reform Club. Awarded CBE New Year Honours 1982, D.Sc(Econ) Honorary Degree by Queen's University Belfast 1989 and Knight Bachelor New Year Honours 1990.

JOHN A. McELHINNEY
Chartered Accountant
7 Seville Place, Dublin 1
(01) 363388)
Born to John and Eileen McElhinney (née Nash) at Dublin on 3 October 1946. Educated at Belgrove NS, O'Connell Schools, Blackrock College and UCD whence he graduated with a BA degree. Married to Mary Byrne with six daughters and two sons. Formerly with Reynolds McCarron & Co. At present partner John McElhinney & Co. Member Irish Hill Running Association, Setanta Orienteers, Compagnons de Bordeaux (Délégation Irlandaise), Knights of Columbanus and Tiller Club.

HAROLD LESLIE McKEE
Consultant
Clanwilliam Place, Dublin
(01) 609433
Born to James and Sarah McKee (née Furey) at Dublin on 8 September 1928. Educated at Lindsay Road National School and Mountjoy School (now Mount Temple). Married to Margaret Higgins with two daughters. Formerly secretary/financial controller Glaxo Ireland, partner Kinnear & Co and partner/managing partner Ernst Young Ireland. At present consultant Ernst Young Dublin, chairman Midland International Cavan and St Andrew's College Dublin. Director Staffords Wexford and Dublin Business Innovation Centre. Member Hibernian United Service Club and Killiney Golf Club.

WILLIAM NOLAN
Certified Accountant
41 MacCurtain Street, Cork
(021) 503863
Born to William and Norah Nolan (née Tobin) at Cork on 31 August 1939. Qualified as certified accountant and admitted to fellowship. Also fellow Chartered Institute of Secretaries. Holds a diploma in marketing. Married to Catherine Patricia Barry with three daughters. Formerly with Irish Refining Company Ltd, E. Love and Son (W. Foreman and Co. Ltd), director and secretary Fitzgerald and Co (Cork) Ltd, managing director and secretary of OKR Group Ltd (formerly Old Kentucky Restaurants Ltd), also part-time lecturer in accounting and business administration. Chairman Cork Harbour Commissioners, president Irish Restaurant Owners' Association, president Munster and Connaught Society of the Chartered Association of Certified Accountants, chairman Southern Region Irish Management Institute and member executive committee of

Cork Chamber of Commerce. At present chairman and managing director of Nolan Financial Services Ltd and of MFS Food Services Ltd. Director Cork/Kerry Tourism. Member of Cork Harbour Commissioners and elected member (since 1979) of Cork Corporation. Member Cork Toastmasters' Club, An Taisce and many business organisations.

MARTIN RAFFERTY
Chartered Accountant
32 Upper Fitzwilliam Street, Dublin 2
(01) 764340
Born to Martin and Mary Rafferty (née Connolly) at Galway on 22 February 1933. Educated at Kilkerrin NS, Castleknock College, UCD and University of California, Los Angeles. Married to Elizabeth Walsh with five children. Formerly managing director of Allied Irish Investment Bank and chairman BWG Group. At present chairman United Drug plc, Readymix plc, Ulster Investment Bank, Lombard & Ulster Banking and Ulster Investment Managers. Director Ulster Bank, Norish plc, Lyons Irish Holdings plc, Aer Lingus and Industrial Development Authority.

PATRICK FRANCIS SHORTALL
Chartered Accountant
23 Earlsfort Terrace, Dublin 2
(01) 782303
Born to Dermot and May Shortall (née Chambers) at Dublin on 2 September 1938. Educated at Belvedere College, Castleknock College and UCD. Admitted to membership and fellowship of Institute of Chartered Accountants in Ireland. Married to Mary Rafferty with two sons and two daughters. Formerly held a number of positions with Coopers and Lybrand and served as chairman of the Ireland Korea Association and Ireland Japan Economic Association. Former member Insolvency Practitioners' Association and council member European Insolvency Practitioners' Association. At present chairman and president ITI Holdings, consultant to Coopers and Lybrand, and director McInerney Properties plc and several other companies. Member Milltown and Connemara Golf Clubs, Lansdowne and UCD Rugby Clubs, Fitzwilliam Lawn Tennis Club and Royal St George Yacht Club.

CORNELIUS F. SMITH
Consultant and Social Historian
Blackrock, Co. Dublin
(01) 2887958
Born to Fred P. and Isabelle Smith (née Smith) in 1918. Educated at Clongowes Wood College and qualified as a Chartered Accountant. Married to Rhona Higgins with two children. Formerly partner, Briscoe Smith which merged into Deloitte Haskins & Sells and president Institute of Chartered Accountants in Ireland. Author of history of the

Stephen's Green Club. Member Dún Laoghaire Golf Club, Stephen's Green Club and Royal Irish Automobile Club.

PASCHAL SEÁN TAGGART

Financial Consultant
23 Fitzwilliam Square, Dublin 2
(01) 762205

Born to James and Evelyn Taggart (née Duffy) at Antrim on 23 April 1943. Educated at St Comgall's, Antrim, St Mary's CBS and Queen's University, Belfast. Married to Helen Hayes with two sons, Shane and Aidan, and two daughters, Lisa and Elva. Formerly executive officer with UK Inland Revenue, tax manager Spicer and Pegler and with Griffin Lynch and tax partner Bastow Charleton. At present partner Cooney and Taggart and chairman or director of some fourteen companies. Member Castle and Blainroe Golf Clubs, St Vincent's GAA Club and Fitzwilliam Lawn Tennis Club.

THOMAS NIALL WELCH

Chartered Accountant
70 Patrick Street, Cork
(021) 273844

Born to Alexander A. and Bridget Welch (née McCall) at Cobh, Co. Cork on 11 June 1944. Educated at Presentation Brothers NS Cobh, CBC Cork, UCC (B.Comm) and the Insitute of Chartered Accountants in Ireland. Married to Eileen O'Brien with two daughters and one son. Formerly partner Touche Ross, president Cork Lions Club and captain Cork Golf Club. At present principal Welch & Co. Chartered Accountants, chairman Nitrigin Éireann Teoranta, member of Cork Freeport Advisory Board and director Irish Fertiliser Industries Ltd. Member executive committee Cork Chamber of Commerce and Cork Golf Club.

MICHAEL ANTHONY WHITE

Institute Director
44 Upper Mount Street, Dublin 2
(01) 785133

Born to Patrick and Mary White (née O'Shaughnessy at Limerick on 2 October 1944. Educated at Sacred Heart College, The Crescent, Limerick, UCD, UCC and King's Inns. Married to Marian Slowey with one son and two daughters. Formerly assistant registrar National Council for Educational Awards. At present institute director Chartered Institute of Management Accountants, committee member International Advisory Committee Salzburg Seminar, Human Resources Policy Committee Confederation of Irish Industry and Education Committee Institute of Public Administration.

Chapter 8
Philosophy and Religion

He who begins by loving Christianity better than Truth will proceed by loving his own sect or church better than Christianity, and end by loving himself better than all.

Coleridge

While Irish society, like most others, contains a whole range of personal philosophies, it is probably fair to summarise the philosophy of the Irish as being materialistic and conservative.

The growth of materialism has, of course, been accompanied by a frequently reported decline in public worship and religious vocations. Experienced door to door canvassers for political parties have consistently reported increased emphasis on economic issues and reduced interest in others, but the results of recent referenda on divorce and abortion have confirmed the strength of traditional values in areas of morality.

A great variety of religions are practised on the island. There is the Church of Ireland itself, as well as the other main Protestant denominations, Presbyterian and Methodist. But there are also Lutherans, Mennonites, Pentecostalists, Unitarians, Baptists, Christadelphians and Congregationalists. In addition, there are some kindred spirits, such as the Evangelical Presbyterians and the Free Presbyterians. Then there are the members of the Religious Society of Friends, known as the Quakers, and the Salvation Army.

In spite of this great diversity, all of the foregoing constitute only 3 per cent of the population of the Republic while they constitute about 60 per cent of the population of Northern Ireland. The Roman Catholic denomination accounts for about 75 per cent of the population of the island as a whole. Attendance at Church more frequently than once a month has been calculated to be achieved by over 80 per cent of Catholics and over 70 per cent of Protestants.

116

God and Mammon
When the National Lottery launched their Lotto game in April 1988, they marked the occasion with a spectacular fireworks display in the Phoenix Park, Dublin, close to the Papal Cross.

Visitors, especially those coming from predominantly Christian countries, may well express amazement at the conflict in Northern Ireland between fellow Christians. They may point out that all Christian religions are opposed to corruption, deceipt and theft, adultery, polygamy and polyandry, falsehood and fraud, and to rape, murder and violence. All promote the virtues opposite to these vices and all hope, pray for, and believe in the triumph of good over evil.

Even in terms of organisation there are resounding similarities. The four numerically strongest denominations, Roman Catholic, Church of Ireland, Presbyterian and Methodist, are all organised on all-Ireland bases. The leaders of all four are regularly seen to make gestures of friendship to one another. On Christmas Day the heads of the Roman Catholic Church and of the Church of Ireland broadcast together to the people of Ireland.

In spite of all of this, however, a most appalling sectarianism thrives in Northern Ireland where it is witnessed by unspeakable violence with shocking regularity. Any study of this problem must take account of historic factors and in particular the successful seventeenth-century plantation of Ulster with mainly Scottish settlers who introduced the strong Presbyterian tradition. Today in Northern Ireland there are about 350,000 Presbyterians and about 600,000 Roman Catholics, and it seems incredible that after 300 years, members of two Christian denominations with so much in common find themselves so separated by so little.

Study of the problem cannot ignore economic factors and visitors need only spend a very short time in Northern Ireland before realising that the 60 per cent Protestant section of the community controls far more than 60 per cent of the wealth and of the well-paid employment.

Majority rule is difficult if not impossible to operate in a situation such as exists in Northern Ireland. One must wonder if the business community should not be involved in finding a solution. Business leaders are accustomed to finding consensus and giving leadership and, when necessary, taking seemingly insoluble problems by the scruff of the neck and making solutions stick.

A businesslike approach to a medium term solution of the

problem would probably favour integration of primary and secondary education. Bringing fellow Christians together at an early age would seem to be capable of producing nothing but good. Paradoxically, the very religious leaders, who exchange so many gestures of goodwill towards one another, would probably be the first to object to this. On the other hand, when, in a white paper published in the autumn of 1988, it was proposed to support integrated schools with Government funds for the first time, the main thrust of the paper was welcomed by educationalists and trade unions.

Discrimination

Just as it seems a pity not to bring young people of different denominations together, it seems equally sad that events have so come to pass in Northern Ireland that there is now an obligation on employers to monitor the denominational mix of their employees. The legislation which gave rise to this situation was no doubt well intentioned but it has the effect of institutionalising religion in employment where politics and religion should have no place.

In the Republic there is little or no evidence of discrimination and citizens, by and large, go about their business without knowing, or caring to know, the denominational adherence of their colleagues and associates. There is, however, a minority view that the Roman Catholic Church is over-involved in health, education and social services, and the objectives of the Campaign to Separate Church and State include: promoting the provision of publicly-funded health, education and social services on a basis which does not discriminate against any Irish citizen, whatever his or her religious or philosophical disposition; securing strict compliance with the prohibition in the Constitution on the endowment of religion, and securing the maximum freedom of information and free circulation of ideas.

Discrimination on the grounds of denominational adherence is to be condemned, whether it takes place in employment or in trade. In the past, blame for much of the discrimination in these two areas was laid at the doors of organisations, such as the Freemasons, the Knights of Columbanus and Opus Dei. These organisations which became identified with discrimination and undue influence, currently enjoy widespread appreciation of their charitable works, which takes the public mind off the discrimination issue. The Knights are organised throughout the island, and it is said that there are probably few orphanages, industrial schools, children's charities or invalid pilgrimages which have not enjoyed their support. Their good deeds are frequently anonymous with the possible exception of an annual Christmas dinner which they organise in Dublin's Mansion House.

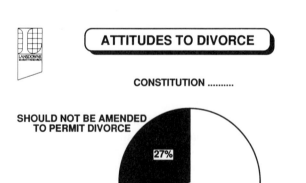

(Reproduced by permission of
Lansdowne Market Research and the *Sunday Press*.)

DIVORCE - IN PARTICULAR CIRCUMSTANCES

%IN FAVOUR   LANSDOWNE 1991
              I.M.S.   1984

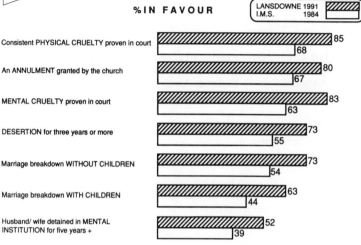

	1991	1984
Consistent PHYSICAL CRUELTY proven in court	85	68
An ANNULMENT granted by the church	80	67
MENTAL CRUELTY proven in court	83	63
DESERTION for three years or more	73	55
Marriage breakdown WITHOUT CHILDREN	73	54
Marriage breakdown WITH CHILDREN	63	44
Husband/ wife detained in MENTAL INSTITUTION for five years +	52	39

(Reproduced by permission of
Lansdowne Market Research and the *Sunday Press* .)

ATTITUDES TO HOMOSEXUALS

LAW REGARDING HOMOSEXUAL
RELATIONSHIPS ....

SHOULD STAY 42

SHOULD CHANGE 39

DON'T KNOW 19

Q: At present, the law in Ireland prohibits physical homosexual relationships:
Do you think the law should be changed to permit homosexual relationships
between consenting adults or should it stay as it is ?

(Reproduced by permission of
Lansdowne Market Research and the *Sunday Press* .)

RAY BATES
Lottery Director
Lower Abbey Street, Dublin 1
(01) 364444
Born to Charles and Elizabeth Bates (née Browne) on 4 October 1947. Educated at O'Connell's CBS and TCD (B.Sc.(Comp) and MEconSc. degrees). Married to Mary Elliott with one daughter and one son. Formerly civil servant Departments of Agriculture, Finance, Public Service and Social Welfare, and head of computer operations, OECD Paris. At present National Lottery Director, An Post National Lottery Company.

MOST REV. JOHN BUCKLEY
Roman Catholic Bishop
Redemption Road, Cork
(021) 301717
Born to John and Hannah Buckley (née Colter) at Inchigeela, Co. Cork on 2 November 1939. Educated at Inchigeela National School, Farranferris College Cork, Maynooth College and at University College Cork.

MOST REV. DONALD A.R. CAIRD
Church of Ireland Archbishop
Church Ave, Rathmines, Dublin 6
(01) 977849
Born to George R. and Emily F. Caird (née Draper) at Dublin on 11 December 1925. Educated at Wesley College and at Trinity College Dublin. Married to Nancy Ballantyne (née Sharpe) with one son and two daughters. Formerly Curate assistant of St Mark's Dundela (Down), chaplain and Assistant Master Portora Royal School Enniskillen, Lecturer in Philosophy St David's College Lampeter (Wales), Incumbent of Rathmichael (Dublin), Assistant Master St Columba's College Dublin, Dept. Lecturer TCD, Lecturer in the Philosophy of Religion, Divintiy Hostel Dublin, Dean of Ossory, Incumbent of Kilkenny and Canon of Aghold, Leighlin, Fellow of St Columba's College Dublin, Bishop of Limerick, Ardfert and Aghadoe, and Bishop of Meath and Kildare. At present Church of Ireland Archbishop of Dublin and Primate of Ireland.

MOST REV. DR EAMONN CASEY
Roman Catholic Bishop
Diocesan Office, The Cathedral, Galway
(091) 63566
Born to John and Helena Casey (née Shanahan) at Firies, Co. Kerry on 23 April 1927. Educated at St Munchin's College, Limerick and at May-

INTRODUCING IRELAND

nooth University whence he graduated in 1947 with a BA degree. Ordained for Diocese of Limerick 1951. Formerly curate at Monaleen and at St John's Cathedral Limerick, chaplain to the Irish at Slough. Worked to help migrant population integrate into local church and civic community, national director Catholic Housing Aid Society, founder of Family Housing Association, director British Churches Housing Trust, trustee of Housing the Homeless Central Fund, founder trustee Shelter National Campaign for the Homeless, council member National Federation of Housing Societies, member Commission for Social Welfare, founder member of Marian Employment Agency, chairman National Youth Resource Group and member Maynooth College Executive Council. Ordained Bishop of Kerry on 9 November 1969. At present Bishop of Galway (1976), executive chairman Trócaire, member standing committee of Irish Hierarchy, secretary Episcopal Commission for Emigration, member Episcopal Commission for Universities, member Governing Body of University College Galway, founder Galway Diocesan Mission to Malawi, Moderator Galway Marriage Tribunal, Western Regional chairman of CURA, president Galway Social Service Council, founder of Galway Adult Education Centre. Has had a number of works published and has been giving retreats for clergy since 1967.

MOST REV. JOSEPH REGINALD CASSIDY
Roman Catholic Archbishop
Tuam, Co. Galway
(093) 24166
Born to John and Mary Cassidy (née Gallagher) at Charlestown, Co. Mayo on 29 October 1933. Educated at Lowpark National School Charlestown, St Nathy's College Ballaghadereen, St Patrick's College Maynooth and University College Galway. Formerly president of Garbally College Ballinasloe, Coadjutor Bishop of Clonfert and Bishop of Clonfert. At present Archbishop of Tuam.

BISHOP BRENDAN COMISKEY
Roman Catholic Bishop
Bishop's House, Wexford
(053) 22177
Born at Tasson, Clontibret, Co. Monaghan on 13 August 1935. Educated at Annyalla, Castleblaney Boys' School and at St Macartan's College, Monaghan. Studied philosophy and Theology in USA. Ordained 25 June 1961. Post-graduate studies in theology and classics at Catholic University of America and Lateran University, Rome. Formerly teacher in USA, Provincial Anglo-Irish Province of the Congregation of the Sacred Heart, Secretary General Conference of Major Religious Superiors, and Auxiliary Bishop of Dublin. At present Bishop of Ferns, member of National

Episcopal Conference, chairman of Bishops' Commission for Communications and president of Catholic Communications Institute of Ireland. Also member of Bishops' Commission for Ecumenism, Joint Commission of Bishops and Religious Superiors, and Commission for Youth. Member of Academic Council of the Irish School of Ecumenics, chairman of Irish Churches' Council for Television and Radio Affairs, and member of Standing Committee of the Glenstal Ecumenical Conference. Was made a Freeman of Wexford Town in June 1990 and is patron of the Wexford Festival Opera.

ARCHBISHOP DESMOND CONNELL
Roman Catholic Primate
Archbishop's House, Drumcondra
(01) 373732
Born to John B. and Maisie Connell (née Lacy) at Dublin on 24 March 1926. Educated at St Peter's NS Phibsboro, Belvedere College, Clonliffe College and University College Dublin whence he graduated with BA and MA degrees. Further studies at Maynooth and Louvain. Ordained at Clonliffe College by Archbishop McQuaid on 19 May 1951. Formerly assistant in the Department of Metaphysics, UCD and Professor of general metaphysics at UCD. Elected Dean of the Faculty of Philosophy and Sociology in November 1983 and re-elected in 1986. Served as chaplain to three communities of contemplative nuns, the Poor Clares, Donnybrook, the Carmelites, Drumcondra, and the Carmelites, Blackrock. At present Roman Catholic Archbishop of Dublin and Primate of Ireland. Published works on philosophical and theological subjects. Awarded a D.Litt degree in 1981 by the National University of Ireland. Fluent in French with a knowledge of German and Italian.

HIS EMINENCE THE MOST REV CARDINAL CAHAL B. DALY
Primate
Ara Coeli, Armagh
(0861) 522045
Born to Charles and Susan Daly (née Connolly) at Loughguile, Co. Antrim on 1 October 1917. Educated at St Patrick's NS, St Malachy's College and Queen's University, Belfast, St Patrick's College Maynooth, and at Institut Catholique Paris. Ordained 23 June 1941. Formerly classics master at St Malachy's College Belfast, lecturer and later reader in scholastic philosophy, Queen's University Belfast, Bishop of Ardagh and Clonmacnois and Bishop of Down and Connor. Member Religious Advisory Committee BBC Northern Ireland and Committee of Northern Ireland Independent Television, chairman Christus Rex Society. At present Archbishop of Armagh, and Primate of all Ireland. Peritus at Second Vatican Council.

Price of Peace
His Eminence Cardinal Cahal Daly of Armagh, reading from his book, *The Price of Peace*, at its launch in St Patrick's College, Maynooth, in June 1991.

MOST REV. EDWARD KEVIN DALY

Roman Catholic Bishop

Bishop's House, St Eugene's Cathedral, Derry BT 48 9AP

(0504) 262302

Born to Thomas and Susan Daly (née Flood) at Belleek, Co. Fermanagh on 5 December 1933. Educated at Belleek PS, St Columb's College, Derry, and afterwards at Irish College and Lateran University, Rome. Formerly curate at Castlederg, Co. Tyrone and at St Eugene's Cathedral, Derry, Religious Advisor to RTE, member of Central Religious Advisory Council to BBC and IBA (London). At present Bishop of Derry. Greatest disappointment is the lack of community harmony and peace. He admires people of Derry.

THE RIGHT REV. EDWARD FLEWETT DARLING

Church of Ireland Bishop

Bishop's House, North Circular Road, Limerick

(061) 51532

Born to Vivian William and Honor Francis Garde Darling (née Flewett) at Cork on 24 July 1933. Educated at Cork Grammar School, Midleton College and St John's School Leatherhead, Surrey and at Trinity College Dublin. Married to Edith Elizabeth Patricia Mann with three sons, David, Colin and Philip, and two daughters, Alison and Linda. Formerly Incumbent of St Gall's, Carnalea, Co. Down, and Rector of St John's, Malone, Belfast. At present Bishop of Limerick and Killaloe.

MOST REV. DR ROBERT HENRY ALEXANDER EAMES

Church of Ireland Archbishop

Cathedral Close, Armagh BT61 7EE

(0861) 527144

Born to William Edward and Mary Eleanor Thompson Eames (née Alexander) at Belfast on 27 April 1937. Educated at Belfast Royal Academy, Methodist College and Queen's University Belfast, and at Trinity College Dublin. Holds LL.B and PhD from Queen's University. Married to Ann Christine Daly with two sons, Niall William Adrian and Michael Harvey Alexander. Formerly research scholar and tutor Queen's University Law Faculty, Bishop of Derry and Raphoe, and Bishop of Down and Dromore. At present Archbishop of Armagh, Primate of All Ireland and Metropolitan, select preacher University of Oxford, member Board of Governors Church Army, chairman Board of Governors Royal School Armagh, chairman Board of Governors Observatory and Planetarium Armagh and member of boards of Dublin hospitals and schools. Chairman of Archbishop of Canterbury's Commisson on Women in the Episcopate and Chairman of Inter-Anglican International Commission on Theology and Doctrine. Member University Club and Friendly Brothers House, Dublin.

REV. CHARLES GEORGE EYRE

Methodist Minister
9 Londonderry Park, Comber, Belfast BT23 5EU
(0247) 873076
Born to Thomas Alexander and Elizabeth McClintock Eyre (née Giffin) at Belfast on 2 June 1925. Educated at Coleraine Model School, Coleraine Academical Institution, Queen's University Belfast and Edgehill Theological College Belfast. Married to Betty Muriel Shier with one son, Maurice John, and two daughters, Jane Muriel and Ruth Elizabeth. Formerly in ministerial positions at Londonderry, Belfast, Waterford, Portadown and Jamaica. President Methodist Church in Ireland 1982/3. Secretary of Conference 1977–90. Chairman Irish Council of Churches and Co-Chairman Irish Inter-Church Meeting 1988–90. At present Treasurer of Trustees of Methodist Church in Ireland, and Circuit Superintendent of Methodist Church in Ireland.

MOST REV. ANTHONY JAMES FARQUHAR

Roman Catholic Auxiliary Bishop
Belfast BT15 4DE
(0232) 773935
Born to Alexander and Bridget Farquhar (née Larkin) at Belfast on 6 September 1940. Educated at Rosario Boys PS, St Malachy's College, Queen's University Belfast, Pontifical Lateran University and at Irish College Rome. Formerly Assistant Priest in Ardglass, Co. Down, Chaplain to hospitals and Boys' Training School, Teacher in St MacNissis College, Assistant Chaplain in Queen's University Belfast and Chaplain in New University of Ulster at Coleraine. At present Auxiliary Bishop of Down and Connor, chairman of the Commission on Ecumenism of Irish Bishops Conference and of Youth Resource Group (Diocesan Youth Directors of Ireland), member of Ballymascanlon Inter-Church Committee and of Pastoral Commission of the Irish Bishops Conference and Episcopal Promoter of the Apostleship of the Sea, chairman of Board of St Patrick's Training School and member of Religious Advisory Panel of Ulster Television. Patron of University of Ulster Association Football Club, Coleraine, and of Irish Universities Football Union and president of Queen's University Football Club Belfast.

MOST REV. THOMAS ANTHONY FINNEGAN

Roman Catholic Bishop
Ballina, Co. Mayo
(096) 21518
Born to Patrick and Margaret Finnegan (née Connaughton) at Castlerea, Co. Roscommon on 26 August 1925. Educated at Runnamoat and CBS Roscommon, Summerhill College Sligo, St Patrick's College Maynooth and University College Dublin. Formerly dean Maynooth College, president Summerhill College Sligo, director Regional Marriage Tribunal

Galway, national chairman Catholic Headmasters' Association, Parish Priest Roscommon and Governing Body Thomond College of Education. At present Bishop of Killala and member of executive council Maynooth College, Episcopal Commissions for Education, Emigration and Catechetics and Rural Resettlement Ireland. Founder member Sligo Historical Society and member North Mayo Historical and Archaeological Society. Published works include *Sligo: Sinbads Yellow Shore*, *Branch of the Vine* and *Sligo Tourist Trail*.

MOST REV. MICHAEL A. HARTY

Roman Catholic Bishop
Westbourne, Ennis, Co. Clare
(065) 28638
Born to Patrick and Eileen Harty (née Cleary) at Toomevara, Co. Tipperary on 6 February 1922. Educated at Ballinree National School, St Flannan's College, St Patrick's College Maynooth and University College Galway. Ordained in 1946. Formerly teacher in St Flannan's College, dean of students in St Patrick's College and assistant priest in Los Angeles USA. At present Catholic Bishop of diocese of Killaloe since 1967. Chairman of Irish Episcopal Commission for Liturgy, trustee and visitor of St Patrick's College, member of Governing Body of UCG and patron of Rural Resources Organisation. Awarded Honorary Doctorate of Divinity.

REV. MICHAEL HURLEY

Jesuit Priest
683 Antrim Road, Belfast BT15 4EG
778009
Born to Martin and Johanna Hurley (née Foley) at Ardmore, Co. Waterford on 10 May 1923. Educated at Ardmore NS, Mount Melleray Seminary, UCD, Faculté Saint Albert Eegenhoven-Louvain and Gregorian University Rome. Formerly lecturer in Systematic Theology Milltown Institute Dublin and director Irish School of Ecumenics Dublin. At present member Columbanus Community of Reconciliation.

SARAH CHARLOTTE JACKSON

Recording Clerk (Administrator)
Swanbrook House, Bloomfield Avenue, Dublin 4
(01) 683684
Born to David Keith and Joan Elizabeth Keith Hardy (née Hare) in Hong Kong on 8 August 1948. Educated at Greenwich Academy Greenwich CT, USA, Vassar College New York USA and at Trinity College Dublin. Married to Timothy Richard Jackson with one son and two daughters. Formerly assistant director Barnardos and copy editor Gill and Macmillan. At present recording clerk (administrator) with Religious Society of Friends in Ireland. Member MBA Association.

MOST REV. JOHN KIRBY
Roman Catholic Bishop
St Brendan's, Coorheen, Loughrea, Co. Galway
(091) 41560
Born to Patrick and Rose Kirby (née McCormack) at Athlone in October 1938. Educated at St Peter's Convent National School, Dean Kelly Memorial School, St Joseph's College Ballinasloe, St Patrick's College Maynooth and University College Galway. Formerly Curate to Ballymacward and Gurteen and to Kilrickle, mathematics teacher, rugby coach, vice president and president Garbally College. At present Bishop of Clonfert, chairman Board of Governors of Garbally College, member Episcopal Commissions on Catechetics, social welfare and vocations.

MOST REV. FRANCIS JOSEPH MacKIERNAN
Roman Catholic Bishop
Bishop's House, Cullies, Cavan
(049) 31496
Born to Joseph and Ellen MacKiernan (née MacTague) at Co. Leitrim on 3 February 1936. Educated at Aughawilliam NS, St Patrick's College Cavan, St Patrick's College Maynooth and at University College Dublin. Formerly president St Felim's College, Ballinamore and chairman of the National Committee for the Papal Visit in 1979. At present Bishop of Kilmore and chairman of the Episcopal Commission on Education.

RIGHT REV. GORDON McMULLAN
Church of Ireland Bishop
The See House, Belfast BT5 7AB
(0232) 471973
Born to Samuel and Annie McMullan (née Payne) at Belfast on 31 January 1934. Educated at Park Parade Elementary School, Belfast Technical High School, Queen's University Belfast, Ridley Hall Cambridge, Trinity College Dublin and Irish School of Ecumenics Dublin. Married to Kathleen Davidson with two sons. Formerly administrator with Short Bros and with Shell/BP, Curate of St Patrick's Ballymacarrett Belfast, central adviser on Christian Stewardship to Church of Ireland, Curate of St Columba's Knock, Belfast, Bishop's Curate, St Brendan's, Sydenham, Belfast, Rector of St Columba's, Knock, Belfast, Archdeacon of Down and Bishop of Clogher. At present Bishop of Down and Dromore. Associate Member of Chartered Institute of Secretaries and Administrators, chairman BBC (Northern Ireland) Religious Advisory Committee and member Central Religious Advisory Committee (BBC/ITV).

RIGHT REV. JAMES MEHAFFEY
Church of Ireland Bishop
Londonderry, Northern Ireland
262440
Born to John and Sarah Mehaffey (née McKerr) at Portadown on 29 March 1931. Educated at Derryhale Primary School, Portadown College, Trinity College Dublin and Queen's University Belfast. Married to Thelma Jackson with two sons and one daughter. Formerly Curate of St Patrick's Belfast, St John's Deptford London, and of Down Parish Church and Minor Canon of Down Cathedral. Curate in charge of St Christopher's Belfast, Rector of Kilkeel and Rector of St Finnian's Cregagh Belfast. At present Bishop of Derry and Raphoe. Received Richmond (Virginia USA) Peace Award 1988.

RABBI EPHRAIM MIRVIS
Herzog House, 1 Zion Road, Rathgar, Dublin 6
(01) 967351
Born to Rabbi Dr Lionel and Freida Mirvis (née Katz) at Johannesburg on 7 September 1956. Educated at Benoni West Primary School and Herzlia High School, Cape Town, and at University of South Africa whence he graduated with a BA degree. Holds the High School Teacher's Diploma issued by the Ministry of Education of Israel where he studied for seven years in Rabbinical Academies. Married to Valerie Lynn (née Kaplan) with four children, Liora, Hillel, Daniel and Noam. Formerly held positions in religion and education in Israel and in South Africa, and Rabbi of the Dublin Hebrew Congregation, Adelaide Road. At present Chief Rabbi of Ireland and member of a number of European and World Jewish organisations.

BISHOP MICHAEL MURPHY
Redemption Road, Cork
(021) 301717
Born at Kilmichael, Co. Cork on 18 February 1924. Educated at Toames, Macroom, Tarelton, St Patrick's College Maynooth and UCC. Ordained in 1949. Formerly President St Finbarr's Seminary, six years in a Washington DC parish, St James Society and Padres de Santo Toribio, Peru. At present, and since 1980 Roman Catholic Bishop of Cork and Ross. Holds All Ireland hurling medal for Cork.

RIGHT REV. BISHOP JOHN NEILL
Church of Ireland Bishop of Tuam
Crossmolina, Co. Mayo
(096) 31317
Born to Erberto Mahon and Rhoda Anne Georgina Neill (née Winder) at Dublin on 17 December 1945. Educated at Avoca School, Blackrock, Sandford Park Dublin, Trinity College Dublin, Jesus College Cambridge

and Ridley Hall Theological College Cambridge. Married to Betty Anne Cox with three sons. Formerly Rector of Abbeystrewry Cork, St Bartholomew's Leeson Park and Dean of Waterford. At present Bishop of Tuam and Secretary to House of Bishops.

DR JEREMIAH JOSEPH NEWMAN
Roman Catholic Bishop
66 O'Connell Street, Limerick
(061) 315856
Born to Joseph and Catherine Newman (née Kiely) at Dromcollogher, Co. Limerick on 31 March 1926. Educated at Dromcollogher NS, St Mary's Secondary School, St Munchin's College Limerick, Maynooth College, Catholic University of Louvain and Oxford University. Ordained priest 1950. Appointed bishop 1974. Formerly lecturer in philosophy Queen's University Belfast, professor sociology, Maynooth College, registrar, vice president and president of Maynooth. At present Bishop of Limerick. Publications include *Foundations of Justice, A Time for Truth, Co-Responsibility in Industry, What is Catholic Action?, The Christian in Society, Studies in Political Morality, Principles of Peace, Change and the Catholic, The Christian Layman, New Dimensions in Regional Planning*, and twelve others. Most recent book: *The Postmodern Church* (1990).

THE VERY REV. DR DÓNAL Ó CUILLEANÁIN
Regional Vicar
Cunningham Road, Dalkey
(01) 285 9877
Born to Tomás and Máirín Ó Cuilleanáin (née Ní Locain) at Dublin in 1949. Educated at Coláiste Mhuire and University College, Dublin, whence he graduated in mechanical engineering. Further studies at the University of Navarre whence he graduated with a doctorate in theology. Formerly employed in the facilities engineering section of Aer Lingus, Dublin Airport, and studied airport facilities systems in Germany. Also actively involved in the administration of the Nullamore university residence in Dartry. Ordained in 1978. Chaplain to Ely University Centre, Hume Street, and Cleraun Study Centre, Mount Merrion. At present Regional Vicar, Opus Dei.

REV. MICHAEL O'DOHERTY
Council Director
All Hallow's College, Dublin 9
(01) 375649
Born to Séamus and Susan O'Doherty (née Murphy) at Glenbeigh, Co. Kerry on 15 November 1929. Educated at Glenbeigh NS, St Brendan's College Killarney, St Patrick's College Maynooth, UCD and Loyola University, Chicago. Formerly teacher in postprimary schools in Co. Kerry and held a number of pastoral appointments in the Kerry Diocese. At present National Director Catholic Marriage Advisory Council.

REV. BRENDAN E. O'MAHONY

Priest and University Professor
University College Cork
(021) 276871
Born to Séamus and Maura O'Mahony (née Tobin) at Castlemartyr, Co. Cork on 30 August 1934. Educated at CBS Youghal, St Francis College, Rochestown, Cork, University College Cork, Gregorian University of Rome and Louvain University. Formerly Provincial of the Irish Province of Capuchins, Governor of University College Cork, member of the Senate of NUI and Dean of Arts Faculty, UCC. At present professor and head of Department of Philosophy at UCC. Founder member and first president Irish Philosophical Society, founder member, trustee and first chairman of Franciscan Institute of Ireland.

PATRICK O'MARA

Counsellor
Greystones, Co. Wicklow
(01) 2875743
Born to Stephen and Osra O'Mara (née O'Dwyer) at Dublin on 31 March 1955. Educated at Killashee Naas and at Clongowes Wood College. Chartered Accountant. Married to Rosemary Magill with three children. Formerly manager Price Waterhouse/Craig Gardner and secretary general National Spiritual Assembly of Bahais of Ireland. At present member Continental Board of Counsellors of Bahai Faith in Europe (involving responsibility for development of European Bahai Community). Member Kildare Street Club.

RIGHT REV. SAMUEL G. POYNTZ

Church of Ireland Bishop
12 Talbot Street, Belfast BT1 2QH
322268
Born to Rev. James and Katherine Jane Poyntz (née Greenfield) in Canada on 4 March 1926. Educated at Fairgreen NS Belturbet, Co. Cavan, Portora Royal School Enniskillen and TCD. Married with one son and two daughters. Formerly Curate St George Dublin, Bray, St Michan and St Paul Dublin. Incumbent of St Stephen Dublin, St Ann Dublin and St Ann with St Stephen Dublin. Secretary and Inspector of Schools, Church Education Society for Ireland, Select Preacher to the University of Dublin, Archdeacon of Dublin, Examining Chaplain to Archbishop of Dublin, Chairman ICC and vice president BCC. At present Bishop of Connor.

MOST REV. MICHAEL SMITH

Roman Catholic Bishop
Dublin Road, Mullingar, Co. Westmeath
(044) 48841
Born to John and Bridget Smith (née Fagan) at Oldcastle, Co. Meath on 6

June 1940. Educated at Gilson National School Oldcastle, St Finian's College Mullingar, and Faculty of Canon and Civil Law, Lateran University Rome. Formerly executive secretary of organising committee for visit of Pope John Paul II's visit to Ireland, Autumn 1979, Curate Clonmellon, Chaplain St Loman's Hospital Mullingar and St Francis Medical Centre Mullingar, executive secretary Irish Bishops' Conference, Diocesan Secretary Diocese of Meath and Auxiliary Bishop of Meath. At present Bishop of Meath and Episcopal Secretary Irish Bishops' Conference. Honorary member of a number of golf clubs.

DICK SPICER
Teacher
Rialto Cottages, Dublin 8
Born to Norman and Frances Spicer (née Hughes) at Dublin on 23 June 1946. Educated at All Saints Blackrock, High School Dublin and London (European Studies). Married with three children and one child from a previous marriage. Formerly honorary secretary of Campaign to Separate Church and State. At present chairman Campaign to Separate Church and State. Member Irish Inland Waterways Association and of the Reform Society.

MICHAEL WILLIAM WALKER
Secretary
17 Molesworth Street, Dublin 2
(01) 761337
Born to James W.B. and Rosemary Walker (née Taylor) in the Channel Islands on 14 April 1936. Educated at Aravon School Bray, St Columba's College, Leeds University and University College Cork. Married to Maurethe Varley with one daughter and one son. Formerly teacher of Agricultural Science and farm manager at Bandon Grammar School, development officer Goulding Chemicals and agricultural consultant. At present secretary of the Grand Lodge of Freemasons of Ireland. Member Kildare Street and University Club and Royal Irish Automobile Club.

RIGHT REV. ROBERT ALEXANDER WARKE
Church of Ireland Bishop
Bishop Street, Cork
(021) 271214
Born to Alexander and Annie Warke (née Pennington) at Belfast on 10 July 1930. Educated at Mountmellick National School, The King's Hospital, Trinity College Dublin and at Union Theological Seminary New York. Married to Eileen Skillen with two daughters. Ordained 1953 in St Mark's Church Newtownards (Diocese of Down). Formerly Archdeacon of Dublin and Rector of Zion Parish Dublin. At present Bishop of Cork, Cloyne and Ross, chairman Church of Ireland Bishops' Appeal Committee and member of Board of Christian Aid (London).

THE RIGHT REV. NOEL VINCENT WILLOUGHBY
Church of Ireland Bishop
The Palace, Kilkenny
(056) 21560
Born to George and Mary Jane Willoughby (née Rothwell) in Co. Wicklow on 15 December 1926. Educated at Kilcommon National School, Tate School Wexford and Dublin University. Married with three children. Formerly Canon St Patrick's Cathedral, Archdeacon of Dublin Diocese, honorary secretary General Synod and Rector of Delgany and Glenageary Parishes. At present Bishop of Cashel, Waterford, Lismore, Ossory, Ferns and Leighlin.

Chapter 9
The Security Forces

For he who fights and runs away
May live to fight another day;
But he who is in battle slain
Can never rise and fight again.

Oliver Goldsmith

Modern armies, police forces and prison officers need the support and help of public opinion, and in both parts of the island, there is a very positive approach to public relations in the broad sense and to media relations in particular. Obviously there is a serious problem with release of information where security is involved but in spite of this the press offices do an excellent job and are extremely helpful to journalists and to others. Songs like 'I am the very model of a modern Major General' and 'The Laughing Policeman' help, as do performances by the Army bands and Garda Choir, to keep a human face on the security forces.

In the Republic these include the Garda Síochána (guardians of the peace), the permanent and reserve defence forces, which include the army, air corps, naval service, An Fórsa Cosanta Áitiúil (Army Reserve) and An Slua Muirí (Naval Service Volunteer Reserve) and in Northern Ireland the British Army, the Ulster Defence Regiment and the Royal Ulster Constabulary.

Police in both parts of the island must adapt their structures and procedures to changes in society itself and in criminal activity within society. The changes in Irish society over the past thirty years have been profound, in particular the move towards an urban consumer society with more money and more disposable income than ever before. Planning decisions, especially those which involve rehousing large numbers of local authority tenants in outer suburbs, destroyed social cohesion at a time when a major increase in violence in Northern Ireland was witnessed.

Criminologists and greater police resoucres were badly needed, as were preventative measures, such as bullet-proof screens in banks, building societies and post offices, more secure doors and windows in private houses, more alarms installed in cars and houses, more wages paid by non-cash methods and more armed escorts for cash in transit.

The Garda Síochána was founded in 1922 and is responsible, like the prison officers, to the Minister for Justice. It has a strength in excess of 11,000 and is headed by a commissioner, who is appointed by the Government and based at Garda Headquarters in the Phoenix Park. The force is divided into divisions, districts and sub-districts. Police training is based at Templemore, Co. Tipperary.

The permanent and reserve defence forces are, according to the Constitution of the Republic, under the supreme command of the President. All officers receive their commissions from her and under her direction military command is exercised by the Government through the Minister for Defence. He, in turn, is advised on military matters by a council of defence and in this regard it should be borne in mind that the Republic is not a member of any military alliance. This is not to be confused with neutrality, of course. Many people speak passionately in 'defence' of Irish neutrality, a vague concept, born of a policy adopted fifty years ago for reasons of expediency. In so far as Ireland is a western democracy with very heavy involvement in organisations, such as the European Community, it is probably fair to describe a policy of Irish neutrality as poppy-cock.

The defence forces are commanded by the Chief of Staff based at Defence Forces Headquarters at Parkgate in Dublin. The regional structure contains an Eastern Command with headquarters in Dublin, a Curragh Command covering the South East and with headquarters at the Curragh in Kildare, a Southern Command with headquarters in Cork, and a Western Command with headquarters in Athlone. Of the 38 bases, 27 are expected to have computer terminals for logistics use in 1992. The apprentice schools are at Naas and Baldonnel, the Army School of Music at Cathal Brugha Barracks, the Equitation School at McKee Barracks and the Military College in the Curragh. The Air Corps is based at Casement Aerodrome near Dublin and also operates from Gormanstown in Co. Meath. The Naval Service operates from its headquarters in Dublin and a base at Haulbowline in Co. Cork. Civil defence has been established as part of the national defence structure with the main aim of protecting the civilian population in war time.

For Yugoslavia
Chief of Staff Lt Gen James Parker, right, with Lt Col Colm Mangan
and Lt Col Michael Mullooly prior to their departure in July 1991 to
take part in the EC Monitoring Mission in Yugoslavia.

Participation in many United Nations peace-keeping missions
including the Congo, Middle East, Zaire, Cyprus, Lebanon and
many other troubled places, has been a feature of Irish military
activity since 1958. Involvement with United Nations missions
benefited army morale by providing the ordinary soldier with a
break from routine, and the officers with international experience
which increased professionalism. In recent years, public sector
cutbacks, together with unsatisfactory promotion arrangements
and dissatisfaction over pay and conditions, led to the appointment of the Gleeson Commission which made significant recommendations in a number of key areas such as pay, conditions of
service, and the promotion structure. These recommendations
have in the main been accepted by Government, and are at this
time in the process of being implemented.

The Air Corps Pilots have skills which make them highly
sought after by private sector employers. Applications to resign
from the Air Corps need to be approved by the Minister for

Defence, who is not always amused at the spectre of the State's highly skilled pilots being head-hunted by the airlines.

Life in Northern Ireland was never quite the same since the then Taoiseach Seán Lemass took tea with the then Unionist Prime Minister Captain Terence O'Neill whose attempts to introduce some modest changes in Northern Ireland were met with violent opposition. This opposition led to a breakdown in law and order and to the decision of the Westminster Government to commit the British Army to the impossible task of keeping the peace between the extremists on both sides of the tribal divide.

The police force known as the Royal Ulster Constabulary (RUC) is headed by a chief constable and is over 8,000 in strength. There is also an RUC Reserve with over 2,000 full-time and 2,000 part-time members. The Ulster Defence Regiment is a constituent part of the United Kingdom Defence Forces and is over 7,000 in strength. It is confined to security duties in Northern Ireland, and is to become part of the Royal Irish Rangers regiment in 1992.

The principal prisons in the Republic are Arbour Hill, Cork, Fort Mitchel, Limerick, Mountjoy, Portlaoise, Shanganna Castle and Shelton Abbey with a new juvenile and women's prison at Wheatfield near Clondalkin. Conditions here are modern by any standards, but conditions in some of the other prisons are frequently less than satisfactory with overcrowding a major problem. There is widespread concern about the juvenile system and it is generally agreed that there is a need for new laws, a new approach to young law breakers, and a need to move away from the situation in which three government departments are responsible (health, education and justice) and concentrate the responsibility in one. The principal prisons in Northern Ireland are Crumlin Road, Magilligan, the Maze and Armagh prison for women.

Interested observers of the work of the Security Forces include the Irish Association of Civil Liberty, the Irish Council for Civil Liberties, and the Irish section of Amnesty International.

MAJ. GEN. NOEL BERGIN

Glasnevin, Dublin 9

(01) 771881

Born to James and Kathleen Bergin (née Carroll) at Kildangan Co. Kildare on 25 December 1931. Educated at CBS Athy, Patrician College Ballyfin, University College Dublin and Military College, Curragh. Married to Sheila Barry with two daughters and one son. Formerly director of operations, officer commanding ECIF, officer commanding Cadet School and Army Apprentice School Naas. Overseas service in Congo, Cyprus and Lebanon. Served as Military Advisor to Conference on Security and Co-operation in Europe in Stockholm in 1983. At present Adjutant General of the Defence Forces.

JOE COSTELLO

Teacher

43 North Great George's Street, Dublin 1

(01) 365698

Born to Joe and Mary Theresa Costello (née McHugh) at Geevagh, Sligo on 13 July 1945. Educated at Geevagh, Sligo, Summerhill College Sligo, Maynooth College and UCD. Single. At present chairman Prisoners' Rights Organisation, executive member of Amnesty International and Irish Council for Civil Liberties, standing committee member Association of Secondary Teachers of Ireland, chairman Dublin North One Branch, ASTI. Labour party representative and Dáil candidate for Dublin Central constituency.

PATRICK J. CULLIGAN

Commissioner

Phoenix Park, Dublin 8

(01) 771156

Born at Killarney on 21 July 1936. Married with three children. Joined Garda Síochána on 9 May 1957. Holds degree of MSc (Mgmt). Formerly Sergeant, Inspector, Superintendent, Chief Superintendent, Assistant Commissioner and Deputy Commissioner. Served in Cork, Technical Bureau, Crumlin, Castlebar, Crime and Security, HQ Private Secretary to Commissioner for three years. At present Commissioner.

COMMODORE JOSEPH A. DEASY

Parkgate, Dublin 8

(01) 771881

Born to Michael and Geraldine Deasy (née Blanchfield) in Dungarvan, Co. Waterford on 19 April 1932. Educated at CBS Dungarvan, Britannia Royal Naval College Dartmouth, Royal Naval Staff College Greenwich, Military College Curragh. Specialised in Anti-Submarine Warfare and Diving. Married to Carmel Fleming with one son, Conor, and three daughters, Orla, Carol-Anne and Susan. Formerly held various appointments ashore at Naval Base Haulbowline and Naval HQ Dublin and afloat, including Officer Commanding Corvettes, Minesweepers and Patrol Vessels. Officer Commanding Naval Depot, and Officer Commanding Naval Base and Dockyard. At present Flag Officer Commanding Naval Service in the rank of Commodore. President Naval Golf Association, Commodore Naval Sailing and member of Management Committee Coiste Asgard.

BRIG-GEN. MAURICE DOWNING
Parkgate Street, Dublin 8
(01) 771881
Born to Jack and Ellen Downing (née Manning) in Glengarrif, Co. Cork on 16 May 1931. Educated at Capuchin College Rochestown, Co. Cork and Military College Curragh. Married to Maeve Breen with two daughters Margaret and Maeve and four sons John, Maurice, Paul and Finbarr. Formerly Commandant Military College, Director of Planning and Research, Officer Commanding 2nd Infantry Battalion, and Officer Commanding 20th Infantry Battalion (FCA). Overseas service in Cyprus. Currently Assistant Chief of Staff. Member Terenure College RFC and president Defence Forces Rugby Committee.

Police Chiefs
Garda Commissioner P.J. Culligan seen with Minister for Justice Mr Ray Burke TD and Chief Superintendent Morgan Walshe.

MAJ. GEN. KEVIN FRANCIS DUFFY

Parkgate, Dublin 8

(01) 771881

Born to Francis and Kathleen Duffy (née Fitzgerald) in Dublin on 20 September 1932. Educated at CBC Dún Laoghaire and Military College Curragh. Married to Alice O'Neill with two sons, Kieran and Brian, and two daughters, Ann-Marie and Catherine. Formerly instructor Cadet School, Officer Commanding 1st Field Artillery Regiment, General Officer Commanding Curragh Command. Has served with the United Nations in Congo, Cyprus and Sinai and as Deputy Chief of Staff of the United Nations Treaty Organisation. At present Quartermaster General of the Defence Forces.

GEORGE MAYBURY

General Secretary

Phibsboro, Dublin 7

(01) 303752

Born to John A. and Kathleen Maybury (née Treanor) at Kenmare, Co. Kerry on 13 January 1954. Educated at Kenmare Poor Clare Convent, Boys' National School Kenmare, Holy Cross College Kenmare, Institute of Public Administration and Trinity College. Married to Anne Griffin with two sons and one daughter. Joined Garda Síochána 27 September 1972 and promoted to Sergeant in June 1979. At present secretary general association of Garda Sergeants and Inspectors. Member of St Brigid's Athletic Club, Blanchardstown, Garda Boat Club and Garda Recreation Club. Represented Garda Síochána on Rotary Group Study to Holland in 1986. Has competed internationally for An Garda in athletics on many occasions, particularly in Marathon.

BRIG-GEN. MICHAEL F. MINEHANE

Collins Barracks, Cork

(021) 397577

Born to Patrick and Ann Minehane (née Driscoll) at Bantry, Co. Cork on 2 June 1933. Educated at Bantry NS, St Augustine's Dungarvan and Military College Curragh. Married to Maura McCarthy with two sons, Michael and Cathal and two daughters, Ann and Niamh. Formerly Deputy Adjutant General Defence Forces, and Military Advisor Conference on Security and Co-operation in Europe. Overseas service in Congo, Cyprus and Lebanon. At present General Officer Commanding Southern Command. Member Cork Golf Club and Elm Park Golf and Sports Club.

PATRICK JOSEPH MORAN

Deputy Commissioner

Phoenix Park, Dublin 8

(01) 771156

Born at Newport, Co. Mayo in 1933. Educated at St Jarlath's College

Tuam, St Patrick's College Maynooth and University of Manchester. Holder of Post Graduate Diploma in Adult and Community Education and Masters Degree in Education from University of Manchester. Married to Maureen McManus with three sons and one daughter. Formerly served as Garda, Sergeant and Inspector in Cork, Monaghan, Westmeath, Galway, Tipperary and Dublin, Superintendent in Training Branch at Garda HQ and Chief Superintendent and Assistant Commissioner and director of Garda College Templemore. At present Deputy Commissioner currently responsible for the administration of Garda Síochána — Personnel, Finance and Training and Research.

MICHAEL DEREK NALLY
Company Chairman
Carrickduff, Bunclody, Co. Wexford
(01) 711444
Born to Michael and Hilda Nally (née Thompson) at Thurles, Co. Tipperary on 4 December 1936. Educated at Holycross NS, Thurles CBS and College of Industrial Relations. Married to Joan Bonass with two daughters. Formerly member of An Garda Síochána, general secretary Association of Garda Sergeants and Inspectors and president Irish Conference of Professional and Service Associations. At present chairman Irish Association for Victim Support and chairman European Forum of Victims Service. Member of Board of Trustees of Irish Youth Foundation and executive chairman of International Investigations Ireland. Chairman River Slaney Rodfishers' Association and Bunclody Amenities Ltd.

LT GEN. TADHG O'NEILL
Retired Chief of Staff
Born to Thomas and May O'Neill (née Gray) at Kilkenny on 16 October 1926. Educated at CBS Monaghan and Carlow, and Military College Curragh. Married to Emer O'Connell with three daughters, Emer, Niamh and Orla. Formerly Officer Commanding 2nd Field Artillery Regiment, Officer Commanding 2nd Brigade, General Officer Commanding Western Command, and Chief of Staff. Overseas service ONUC, UNFICYP and UNIFIL. Decorated UN Medal (ONUC), UN Medal (UNFICYP), UN Medal (UNIFIL), Service Medal and Bar. At present chairman Army Pensions Board and director Omnitron Ltd. Member Newlands Golf Club and honorary member Athlone and Dublin no. 1 Rotary Clubs.

THOMAS J. O'REILLY
Deputy Commissioner
Phoenix Park, Dublin 8
(01) 771156
Born in Dublin on 25 May 1934. Married with five children. Holds BA and MSc (in Economics and Statistics) Degrees. Joined Garda Síochána on 22 May 1958. Formerly Sergeant, Inspector, Superintendent, Chief Superintendent and Assistant Commissioner. Most of service has been in Dublin Metropolitan Area. At present Deputy Commissioner.

Comrades in Arms
Second Lieutenant Ann Hanniffy and Second Lieutenant Conor Lynch
share the jubilation of receiving their commissions at a ceremony at the
Curragh in May 1988.

LT GEN. JIM PARKER
Parkgate, Dublin 8
(01) 771881

Born to Edmund and Norah Parker (née Sheehan) at Mitchelstown on 15 April 1929. Educated at CBS Mitchelstown, Military College Curragh, Infantry School Warminster, Staff College Camberly and University College Dublin. Married to Breda Roche with five sons, Eamonn, Liam, Michael, Kieran and Diarmuid and one daughter, Siobhán. Formerly Officer Commanding 3rd Infantry Battalion, Director of Reserve Forces, Officer Commanding 2nd Infantry Brigade, Executive Officer of both Western and Curragh Commands and Adjutant General of the Defence Forces. Has had extensive overseas service with United Nations including service in the Congo, Cyprus, Sinai where he was Officer Commanding 26th Infantry Group, Lebanon and India/Pakistan where he was Chief Military Observer with the UN Military Observer Group for India and Pakistan. At present Chief of Staff of the Defence Forces. Member of Curragh Golf Club.

BRIG-GEN. JOSEPH PATRICK PURCELL
Custume Barracks, Athlone
(0902) 92631

Born to Nicholas and Julia Purcell (née O'Gorman) at Kilkenny on 20 May 1933. Educated at CBS Kilkenny, Military College and Institute of Science and Technology Dublin. Married to Joan Rogers with one daughter, Siobhán, and one son, Fergal. Formerly Instructor Command and Staff School Military College, Officer Commanding Depot Signal Corps and Ceannt Barracks Curragh and Director of Signals. Overseas service with the United Nations in Congo, Lebanon and Central America. At present General Officer Commanding Western Command.

BRIG-GEN. T.A. WALL
Curragh Camp, Co. Kildare
(045) 41301

Born to Patrick and Brigid Wall (née Cleary) at Clonmel, Co. Tipperary in May 1934. Educated at Thurles CBS and Military College Curragh. Married to Elisabeth Barclay with two daughters, Sharon and Alice. Formerly held appointments at Magee Barracks Kildare, Sarsfield Barracks Limerick, Ballincollig, Spike Island, Defence Forces Headquarters, Command Adjutant Eastern Command and OC 2nd Regiment. Overseas service in Cyprus, Lebanon and as Chief Operations Officer with United Nations in Honduras, Central America. At present General Officer Commanding Curragh Command. Holder of five All-Ireland Senior Hurling Championship medals with his native Tipperary.

Chapter 10
Women and Progress

*The hand that rocks the cradle
Is the hand that rules the world.*

William Ross Wallace

The amazing contributions made to Irish life by women such as Lady Gregory, Maud Gonne and Countess Markievicz were blinding in a way. They may have caused a great many people to believe for a very long time that, as certain women got to the top, the way was open for any woman to get to the top. One could argue whether the way was half open, fully open or not open at all, but it cannot be denied that women in Ireland, like women elsewhere, were handicapped by legal discrimination and stereotyping.

Feminism in Ireland has been striving for equality for women in economic and social matters and, in looking at this situation one must, of course, distinguish between issues which are relevant to women only and those which apply to both sexes.

It may be true that there is always room at the top but, according to the report of the Advisory Committee on Management Training, over 80 per cent of public and private organisations have no women at top management level; between 30 per cent and 50 per cent of private and public organisations have no women in middle management; and just under a third have no women in junior management. A survey by the Council for the Status of Women on the position of women on boards of state-sponsored bodies reveals that in 1981 participation by women on all state boards amounted to 10 per cent, but this had increased to 12 per cent in 1985, and to 15 per cent in 1990. There can be no doubt that this situation will continue to change as more and more women join the pool of potential managers and, as the report stated, it is 'sound business practice' to encourage and assist all employees, male and female, to develop their full potential. Equally, according to Jim O'Donnell's *Wordgloss Current Affairs Dictionary*, there are still parts of the country where 'herself' thinks it best to say nothing!

The Commission on the status of women published its first

statement in April 1991 identifying some key areas which Government could work on immediately. The first of these was a proposal that Government introduce legislation to give each spouse equal rights of automatic ownership of the family home and household chattels. Other recommendations concerned the inclusion of a paragraph in all memoranda to Government outlining the probable impact on women of any proposed policy change; representation of women on the boards of state-sponsored bodies; non-allocation of national lottery and other public funds to private clubs, sporting, social or recreational, which operate discriminatory policies against women; the appointment of a woman as a fifth member of the Top Level Appointments Committee; the prevention of age being a barrier to recruitment; and that Government through the Minister for Education directs the National Council for Curriculum and Assessment to review the primary school curriculum handbook with a view to the elimination from it of sexism and sex-stereotyping. Organisations working solely or mainly for women include the Aim Group for Family Law Reform, Ally, Cherish, several Rape Crisis Centres, La Leche League of Ireland, Women's Aid and many others.

Network is a growing organisation for women in business, with five regional branches and over 300 members, who have adapted the traditional old boys' network for business contacts, slipped into the system, and made it an old girls' network. As a result, the organisation is a source of information about promotion and career prospects, expansion plans and investment opportunities for its members.

The Employment Equality Agency in the Republic and the Equal Opportunities' Commission in Northern Ireland do not, strictly speaking, belong in this chapter, as they aim to eliminate sex discrimination. Similarly, the work of the Council for the Status of Women is of interest to anyone male or female taking a broad view of society.

The Irish Country Women's Association has established over 1,000 Guilds throughout the country where local women exchange ideas on various aspects of home and farm management, handcrafts and cultural activity. Formed originally as the United Irish Women, it changed its name in 1934. Its adult education centre, An Grianán, is situated five miles from Drogheda and was purchased by the W.K. Kellogg Foundation of America and entrusted to the ICA in 1954. The Foundation financed an expansion in 1979 which brought the total Kellogg investment to over US$2 million. ICA is the only full member of COFACE (The Confederation of Family Associations in Europe) which acts as an advisory body to the European Commission. The Irish Housewives Association defends consumers' rights as well as dealing with all matters affecting homes. The National Association of Widows in Ireland aims to help widows adapt to their altered role in society.

The Soroptomists Service Clubs exclude men from membership, just as Rotary Clubs exclude Women. There is no apparent justification for this, nor does there appear to be any real reason why women find it necessary to have separate organisations to campaign for Disarmament and Soviet Jewry and so on. The Women's Committee of the Irish Congress of Trade Unions advises Congress on matters of special concern to women workers, and the Women's Political Association encourages participation in public life. The last local elections in the Republic showed an increase in the number of women elected to local authority membership from 8 per cent in 1985 to 11 per cent in 1991.

Role reversal still raises eyebrows and it goes without saying that when television viewers saw Gráinne Cronin going up the aircraft steps accompanied by a rather bulky male, the vast majority must have been surprised to learn that she was the pilot and he was the co-pilot! But that piece of television was, in fact, the first Aer Lingus flight to be captained by a woman. The surprise was natural and stemmed only from the novelty of the scene. Similar changes are taking place throughout the business world. Miriam Hederman O'Brien sits on the Board of AIB Bank, Margaret Downes on the Board of the Bank of Ireland, and Carmencita Hederman on the Board of First National Building Society, to name but three examples of progress. The novelty of these situations soon wears off.

Role reversal will also slowly bring about a greater appreciation of work which in the past was normally done by women. Parenting is now being experienced by men, who may be unemployed at a time when their wives are in employment. These situations, which are rare but becoming less so, bring about an appreciation of parenting as one of the hardest jobs in the world, with long hours, low status and no payment.

A number of groups campaign for civil divorce and re-marriage where marriages have broken down, but this facility is not available in the Republic. Following a unanimous decision of the Supreme Court in March 1988, counselling and information services which would assist the procuring of an abortion — and thus the violation of the Constitutional Right to Life of the Unborn — are perpetually 'restrained' or, in other words, banned.

And the co-pilot was male
Captain Gráinne Cronin seen above at the controls of a Belfast-made shorts 360, became, during 1988, the first woman captain to fly for Aer Lingus.

MONICA BARNES
Public Representative
Leinster House, Dublin 2
(01) 789911
Born to James and Helena McDermott (née Murren) at Kingscourt, on 12 February 1936. Educated at Kingscourt National School, St Louis Convent Carrickmacross and Orange's Academy Belfast. Married to Robert Barnes with three children. Formerly board member Employment Equality Agency, member Women's Representative Committee and Senator. At present and since 1982, Fine Gael TD, chairwoman Joint Oireachtas Committee on Women's Rights, spokesperson on Women's Rights and on Marine and Urban Affairs, and vice president Fine Gael. Appointed member of the Council of State by President of Ireland in January 1991.

GILLIAN BOWLER
Managing Director
134 Lower Baggot Street, Dublin 2
(01) 613122
Born to Maurice and Josephine Bowler (née Easton-Taylor) at London on 18 November 1952. Educated at Sandhurst and Carisbroore Schools, England. Married to Harry Sydner. Formerly director Irish Goods Council. At present director Granada Travel, Budget Travel and Leisure World, and chairman of Irish Museum of Modern Art at Kilmainham. Awarded honorary doctorate by the National Council for Educational Awards.

MARY T. CANNING
Manager
27/33 Upper Baggot Street, Dublin 4
(01) 685777
Born to Patrick and Eileen Carden (née Kelly) at Dublin on 19 June 1944. Educated at Notre Dame des Missions and UCD and later at Rome University. Married to the late Brendan Canning, with one son, Ronan, and one daughter, Sinéad. Formerly assistant general manager Altergo Training, English lecturer at Rochester State Junior College, Minnesota, assistant manager AnCo Training Centre, Loughlinstown and Manager International Services FÁS with responsibility for Eastern Europe. At present chief technical advisor for the European Commission to the Ministry of Labour, Hungary. Board member DEVCO; Services to Industries Research Centre (UCD); Loreto High School (Dalkey).

MARGARET DOWNES
Chartered Accountant
Fitzwilton House, Wilton Place, Dublin 2
(01) 682222
Born to Charles Edmond and Mary Gavin (née Hunt) at Ballina, Co. Mayo in 1934. Educated at Convent NS Ballina, Loreto Abbey Rathfarnham and University College Dublin whence she graduated with a BComm degree. Later admitted to membership of the Institute of Chartered Accountants in Ireland. Married to Desmond Downes with one son, Alexander, and two daughters, Rachel and Lucy. Formerly with Price Waterhouse, London, Accountant UCD, partner, Peterson Morrison and Co, partner, Coopers and Lybrand. President Institute of Chartered Accountants in Ireland. Chairman Finance Council Archdiocese of Dublin and Government-appointed chairman of Cable Systems' Committee. At present member of Court of Directors of Bank of Ireland, director of Irish Glass plc, Gallagher (Dublin) Ltd, Storehouse plc and other public and private companies. President European Federation of Accountants. Chairman President's Development Council UCD, director Douglas Hyde Gallery TCD, trustee Chester Beatty Library, director Moy Valley Resources, Ballina, Co. Mayo and director New City Initiative (NCI). Member Kildare Street and University Club, UCD Association and Women's Political Association. Awarded honorary degree by NUI.

MARY PATRICIA McALEESE
Institute Director
Queen's University, Belfast BT7 1NN
(0232) 245133
Born to Patrick Joseph and Claire Thérèse Leneghan (née McManus) at Belfast on 27 June 1951. Educated at Convent of Mercy, Crumlin Road and St Dominic's High School, Falls Road and Queen's University Belfast and at The Inn of Court, Northern Ireland. Married to Martin McAleese with one son, Justin, and two daughters, Emma and Saramai. Formerly Reid Professor of criminal law, criminology and penology at TCD, reporter and presenter for RTE television Current Affairs, Co-Chairperson Inter-Church Working Party on Sectarianism (1991). At present director Institute of Professional Legal Studies at Queen's University. Member BBC Broadcasting Council of Northern Ireland (1989–92). Non-executive director Northern Ireland Electricity. Member Irish Commission for Justice and Peace. Was a member of the Roman Catholic Episcopal Delegation to the New Ireland Forum.

NELL McCAFFERTY
Journalist
(01) 973896
Born to Hugh and Lily McCafferty (née Duffy) at Bogside, Derry City on

28 March 1944. Educated at St Eugene's Girls' School Derry, Thornhill Grammar School and Queen's University Belfast. Formerly secretary Derry Labour Party and founder member Irish Women's Liberation Movement. At present freelance journalist. Publications include *Armagh Women*, *Eyes of the Law*, *The Best of Nell*, *Women to Blame*, *Goodnight Sisters*, *Peggy Deery*, and *Warm in the Heart*.

CATHERINE McGUINNESS
Senior Counsel
Four Courts, Dublin 7
(01) 720622
Born to Rev. Canon Robert C. and Sylvia Ellis (née Craig) at Belfast on 14 November 1934. Educated at Dunmurry Public Elementary School Belfast, Alexandra College and School Dublin, TCD and King's Inns. Married to Proinsias MacAonghusa with two sons and one daughter. Formerly member of Seanad Éireann, Council of State, Adoption Board and Voluntary Health Insurance Board and chairperson National Social Service Board. At present chairperson Employment Equality Agency and National College of Art and Design, and member of Commission on Status of Women. Member Culwick Choral Society, International Academy of Matrimonial Lawyers, Family Lawyers' Association and of the General Synod of the Church of Ireland.

SYLVIA MEEHAN
Chief Executive
36 Upper Mount Street, Dublin 2
(01) 605966
Born to Dr John and May Shiel (née Lennon) at Dublin on 2 April 1929. Educated at Loreto College North Great George's Street and UCD. Married to the late Denis Meehan with three sons and two daughters. Formerly vice principal, Cabinteely Community School and member National Economic and Social Council. At present Chief Executive, Employment Equality Agency and member EC Advisory Committee on Equal Opportunities for men and women.

STELLA G. MEW
School Principal
Glenageary, Co. Dublin
(01) 853133
Born to Col. R.G. and Maureen Mew (née Palmer) at Dublin on 27 April 1942. Educated at Chapelizod NS, Alexandra Junior School, Alexandra School and College and at Trinity College Dublin. Single. Formerly assistant teacher, Clarendon School, North Wales and Heathfield School Ascot Berkshire. At present principal Rathdown School. Member Royal Overseas Club, Dublin University Women Graduates' Association, Irish

School Masters' Association, and Joint Managerial Body, General and Diocesan Synods, General and Diocesan Boards of Education.

MARY REDMOND

Solicitor
3 Fitzwilliam Place, Dublin 2
(01) 789699

Born to John and Mary Redmond (née Lannin) at Dublin on 25 August 1950. Educated at Dominican Convent Muckross Park and Loreto College St Stephen's Green, University College Dublin, Somerville College Oxford, Christ's College Cambridge and University of Cambridge. Graduated with BCL, LL.M and PhD degrees. Married to Dr Patrick Ussher LL.D, FTCD with one son. Formerly lecturer UCD Law Faculty, fellow and director of Studies in Law, Churchill College, Cambridge, fellow and director of Studies in Law and tutor at Christ's College, Cambridge. At present solicitor and chairperson Irish Hospice Foundation. Author of a number of books on labour law.

Chapter 11
Economy and Economists

Annual income twenty pounds, annual expenditure nineteen nineteen six, result happiness. Annual income twenty pounds annual expenditure twenty pounds ought and six, result misery.

Dickens

Public awareness of the economy is growing, although it has a long way to go. Public interest in the world of business is lively and growing also. While the degrees of awareness and interest may be low, their growth is encouraging. We may never reach the stage where a serious programme on the latest economic situation will attract more viewers than the latest episode of a television soap opera, but party canvassers have reported during recent election campaigns on the growing interest in Budget Deficits and the State of the Nation.

The Economic and Social Research Institute is a non-profit making organisation which enjoys full academic independence. It is governed by a Council consisting of 30 members appointed from the general membership of the Institute representative of business, trades unions, government departments, state agencies, universities and other research institutes. The most important resource of the Institute is its high quality staff including a total of 25 full time research staff. In June 1991 the Institute published a Medium-Term Review: 1991–1996 which highlighted the sharp recovery in Irish growth post 1987 and, from the experiences of the 1980s, drew the following 'salutary lessons' —

* the Irish economy is extremely vulnerable to influences from the world trading environment.
* competitiveness is important, and close attention must be paid to any factors which might cause a deterioration.
* fiscal expansions can be a negative sum game in the medium term and in very particular circumstances.
* wage determination mechanisms are crucial to the growth of the economy.
* the benefits to the economy from foreign-owned high technology companies are manifest.
* the recovery in the period 87/90 was driven largely by

154

the growth in the world economy and by stronger private consumption and investment, which more than offset the negative effect of public expenditure cutbacks which were needed to restore confidence in and balance to the public finances.

The 1989 Government in the Republic continued the efforts of the previous Government to curb expenditure and to reduce the National Debt which at the end of 1989 was over IR£26,000 million. Of this over IR£17,000 million was domestic debt and over IR£9,000 million was foreign debt. The Official External Reserves amounted to IR£2,829 million.

The Budget for 1991 foresaw a Current Budget Deficit of IR£245 million and an Exchequer Borrowing Requirement for capital purposes of IR£215 million to bring Total Exchequer Borrowing to IR£460 million.

The principal public concerns include Unemployment, Tax Harmonisation, and Inflation.

Jobs

The importance of the services sector in terms of employment has been growing steadily as follows:

	1956 %	1988 %
Services	38	57
Industry	24	28
Agriculture, forestry and fishing	38	15

Within the services sector the most important areas are professional services and distribution followed by public administration and defence, transport, communications and storage, personal services and financial services. A similar picture emerges in Northern Ireland with the services sector being by far the most important in terms of sustaining employment, followed by industry, which in turn, is followed by agriculture. Agriculture is really important accounting for 10.5 per cent of GDP compared with an EC average of 3.2, and accounting for 15 per cent of employment compared with an EC average of 7.7 per cent.

It is impossible to overstate the importance in human terms of job opportunities. For so many people it is important that there be a choice between job opportunities at home and job opportunities abroad. Lack of these opportunities is a major source of concern. Irish youth rebels against a system which imposes sustained periods of dependency long after it aspires to independence. Finding a solution to this state of affairs is one of the greatest challenges facing our political and business leaders.

The continued decline in construction, lack of growth in agriculture, and continued cut-backs in the public sector, all combine to bring about in 1991 a steady rise in unemployment which the Republic has been experiencing since Summer 1990. This reached 19.4 per cent in August 1991, one of the highest rates in the EC. The following picture, at end 1990, uses OECD standardised figures for valid international comparisons:

	% End 1990
Ireland	14.2
UK	7.6
Germany	4.6
France	9.0
Italy	9.8
Spain	15.8
Belgium	8.2
Netherlands	7.3
EC average	8.5

In the longer term, the consequences for Ireland of declining birth rates in Europe, may be favourable. Fertility or the average number of children born per woman is 2.2 in the Republic compared with 2.0 in the United Kingdom, and even lower rates in other European countries. The phenomenon is to be seen in East European countries also, and in Hungary the birth rate dropped from 23 per 1,000 in 1945 to less than 12 today. The Irish birth rate at 17.6 is substantially ahead of Italy at 10.1 and Portugal at 12.8 for example.

The birth rate peaked in 1980 and as a result a rapid fall in the number of new entrants to the work force can be predicted with certainty for the early part of the next century. The number is expected to be between 20,000 and 25,000 until the year 2000 and it will then fall rapidly to about 8,000 by the year 2005. This means that without any emigration, and without any increase in the number of married women working, employment must grow by between 1.5 per cent and 2 per cent each year in order to provide enough jobs for this natural increase in the working population.

Border Business

After Income Tax, Value Added Tax and Excise Duties are the two most important sources of revenue for the Republic. The Government looks with dismay at the idea of harmonisation by 1993, which could cost IR£450 million in loss of revenue out of a total estimated tax revenue of IR£8,000 million. Nevertheless, it is to be hoped that Government will not seek any derogation from the 1993 target date. Developments in this area will be subjected to the closest scrutiny on both sides of the border.

The phenomenon of cross border shopping from the Republic to the North had an estimated value of IR£200 million, in terms of spending on petrol, foodstuffs, soft and alcoholic drinks, TV and electrical goods. Only an estimated IR£7 million flowed from Northern Ireland into the Republic, being spent mostly on clothing, which carries a lower rate of Value Added Tax in the Republic than in the North. Not all of the price differential can be attributed to factors under Government control.

For example, Northern Ireland is frequently regarded by United Kingdom manufacturers as being part of their internal market and a uniform costing approach is applied to distribution costs. In other words, a retailer in Northern Ireland may buy at the same price as a retailer in London, notwithstanding the expensive strip of water to be crossed in order to bring the goods home. When the same UK manufacturer comes to deal with the Republic of Ireland, however, he quotes on an ex-factory basis, leaving his Irish agent or distributor to add on the actual freight costs to Dublin, the costs of the customs clearance and the distributor's mark-up. Given that the population is small and the density low, the mark-up has to be reasonably substantial to cover the distributor's costs.

The scale of the problem is illustrated by the following tables which compare current Irish excise rates with EC minimum rates, EC target rates, and current UK rates:

Alcohol — Excise Rates (nearest IR£)

	Current Irish Rate IR£	Commission Minimum Rate IR£	Commission Target Rate IR£	UK Rate IR£
Beer per std. barrel	152.595	12.715	25.429	104.85
Spirits per litre of alcohol	20.085	8.632	10.790	20.835
Still Wine per litre	2.04	0.072	0.144	1.325
Sparkling Wine per litre	4.08	0.127	0.255	2.187
Intermediate Products per litre	2.96	0.577	0.722	2.285

Tobacco — Excise Rates (nearest IR£/nearest %)

	Current Irish Rate IR£	Commission Minimum Rate IR£	Commission Target Rate IR£	UK Rate IR£
Cigarettes (per 1,000)	£43+34%	£12+45%	£17+54%	£44+36%
Price per pack of 20	£2.10	£1.40	£1.90	£2.22
Total tax take at new price	£1.56 74%	£0.86 61%	£1.36 72%	£1.68 76%

Hydrocarbon Oils— Excise rates per hectolitre (nearest IR£)

	Current Irish Rate IR£	Commission Minimum Rates/Bands IR£		UK Rates IR£
		Min	Target	
Petrol (leaded)	30.35	26.01	38.20	28.407
Petrol (unleaded)	27.79	22.15	34.34	24.626
Derv	22.31	18.91	20.84	24.033

Prices and Earnings

According to a recent global survey conducted by the English company, Employment Conditions Abroad Limited, the Irish cost of a shopping basket of essential items, comes in twenty-fourth dearest in a league table of 68 countries. Finland and Japan were the two dearest countries, with Italy eleventh, Germany nineteenth and Hong Kong thirty-sixth — all ahead of the UK which came in thirty-eighth place.

Inflation in the Republic has been slowing down and amounted to only 3.4 per cent in 1990, and to only 4 per cent in 1989. The August 1991 Economic Review published by National Irish Bank provided the following international comparison on inflation trends:

	% Current	% 1992 Forecast
Ireland	3.1	3.3
UK	5.8	4.0
US	4.6	4.1
Japan	3.4	2.5
Germany	3.5	3.6
France	3.3	3.0
Italy	6.7	5.5
Belgium	3.6	3.5

It is good to have the Republic's inflation below the EC average, especially in the context of the Union Bank of Switzerland survey based on research carried out in spring 1991, which showed Dublin as a slightly more expensive city than for example Frankfurt (on a rent exclusive basis) with lower salary and wage levels which were subject to higher tax and social insurance contributions, and lower domestic purchasing power:

	Dublin	Frankfurt	New York	Tokyo
Price Level	76.0	74.5	83.3	115.0
Price Level Rent Inclusive	74.2	79.8	103.9	141.4
Salary and Wage Level	45.4	72.2	68.2	63.9
Purchasing Power Level	59.9	97.0	81.8	55.6

Levels based on Zürich = 100

When income tax is taken in isolation, the Ireland/United Kingdom disparity is highlighted as follows:

	R. of Ireland IR£	N. Ireland IR£
Pre-tax income	25,000	25,000
Income Tax Single	11,348	7,035
Income Tax Married	8,251	6,565

QUALITY OF LIFE
IRELAND vs. OTHER COUNTRIES

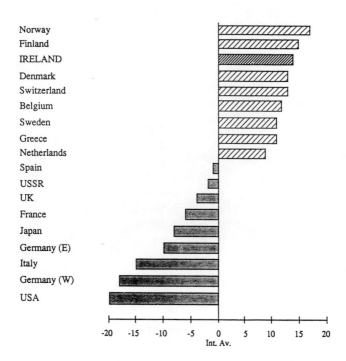

(Reproduced by permission of Lansdowne Market Research
and the *Sunday Press*.)

Money Men
The Chairman of the Revenue Commissioners, Mr Cathal Mac Domh-
naill, with Mr Bertie Ahern, Minister for Finance, at an Open Day for Tax
Practitioners in December 1991.

JOHN DONOVAN COYLE
Company Director
Áras Hygeia, Oranmore, Co. Galway
(091) 94722
Born to David Donovan and Róisín Coyle (née MacNeill) at Dublin on 20 August 1946. Educated at Coláiste Iognaid Galway, Glenstal Abbey, UCD and Collège d'Europe, Bruges. Married to Sarah Doyle with three sons, Ronan, David and Eoin, and three daughters, Zoë, Róisín Mary and Sophia. Formerly president Galway Chamber of Commerce and Industry, president Chambers of Commerce of Ireland, and vice president Eurochambres. At present chairman of Hygeia Chemicals Ltd, Renvyle Hotel Ltd, Steelforms Ltd, and director of several companies. Member Galway Race Committee, Marketing Institute, Institute of Directors, Galway Oyster Festival, Galway County Club and Galway Bay Sailing Club.

ALAN WILLIAM GRAY
Economic Consultant
25 Wellington Quay, Dublin 2
(01) 777144
Born to Albert and Sarah Gray (née Boucher) at Dublin on 10 December 1957. Educated at Rathgar National School, The High School Dublin and at TCD. Married to Caroline O'Donovan with one son, Robert. Formerly chief economic consultant with pan-European consultancy practice, Price Waterhouse. Also with Central Bank of Ireland, Irish Goods Council, Department of Industry and Energy. Chairman of Government Review Group on Whitegate Oil Refinery and Irish Oil Prices and of Interdepartmental Monitoring Group on Industrial Costs. At present managing director Indecon International Economic Consultants, chairman Montilla Investments and director Gray Murray and Associates (Strategic Marketing Advisors). Member of Financial Services Industry Association and Committee on European Integration.

GRAHAM GUDGIN
Economist
46 University Road, Belfast BT5 6DJ
(0232) 325594
Born to Harold and Ethel Gudgin (née Reid) at Aberdeen on 2 January 1946. Educated at Weeton Church of England Primary School and Kirkham Girls' School, Newark Girls' School and University of London Queen Mary College. Married with two children. Formerly senior research officer Department of Applied Economics University of Cambridge. At present director Northern Ireland Economic Research Centre. Member East Down Yacht Club and Institute of Directors.

PHILIP ANTHONY HALPIN

Economist
27 College Green, Dublin 2
(01) 6798788

Born to Noel and Philomena Halpin (née Marcantonio) at Dublin on 14 June 1955. Educated at Árd Scoil Éanna and UCD. Married to Ursula Gerding with one daughter, Donata. Formerly economist with Dudgeon Stockbrokers, lecturer at Institute of Public Administration and University of Gezira (Sudan), gilt dealer with Solomons Abrahamson Stockbrokers and investment manager with Abbey Life Association (Ireland) Ltd. At present group economist and senior fund manager National Irish Bank. Member Economics and Taxation Policy Committee (Confederation of Irish Industry) and of Consultative Committee on EMU (Institute of European Affairs). Member Riverview Tennis and Racquet Club.

KIERAN ANTHONY KENNEDY

Economist
4 Burlington Road, Dublin 4
(01) 760115

Born to Patrick and Margaret Kennedy (née Callaghan) at Newbridge, Co. Kildare on 14 July 1935. Educated at Clontuskert NS, CBS Limerick, University College Dublin, Nuffield College Oxford and at Harvard. Married to Finola Flanagan with three sons, Kieran Francis, Michael Brendan, and Francis John Bernard, and three daughters, Ruth Margaret, Susan Edel and Lucy. Formerly executive officer, administrative officer and assistant principal officer in the Civil Service and senior research officer at Economic and Social Research Institute. Spent a period on secondment to Central Bank of Ireland as economic consultant. At present director Economic and Social Research Institute, president Statistical and Social Inquiry Society of Ireland, member American Economic Association, and International Association for Research Income and Wealth, and chairman Swiss-Irish Business Association. Elected member Royal Irish Academy 1973. Has published numerous books and pamphlets.

PATRICK LYNCH

Retired University Professor

Born to Daniel and Brigid Lynch (née Kennedy) at Dublin on 5 May 1917. Educated at Holy Faith Convent, Synge Street CBS, Catholic University School Dublin, University College Dublin, and Peterhouse Cambridge. Widowed. Formerly professor of Political Economy UCD, chairman Aer Lingus, deputy chairman Allied Irish Banks and assistant secretary Department of the Taoiseach. Director of OECD/Government Surveys 'Investment in Education' and 'Science & Irish Economic Development'. Member of Higher Education Authority, Senate NUI and Club of Rome. Chairman Economic and Social Research Institute and Medico-Social Research Board, treasurer Royal Irish Academy, member of National Science Council, patron British Irish Association, president Irish Anti-Apartheid Association and deputy chairman Co-operation North. Member Royal Irish Academy.

JOHN McCARRICK
Business Consultant and Company Director
Laraghcon House, Lucan, Co. Dublin
(01) 281059
Born to Conor and Annie McCarrick (née McIntyre) at Tobbercurry, Co. Sligo on 13 July 1945. Educated at Dean Kelly School Athlone, Patrician College Ballyfin, University College Galway (BComm) and University College Dublin (BAgrSc Econ). Fellow of Chartered Institute of Management Accountants. Married to Helen Regan with three sons and four daughters. Formerly chief agricultural advisor Bank of Ireland, director general Irish Co-operative Organisation Society, chairman National Association of Community Broadcasting and Gorta volunteer Kenya. At present engaged in international development co-operation and corporate strategic planning. A director of Renewable Energy Ireland Ltd, McCarrick Bros Ltd and Irish Life plc. Also pursues farming interests.

PATRICK J. MOORE
Economist
Clanwilliam Court, Lower Mount Street, Dublin 2
(01) 685155
Born to Thomas and Mary Moore (née Delaney) at Laois on 24 November 1942. Educated at Ballacolla NS, Patrician College, Ballyfin and University College Dublin whence he graduated with an honours agricultural economics degree. Married to Nuala Campion with three sons and one daughter. Formerly economist with marketing division Canadian Department of Agriculture in Ottawa and agricultural specialist with USDA at American Embassy, Dublin. At present chief executive CBF, the Irish Livestock and Meat Board. Awarded the 1990 Bastow Memorial Award for his contribution to the Irish livestock and meat industry.

JEREMIAH SEXTON
Research Professor
4 Burlington Road, Dublin 4
(01) 760115
Born to Cornelius and Mary Sexton (née Murphy) at Cork on 6 March 1939. Educated at Sullivan's Quay CBS Cork, and at University College Cork whence he graduated with an MSc degree. Married to Kathleen Galvin with five children. Formerly senior statistician Central Statistics Office. At present research professor, Economic and Social Research Institute. Member Royal St George Yacht Club.

JOHN ERVINE SPENCER

University Professor
Queen's University Belfast BT7 1NN
(0232) 245133
Born to Wilfred John and Emily Edith Spencer (née Ervine) at Portadown, on 22 December 1942. Educated at Portadown College and Queen's University Belfast. Married. Formerly Henry Fellow, Yale University, president Irish Economic Association, lecturer London School of Economics and political science professor University of Ulster. At present profesor of economics Queen's University Belfast. Member American Economic Association, Econometric Society, Royal Economic Society and Irish Economic Association.

PATRICK TEAHON

Civil Servant
Upper Merrion Street, Dublin 2
(01) 610346
Born to John and Mary Teahon (née Prendeville) at Co. Kerry in 1945. Educated at Coolick NS, St Brendan's College Killarney, at UCD whence he graduated with BA degree and Diploma in Public Administration, at TCD whence he graduated with MScEcon degree, at TCD/IMI whence he graduated with MSc management (org. behaviour) and at Netherlands Institute of Social Studies (diploma in economic planning). Married to Mary Morrissey with one son, John, and two daughters, Caroline and Marion. Formerly held a number of senior positions in the Civil Service including executive officer in Department of Post and Telegraphs, administative officer and assistant principal, Department of Finance, assistant principal and principal Department of Economic Planning and Development, and principal and assistant secretary in the Department of the Taoiseach. At present assistant secretary in charge of economic and social policy at the Department of the Taoiseach, and managing director of Temple Bar Properties Ltd, the company formed to renew the Temple Bar area of Dublin.

BRENDAN M. WALSH

University Professor
Belfield, Dublin 4
(01) 693244
Born to Jeremiah and Mary Walsh (née Curtin) at Dublin on 6 May 1940. Educated at Gonzaga College and University College Dublin (BA) and Boston College (PhD). Married to Patricia Noonan with two sons, Colm and Ben, and one daughter, Nessa. Formerly assistant professor, Department of Economics, Tufts University, Medford, Mass. and research professor, the Economic and Social Research Institute Dublin, member of National Planning Board 1983/84. Project advisor in The Gambia, West

Africa 1989–91 as consultant for Harvard Institute for International Development. At present professor of the national economics of Ireland at UCD. Member Royal Irish Academy, Irish Economics Association, Economic and Social Research Institute and Statistical and Social Inquiry Society of Ireland. Served on many national and international commissions and has had numerous publications.

Chapter 12
Agriculture and Food

And he gave it for his opinion, that whoever could make two ears of corn or two blades of grass to grow upon a spot of ground where only one grew before, would deserve better of mankind, and do more essential service to his country than the whole race of politicians put together.

Jonathan Swift

Agriculture

Although the numbers employed in agriculture have been in decline, the industry is of prime importance to the economy of the whole island. It accounts for more than 20 per cent of the Republic's exports and around 10 per cent of gross domestic product. These figures are above EC averages, and uniquely within the EC, over 75 per cent of farming production comes from milk and beef. As a result, there is a great vulnerability to any adverse changes in milk quotas or beef price restrictions.

Much attention is paid to marketing and to the image of Ireland as an unpolluted source of fresh healthy food. The added value available from processing has been highlighted, and the drift away from the export of live cattle into boned and vacuum-packed beef products is encouraged. There is also a major emphasis on quality in beef, dairy products, sheepmeat, pigmeat and poultry.

Priority is given to agricultural research and the scope of the research programme includes, for example, meat production from rabbits, twinning in the dairy herd, developing a mastitis-free herd, maximising beef output from dairy herds, in addition to programmes on alternative crops and alternative uses for crop products, potato breeding, new methods of pasture regeneration and slurry utilisation, the integration of hill and lowland sheep sectors, plant biotechnology, and the compilation of food and agricultural data bases.

An Bord Bainne exports a wide range of dairy and related food products, many of them sold under the Kerrygold label — a brand launched by the Board in 1962, and now internationally famous. It has subsidiary companies in the United Kingdom,

Belgium and USA. 25 per cent of exports go to the UK with 33 per cent to other EC countries and 1 per cent to other European countries. Middle and Far Eastern countries take 4 per cent, North America 12 per cent, Africa 6 per cent and Latin America 19 per cent. The Bord has a pan-European advertising strategy, and sponsors the Kerrygold Dublin Horse Show.

Horticulture

New attention is being paid to horticulture. A Minister of State for Horticulture was appointed and a new State body, An Bord Glas, is responsible for horticultural development. There has been widespread concern about the extent of the imports of fruit and vegetables which can be grown in Ireland.

A major study has been carried out to identify the influences on tomato quality and the various factors influencing quality in mushrooms. There is also considerable interest in so-called 'alternative' crops, such as peas, beans, oil-seed rape, flax, linseed, lupins and borage.

Food

A feature of the Irish food scene in recent years has been the development of new products and exciting new ways of presenting old ones. Typical of developments in this area are cheeses, mustards, homemade biscuits, shortbread and cookies, chutneys, preserves and pickles, chocolate truffles, cream liqueurs, bottled mineral waters and the traditional black pudding. In Mallow, Michael O'Callaghan of Longueville has managed to make wine in small quantities, and there could be potential for growth in this idea, especially if more suitable vines were bred.

The food research centre at Dunsinea is a key recent development. It has as its goals: the enhancement of technological excellence through a wide range of projects; the technological development of targeted food manufacturing companies; the promotion of a greater awareness of the market place; the upgrading of national hygiene standards; the support of specific product development ventures, and the identification of constraints which inhibit the growth of the food industry, as well as advising Government on the appropriate policy initiatives to address these problems.

Expert Eye
Mr John Treacy of Carlow competing in the senior tractor class during the All-Ireland Ploughing Championships at Woodsgift, Urlingford, Co. Kilkenny.

Product development is of particular importance to the Irish economy and areas studied in recent times include the stability of cultured milk products — like buttermilk, whole milk and cream — during storage. A major project was carried out on low-fat dairy spreads and on cheese-flavoured concentrates. Quark was virtually unknown in Ireland until recently and yet this low-fat, unripened cheese is used extensively on the Continent as a base for consumer dairy products.

There is a growing consumer lobby on food and health, and research in the human nutrition field has received particular attention. The National Dairy Council, for example, funded a research study on the dietary fibre content of a wide range of brown breads on retail sale in Ireland. Flahavans funded a study on the incorporation of oat fractions in soda and yeast breads. The idea behind the study was to broaden the use of oats which are consumed mainly as muesli or porridge. Research studies, based on close co-operation between science and business, may well hold the key to the future development of the Irish food industry.

The spring 1991 Union Bank of Switzerland survey of food prices, based on a weighted food basket of thirty-nine different food and beverage items, showed Dublin prices comparing favourably with those examined in forty-seven other cities. The basket which cost US$316 in Dublin, cost $743 in Tokyo and $476 in New York. EC prices ranged from Lisbon at $232 to Madrid at $410, with London slightly lower than Dublin at $301.

Agriculture and food are presided over from Agriculture House, the Dublin Head Office of the Department of Agriculture, and by Teagasc, the body which contains the former Agricultural Institute and the former Council for Development in Agriculture. The industry representatives, are the Irish Farmers' Association, the Irish Creamery Milk Suppliers' Association and the Irish Co-Operative Organisation Society.

In Northern Ireland, the Ulster Farmers' Union was formed in 1918, and when the first annual meeting of the NFA (now IFA) was held in Dublin, the good wishes of the UFU were conveyed to it in Irish by their then President, Arthur Algeo. Liaison meetings between the two organisations are held as required. The Ulster Agricultural Organisation Society, based at Portadown, is the central body for co-operatives in Northern Ireland. Developments there are watched over by these two organisations, by the Department of Agriculture and the Northern Ireland Agricultural Producers' Association.

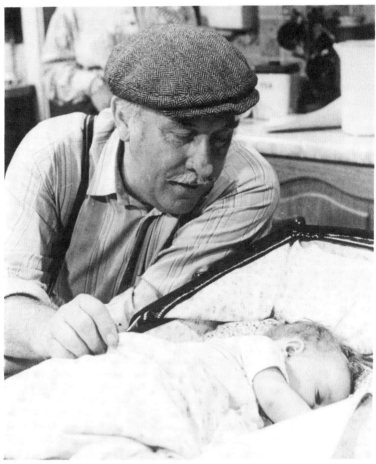

Country Life

An urban/rural divide in Irish society would be most undesirable and RTE plays its part in preventing it by giving town dwellers a glimpse of country life through their highly popular serial, Glenroe. The Byrne family, farmers and market-gardeners, are as a result the best-known country family in Ireland. Grandfather Dinny Byrne (actor Joe Lynch) is seen here with granddaughter Mary Denise (Bláthnaid Uí Threasaigh).

PROFESSOR J. DESMOND BAGGOT
Pharmacologist
Johnstown, Co. Kildare
(045) 66266
Born to John and Patricia Baggot (née Maher) at Abbeyleix, on 11 October 1939. Educated at Newbridge College, University College Dublin, The Ohio State University. Fellow American College of Clinical Pharmacology, Member Royal College of Veterinary Surgeons, Member Australian College of Veterinary Scientists. Formerly professor of Clinical Pharmacology, Department of Medicine, and Foundation chairman, Department of Veterinary Pharmacology and Toxicology, School of Veterinary Medicine, University of California, Davis. Associate professor of Pharmacology and Chemotherapy School of Veterinary Studies, Murdoch University, Perth, Western Australia and associate professor of Comparative Pharmacology and director, Equine Pharmacology Research Unit, College of Veterinary Medicine, The Ohio State University, Columbus, Ohio. At present director Irish Equine Centre, and research professor of clinical pharmacology, School of Veterinary Medicine, the University of California, Davis. Holds the Merck Award for teaching and research in Veterinary Clinical Pharmacology.

CHRISTOPHER KIERAN COMERFORD
Managing Director
Born to Thomas and Margaret Comerford (née Purcell) at Kilkenny on 24 December 1933. Educated at St Kieran's College Kilkenny and University College Dublin. Married to Teresa Fitzmaurice with two sons, Noel and Jonathan, and two daughters Fiona and Hilary. Formerly teacher at St Kieran's College Kilkenny, researcher at Irish Agricultural Research Institute; since 1964 with the Irish Sugar Company as manager Seed Breeding and Research Centre, agricultural development officer, manager Agricultural and Horticultural Services, general manager Agricultural and Horticultural Services, deputy chief executive, group general manager, and chief executive designate. Resigned in September 1991 as managing director Greencore plc, chairman Siúicre Éireann cpt, Grassland Fertilizers Ltd, Odlum Group Ltd, Yeast Products Ltd, James Budgett & Son Ltd (UK), Sugar Distributors Holdings Ltd, Premier Molasses Co. Ltd, director United Molasses (I) Ltd, W. McKinney Ltd.

R. GERARD CULLEN
Veterinary Surgeon
Agriculture House, Kildare Street, Dublin 2
(01) 789011
Born to Daniel and Mary Cullen (née Taylor) in Dublin on 20 May 1929. Educated at Synge Street CBS, Blackrock College, University College Dublin, Veterinary College Dublin and the Royal Veterinary College, University of London. Married to Hilda Osborne. Formerly veterinary

officer at Ministry of Agriculture, Fisheries and Food, Great Britain and Agricultural Counsellor, Irish Embassy Washington DC. At present director of veterinary services at the Department of Agriculture and Food. Member of the Veterinary Council of Ireland, Irish Veterinary Association, British Veterinary Association. Governor of Irish Equine Centre, Kill, Co. Kildare.

PATRICK LEONARD CURRAN
University Lecturer
UCD, Belfield, Dublin 4
(01) 693244
Born to Patrick and Helen Curran (née Lyons) at Oranmore, Co. Galway on 3 October 1932. Educated at Oranmore NS, St Joseph's Seminary (Patrician Brothers) Galway, at UCG, UCD and at Cornell. Married to Mary Walsh with one son, David, and two daughters, Maria and Elizabeth. Formerly head of Agricultural Botany Department and one time Dean of the Faculty of General Agriculture at UCD. Currently lecturer on grassland and environmental conservation.

DAVID JOHN DILGER
Chief Executive
Iveagh Court, Harcourt Road, Dublin 2
(01) 781511
Born to John and Olivia Dilger (née English) at Dublin. Educated at Monaleen primary school Limerick, Clongowes Wood College, Dublin University and Institute of Chartered Accountants in Ireland. Married to Katherine Boylan with four children. Formerly finance director Woodchester Investments plc. At present chief executive Food Industries plc. Member Ballybunion and Blainroe Golf Clubs.

LAURENCE FALLON
Farmer
Knockcroghery, Co. Roscommon
Born to Michael and Margaret Fallon (née Moran) at Roscommon on 7 March 1957. Married to Bernadette Briody. Formerly national president Macra na Feirme. At present vice president CEJA the European Council of Young Farmers. Member Macra na Feirme (Roscommon) and of the Irish Farmers' Association.

JOHN FERRIS
Cattle Farmer
Arran Chambers, 6 Arran Quay, Dublin 7
(01) 215424
Born to Edward and Alice Ferris (née Reid) at Dublin on 29 March 1944. Educated at Dominican Convent Cabra, Castleknock College, University College Dublin and Flying Schools in USA. Married to Filipina Bilotte

with two children. Formerly with Aerial Photo Company in Germany and bush pilot and flying instructor in South Africa. At present cattle farmer and honorary Philippine Consul. Member Irish Filipino Association and Irish-Thailand Association.

FRANCIS FLANAGAN
General Manager
Killeshandra, Co. Cavan
(049) 34334
Born at Strokestown, Co. Roscommon on 27 December 1933. Educated at Strokestown Marist Brothers, Summrhill College, Sligo, and at UCC. Married to Eithne (née Shiel) with five children, Desmond, Ronan, Siobhán, Connor and Coman. Formerly held a number of senior positions with Killeshandra Co-Operative Agricultural and Dairy Society Ltd. At present general manager and secretary of Killeshandra, director Bord Bainne, Cavan County Enterprise Fund, Western Industries and area director Ulster Bank.

SEÁN FLANAGAN
Principal Research Officer
Belclare, Tuam, Co. Galway
(093) 55455
Born to John P. and Rose Anne Flanagan (née Coen) at Roscommon. Educated at CBS Roscommon, UCG, UCD and University of Edinburgh. Married to Madeleine O'Hurley with four children. Formerly head of Animal Husbandry Department, Western Research Centre and secretary, Executive Committee, European Grassland Federation. At present farm director Knockbeg Sheep Farm, Carlow. Honorary secretary Irish Grassland Association and member of British Society of Animal Production, British Grasslands Society and National Sheep Association (UK).

PATRICK F. FOX
University Professor
University College, Cork
(021) 276871
Born to Patrick and Kathleen Fox (née O'Brien) at Mitchelstown, Co. Cork on 20 November 1937. Educated at Knockadea NS Ballylanders, at Christian Brothers School, Mitchelstown, at UCC and at Cornell University whence he graduated with a PhD degree in 1964. Formerly postdoctoral research fellow at Michigan State University, research biochemist at University of California, senior research officer with An Foras Talúntais and visiting professor (food science) at Universities of California, Minnesota and Wisconsin. At present Professor of Food Chemistry (since 1969) at UCC. Co-ordinates an active research programme on various aspects of food chemistry.

ALAN LESLIE GILLIS

Farmer
Wilton Park House, Wilton Place, Dublin 2
(01) 600611
Born to George and Veronica Gillis (née McLeod) at Dublin on 22 September 1936. Educated at Zion National and High School, Dublin, and at Bolton Street College of Technology. Married to Irene (née Harris) with three sons, Nigel, Stephen and Barry, and two daughters, Hazel and Anna. Formerly deputy president Irish Farmers' Association, chairman Leinster Milk Producers, chairman Animal Health Committee and Animal Feedstuffs' Committee and chairman advisory council on Animal Health Disease Eradication, member National Enterprise Agency, chairman Tír Laighean Co-Operative. At present president Irish Farmers' Association, chairman Aquahatch Ireland Ltd, Galway Aquatic Enterprises Ltd, board member Tír Laighean Co-Operative, Health Promotion Council and Disease Eradication Board. Member of General Synod of Church of Ireland, and of the National Heritage Council.

LAURENCE JOSEPH GOODMAN

Company Director
Ardee, Co. Louth
(041) 53754
Born to Laurence and Kathleen Goodman (née Beattie) at Dundalk on 15 September 1937. Educated at Marist School Dundalk. Married to Kitty Brennan with two sons. At present chief executive Goodman Group of companies and of the Holding Company, Glyde Holdings.

DR D.E. HOOD

Consultant
Dundrum, Dublin 14
(01) 986367
Born to Samuel and Harriett Hood (née Brown) at Bessbrook, Northern Ireland on 8 February 1936. Educated at Masonic Boys' School Dublin, Queen's University Belfast and Trinity College Dublin. Married to Vivien Marshall with two sons, Alan and Timothy, and one daughter, Susan. Formerly lecturer Belfast College of Technology and Queen's University, and scientist Denny Group Laboratory. Head of Meat Research Department, National Food Centre until 1989. At present technical consultant to Food Industry. Secretary-General and president-elect of IUoFST (International Union of Food Science & Technology). Fellow Institute of Food Science and Technology of Ireland, Royal Institute of Chemistry and Institute of Food Science and Technology of United Kingdom.

PATRICK JORDAN
Trade Association Director
Confederation House, Kildare Street, Dublin 2
(01) 779801
Born to Michael Anthony and Kathleen Jordan (née Woods) at Kilkenny on 30 May 1941. Educated at CBS Synge Street, Dublin, at City University New York and Institut de Touraine, Tours, France. Married to Helen Oates with two sons and three daughters. Formerly executive officer in Department of Industry and Commerce, manager New York and Paris offices of CTT and marketing manager Robert Usher Ltd, Drogheda. At present director Food and Drink Federation, with the Confederation of Irish Industry. Member Fitzwilliam Lawn Tennis Club.

BRIAN A. JOYCE
Company Director
Heritage House, 23 St Stephen's Green, Dublin 2
(01) 766333
Born 10 September 1940. Educated at St Mary's College and University College Galway. Fellow of the Chartered Institute of Management Accountants. Married to Margaret Glynn with one son and one daughter. Formerly accountant with Fords, Dagenham, managing director, Bord Bainne and with Adams Foods Ltd of Leek in Staffordshire. At present chairman Williams Waller Ltd, Tara Meats Ltd, International Development Ireland Ltd, Business and Trading House Investment Company Ltd, Allegro Ltd, and director Educational Building Society.

JOHN GEORGE DALKEITH LAMB
Research Officer (retired)
Born to Francis William and Constance Charlotte Lamb (née Plunkett-Johnston) at Blackrock, Co. Dublin on 19 August 1919. Educated at Shortenills, Chalfont St Giles, Bucks, Wrekin College, Wellington, Shropshire and at University of Reading and UCD. Married to Helen Margaret Tobias with one son, Henry Francis, and two daughters, Eleanor Margaret and Melissa Jane. Formerly chief horticultural research officer, An Foras Talúntais and president Royal Horticultural Society of Ireland. At present honorary life member Royal Dublin Society and International Plant Propagation Society, member An Taisce, Irish Wildbird Conservancy and Irish Garden Plant Society. Co-author of *Nursery Stock Manual 1975* and of *A History of Gardening in Ireland*.

PHILIP LYNCH
Group Managing Director
151 Thomas Street, Dublin 8
(01) 717131
Born at Cork on 1 May 1945. Educated at Hamilton High School, Copswood Agricultural College Palleskenry and Waterford RTC.

Married to Eileen Crowley with one son and three daughters. Formerly with Odlum Group and R & H Hall plc. At present group managing director IAWS Group plc. Member Stephen's Green Club.

CHARLES AIDAN McCARTHY
Chief Executive
Grattan House, Lower Mount Street, Dublin 2
(01) 619599
Born at Dunmanway, Co. Cork on 3 July 1944. Educated at Gormanston College and UCC, whence he graduated with a BE degree. Married to Breda Keegan with two sons and one daughter. Formerly marketing manager P. J. Carroll. At present chief executive National Dairy Council.

WILLIAM LESLIE McCAULEY
Company Director
Dublin
(01) 364306
Born to William George and Essie McCauley (née Stuart) at Castleblayney on 20 July 1944. Educated at Castleblayney NS, Sligo Grammar School and Trinity College/Irish Management Institute Dublin where he was awarded an MSc(Mgmt) degree in 1984. Married to Marguerite Emma Deegan with three sons, Craig, Russell and Fern. Formerly general manager Norish plc. At present chief executive Norish plc and director, Food Venture Fund, Donegal Foods, Camus Salmon Holdings and Valley Ice Cream. Member Mensa, Baltray Golf Club and Board of Trustees Irish Youth Foundation.

DANIEL MICHAEL McGING
Chartered Accountant
ACC House, Hatch Street, Dublin 2
(01) 780644
Born to Daniel and Maureen McGing (née Pelly) at Castlebar on 17 February 1940. Educated at CBS Westport, Mungret College Limerick and UCD whence he graduated with a BComm degree. Later admitted to membership of Institute of Chartered Accountants in Ireland. Married to Mary Molloy with two sons and two daughters. Formerly partner Coopers and Lybrand, director Voluntary Health Insurance Board and member of Commission on Health Funding. At present chairman Agricultural Credit Corporation plc and Irish Press plc, director Irish Press Newspapers Ltd and Irish Press Publications Ltd. Member Stephen's Green Club and Fitzwilliam Lawn Tennis Club.

ANNA MAY McHUGH
Housewife
Fallaghmore, Athy, Co. Kildare
(0507) 25125
Born to James and Elizabeth Brennan (née Wall) at Clonpierce, Bally-

linan, on 11 May 1934. Educated at St Patrick's NS, Ballylinan and St Brigid's, Athy. Married to John McHugh with one son and one daughter. At present managing director and secretary of National Ploughing Association of Ireland Ltd, Irish Representative on World Ploughing Board and member of ICA Community Council.

PETER CLANCY McKIMM
Company Director
Grattan House, Lower Mount Street, Dublin 2
Born to John and Josephine McKimm (née Elliot) at Skerries, Co. Dublin, on 25 April 1930. Educated at Christian Brothers Dún Laoghaire and University College Dublin. Married to Marie Hearn with four sons, Andrew, Frazer, Barry and Lesley. Formerly secretary An Bord Bainne and president Irish Exporters' Association. At present chairman, National Dairy Council, Arab/Irish Chamber of Commerce and trustee Irish Exporters' Association. Director of Sheedy Communicaitons Ltd and chairman Cider Industries Group. Member Dún Laoghaire Golf Club.

RAY MacSHARRY
EC Commissioner
Rue de la Loi 200, 1049 Brussels
Born at Sligo in April 1938. Educated at St Vincent's NS, Ballincutranta NS, Marist Brothers NS and Summerhill College Sligo. Married to Elaine (née Neilan) with three sons and three daughters. Formerly member Sligo County Council, Minister of State at the Department of Finance and Public Service, Minister for Agriculture, Tánaiste and Minister for Finance, Governor European Investment Bank and member of New Ireland Forum, Fianna Fáil TD for Sligo/Leitrim, and MEP for Connaught/Ulster. At present EC Commissioner for Agriculture and Rural Development.

PEADAR MURPHY
Chief Executive
Irish Farm Centre, Bluebell, Dublin 12
(01) 551036
Born to Martin and Bridget Murphy (née Roche) at Wexford on 26 February 1941. Educated at Ferns Boys' National School, St Peter's College Wexford and at University College Dublin. Married to Bríd Dempsey with four children. Formerly agronomist Shell Chemicals, agricultural advisor, general secretary Macra na Feirme, president of European Committee for Young Farmers' Organisations and member Committee Co-ordinating Young Farmers' Organisations. At present chief executive IFAC Irish Farm Accounts Co-Op, director IFAC Accounting Services, Irish Farm Centre and Irish Agricultural Museum (Johnstown Castle Wexford). Member Agricultural Science Association, Agricultural Economic Society, Irish Grassland Association and Newlands Golf Club.

PHILIP FREDERICK MYERSCOUGH
Bloodstock Auctioneer
Kill, Co. Kildare
(045) 77211
Born to Cyril Frederick and Joyce Evelyn Myerscough (née Cunningham) at Dublin on 15 March 1948. Educated at Castle Park, St Columba's College and TCD. Married to Jane O'Brien with two sons and two daughters. Formerly marketing director Goffs Bloodstock Sales. At present managing director Goffs Bloodstock Sales Ltd, director Coyle Hamilton Group Ltd, International Bloodstock Finance Ltd and Irish Thoroughbred Marketing Division. Member Partmarnock Golf Club, Kildare Street and University Club and Thurles Golf Club.

MATT O'KEEFFE
Farmer
Irish Farm Centre, Bluebell, Dublin 12
(01) 508000
Born to Nicholas and Carmel O'Keeffe (née Kehoe) at Clara, Kilkenny on 31 August 1957. Educated at Clara National School, St Kieran's College Kilkenny and Carlow Regional College. Single. Formerly Leinster vice president and chairman Agricultural Affairs Committee Macra na Feirme. At present national president Macra na Feirme.

PADDY O'KEEFFE
Farmer and Journalist
Farm Centre, Bluebell, Dublin 12
(01) 501166
Born to Jack and Margaret O'Keeffe (née Ahearne) at Fermoy, Co. Cork on 6 May 1923. Educated at CBS Fermoy, Athenry Agricultural College, Albert Agricultural College and UCD. Married to Anne O'Connor with one son and three daughters. Formerly editor *Farmers' Journal*, chairman Agricultural Institute and board member RTE Authority. At present chief executive *Farmers' Journal*, chairman FBD Holdings and Irish Farm Centre Ltd, and dairy farmer. Awarded honorary LL.D by NUI and elected Honorary Life Member RDS.

PATRICK A. O'NEILL
Group Managing Director
Kilkenny
(056) 22907
Born to William and Mary O'Neill (née Flynn) at New Ross, Co. Wexford on 8 August 1938. Educated at CBS New Ross. Married with one son and three daughters. Formerly director of administration An Bord Bainne, chairman Pigs and Bacon Commission and of the Irish Livestock and Meat Board. At present group managing director Avonmore Foods plc. Member Chartered Institute of Management Accountants, Kilkenny Rotary Club and Kilkenny Golf Club.

JOSEPH FRANCIS REA

Farmer

19 Sandymount Avenue, Ballsbridge, Dublin 4

(01) 688188

Born to Michael and Kathleen Rea (née O'Keeffe) at Cahir on 2 May 1938. Married to Margaret (née Ryan) with two sons and one daughter. Formerly president Macra na Feirme, chairman Farm Apprenticeship Board, director Mitchelstown Creameries, president and deputy president Irish Farmers' Association and director FBD Insurance Company. At present chairman of Teagasc.

PIERCE RYAN

Director General

19 Sandymount Avenue, Ballsbridge, Dublin 4

(01) 688188

Born to Michael P. and Mary B. Ryan (née Shortle) at Wexford on 10 August 1928. Educated at Glynn NS and St Peter's College Wexford and UCD whence he graduated with an honours BAgrSc degree. Later studied at Iowa State University, graduating with MSc degree, and at TCD, graduating with PhD degree. Married to Katherine V. Meyler with two daughters, Christina and Suzanne. Formerly director An Foras Talúntais, scientific officer Department of Agriculture and Fisheries, Johnstown Castle Research Station, technical staff officer Food and Agricultural Organisation Rome, research assistant at Iowa State University, head of National Soil Survey at An Foras Talúntais and deputy director An Foras Talúntais. At present director of Teagasc, the agriculture and food development authority. Member Royal Dublin Society, Japan Ireland Society and Fitzwilliam and Donnybrook Lawn Tennis Clubs. Decorated Order of Merit by French and Portuguese Governments, and elected life-member of the Royal Irish Academy (in recognition of scientific merit and achievement) in 1967.

J.V. SMYTH

Union General Secretary

475 Antrim Road, Belfast

(0232) 370222

Born in Lisburn Co. Antrim. Educated in Wallace High School Lisburn. Post graduate research work in crop husbandry and animal nutrition at the Agricultural Research Institute for Northern Ireland. Formerly in commercial agricultural advisory service and farm management and on Ulster Farmers' Union staff as an administrative officer. At present general secretary Ulster Farmers' Union. Member of the Ulster Farmers' Union, the Royal Ulster Agricultural Society and the Northern Ireland Institute of Agricultural Science.

RORY E. TOAL
Company Executive
151 Thomas Street, Dublin 8
(01) 717131
Born to Charles and Maeve Toal (née Hamilton) at Cavan on 10 November 1945. Educated at Killeshandra National School, St Patrick's College Cavan and Columbia University Missouri. Married to Angela Buckley with five children. Formerly Cavan footballer. Has held various executive positions within IAWS Group plc. At present managing director R & H Hall and executive director IAWS Group plc. Member Cork Golf Club and Castleknock Tennis Club.

HUGH THOMAS TUNNEY
Company Chairman
O'Connell Street, Dublin
(01) 748138
Born to James and Mary Anne Tunney (née Gallagher) at Trillick, Co. Tyrone. Educated at De La Salle College, Ballyshannon. Married with two sons and two daughters. Founder/chairman Tunney Meat Packers. Founder/owner Tunney Group of Companies. Member Mullaghmore Yacht Club, Antique Collectors Club and Institute of Meat, London.

Chapter 13
Fishery and Forestry

Fly fishing may be a very pleasant amusement; but angling or float fishing I can only compare to a stick and a string, with a worm at one end and a fool at the other.

Johnson

There is a romance about fishermen — about the rugged hunters of shoals of herring and the quiet fly fishermen by river pools. The public, by and large, appreciate the dangers faced by trawlermen, but very few, apart from industry professionals, realise what a big business fishing is. Trade statistics published by BIM the Irish Sea Fisheries Board reveal total values of sea fish landings and farmed fish production in 1986 of IR£76 million, which increased to IR£96 million in 1987 and which further increased to IR£114 million in 1989. These figures relate to the Republic only. Of the IR£114 million, aquaculture accounted for IR£25 million or 22 per cent.

The island lies in the path of the Gulf Stream, has 3,500 miles (or 5,600km) of coastline and great opportunities to make a living from the sea. Main landings include plaice, cod, whiting, haddock, herring, mackerel, ray and skate, with shell fish, such as lobster, cray fish and oysters.

BIM or Bord Iascaigh Mhara is the State Company responsible for developing the Republic's sea fishing industry and it provides grants and assistance towards acquisition of vessels and development of markets, as well as assisting in the education and training of fishermen. BIM announced an ambitious three-year development strategy for the seafish industry in October 1988. The stated objectives are worthy of quotation:

> The overall aim of the strategy is to exploit fully the potential of the sea fishing and aquaculture industry both at sea and ashore, to enable it to make its full contribution to the economy of the coastal regions, and to the country as a whole. The principal objectives that must be satisfied to achieve the overall aim are:
> — Vigorous marketing of a quality product on home and export markets.
> — Improved utilisation through greater processing.
> — Strengthening the fish supply base.

IFPO (the Irish Fish Producers' Organisation) is a body established by fishermen at the instigation of, and with the support of, the EC. It is regarded as part of the structure necessary to operate the Common Fisheries Policy, and represents the owners of commercial sea-fishing vessels.

The Irish Fishermen's Organisation and Killybegs Fishermen's Organisation have the aim of promoting the interests of fishermen, of lobbying for Government and EC support, as well as assisting individual IFO members with their specific problems. The Irish Fish Processors' and Exporters' Association services the on-shore segment of the industry.

The Common Fisheries Policy deals with the following items on a community basis and is of equal concern to fishermen in the Republic and in Northern Ireland:

— Managing and rationally exploiting fish stocks by a system of total allowable catches or TACs divided into quotas allocated to individual member states.

— Assuring supply of fish to the community.

— Protecting the living standards of fishermen.

— Balancing fishing capacity with fish resources.

— Negotiating international agreements to secure access to additional resources.

The Commission does not carry out any research of its own, but relies on advice from the Scientific and Technical Committee for Fisheries which in turn bases its advice on the work of the International Council for the Exploration of the Sea. The mid-term review of the Common Fisheries Policy was due for completion by the end of 1992. All elements of the industry came together with BIM, the Department of the Marine, and some independent specialists, under the chairmanship of Dr T.K. Whitaker, and presented a detailed report seeking real improvements from the review. The 1990 Irish quotas and community TACs were as follows:

Species	Irish Quota	EC TAC	Irish Quota as % of TAC
	Tonnes	Tonnes	%
Quota:			
Cod	11,720	253,150	4.6
Haddock	3,220	80,330	4.0
Saithe	4,640	110,600	4.2
Whiting	16,760	125,560	13.4
Plaice	3,560	213,790	1.7
Sole	650	39,570	1.6
Hake	2,030	85,100	2.4
Monkfish	3,370	63,690	5.3
Megrim	3,260	35,940	9.1
Pollack	1,230	19,100	6.4
Nephrops	9,805	55,070	17.8
Mackerel	70,550	380,120	8.6
Herring	52,050	445,610	11.7
Sprat	—	78,750	—
Scad	—	86,000	—
Blue Whiting	—	70,000	—
	182,845	1,907,630	9.6

The coastal waters are ideally suited for fish farming and BIM supports this new industry because the quality of Irish salmon enjoys high status in the market and because salmon farming provides direct employment for about 1,000 people.

The Irish Aquaculture Association was formed about twelve years ago, bringing together the many individuals, co-operatives and companies involved both in sea and fresh water environments. Production includes mussels, oysters and salmon. There is said to be about IR£65 million invested in salmon farming with about 1,000 people employed, and there is considerable economic advantage also from all of the activities, resulting very often in extremely valuable employment in romantic but remote coastal communities.

Rathlin Danger
This spectacular shot was taken from Portrush Lifeboat as she
towed the stricken Rosnakill fishing boat from danger off Rathlin
Island to the safety of Portstewart Harbour.

Processing the catch is one such activity and other lesser known ones include the production of purpose moulded mussel longline barrels, cages for salmon farming, net-making, boatbuilding, food manufacturing, as well as disease eradication, research and development. The national fishery training centre is operated by BIM at Greencastle, Co. Donegal. BIM is the authority responsible for the industrial training and education of new entrants, established fishermen and fish farmers within the fishing industry.

The Atlantic Salmon is the most important species of fish in inland waters, followed by trout, eel and the coarse varieties, such as pike, perch, roach and bream.

Ireland's third largest export earner is tourism and, needless to say, fishing is one of the major tourist attractions throughout the island. And fishermen-tourists are excellent tourists, as they return year after year to enjoy the pleasures of fly fishing on the great salmon rivers, or coarse fishing on inland waterways, or even deep sea angling off the coast.

Management and development of inland fisheries is the responsibility of the seven Regional Fisheries Boards, acting under the Central Fisheries Board.

Forestry
Planting in the Republic runs at about 14,000 hectares (34,000 acres), with Coillte Teo accounting for about 70 per cent and others about 30 per cent. 1990 was the third successive year in which the 10,000ha planting target was exceeded by Coillte, whose forest operations extend over 198 forests organised in 28 districts and seven regions. In 1990 7,500ha of land were acquired at an average of IR£1,048/ha. It has been forestry policy to avoid using productive farmland, and broad leaved trees are not generally planted. Sitka spruce and lodgepole pine comprise the greater part of contemporary planting. The remaining 12 per cent includes Norway spruce, Japanese larch, Douglas fir and other conifer and some broad leaf species. Over 600,000 people visited Coillte's twelve forest parks in 1990. Since then the company completed resoration of Avondale House, the birthplace of Charles Stewart Parnell, on the occasion of the centenary of his death in 1991.

The island has natural advantages in timber growing, including a pollution-free atmosphere and rapid growth rates which are attained with ease. The industry gives long term employment and raises amenity and conservation values in forestry areas. Irish saw mills have a 55 per cent overall share of the timber market, and this includes 100 per cent of the Irish pallets/fencing market and 60 per cent of the construction timber market. About 35 per cent of Irish timber is exported, mainly to British pallet fencing and garden product markets.

Floriculture is closely associated with forestry and is emerging as a 'new' industry. Not that growing daffodils, heathers, and other common flowers is new, but air freighting them to New York caused some surprise when it became known in 1989. It seems that there is a market both for freshly cut daffodils and also for disease-free bulbs. Flowers may be exported also to meet the demands of the dried and dyed fashion trade.

Interested observers of the forestry scene in Ireland include the Irish Timber Council, the Wood Marketing Federation, the Tree Council of Ireland, and Crann.

Forestry is the responsibility of the Department of Energy, and the game and wildlife service, which employs sixty rangers, is the responsibility of the Office of Public Works.

PETER EUGENE CAMPBELL
Trawler Skipper
Skerries, Co. Dublin
(01) 490267
Born to Dr John and Mrs Joyce Campbell (née McCarren) at Belfast on 25 October 1953. Educated at Terenure College and at Moville Fishing College. Married to Norma (née McClean) with two daughters, Emma and Sara. Formerly chairman, Skerries Fishermen's Organisation. At present vice chairman, Irish Fishermen's Organisation and representative for Skerries and Galway. Member Skerries Rugby Club and of the management board of Galway and Aran Fishermen's Co-operative.

PATRICK JOSEPH COONEY
Managing Director
32 Cookstown Industrial Estate, Dublin 24
(01) 510055
Born to Peter and Mary Cooney (née Carberry) at Drogheda on 4 June 1947. Educated at CBS Drogheda and at London University. Married to Marie White with three sons, Peter, Patrick and James, and two daughters, Sally-Anne and Celestine. Formerly senior accountant with Deloittes, London, and management consultant with Coopers and Lybrand, Dublin. At present managing director Gleeson Group of Companies, Tipperary Natural Mineral Water Co, and chairman of Coillte Teo (The Irish Forestry Board).

JOHN de COURCY IRELAND
Lecturer
St Mary Street, Dublin 1
(01) 859588
Born at Lucknow, India on 19 October 1911. Educated at Marlborough College, New College Oxford, and Trinity College Dublin. Married to Betty Haigh with one son and two daughters. Formerly worked at sea, for Government of China, in freelance journalism, lumber, coast and border watch, harbour construction and various teaching posts, St Patrick's Cathedral GS, Drogheda GS, Kingstown School and Avoca and Kingstown School in charge of Newpark CS. At present president Irish CND, Irish Nautical Trust, and Dún Laoghaire Life Boat. Honorary research officer Maritime Institute of Ireland and president Ireland-Portugal Cultural Society. Member Workers Party and Dún Laoghaire Harbour Watch. Decorated by Argentina, France, Yugoslavia and Portugal.

DR JOHN ROBERT JOYCE
Chief Executive
Farm Centre, Bluebell, Dublin 12
(01) 500266
Born to Robert and Patricia Joyce (née Murphy) at Dorset, on 15

November 1951. Educated at Holy Trinity Infants and Junior School, Weymouth Grammar School, University College Swansea, University East Anglia School of Environmental Sciences, and University College Cork. Married to Jane Keyes McDonnell with two daughters and one son. Formerly scientific officer to Irish Underwater Council, resource development officer Bord Iascaigh Mhara, Research fellow NBST, and research assistant Ministry Agriculture and Fisheries UK. At present chief executive Irish Salmon Growers' Association, president European Aquaculture Society, Chairman International Salmon Farmers' Association Environmental Group, secretary Irish Aquaculture Association and editor *Aquaculture Ireland Magazine*. Member Dún Laoghaire Toastmasters and Dundrum Gym. Awarded Glaxo Fellowship for EC Science Writers and UK Patent Holder on Oceanographic Sampling Device.

SÉAMUS KIRK
Public Representative
Department of Agriculture, Kildare Street, Dublin 2
(01) 789011
Born in Co. Louth in April 1945. Educated at Drumsinnot National School and CBS Dundalk. Married to Mary McGeough with three sons and one daughter. Formerly front bench spokesman on horticulture with special responsibility for the party's policy document for the development of the horticulture industry, member of Louth County Council and of subsidiary bodies. Was appointed Minister of State at the Department of Agriculture and Food (with special responsibility for horticulture) in March 1987. Reappointed to this position in July 1989. At present Fianna Fáil TD for Louth.

BRENDAN P. MacEVOY
Executive
Crofton Road, Dún Laoghaire
(01) 2841544
Born to Patrick and Helena Mac Evoy (née McDermott) at Dublin on 22 June 1944. Educated at St Finbarr's Cabra, Reading University and TCD whence he graduated with an MSc Degree. Married to Ruth Richardson. Formerly with Arthur Guinness, Bord Bainne, W.R. Grace (New York) and Bord Fáilte (London). At present executive for EC Affairs with An Bord Iascaigh Mhara (Irish Sea Fisheries Board) also lecturer College of Commerce Rathmines, and College of Marketing and Design. Chairman Institute of Foreign Trade, Member Education Committee Irish Exporters' Association, and Irish Secretary of the International Association of Institutes of Export. Member Trinity College Association, National Yacht Club and Kilternan Parish Tennis Club. Author of three books on foreign trade. Has lectured on foreign trade in Europe and USA.

190

RICHARD ANTHONY MEANEY
EC Official
Brussels
Born to Thomas and Mary Meaney at Clonmel on 16 January 1942. Educated at CBS Clonmel, University College Galway whence he graduated with a BSc degree and Trinity College whence he graduated with PhD degree. Married to Patricia Ann Walsh with three sons and one daughter. Formerly research officer, head of research and development and chief executive Bord Iascaigh Mhara. At preseent with the EC Commission Directorate of Fisheries in Brussels.

MICHAEL JOHN ORREN
Oceanographer
University College, Galway
(091) 67894
Born to Hazelton Russell and Iris Veronica Orren (née Frost) at London on 9 June 1940. Graduated with hons. BSc degree in chemistry, later MSc in chemistry and PhD in geochemistry. Married to Angela Jackson with two daughters, Sally Nora and Jennifer Ann. Formerly chairman School of Chemical Sciences, University of Capetown. At present head of Department of Oceanography at UCG. Member of Rotary and of American Association for Advancement of Science. Fellow of the Royal Society of Chemistry; Chartered Chemist.

Chapter 14
Construction and Property

Well! some people talk of morality, and some of religion, but give me a little snug property.

Maria Edgeworth

The Construction industry is primarily dedicated to the building of roads and bridges, and the erection of homes, schools, hospitals, churches and places of employment — a calling as old as the history of mankind itself, and one which employs about 30,000 people in the Republic and about 20,000 in Northern Ireland. Any general recession in the economy of either part of the island, quickly depresses the Industry and related services. In the Republic, house registrations rose by 40 per cent from 8,297 in 1988 to 11,627 in 1989, but fell by 2 per cent to 11,346 in 1990.

Fortunately, for all concerned, there was a billion-pound construction boom in London and in the South East of England generally in 1989. This did not mean that life was a bed of roses for those who transferred operations to the bigger island but it did at any rate mean that architects, builders and property men could find gainful employment there almost on a commuter basis because of the availability of low airfares.

The spring 1991 survey by Union Bank of Switzerland showed the following picture for gross earnings per year in $US:

	Construction Workers	Electrical Engineers
Amsterdam	19,600	44,300
Brussels	20,900	49,800
Copenhagen	28,500	54,300
Dublin	12,500	43,400
Frankfurt	21,900	51,500
Lisbon	3,900	20,200
London	13,500	24,400
Luxembourg	16,700	68,300
Madrid	10,100	36,900
Paris	13,300	38,800
New York	30,000	48,000
Tokyo	27,200	34,900

The Construction Industry Federation participated in a project with the Export Board in 1987 to help Irish building firms to set up operations in the United Kingdom. This was a highly laudable project in so far as 1987 was the greatest year for construction in the United Kingdom since 1973, and 1988 was expected to be not too far removed from 1987. Not surprisingly, the UK boom was of benefit also to Irish exporters of building materials, such as pipes, felts, tiles and joinery.

Visual Effects

Visitors often judge the societies they visit by the appearance of the principal buildings, streets, parks and squares. There can be little doubt that a sense of proportion and harmony between neighbouring buildings produces a soothing and civilised effect. The Local Authorities are the Planning Authorities, and within them there are clearly two groups — the elected representatives and the management. When problems arise, the former are very happy if they can transfer their responsibilities to the latter, but on some occasions, the elected representatives overrule management under a procedure known as 'Section 4'.

Proper planning is vital if good order, taste and harmony are to be achieved and maintained. Clear policies are needed on issues such as the desire of financial institutions to establish themselves in the the principal shopping streets. All too often these streets, weakened by their lack of car parking facilities and competition from suburban shopping centres, have been invaded by the institutions who want to be where the people are. Their invasion weakens the high street even more, to such an extent that the financial institutions end up by being in a shopping street which is not a principal shopping street any more. Visitors may ask how the authorities can prevent this and the answer is simply in the 'change of use' rules under which permission is required to change the use of a building from, say, retail to banking.

The financial institutions invasion has often been noted for its lack of harmony and in many instances these institutions, who were best able to afford to adapt their requirements to the existing streetscape, were allowed build, say, four-storey flat-roofed glass and concrete boxes in streetscapes of two or three-storey pitched-roof houses. That is not, of course, to imply that financial institutions have contributed nothing to the preservation and erection of fine buildings and, indeed, the two largest Irish institutions, AIB Bank and Bank of Ireland, have both erected impressive headquarters in Dublin. AIB has had the more fortunate result, and has occupied since 1979, premises known as Bankcentre which consists of eight interlinked buildings, the tallest being only five storeys high. This complex is set well back from the road on a tastefully landscaped site. Bank of Ireland Headquarters, though equally impressive, are, however, constructed on a corner site in Baggot Street and are not quite in harmony with their Georgian neighbours.

Controversial planning situations involve State companies too. The Electricity Supply Board, for example, was involved in a major controversy in the early 1960s when it demolished fourteen houses in what was Dublin's longest Georgian streetscape. The pendulum swung back with the passing of time, however, and ESB recently completed the restoration of ten Georgian houses adjoining the headquarters building which it constructed on the site of the demolished fourteen.

Safety
The construction industry is not all about aesthetics, of course. It is primarily dedicated to the erection of homes, schools, hospitals, churches and places of employment — a calling as old as the history of mankind itself.

There is great emphasis in the industry today on reducing fire risk in the design of buildings. Building regulations to minimise the risk of fire were to be introduced in the Republic under the Local Authority (Planning and Development) Act of 1963. Eighteen years later, forty-eight lives were lost in a fire at the Stardust Discotheque. In 1982 the report of the Stardust Tribunal said that the delay in introducing these building regulations 'was wholly unacceptable'. Proposed building regulations to take account of the Stardust recommendations, and comments on older drafts were issued in May 1984 and, although the Building Control Bill to give legislative effect to the regulations was introduced in 1984, it has never become law. There are, however, special requirements for buildings of five storeys and more, and both fire officers and planning officers make demands to enhance safety in all buildings.

Regulations were introduced in 1985 to make the locking of exits or blocking of escape routes an offence. The penalty for this is a fine of £10,000 or two years in prison. The need for proper controls in this area extends to upholstered furniture, in which the foam filling can cause death by fume poisoning. In this area, technological advances enable the authorities to demand higher levels of fire resistance than before.

Landscape and Developers
In 1990 new regulations were introduced in the Republic to implement an EC Directive on Environmental Impact Assessment. These set thresholds for certain types of development, which if exceeded call for environmental impact studies to be carried out. The developments concerned include initial afforestation, pig and poulty rearing, and salmon breeding, all of which have been the subject of some public concern.

The beauty of the countryside is a great natural resource and there has been some understandable concern about a disease known as 'bungalow blight' which manifests itself in modern bungalows popping up all over the countryside. Visitors ask why the Planning Authorities do not prevent this, but there are different considerations to be borne in mind.

In one situation the bungalow may be a weekend home for a family living in a nearby town or city for whom location is not critical, and in the other the bungalow may be the principal private residence of a farmer, for whom choice of location may well be very limited and very critical.

Early in 1988 the establishment of a trust was announced which was to have as its priority the buying, restoring and reselling of thatched dwellings. The thatched roof has always had great charm and attraction for visitors and efforts to preserve thatch and the skill of the thatcher seem highly laudable.

The creation of new buildings requires a whole range of talents. Building skills, even when money is available to go with them, are not sufficient to get things moving. Similarly the individual skills of the architect, the engineer, and the chartered surveyor are not sufficient. Somebody has to bring all of these talents together and this is the role of the property developer. Many attempts are made to lay the blame for planning and other disasters on the doorstep of the property developer. The builders say that they build what the architects design, and the architects say they design what the developers want. Praise for successful and tasteful developments tends, therefore, to find its way to the doorstep of the developer, along with the blame for the projects which are not quite so successful. A key skill in this whole area is the valuation of property and its potential. This is the role of the valuers who are established like the other property professions throughout the country.

The Departments of the Environment in the Republic and in Northern Ireland are responsible for town and country planning, housing, roads and traffic. Other organisations keeping a watchful eye on developments include the Construction Industry Federation, the Irish Auctioneers' and Valuers' Institute, the Chartered Institute of Building, the Society of Chartered Surveyors, the Royal Institute of the Architects of Ireland, the National Safety Council, the House Builders' Association, the Federation of Building and Civil Engineering Contractors (Northern Ireland), An Taisce: the National Trust in the Republic, the UK National Trust in Northern Ireland, and the Association of Consulting Engineers of Ireland.

ANTHONY DERMOT BARRY

Chief Executive
Belgard Castle, Clondalkin, Dublin 22
(01) 591111
Born to Anthony and Rita Barry (née Costelloe) at Cork on 19 January 1935. Educated at CBC Cork, and later at UCC. Having held a number of senior positions within CRH plc, was appointed group chief executive in January 1988.

MARK BENCE-JONES

Writer
Born to Philip and May Bence-Jones on 29 May 1930. Educated at Ampleforth and Pembroke College, Cambridge. Married to Gillian (née Pretyman) with one son and two daughters. At present writer and vice president Irish Association, Sovereign Military Hospitaller Order of Malta. Publications include *Paradise Escaped*, *Nothing in the City*, *The Remarkable Irish*, *Palaces of the Raj*, *Clive of India*, *The Cavaliers*, *Burke's Guide to Irish Country Houses*, *The British Aristocracy*, *The Viceroys of India*, *Ancestral Houses*, *Twilight of the Ascendancy* and *Guide to Irish Country Houses*. Member Irish Georgian Society, Cork Preservation Society, Munster Agricultural Society, Kildare Street and University Club and Royal Irish Automobile Club. Knight of Obedience, Sovereign Military Hospitaller Order of Malta. His home is in Co. Cork.

FINBAR CALLANAN

Institute Director
22 Clyde Road, Dublin 4
(01) 684341
Born to Denis and Annie Callanan (née Fry) at Cork on 15 March 1931. Educated at Kilrane NS Co. Wexford, Mt Sion CBS Waterford and UCC. Married with four children. Formerly held positions with local authorities, the OPW, Harbour Commissioners and Consultants and assistant development engineer, project engineer, head of production and planning, chief operations engineer and chief civil engineer with Bord na Móna. At present director of Institution of Engineers of Ireland. Member Irish Club London. Fellow of Institution of Engineers of Ireland, Institution of Civil Engineers London, and of the Institution of Engineers Australia. Member American Society of Civil Engineers European Engineer Eur Ing and chartered engineer Ireland and UK.

SEÁN CANNON

Chief Executive
27 Herbert Place, Dublin 2
(01) 618744
Born to Frank and Kitty Cannon (née Melody) at Ballina on 30 September 1940. Educated at Ballina Boys' NS, St Muredach's College

Ballina, UCD and Institute of Chartered Accountants in Ireland. Married to Anita Farley with two daughters and one son. Formerly audit senior Deloitte & Co, Paris and finance manager Burmah Castrol (Ireland) Ltd. At present chief executive McInerney Properties plc. Member Howth Golf Club and Leinster Society of Chartered Accountants.

JOHN A. CARROLL
Executive
Irish Life Centre, Lower Abbey Street, Dublin
(01) 728001
Born to John and Hannah Carroll (née Hyde) at Mallow, Co. Cork on 17 July 1934. Educated at Patrician Brothers Mallow and Patrician Academy Mallow. Married with two children. Formerly managing director Housing Finance Agency and director National Building Agency. At present chief officer An Bord Pleanála.

JOHN VINCENT GREER
University Lecturer
University Road, Belfast BT7 1MN
(0232) 245133
Born to John and Anne Greer (née Daly) at Portadown on 20 September 1942. Educated at Presentation Convent and St Columba's Portadown, St Patrick's College Armagh and Queen's University Belfast. Married to Dymphna Farrell with three children. Formerly planner Craigavon Development Commission and research student Queen's University Belfast. Contributor to Masters of Rural Development Programme UCG and external examiner Dublin Institute of Technology. At present senior lecturer and undergraduate course leader Department of Architecture and Planning Queen's University Belfast and president of the Irish Planning Institute. Member of the Royal Town Planning Institute.

DESMOND GUINNESS
Architectural Preservationist
Born to Bryan and Diana Guinness (née Mitford) at London on 8 September 1931. Educated at Gordonstoun and Christ Church, Oxford. Married first to Princess Hermione Marie-Gabrielle Petronella Sophia Devota Florestine, daughter of HSH Prince Gero Maria Albrecht von Urach, Count of Württemberg. One son, Patrick, and one daughter, Marina. Second to Penelope Cuthbertson. Formerly Lieutenant 7th Hussars. Founder of The Irish Georgian Society. Several publications.

BRIAN DOMINIC HOGAN
Architect
1 Mount Street Crescent, Dublin 2
(01) 760915
Born to Sarsfield and Sheila Hogan (née Boland) at Dublin in 1928.

Educated at UCD and admitted member of the Royal Institute of the Architects of Ireland and Royal Institute of British Architects. Married to Marie Lawton with three sons. Formerly resident architect for Kuwait Technical College and architect in the Ministry of Public Works. Designed over twenty office buildings in Ireland between 1965 and the present, mainly in Dublin, including Lansdowne House (1967) and IDA Headquarters, Wilton Place (1985). Joint designer of the Mater Private Hospital (1981–6). Designed hospitals in Kuwait and Libya, housing in Baghdad and the System Control Centre for the national power network in Bahrain. At present practising as Brian Hogan Architects, he founded Tyndall Hogan & Associates in 1960, succeeded by Tyndall Hogan Hurley Architects in 1968. Partnership dissolved amicably in 1988. Formerly president Architectural Association of Ireland, admitted fellow and later elected vice president Royal Institute of the Architects of Ireland. Council member 1986–91 of National Council of Education Awards and chairman of NCEA Engineering/Construction Board. Chairman Schizophrenia Association of Ireland 1988–90.

FELIX ALFRED JONES
Architect.
7 Adelaide Street, Dún Laoghaire
(01) 2800378
Born to Alfred Edwin and Mary Jones (née Ardiff) at Dublin on 1 August 1925. Educated at Synge Street CBS, Belvedere College and Royal Institute of the Architects of Ireland. Married to Colleen Veronica Twohig with three sons and four daughters. At present senior partner Jones and Kelly Architects and Fellow of Royal Institute of the Architects of Ireland. President of the Irish Amateur Boxing Association, vice-president of the European Amateur Boxing Association and member of the executive committee of the World Amateur Boxing Association. Life member Old Belvedere, Blackrock and Terenure RFCs, and member National Yacht Club, Dún Laoghaire.

JOHN A. KAVANAGH
Consulting Engineer
76 Merrion Road, Dublin 4
(01) 606966
Born to John and Sarah Kavanagh (née Byrne) at Dublin on 5 July 1943. Educated at CBS Dún Laoghaire and University College Dublin. Married to Felicity O'Donoghue with one son and three daughters. Formerly president Association of Consulting Engineers of Ireland and chairman of the Engineering Institutions' Joint Committee on Resistance of Buildings to Accidental Damage. At present managing director Kavanagh Mansfield & Partners, director KMK Project Management, Irish delegate to CEDIC (Comité Européen des Ingénieurs Conseils), member of NSAI's Concrete Consultative Committee of the Masonry Panel and of

several other technical and professional committees. Member Woodbrook Golf Club. Recipient of the Institution of Engineers of Ireland's Institution Prize for work of exceptional merit. Fellow of Institution of Engineers of Ireland, Institution of Structural Engineers (London) and member Institution of Civil Engineers (London).

AUGUSTIN KEARNEY
Corporate Chief Executive
Gortnafluir, Clonmel, Co. Tipperary
(052) 22811
Born to Patrick and Mary Kearney (née Lynch) on 13 January 1945. Educated at Christian Brothers and High School Clonmel, and Harvard School of Business. Married with three sons and one daughter. At present Chief Executive of M.F. Kent.

KEVIN CORNELIUS KELLY
Builder
Naas Road, Clondalkin, Dublin 22
(01) 504589
Born to Jeremiah and Sheila Kelly (née O'Shea) at Cork on 6 November 1939. Educated at Lehanmore NS, at St Colman's College Fermoy and College of Technology Bolton Street. Fellow of the Chartered Institute of Building. Married to Nuala Hourigan with four sons and one daughter. Formerly chairman of the Irish branch of the Chartered Institute of Building and holder of a number of senior positions with the Sisk organisation. At present managing director John Sisk and Son Ltd, director John Sisk and Son (UK) Ltd managing director John Sisk & Son GmbH (Germany) and member of the Construction Industry Development Board. Member St Mary's Rugby Club, Hermitage and Ballybunion Golf Clubs and Hibernian United Service Club.

MATT LARKIN
General Secretary
35 Meath Place, Dublin 8
(01) 543842
Born to Hugh and Catherine Larkin (née Kelly) at Dublin on 26 November 1932. Educated at Basin Lane Convent, St James' CBS and School of Commerce Rathmines. Married to Eleanor Moloney. Formerly chairman Guinness Boxing Club, committee member Bull Alley VEC and Travellers' Review Body. Member advisory committee Year of the Disabled, committee Year of the Aged. Executive committee member Irish Goods Council and Combat Poverty Agency first programme, chairman, contracted-out projects, Combat Poverty Agency first programme, shop steward Workers' Union of Ireland, founder member, first chairman and currently secretary South Inner City Community Development Association and honorary secretary Dublin Corporation

Tenants' Central Council. At present honorary secretary Marrowbone Lane Tenants' Association (NATO Branch), South Inner City Community Development Association, honorary general secretary National Association of Tenants' Organisations and member Irish Anti-Apartheid Association.

THOMAS AUGUSTINE LOMBARD
Chartered Surveyor
13 Merrion Row, Dublin 2
(01) 616198
Born to John Vincent and Florence Mary Lombard (née Curran) at Tipperary Town on 9 December 1937. Educated at Christian Brothers, Gorey, Castleknock College Dublin and College of Commerce, Liverpool. Married Joan Nestor (separated) with two sons and two daughters. Formerly real estate representative for Shell-Mex and BP in UK, senior partner Jones Lang Wootton and principal of Lombards. At present director, Sherry FitzGerald. Member Milltown and Woodenbridge Golf Clubs and Hibernian United Service Club.

ADRIAN ERNEST LONG
Civil Engineer
Queen's University Belfast BT7 1NN
(0232) 245133
Born to Charles and Sylvia Long (née Mills) at Dungannon on 15 April 1941. Educated at Benburb P.E. School, Royal School Dungannon and Queen's University Belfast. Married to Elaine Margaret Thompson with one son and one daughter. Formerly bridge design engineer FENCO Toronto, assistant professor Queen's University Kingston Ontario, lecturer Queen's University Belfast and dean Faculty of Engineering Queen's University Belfast. At present professor of civil engineering and director of the School of the Built Environment. Fellow of the Institutes of Engineers, Civil Engineers and Structural Engineers. Member of American Concrete Institute, Concrete Society (UK) and AUT Fellow of the Fellowship of Engineers (1989).

J.J. (SEÁN) LUCY
Engineer and Town Planner
Lower Abbey Street, Dublin 1
(01) 728011
Formerly with Dublin Corporation before spending some years with P.H. McCarthy, Son and Parnters, Consulting Engineers, Dublin, where he undertook the design of water and sewerage schemes. Resident Engineer on the South Wexford Regional Water Supply Scheme. Assistant county engineer with Wexford County Council responsible for road design and construction. Chief planning assistant with Westmeath County Council 1965–76 during which time was responsible for the

preparation of the first provisional and statutory development plans for that county and its principal towns, Athlone and Mullingar. Was also responsible for development control and work on the development of the amenity and industrial resources of the county. Appointed chief assistant county engineer with Westmeath County Council in 1976, Roscommon county engineer in 1980 and Offaly county engineer in 1983. At present chairman of An Bord Pleanála — appointed on 2 March 1987 for a term of 7 years. Member of the Institute of Engineers in Ireland and founder member of the Irish Planning Institute.

PAUL McNEIVE
Estate Agent
32 Molesworth Street, Dublin 2
(01) 760251
Born to James and Pauleen McNeive (née Connolly) at Dublin on 16 May 1962. Educated at CBC Monkstown and St David's Co-Ed Greystones. Married to Barbara Cole with one child. Chartered Surveyor and Member of the Irish Auctioneers & Valuers Institute. At present director Hamilton Osborne King and member Trials Drivers' Club.

JOHN EDWARD MEAGHER
Architect
42 Dawson Street, Dublin 2
(01) 770288
Born to Gerard A. and Teresa Meagher (née O'Beirne) at Dublin on 15 May 1947. Educated at Pembroke School, St Michael's College, Blackrock College, the School of Architecture, College of Technology Dublin 1966–71 and at Helsinki University of Technology, School of Architecture, Otaniemi, Finland 1971–2. Single. Formerly lecturer, at University of Helsinki and at University College Dublin. Admitted to membership of the Royal Institute of Architects of Ireland (1973) and fellow (1986). At present partner De Blacam and Meagher, Architects, which he founded with Shane de Blacam in 1976. Council member of ROSC, member of Local Appointments Commission, member of Art Advisory Board of Hugh Lane Municipal Gallery of Modern Art, member of editorial board of *Irish Arts Review*, trustee of the Dublin Graphic Studio Gallery and board member Irish Museum of Modern Art

GORDON STOPFORD MILLINGTON
Consulting Civil Engineer
2 Elmwood Avenue, Belfast BT9 6BA
(023) 667914
Born to Percy and Rene Millington (née Forster) at Belfast on 29 June 1935. Educated at Cabin Hill and Campbell College, Belfast, and at Queen's University Belfast. Married to Margaret Pegler with two sons, Mark and Gavin, and one daughter, Kathryn. Formerly held various

posts in the firm of Kirk McClure Morton Consulting Civil and Structural Engineers. At present senior partner, Kirk McClure Morton.

BRIAN DALTON O'CONNELL
Architect
9 Fitzwilliam Place, Dublin 2
(01) 767408
Born to C.D. and M.T. O'Connell (née Murphy) at Dublin on 30 January 1944. Educated at Gonzaga College, University College Dublin and King's Inns. Married with two children. Formerly president Architectural Association of Ireland. At present president Royal Institute of the Architects of Ireland and partner Brady Stanley O'Connell Associates, Architects. Member Royal Institute of British Architects.

CORNELIUS AUGUSTINE ODLUM
Consulting Engineer
Springville House, Blackrock Road, Cork
(021) 966400
Born to Patrick and Ellen Odlum (née Buckley) at Cork on 22 August 1933. Educated at Presentation Brothers College and University College, Cork. Married to Madeline Hickey with three sons and one daughter. Formerly president Cork Chamber of Commerce. At present chairman and managing director E.G. Pettit and Co. and Pettit International and member Association of Consulting Engineers of Ireland.

CATHAL O'NEILL
Professor, Architect
33 Pembroke Road, Dublin 4
(01) 684622
Born to Charles and Mary O'Neill (née Moran) at Dublin on 23 November 1930. Educated at Scoil Colmcille, Coláiste Mhuire, UCD and at Illinois Institute of Technology. Married to Deirdre Monks with five children. At present head of School of Architecture, UCD. Private practice in partnership with Garrett O'Neill. Member Howth Yacht Club, Fitzwilliam Lawn Tennis Club and Lough Ree Yacht Club.

SEÁN PADRAIG O'NUALLÁIN
Senior Archaeologist
Phoenix Park, Dublin
(01) 213171
Born to Albert Edward and Christina Nolan (née McCormack) at Dublin on 17 October 1926. Married to Ursula Dooley with four sons and one daughter. Formerly chairman Irish Association of Professional Archaeologists, and Royal Irish Academy National Committee for Archaeology. At present president Royal Society of Antiquaries of Ireland and senior archaeologist at the Ordnance Survey Office. Fellow

Royal Society of Antiquaries of Ireland and member of the Ulster Archaeological Society and of the Prehistoric Society (London).

JOHN TRAQUAIR PAUL
Group Chief Executive
Windy Arbour, Dublin 14
(01) 983044
Born to John T. and Elizabeth Paul (née Stewart) on 19 June 1937. Educated at The High School Dublin and TCD. Married to Jean Elizabeth Blyth with four children. At present managing director John Paul & Co. Ltd. Member Fitzwilliam Lawn Tennis Club and Kildare Street and University Club.

PIERCE T. PIGOTT
Chartered Engineer
51 St Stephen's Green, Dublin 2
(01) 613111
Born to John J. and Nora Pigott (née Looney) at Dublin in 1931. Educated at St Patrick's NS Drumcondra, Coláiste Mhuire Parnell Square, UCD and Stanford University California. Married with one son and two daughters. Formerly chief technical adviser An Foras Forbartha and president Institution of Engineers of Ireland. At present director of engineering services Office of Public Works, fellow of Institution of Engineers of Ireland and chairman Irish Concrete Society. Awarded President's Award 1991. Member of Association of Consulting Engineers of Ireland.

DIARMUID F. QUIRKE
Managing Director
Belgard Castle, Clondalkin, Dublin 22
(01) 591111
Born to Eamonn and Christina Quirke (née Toner) at Dublin on 25 August 1931. Educated at CBC Dún Laoghaire, UCD and Imperial College of Science and Technology, London. Married to Joan Glover with three sons and one daughter. Formerly works manager, operations manager, deputy managing director, and managing director of Irish Cement. At present managing director — Ireland and Britain, CRH plc, director Irish Steel, Heiton Holdings plc, and treasurer Federation of Irish Employers.

P. ANTHONY REDDY
Architect
26 Upper Mount Street, Dublin 2
(01) 764127
Born to Peter and Philomena Reddy (née Murphy) at Dublin on 17 April 1952. Educated at St Teresa's CBS, Synge Street CBS, UCD and TCD.

Married to Aoife O'Neill with one son, Shane, and two daughters, Ciara and Deirdre. Formerly worked with architectural practices in USA, architect with Murray Pettit and Partners and with Stephenson Associates, and president Architectural Association of Ireland. At present partner Fitzgerald Reddy and Associates, council member Royal Institute of Architects of Ireland, director RIAI Insurance Services, and director National Building Agency. Member Royal Institute of British Architects and associate Chartered Institute of Arbitrators.

THOMAS REYNOLDS
Federation Executive
Canal Road, Dublin 6
(01) 977487
Born to Col. David and Rita Reynolds (née Nolan) at Cork on 31 July 1935. Educated at Crescent College and Mungret College, Limerick, at UCD and King's Inns Dublin, and at Universidad Hispano-Americana de Santa Maria de la Rabida. Married to Niala Purcell with three sons, David, Garrett and Brian. Formerly general secretary Local Government Services' Union, council member AnCo and committee member National Industrial Safety Organisation. At present managing director, Construction Industry Federation and chairman Construction Guarantee and General Insurance Co Ltd. Member Fitzwilliam Lawn Tennis Club, the Lighthouse Club, Lansdowne Football Club, UCD and Old Crescent Rugby Football Clubs and UCD Alumni Association. Fellow Institute of Directors.

REGINALD BRYAN SCHOFIELD
University Professor Emeritus
Consultant
Born to Charles Reginald and Doris Schofield (née Smith) at Harworth, Nottinghamshire on 31 December 1929. Educated at Walkden Moor Methodist School Manchester, Bolton School, Corpus Christi College, Cambridge University. Married to Brenda Allcott with two sons, Robert David and Neil Charles, and one daughter, Gillian. Formerly project engineer with John Laing Construction Ltd, Lecturer and Senior Lecturer in the University of Salford at Jordanstown. Elected Professor Emeritus in 1989. Past chairman of the Institution of Civil Engineers (Northern Ireland). At present vice chairman of the Northern Ireland Water Council. Member of the Newcomen Society for the Study of the History of Science and Technology, and the Railway and Canal Historical Society. A keen fisherman.

MORGAN SHEEHY
Consulting Engineer
10 Wellington Road, Ballsbridge, Dublin 4
(01) 683112
Born to Morgan Michael and Catherine Sheehy (née Murphy) at

Clonakilty, Co. Cork on 18 August 1936. Educated at St John's NS Kinsale, Presentation Brothers College Cork, UCC and Colleges of Technology London. Married to Olivia Salinas with six children. Formerly president the Institution of Engineers of Ireland and member of Round Table on the Economy — Confederation of Irish Industry. At present chairman Institute of Directors Republic of Ireland Branch, chairman Accreditation Board the Institution of Engineers of Ireland, chairman College of Education Confederation of Irish Industry. Member Advisory Board Centre for the Development of Industry Brussels, member Board of Studies National Council for Educational Awards, managing director Ove Arup & Partners Ireland, board member The Arup Partnerships and external examiner for courses at TCD and College of Technology Bolton Street. Member Stephen's Green Club, Royal St George Yacht Club, Carbury Foxhounds, Fitzwilliam Lawn Tennis Club and Kinsale Yacht Club. Awarded MA MAI Honoris Causa TCD 1991, fellow Institution of Engineers of Ireland, Insititution of Civil Engineers, Institution of Structural Engineers and member American Society of Civil Engineers.

PHILIP DEXTER SHIPMAN
Landcsape Architect
26 Temple Road, Dartry, Dublin 6
(01) 979651
Born to George and Gladys Shipman (née Dexter) in England on 16 January 1936. Educated at Thurrock Primary School, Harlow College Essex, The Polytechnic London and University of Pennsylvania Philadelphia. Married to Siobhán Margaret Downes with three children. Formerly chairman Irish Chapter of the Landscape Institute (UK) and course lecturer 'Landscape Planning' UCD — Regional and Urban Planning Department. At present partner Brady Shipman Martin and chairman Irish Institute of Landscape Architects. Member Irish Ramblers' Club and Irish Wildbird Conservancy.

RONALD TALLON
Architect
19 Merrion Square, Dublin 2
(01) 760621
Born to Michael and Jennie Tallon (née McDermot) at Dublin in 1927. Educated at Coláiste Mhuire and School of Architecture, UCD. Married to Nora Vize with one son, Michael, and four daughters, Joan, Patricia, Yvonne and Deirdre. At present senior partner at Scott Tallon Walker Architects of Dublin, London and Galway. Works include Electrical Factory Dundalk, Knockanure Church, Co. Kerry, Abbey Theatre, RTE Buildings, Tobacco Factory Dundalk, Bank of Ireland Headquarters, New University Buildings and master planning for UCG, and buildings at UCD and TCD. Knight of the Order of St Gregory 1980, and recipient of Triennial Gold Medals of the Royal Institute of the Architects of

Ireland for the periods 1959–61, 1962–4, and House Medal 1965–7. Doctor of Laws (Honoris Causa) National University of Ireland 1990. Director Gate Theatre Dublin.

DAVID MICHAEL ROBERT TAPLIN
University Professor
Trinity College, Dublin 2
(01) 772941
Born to Alfred and Winifred Taplin (née Snell) at Derbyshire on 19 July 1939. Educated at Highfield Hall Derbyshire, Christ's Hospital Sussex and Oxford University. Married to Marian (née O'Neill) with two sons, Justin and Toban. Formerly president International Congress on Fracture, professor of engineering in Canada and lecturer in Australia. At present Professor of Engineering at Trinity College. Member Royal Irish Yacht Club.

MICHAEL J.T. WEBB
Chartered Quantity Surveyor
24 Lower Hatch Street, Dublin 2
(01) 763671
Born to John H. and Betty B. Webb (née Pollard) at Dublin on 29 July 1942. Educated at Baymount, Mountjoy and College of Estate Management. Married to Melissa D. (née Stanford) with one son, Richard, and three daughters, Sarah, Kate and Emma. Formerly chairman National Youth Council of Ireland and chief commissioner Scout Association of Ireland. At present senior partner Patterson Kemster and Shortall, director Avering plc, and Youth Exchange Bureau. Member National Economic and Social Council, chairman Society of Chartered Surveyors (1988), member of Engineering Board National Council for Education Awards. Member Kildare Street and University Club, Royal St George Yacht Club, fellow Royal Institution of Chartered Surveyors and fellow Chartered Institute of Arbitrators.

Chapter 15
Health and Welfare

The greatest pleasure I know, is to do a good action by stealth, and to have it found out by accident.

Charles Lamb

Promoting good health and healthy living is the praiseworthy pursuit which prompted the Republic's then Minister for Health Dr O'Hanlon to appoint the Advisory Council on Health Promotion in January 1988. The Council is to advise on health promotion policies, and make recommendations on preventive measures and on health education. The membership of the Council includes communications experts and cardiologists and this, perhaps, best sums up the desire to propagate information about good health and good lifestyle. Concern for healthy lifestyle will almost certainly lead to lower consumption of red meat, tobacco and alcohol. In fact, visitors who have encountered drunken Irishman images, will be interested to know that adult consumption of alcohol measured in litres of pure alcohol in 1987 was 8.7 lower than any other EC country and well below the level for France at 16.6 litres. There is a Health Promotion Unit within the Department of Health and this is the National Executive Unit engaged in a broad range of programmes on issues such as immunisation, drug abuse, food hygiene, Aids and cancer. The programmes are carried out in liaison with a wide network of voluntary, statutory, professional and commercial organisations. There is also a Cabinet Sub-Committee on health promotion composed of the ministers for agriculture, education, energy, environment and labour under the chairmanship of the Minister for Health. The Department has sponsored a Chair in Health Promotion at University College Galway.

Visitors will probably presume correctly, that the factors influencing health on this island are no different from those in other Western European countries — factors, such as atmospheric pollution, tobacco, abuse of alcohol and other drugs, housing, stress, marital breakdown, and unemployment. There is evidence that long-term unemployment leads not only to depression and malaise, but sometimes even to suicide. Similarly, homelessness has a debilitating effect, and a great many people believe that local authorities should be compelled, and not merely obliged, to provide housing for the homeless.

State Services

Over 35 per cent of total central government expenditure is devoted to health and social security. The health services in the Republic are administered by eight regional health boards with a view to promoting the highest possible level of general health in the population. The general medical service involves over 1,400 doctors with an average of 900 patients on each panel. Doctors can have private patients in addition to those whose care is state-funded. There are 12 doctors and 2.8 dentists per 10,000 of population in the Republic, and over 1,000 privately owned and operated retail pharmacies. Hospitals are run either by the health boards or by religious communities or other private organisations with state-funding.

In Northern Ireland the Department of Health and Social Services operates through four health and social services boards. There are over eighty hospitals with 18,000 beds and over 800 doctors with an average number of patients of about 1,900.

Private Services

In the Republic about one third of the population participates in the Volunatary Health Insurance scheme. The Voluntary Health Insurance Board, a state-sponsored corporation, has as its primary objective the provision of an insurance system for health care costs for those who have no entitlement to benefit under the tax-based state system. It also has the duty of sponsoring a spirit of self-reliance by expanding and improving its services in such a way that those who can afford to do so provide for their care without imposing any burden on the exchequer. Voluntary Health Insurance — a non-profit organisation — is, in essence, a co-operative movement. Through insurance, members band together to help each other in times of illness and high expenditure. It is essentially a consumers' organisation which is wholly financed by its members and which exists solely for their service.

In recognition of these characteristics, government has given VHI two valuable practical supports. Firstly, in view of the relatively small market, it was given a special position in health care insurance, and it has always treated its virtual monopoly with respect, placing much emphasis on cost containment and excellence in its member service. Secondly, VHI subscriptions are fully deductible for income tax purpose. This recognises that all citizens pay for the public health services through their health contributions and general taxes and that those who elect to pay for health care privately should receive some reasonable rebate of tax. VHI has been incurring losses in spite of increasing membership. Costs are rising faster than the rate of inflation, and the average age of the population is rising also.

A number of new private hospitals have opened their doors in recent years including the Blackrock Clinic and the Mater Private Hospital in Dublin and the Galvia Private Hospital in Galway.

Social Welfare
Social security services are similar throughout the island and those in Northern Ireland are almost identical to those available in other parts of the United Kingdom. The rules and qualification conditions are complex, and bearing this in mind, two examples are given—

Unemployment benefit which is payable for up to fifteen months under certain conditions was at a rate of IR£50 per week in 1991 with an additional IR£33 per week for an adult dependent.

Old age contributory pension payable to people aged sixty-six or over under certain conditions at a 1991 rate of IR£64 per week with an additional IR£40.80 per week for an adult dependent under age sixty-six or IR£46 per week for an adult dependent over age sixty-six.

In the Republic, children's allowances are paid to all families of children up to 16 years of age or up to 18, if in full-time education, and in addition there are two other main categories of social welfare benefit, known as social insurance and social assistance.

Social insurance payments are the subject of reciprocal arrangements with other EC member states and the payments themselves are related to the level of Pay Related Social Insurance (PRSI) contributions. Payments are made to those who reach the age of 66, take maternity leave, become unemployed or ill.

Social assistance payments are non-contributory and are made on the basis of need rather than qualification. The system of supplementary benefits supports those in particularly dire situations. The Society of St Vincent de Paul, which has enormous welfare experience throughout the island, believes that families frequently are beaten by circumstances, lose hope, and that either whole families or the breadwinners emigrate to a new life in England often to encounter even greater poverty. They believe also that communities are dying because their men feel useless, unwanted and unnecessary in a society that values people primarily in terms of their economic worth as earners or spenders. The Society, whose members see the problems week in week out in the course of their visits to homes in deprived communities, calls for a radical redesign of long-term social welfare and rejects as unimaginative the present system of 'add on percentages'. It suggests that certain benefits already enjoyed by old people should be extended to the long-term unemployed and that restructuring should provide for free electricity and/or gas, free travel at off peak times, free TV licence, and free education, including books and examination fees. It also considers that long-term social welfare should be regarded as normal income with a facility for voluntary deduction at source of some recurring items such as rent.

Voluntary Groups
The work of voluntary groups in the fields of prevention and care is truly wonderful and matches the endeavours of volunteers in any country. Cairde, for example, is a little known organisation supporting and helping AIDS victims, while the Central Remedial Clinic is a very well-known comprehensive medical rehabilitation centre offering physiotherapy, hydrotherapy, occupational and speech therapy. Similarly, Coolmine Therapeutic Community for Drug Abusers is not well-known, while Alcoholics Anonymous, the self-help organisation for those suffering from the disease of alcoholism, is justly famous

Other prominent organisations include the Irish Association of Social Workers, the Cheshire Foundation, Cork Polio and General Aftercare Association, the Disabled Drivers' Association, the Irish Hospice Foundation, Irish Association for the Blind, Irish Cancer Society, Irish Heart Foundation, Irish Wheelchair Foundation, National League for the Blind of Ireland, The Polio Fellowship of Ireland, Rehabilitation Institute and many, many others. The Simon Community is a voluntary organisation which was founded in Britain in 1963 to care and campaign for the homeless.

Not Paying Attention

All was in readiness for Health Minister Mary O'Rourke officially to open St Brídes new school in Oldcastle, Co. Meath, in September 1990 ... that was until four-year-old Edward Naper decided the weather was too fine for his first day at school and turned his back on the proceedings.

MARK ANTHONY BLAKE-KNOX
Adminstrator
20A Herbert Lane, Dublin 2
(01) 614550
Born to Desmond and Monica Blake Knox (née Doyle) at Dún Laoghaire on 30 March 1957. Educated at All Saints' NS, St Andrew's College and TCD. Married to Ann (née Murray). Formerly administrator Cara Cheshire Home, Phoenix Park. At present co-ordinator of Cheshire Foundation in Ireland. Member Dublin University Central Athletics Committee and Union of Voluntary Organisations for the Handicapped.

HENRY DESMOND CASHELL
Insurance Executive
7/9 South Leinster Street, Dublin 2
(01) 767117
Born to Henry Edward and Annie Cashell (née Evans) at Skerries on 28 February 1924. Educated at Holmpatrick National School Skerries and at The King's Hospital. Married to Gemma Good. Formerly manager — Ireland with Norwich Union Fire Insurance Society. At present chairman VHI and consultant to Coyle Hamilton Ltd. Member United Service Club, MCC, Malahide CC and Skerries RFC.

EUGENE DONOGHUE
Chief Executive
31/32 Fitzwilliam Square, Dublin 2
(01) 760226
Born to Thomas and Kathleen Donoghue (née Coss) at Portlaoise on 11 May 1946. Educated at Christian Brothers Schools, University College Cork, Manhattan College and Maynooth College. Married to Nuala Brady with three children. Formerly teacher Vocational Educational Committee Carlow, instructor in Psychiatry and Counsellor Kings Co. Hospital New York, guidance counsellor Vocational Educational Committee Carlow, manager Education and Training at Health Education Bureau and assistant principal Department of Health. At present chief executive An Bord Altranais. Member Stackstown Golf Club, Institute of Health Education and International Union of Health Education.

DAVID DOWNES
Executive Director
1 Ringsend Road, Dublin 4
(01) 602933
Born to Edward F. and Catherine Downes (née Breen) at Dublin on 13 March 1951. Educated at Scoil Mhuire CBS Marino, St Joseph's CBS Fairview and University College Dublin. Married to Joelle Le Cloerec with three sons. Formerly social worker Contact Youth Advisory Service

and St Michael's House, development officer Shelter Referral and probation and welfare officer Department of Justice. At present executive director Irish Youth Foundation.

JOHN DUNNE
Chief Executive
20 Lower Dominick Street, Dublin 1
(01) 729933
Born to Richard and Sheila Dunne (née O'Sullivan) at Dublin on 12 December 1958. Educated at St John Bosco National School, St Declan's CBS, Institute of Public Administration and at Trinity College Dublin. Married to Maria Murray with one son and one daughter. Formerly with the Department of Industry and Commerce, the Department of Foreign Affairs, the Institute of Public Administration, the International Fund for Ireland and private secretary to the Minister for Foreign Affairs. At present chief executive National Youth Federation. Member Political Studies Association of Ireland and Royal Zoological Society of Ireland.

MICHAEL FERRIS
Public Representative
Leinster House, Dublin 2
(01) 785187
Born in November 1931. Educated at Tipperary Christian Brothers School, Tipperary Vocational School, Salesian Agricultural College and attended special courses at University College Cork. Married with six children. Formerly Senator, member of the South Eastern Health Board and of Tipperary SR Local Health Committee. At present Labour Party TD and spokesman on Health, member of the Joint Oireachtas Committees on Secondary Legislation of the European Communities and Social and Economic and Agricultrual Affairs Sub-Committee. Member of the Inter Parliamentary Union and of the Council of Europe for 1991–92.

REV. AENGUS FINUCANE
Chief Executive
1 Upper Camden Street, Dublin 2
(01) 681237
Born to John and Delia Finnucane (née Byrnes) at Limerick on 26 April 1932. Educated at Model School Limerick, CBS Sexton Street Limerick, UCD and University of Wales. Formerly field director for Concern in Gabon, Bangladesh, Thailand, Uganda, Parish Priest of ULI Nigeria, and principal of Premier Secondary School Nigeria. At present chief executive of Concern. Member Newlands Golf Club.

FRANK FLANNERY
Chief Executive
Roslyn Park, Sandymount, Dublin 4
(01) 698422
Born to Patrick and Mary Flannery (née Waldron) at Galway on 4 December 1944. Educated at Attymon and Kiltulla NS, St Clement's College Limerick, University College Galway whence he graduated with an honours BA degree and at University College Dublin whence he qualified with a Master's degree in Business Administration. Awarded a Diploma in Applied Finance by the Irish Management Institute. Married to Marguerite McCurtin. Formerly president Union of Students in Ireland, member of RTE Authority and chairman Cablelink Ltd. At present chief executive Rehabilitation Institute, managing director UK Charity Lotteries Limited, director Rehab Scotland, director National Rehabilitation Board. Member Dublin Chamber of Commerce, Irish Management Institute, Marketing Institute of Ireland, Institute of Directors, Fine Gael, Fitzwilliam Lawn Tennis Club and Loughrea Golf Club.

JOHN FINLAYSON FLEETWOOD
Physician
11 Proby Square, Blackrock, Co. Dublin
(01) 2887329
Born to John and Gabrielle Fleetwood (née Van Esbeck) at Edinburgh on 21 April 1917. Educated at Ursuline Convent Edinburgh, Presentation Colleges Plymouth and Bray, Saint Michel College Brussels, and Blackrock College, UCD, and TCD. Married to Anita Maria O'Connor with two sons, John and Conor, and two daughters, Caroline and Mary. Formerly battalion medical officer Local Defence Force, acting Wicklow County Medical Officer, and house physician St Vincent's Hospital; president Royal Academy of Medicine in Ireland; president Irish Gerontological Society, chairman Irish Council of Royal College of General Practitioners, chairman Dún Laoghaire Old Folks' Association and council member International Association of Gerontological Societies. Member Dún Laoghaire Motor Yacht Club, Irish Writers' Union, GP Writers' Association and British Geriatrics Society. Recipient of Flood Medal for oratory, Bobst Medal for Gerontological Service, Chevalier du Mérite Maritime, People of the Year Award, Bourke Memorial Medal and Doolin Memorial Medal. Author of *History of Medicine in Ireland*, *The Irish Body Snatchers*, *As You Get Older*, *Health Matters*, and four pantomimes.

HUGH CHRISTOPHER FRAZER
Agency Director
8 Charlemont Street, Dublin 2
(01) 783355
Born to Tony and Nesta Frazer (née Hughes) at Cullybackey on 14 October 1949. Educated at Heronwater and Stowe Schools, TCD and

London School of Economics. Married to Hilary Simms with three sons, Owen, Daniel and Benjamin. Formerly youth officer and community information officer Northern Ireland Council of Social Services and director Northern Ireland Voluntary Trust. At present director Combat Poverty Agency.

PETER BARRY BRONTË GATENBY
Medical Doctor
Trinity College, Dublin
(01) 2841443
Born to James Brontë and Enid Kathleen Mary Gatenby (née Meade) at Dublin on 2 November 1923. Educated at Nightingale Hall, St Andrew's College and at TCD. Married to Yvette Jeanne Bonnet with two children. Formerly consultant physician Meath Hospital, Steevens Hospital and Rotunda Hospital Dublin, professor of Clinical Medicine at TCD and Medical Director UN, New York. At present occasional medical consultant UN Organisation and president TCD Medical Alumni Association. Member Kildare Street and University Club and fellow Royal Academy of Medicine in Ireland. Honorary Fellowship American College of Physicians, Royal College of Physicians Edinburgh and of TCD.

PAUL DAVID HANLY
Managing Director
St John Court, Swords Road, Santry, Dublin 9
(01) 429933
Born to Desmond and Lily Hanly (née Maher) at Dublin on 23 March 1944. Educated at St Patrick's NS Drumcondra and O'Connell's CBS. Married to Caroline O'Mahony with four children. Formerly personnel executive with Aer Lingus. At present managing director Parc Group, chairman Comhairle na nOspidéal and director Arab/Irish Chamber of Commerce. Fellow of Institute of Personnel Management, member Irish Management Institute, Irish Marketing Institute, Institute of Directors and St Anne's Golf Club.

MOHAMMED SALEEM KHAN
North Circular Road, Dublin 7
(01) 387699
Born to Atta and Sakina Mohummad (née Bibi) in Pakistan on 17 December 1953. Educated at Government Degree College Faisal Abad, Nishtar Medical College Pakistan and Manjing College China. Married to Bernadette Nard with one child. Formerly general secretary Irish Council for Complementary and Alternative Medicine. At present principal Acupuncture Foundation of Ireland and representative The World Federation of Acupuncture Societies. Member Dublin Islamic Society and associate Royal College of General Practitioners England. Awarded Yellow Emperor's Award for work in Acupuncture.

DESMOND MacHALE
University Professor
University College, Cork
(021) 276871
Born to John and Kathleen MacHale (née Murray) at Castlebar on 28 January 1946. Educated at St Patrick's NS and St Gerald's College Castlebar, UCG and University of Keele. Married to Anne M.E. Gryce with four sons, Peter, Simon, John and Dominic, and one daughter, Catherine. Formerly chairman International Conference on Humour. At present associate professor in mathematics UCC, secretary Irish Association of Non-Smokers, author, writer, broadcaster, curator Library of Humour UCC, member Irish National Committee for History of Science & Philosophy. Member St Michael's Tennis Club.

PATRICK McKEON
Consultant Psychiatrist
James' Street, Dublin 8
(01) 775423
Born to Terence and Eithne McKeon (née Heffernan) at Ballina on 16 March 1950. Educated at St Patrick's NS Castlerea, St Mureadach's College Ballina, UCD and Institute of Psychiatry London. Married to Mary Moran with one son and two daughters. Formerly chairman Charlemont Clinic. At present consultant psychiatrist St Patrick's Hospital Dublin, director Depression Research Unit St Patrick's Hospital, lecturer TCD and chairman AWARE. Fellow of Royal College of Physicians of Ireland, member Royal College of Psychiatrists London and of Royal Irish Academy of Medicine. Awarded Norman Moore Fellowship in Psychiatry 1978 and Peter Beckett Memorial Medal 1980 for Research.

GERARD PATRICK MARTIN
Corrigan House, Fenian Street, Dublin 2
(01) 763474
Born to John and Kathleen Martin (née Blake) at Dublin on 27 March 1941. Educated at Synge Street CBS Dublin. Married to Rosemary Hodgins with one son, Paul, and one daughter, Jennifer. Formerly assistant principal Dept of Health and head of Irish delegation to hospital committee of EC. At present chief officer Comhairle na nOspidéal. Member Institute of Hospital & Health Services Administrators, and International Hospital Federation. Honorary life and founder member Association of Irish Musical Societies, former member and chairman Action Aid (Ire).

DON BOSCO MULLAN
Relief Agency Director
'The Cottage', 63 Harold's Cross Road, Dublin 6W
(01) 966880
Born to Charles and Sara Mullan (née Redden) at Derry on 3 March 1956.

Educated at St Eugene's Primary School Derry, St Joseph's Secondary School Derry, Ulster Polytechnic Co. Antrim and at Iona College, New Rochelle, New York. Married to Margaret Beatty with one son and one daughter. Formerly studied with St Patrick's Missionary Society Kiltegan, Co. Wicklow. Worked with Kiltegan Fathers in Recife, Brazil, PR officer Free Fr Niall O'Brien and the Negros Nine Committee, director Year of St Francis International Conference on World Peace and Poverty. At present Director Great Famine Project and Iona College's Peace Studies Programme in Ireland. PR Officer and Tour Organiser Longtower Folk Group Derry and secrtary Derry Athletic Football Academy. Made honorary chief of the Choctaw Nation of Oklahoma.

UNA O'CONNOR
Chartered Physiotherapist
Trinity College, Dublin
(01) 6266332
Born to William and Freda McMahon (née Durkin) at Dublin on 10 July 1935. Educated at St Louis Convent Rathmines, St Louis Convent Monaghan and at Trinity College Dublin. Married to Philip O'Connor with five children. At present with the Department of General Practice Trinity College Dublin and president Irish Society of Chartered Physiotherapists.

JOHN DANIEL ALEXANDER ROBB
Consultant Surgeon
Route Hospital, Ballymoney, Co. Antrim
Born to John Charles and Jessie Bannatyne Robb (née Wilson) at Downpatrick on 24 February 1932. Educated at Rockport Craigavad and Merchiston Castle School Edinburgh, Queen's University Belfast and Royal College of Surgeons London. Married to Sylvia Sloan with two daughters and two sons. Formerly consultant surgeon Royal Victoria Hospital Belfast, visiting consultant surgeon to Harare Hospital Zimbabwe and member of Seanad Éireann. At present consultant surgeon at Route Hospital Ballymoney, and chairman New Ireland Group.

THOMAS ROSEINGRAVE
Sociologist
2 Rue Ravenstein, Brussels
Born to Thomas W. and Nora Roseingrave (née McMahon) at Gort, Co. Galway on 4 July 1918. Educated at Gort National School, O'Brien Institute Dublin and at University College Dublin. Married to Ellen Goulding with seven children. Formerly director Manpower Studies, Department of Labour Dublin, president of Economic & Social Committee of the EC, former member of National Social Service Council, First National Poverty Committee, Commission on the GAA, Commission on Broadcasting and chairman Commission on Pharmacy in Ireland. At present

senior research fellow Department of Social Science UCD and member of Economic and Social Committee of the EC. Member Irish Sociological Society and of the Regional Studies Association.

RONALD SMILEY
Chief Executive
12 Herbert Street, Dublin 2
(01) 615522
Born to William and Mary Smiley (née Fleming) at Dublin on 29 October 1935. Educated at Synge Street CBS and attended Social Studies Courses at Institute for Adult Education. Married to Mona Dalton with one son and one daughter. Formerly car salesman, parts rep and car rental manager. At present chief executive/company secretary with GORTA, Third World Agency, since 1974. Undertook marathon tractor drive around Ireland to raise IR£30,000 and *Guinness Book of Records* recognised this effort as a world record and has published it.

THOMAS WALSH
Director General
27 Upper Baggot Street, Dublin 4
(01) 603388
Born to Walter and Kathleen Walsh (née Daniels) in Waterford. Married to Elsie Wall with four children. Formerly principal officer Department of Labour, Social Affairs Attaché with Irish Permanent Representation to the EC, Brussels. At present director general National Authority for Occupational Safety and Health.

NIALL GERARD WELDON
Company Director
Beaumont, Dublin 9
(01) 377755
Born to Thomas and Mary Weldon (née Kelly) at Dublin on 11 October 1922. Educated at Rush National School, O'Connell Schools Dublin and at University College Dublin. Married to Elizabeth Sheils with eight children. Formerly airport manager Dublin Airport; services manager, general sales manager, personnel manager, and company secretary and general manager corporate affairs Aer Lingus. At present chairman Beaumont Hospital, director RTE, Jury's Hotel Group plc and of Comhairle na nOspidéal. Member Institute Personnel Management, fellow Institute of Transport and of the Institute of Secretaries and Administrators. Member Skerries Golf Club.

Chapter 16
The Media

The men with the muck-rakes are often indispensable to the well-being of society; but only if they know when to stop raking the muck.

Roosevelt

Publishing and broadcasting are about people and ideas and together they offer each person, group and nation the opportunity to tell a story, express a point of view, or make a statement. Mr Vincent Finn, Director General of RTE said in a 1988 paper, 'The contribution of the broadcasting media in international understanding', is that '... in Ireland, where the most honoured place beside the hearth was that of the seanchaí, the storyteller, poet and historian, we have translated the importance of narrative into our broadcasting function'.

Journalists are professionals. By and large, they observe professional standards of accuracy and fair reporting. They care about their professional standing with their peers, and compete with one another. They are so keen to report events, that very often their attention tempts decision-makers to worry, not about how things really are, but how they are seen to be.

This can produce an unreal situation, such as the interviewing of people concerned with the contents of lengthy reports immediately after the release of the reports. It is regrettable to see people who hold positions of responsibility granting these interviews and hedging their meaningless utterances with caveats like 'Of course, I haven't had an opportunity to read the report myself yet, but ...!'

It can be fatal for public figures to comment publicly on situations which they have not carefully considered, and organisers of conferences such as the British Irish Association for example, invite eminent public figures to discuss topical issues, political, social or economic, during a weekend — in private and unreported. The Association finds that 'both Governments, together with senior spokesmen from the main political parties in both islands, people from business, public service, the churches, universities and the media, all welcome the chance to talk in discussions which are frank and lively'.

Competition

The Republic's National Broadcasting Authority, RTE (Radio Telifís Éireann), competes for audience share with BBC Radio, Radio Luxembourg, Capital and other overseas stations. Similarly RTE Television competes on the East Coast with British TV channels and in all parts of the country where there are licensed local cable monopolies.

When the Irish travel abroad, especially if they travel at a time when some important event is taking place at home, such as an election, they quickly become aware of the lack of an Irish world service. The idea of a short-wave radio station is not new and, in fact, equipment for such a station was at one stage bought and installed in Athlone. The project never came to fruition, however, and the void still exists. It is a void much to be regretted, not only because of the way in which travellers could be facilitated with the latest news from home, but also because the Irish version of the facts would be available to them instead of, or in addition to, the versions promulgated by the world services of greater powers. There may be scope here for some business and some job creation.

There is keen competition between the following daily newspapers: published in Dublin — the *Irish Independent*, the *Irish Press*, *The Irish Times* and *The Star*; published in Belfast — the *Belfast Newsletter* and the *Irish News*; and in Cork — *The Cork Examiner*. In addition, evening papers are published in Dublin, (the *Evening Herald* and the *Evening Press*), and in Belfast and Cork (the *Belfast Telegraph* and the *Evening Echo*). *The Irish Times* is not published on Sunday but the *Sunday Independent* and the *Sunday Press* are joined in Dublin by other weekly papers, *Sunday Tribune*, *Sunday World*, and *Sunday Business Post*, and in Belfast by the *Sunday News* and the *Sunday Life*.

The following analysis of newspaper readerships may be of interest to visitors — it is meant to be humorous, but with a serious undercurrent:

The *Irish Independent* is read by the people who own the country. The *Cork Examiner* is read by people who want to own the country. The *Irish Press* is read by people who know who runs the country. *The Irish Times* is read by people who think they run the country and *The Star* is read by people who don't care who runs the country as long as there's a pretty girl on page three.

Business Bias

Many Irish businessmen, like their counterparts in other countries, feel that the media attitude to business is a mixture of curiosity, suspicion and hostility. Now, there is no doubt that Irish businessmen have, to a large extent, ceased to be the great 'men of affairs' of the last century, and they have drifted away from the centre of trust and respectability which they once dominated. Yet, Irish business has a good story to tell.

A great many Irish businesses are successfully competing with multinational firms at home in the Irish market and in overseas markets. But, the good story must be told. It cannot be taken as read. It must be told particularly to employees, customers, suppliers and shareholders so that these people, who have a stake in the success of Irish business, can join in expressing legitimate concern for a better deal for Irish business.

Public interest in business news has been increasing and it is, therefore, in the best interests of the media to give it fair and generous coverage.

Section 31

RTE is prevented from broadcasting on radio or television interviews or reports of interviews with spokesmen for a number of organisations notably the IRA, Sinn Féin, the UDA, INLA and Republican Sinn Féin. The regulations which arise from Section 31 of the Broadcasting Authority Act 1960 also encompass organisations proscribed in Northern Ireland, such as the UFF, UVF, Saor Éire, Red Hand Commandos, Fianna Éireann and Cumann na mBan.

The operation of this ban has been a source of controversy. Arguments against it include claims that it amounts to a form of political censorship and claims that it had become irrelevant because the interviews and reports which are banned on RTE were available in many parts of the country on BBC and ITV, until Autumn 1988.

Successive governments in the Republic have continued to impose the Section 31 ban on the basis that those who plot to overthrow the State should not be allowed access to the State broadcasting service in order to propagate their views. On one occasion, the ban was referred to the Supreme Court who decided that there was an obligation on the Government:

> to ensure that the organs of public opinion (which include television and radio) shall not be used to undermine public order or morality or the authority of the State ... that the use of such organs of opinion for the purpose of securing or advocating support for organisations which seek by violence to overthrow the State or its Institutions, is a use which is prohibited by the Constitution. Therefore, it is clearly the duty of the State to intervene to prevent broadcasts on Radio or on Television which are aimed at such a result or which in any way would be likely to have the effect of promoting or inciting to crime or endangering the authority of the State.

Reporting Strikes

The way the media deal with the start of a strike often contrasts sharply with the way they deal with the end. For example, Irish trade unionists responded quickly to the August 1987 strike by South African mine workers. August is traditionally a quiet month for news and this may have contributed to the emergence of Cyril Ramaphosa as the Helicopter Messiah who was portrayed in Ireland as being not only about to topple the South African mining companies but also the whole South African régime.

The strike was the subject of the most extensive print and broadcast media coverage focusing especially on Irish pickets and protests and the monies which were collected in Ireland to be sent to relieve the suffering of the mine workers and their families. Three weeks later the strike was over but this received hardly any attention in the Irish media. Another point which did not appear to be worthy of mention was that the strike ended without any increase in pay! So, is the end of a strike newsworthy at all? As Charles Anderson Dana says, 'When a dog bites a man that is not news, but when a man bites a dog that is news.' We need to consider 'news' in the context of our favourite daily newspaper's duty to inform. If the start of a strike is newsworthy, then its end must surely be worthy of some mention in the interests of balanced reporting.

Standards

The Broadcasting Complaints Board, as its name implies, handles complaints from listeners and viewers in the Republic, arising from broadcast material. Unfortunately, there is no similar tribunal for the printed media. Complaints arising from advertisements can be referred to the Advertising Standards Authority.

Quality, in terms of a pendulum, is still tending to swing towards entertainment and away from information, and there may be undue preoccupation with the slick and the trivial especially by headline writers. This must be a source of great frustration to visitors, however fluent, who do not have English as a mother tongue. As pun-headlines go, it must be hard to beat the description by Trevor Danker in the *Sunday Independent* of the aftermath of an Irish-Welsh Rugby International which was headlined: 'Reds, Sales and the Scrum Set'.

Public figures have private lives, but to what extent have they a right to privacy? This is a question which is frequently asked. Certainly if US presidential elections are anything to go by, no one who ever kissed his or her boss at an office party should even dream of going forward for election in the United States, such is the enthusiasm for 'research' into candidates' private lives there. By contrast Irish politicians rest easily on the basis of an understanding which provides that journalists will not comment on top politicians' peccadillos in the press, and politicians will not mention the peccadillos of Managing Editors in Parliament.

MAEVE BINCHY

Writer

Irish Times, Dublin 2

Born to William and Maureen Binchy (née Blackmore) at Dublin on 28 May 1940. Educated at Holy Child Convent Killiney and University College Dublin. Married to Gordon Snell. Formerly girls' school history teacher. At present, *Irish Times* columnist and novelist. Author of two short plays, *End of Term* and *Half Promised Land*; two TV plays, *Deeply Regretted By* and *Ireland of the Welcomes*; four novels, *Light A Penny Candle*, *Echoes*, *Firefly Summer* and *Circle of Friends*, and five collections of short stories. Almost all of her work has been translated into several other languages.

WESLEY BOYD

Broadcaster

Donnybrook, Dublin 4

(01) 642350

Born at Fermanagh on 14 August 1933. Formerly director of news RTE, diplomatic correspondent *Irish Times* and London editor *Northern Whig*. At present director broadcasting developments RTE, member of Administrative Council, European Broadcasting Union and member Oireachtas Broadcasting Control Committee. Member United Arts Club Dublin.

CONOR PATRICK BRADY

Editor

11–13 d'Olier Street, Dublin 2

(01) 6792022

Born to Conor and Amy Brady (née MacCarthy) at Dublin on 24 April 1949. Educated at St Columba's Tullamore, Cistercian Abbey Roscrea and University College Dublin whence he obtained BA and MA (Political Science) Degrees. Married to Ann Byron with two children. Formerly editor *Sunday Tribune*. At present editor and director *The Irish Times*. Member Stephen's Green Club and Tullamore Golf Club.

VINCENT BROWNE

Editor

15 Lower Baggot Street, Dublin 2

(01) 615555

Born to Séamus and Kathleen Browne (née Burns) at Limerick on 17 July 1944. Educated at Broadford Primary School Co. Limerick, St Mary's Drumcollogher Co. Limerick, Castleknock College Dublin and at University College Dublin. Married to Jean Learmond with two children. Formerly editor and founder of *Magill*. At present editor of *Sunday Tribune*.

GAY BYRNE
Broadcaster
RTE, Donnybrook, Dublin 4
(01) 693111
Born to Edward and Annie Byrne (née Carroll) at Dublin on 5 August 1934. Educated at Synge Street CBS. Married to Kathleen Watkins with two daughters, Crona and Suzy. Formerly worked in insurance, cinema management, advertising and as professional broadcaster with Granada Television, BBC 2, TVS and WBZ Boston. At present broadcaster with RTE where he has been presenter and producer of the 'Late Late Show' for twenty-nine years and the Gay Byrne daily radio show for twenty years. The 'Late Late Show' has been written into the *World Who's Who of Television* as longest running live chat show in world with the same presenter/producer. Author of *To Whom It Concerns*. His autobiography *The Time of My Life*, written with Deirdre Purcell, was published in 1990. Also writes a regular column in *The Sunday World*. Awarded an honorary doctorate of letters by Trinity College in Dublin's Millennium Year.

WILLIAM HAROLD CLARKE
Bookseller
80 Middle Abbey Street, Dublin 1
(01) 733811
Born to George and Cathleen Clarke (née Maxwell) at Roscommon on 30 November 1932. Educated at The King's Hospital and at TCD. Single. Having held various positions within Easons he is at present chairman of Eason and Son Ltd and director of a number of associated companies. Editor of the *Irish Heritage Series* of booklets on all aspects of Irish life which began with the booklet he wrote on Georgian Dublin. Restorer of a derelict eighteenth-century house in Dublin 1 to its original elegance. Vice President of the Friends of the National Collections and member Christ Church Cathedral Board. His ambition is to see people in Ireland buying more books per capita than in any other country.

THOMAS EDWARD CROSBIE
Newspaper Publisher
95 Patrick Street, Cork
(021) 272722
Born to Thomas and Gladys Crosbie (née Whitaker) at Cork on 30 April 1931. Educated at CBC Cork and afterwards at UCC where he studied chemistry and physics until 1952. Undertook post-graduate studies in pulp and paper in Sweden in 1953/4. Married to Margaret Rosa Kelleher with three sons and three daughters. Formerly works director of Cork Examiner Publications and director Metal Products. At present director and chief executive Cork Examiner (Publications) Ltd, director Harveys Waterford, and Thomas Crosbie & Co (Printers) Ltd. Member Rotary Club of Cork, Royal Cork Yacht Club and Cork Golf Club.

The Late Late Show

The world's longest running chat show with the same producer-presenter is RTE's Late Late Show. Producer-presenter Gay Byrne is seen here with Olivia Tracey at the announcement of the 1990 People in Need Telethon.

CONOR CRUISE-O'BRIEN
Writer

Born to Francis and Katherine Cruise-O'Brien (née Sheehy) at Dublin on 3 November 1917. Educated at Sandford Park School and TCD. Married to Máire Mac an tSaoi. Formerly worked in Dept of Finance, and Dept of External Affairs. Worked with UN as Secretary General's Personal Representative in Katanga, vice chancellor University of Ghana and Albert Schweitzer Professor of Humanities New York University. At present pro-chancellor Dublin University (Trinity), regular contributor to *The Times* (London) and *Irish Independent* as well as to several American publications and contributing editor to *The Atlantic* (Boston). Member Royal Irish Academy and The Royal Society of Literature (London). Awarded the Valiant for Truth Media Award of the Order of Christian Unity (London) 1979, Granada Television Media Awards as Commentator (1979 and 1983) and Sydney Hillman Award (New York 1987).

CLARE DUIGNAN
Television Producer
Donnybrook, Dublin 4
(01) 643015

Born to Gerry and Mary Duignan (née Glynn) at Dublin on 24 February 1956. Educated at St Louis Monaghan, Loreto Clonmel, Loreto Abbey Dalkey and at UCD. Married to Eugene Doran with one daughter and two sons. Originated 'Women Today' (radio) The 'Women's Programme' (TV), produced/directed 'Today-Tonight', The 'Late Late Show' and member RTE Network 2 Relaunch Group. At present group head Features and Current Affairs TV Programmes RTE. Member Monkstown Lawn Tennis Club, Women's Environmental Network, of the EEC/EBU Equal Opportunities in Broadcasting Committee and of the 1990 jury Bank of Ireland Arts Show Awards.

VINCENT FINN
Director General
Donnybrook, Dublin 4
(01) 642147

Born to James and Margaret Finn (née Dwyer) at Dublin on 22 July 1930. Educated at Belvedere College, UCD and Institute of Chartered Accountants in Ireland. Married to Deirdre Cullen with one daughter and one son. Formerly accountant with Motor Distributors and with Bolands; accountant, financial controller, director of finance and deputy director general with RTE. At present director general RTE. Council member and fellow of Irish Management Institute, council member Confederation of Irish Industry, chairman European Broadcasting Union Finance Group, director International Council, The National Academy of Television Arts & Sciences (NATAS) and of GPA Dublin International Piano Competition. Member Royal St George Yacht Club and Woodbrook Golf Club.

ROBERT KEVIN GAHAN
Assistant Director General
Donnybrook, Dublin 4
(01) 642357
Born to Robert and Mary Gahan (née Atkinson) at Ballina Co. Mayo on 9 February 1930. Educated at O'Connell Schools Dublin, High School of Commerce Rathmines, Harvard Business School and at King's Inns. Married to Josephine Healy with four daughters. Formerly president Publicity Club of Ireland, director commercial affairs, director sales, and sales manager RTE. At present assistant director general and director corporate affairs RTE, director Cable Link, Telegael Spiddal, AGB (Ire) and chairman RTE Commercial Enterprises. Fellow Marketing Institute and holder of McConnell Award for services to Advertising and Marketing. Trustee Advertising Benevolent Society, board member Research Centre Our Lady's Hospital Crumlin, member Elm Park GSC, Fitzwilliam LT & SC. Life member Publicity Club and Advertising Press Club.

EILEEN E. GLEESON
Managing Director
38 Upper Fitzwilliam Street, Dublin 2
(01) 760168
Born to Frank and Nora Gleeson (née Bishop) at Dublin on 20 August 1960. Educated at Booterstown National School, Sion Hill Blackrock and College of Commerce. Married to Gerry Hegarty. Formerly director Irish Goods Council and council member PR Institute. At present managing director Financial and Corporate Communications Ltd, director National Lottery Company and chairman Public Relations Consultants Association. Member NUJ and Network.

MICHAEL GOOD
Managing Editor
Donnybrook, Dublin 4
(01) 642149
Born to Peter and Norah Good (née Tyndall) at Dublin on 27 June 1951. Educated at Highlands Junior School and Falcon College Zimbabwe and at Trinity College Dublin. Married to Marian Richardson with four sons. Formerly reporter Belfast, presenter/reporter 'News at 1.30', 'This Week' and programme editor 'News At One', 'News at 6.30' for RTE. At present managing editor Radio News RTE.

JOE HAYES
Managing Director
90 Middle Abbey Street, Dublin
(01) 731666
Born to Tim and Margaret Hayes (née O'Sullivan) at Tralee, Co. Kerry on 21 April 1947. Educated at Ballyduff NS, Salesian College Co.

Limerick and TCD. Married to Colette Walsh with two sons and three daughters. Formerly marketing director Independent Newspapers and marketing manager Gallaher (Dublin) Ltd. At present managing director Independent Newspapers (Ireland) Ltd and Independent Newspapers Marketing Ltd, director Independent Newspapers plc, Independent Technologies Ltd, The Kerryman Ltd, Drogheda Independent Co Ltd, People Newspapers Ltd, Independent Information Services Ltd, Independent Directories Ltd, Cork Communications Ltd, Independent Wireless Cable Ltd, Westward Horizons Ltd, chairman Independent Star Ltd.

KEVIN HEALY
Journalist
Donnybrook, Dublin 4
(01) 642453
Born to John C and Maureen Healy (née Buckley) at Cork on 3 June 1947. Educated at Christian Brothers College Cork. Separated with one son and two daughters. Formerly managing editor Radio News, duty editor TV News, news features editor and presenter, journalist RTE and journalist *Cork Examiner*. At present director of Radio Programming RTE. Member RTE Managers Association, NUJ.

MICHAEL J. KEANE
Editor
Burgh Quay, Dublin 2
(01) 713333
Born to Gerry and Kathy Keane (née Kealy) in Co. Kildare on 27 December 1946. Educated at Levitstown NS Co. Kildare, CBS Athy and College of Commerce Rathmines. Married to Jennifer Asquith with one daughter and two sons. Joined company as trainee journalist/copy boy 1965, reporter on all three titles, covered northern troubles, worked as Northern editor, and on assignments in US, Norway, Poland, Israel, Lebanon and Germany. Deputy editor/news editor *Sunday Press*, deputy chief news editor, Irish Press Group, assistant editor *Irish Press*, and Northern editor The Irish Press Group. At present editor *Sunday Press*.

DR IVOR KENNY
Professor and Author
94 St Stephen's Green, Dublin 2
(01) 774573
Born to T.J.W. and J.A. Kenny (née McGuinness) at Galway on 15 April 1930. Educated at St Ignatius College and UCG, at TCD, the Institut d'Études Politiques, Paris, the London School of Economics and Harvard Business School. Married to Maureen MacMahon with four sons and one daughter. Formerly director general Irish Management Institute, chancellor International Academy of Management, research professor of political economy at TCD and chairman/member of several government

commissions. At present chairman Smurfit Paribas Bank, Dublin Fine Meats Ltd, Odyssey plc and Typetec Ltd, director Independent Newspapers plc, vice president and Distinguished International professor of Public Policy, the International Management Centres and Senior Research Fellow UCD. Member of the board the Royal City of Dublin Hospital and of the Councils of the Irish Management Institute, Co-Operation North and the Financial Services Industry Association. Member Stephen's Green Club, Royal St George Yacht Club, Fitzwilliam Lawn Tennis Club, London Rowing Club and Garda Síochána Boat Club. Has been awarded a number of honorary doctorates and other international awards, and is a knight commander of the Order of St Gregory the Great. Author of five books including *Government and Enterprise in Ireland* and the best-selling *In Good Company* and *Out on Their Own*.

COLIN BARRY McCLELLAND
Journalist
Terenure, Dublin 6
(01) 901980
Born to William Thomas and Frances McClelland (née Fitzsimmons) at Belfast on 14 February 1944. Educated at Carrs Glen Primary School and Belfast Royal Academy. Married to Helen Ross with one son and one daughter. Formerly manager of 'Stiff Little Fingers', Belfast punk rock group who achieved worldwide fame in the late 1970s, chief sub-editor *Sunday News* Belfast, chief sub-editor and deputy editor *Sunday World* Dublin. At present editor and director *Sunday World*.

GERARD L. McGUINNESS
Newspaper Publisher
Terenure, Dublin 6
(01) 901980
Born to John Eiver and Eileen McGuinees (née Malloy) at Dublin on 1 May 1938. Educated at Presentation Convent Terenure, at Terenure College, and at the London School of Economics. Married first to Alma Carroll, and second to Deborah Wickins. Formerly cinema productions manager Associated British Cinemas, business manager, woman's manager and marketing director of Creation Group. At present chairman Sunday Newspapers, Nutley Investments and Newspread Ltd. and deputy chairman, Atlantic Resources plc. Launched in 1973, the *Sunday World*, which became Ireland's biggest selling paper in 1980. Member Castle, Ballina and Enniscrone Golf Clubs, and the K Club, Straffan, Co. Kildare.

PETER JOHN MONTELLIER
Journalist
124 Royal Avenue, Belfast BT1 1EB
(0232) 331133
Born to Norman and Maureen Anne Montellier (née Cleland) at Rome

on 21 August 1950. Educated at PS 49 New York City, Napa California, Rockport Preparatory School, Co. Down, Portora Royal School Enniskillen and Queen's University Belfast. Single. Formerly deputy chief sub-editor *Belfast Newsletter*, chief sub-editor, assistant editor, executive editor *The Irish News*. At present deputy editor *Sunday Life* Belfast.

CHRISTINA MURPHY

Journalist

D'Olier Street, Dublin 2

(01) 6792022

Born to Tom and Dora Murphy (née O'Malley) at Castlebar. Educated at Breaffy National School, Convent of Mercy, and University College Dublin. Married to Dermot Mullane with one son. Formerly editor *Young Citizen* magazine and women's editor and education correspondent, *The Irish Times*. At present duty editor of *The Irish Times*. Writer of educational advisory columns, and editor of the Working and Living section. Author of *School Report, The Guide to Irish Education*, and *Careers and Living, A Guide to Careers*. Winner of Benson and Hedges award for outstanding work in Irish journalism 1981.

FERGUS D. O'CALLAGHAN

Editor

95 Patrick Street, Cork

(021) 272722

Born to James and Augusta O'Callaghan (née McCarthy) at Cork on 27 September 1937. Educated at CBS Sullivan's Quay, Cork. Married with five children. At present editor *Cork Examiner*.

JAMES DESMOND O'DONNELL

Publisher

Vergemount Hall, Clonskeagh, Dublin 6

(01) 2697011

Born to James and Bridget O'Donnell (née Smyth) at Navan, on 16 October 1936. Educated at Mercy Convent National School, St Finian's College Mullingar, St Patrick's College Maynooth and at University College Galway. Married to Mary Costigan with three daughters. Formerly secondary teacher Garbally Park, Ballinasloe, and president CLÉ the Irish Book Publishers' Asociation. At present assistant director general Institute of Public Administration and director Irish Committee, European Cultural Foundation. Member Executive Committee CLÉ, and council member Public Relations Institute of Ireland. Originator of *Administration Yearbook and Diary*. Author of *How Ireland is Governed*, *Wordgloss*, *Our Lawmakers* and (with Seán de Fréine) *Ciste Cúrsaí Reatha*.

DR A.J.F. O'REILLY
Company Chairman
Lower Hatch Street, Dublin 2
(01) 717277

Born to John and Aileen O'Reilly (née O'Connor) at Dublin on 5 July, 1936. Educated at Belvedere College and UCD, University of Bradford Yorkshire and the Incorporated Law Society of Ireland. Married to Susan Cameron with three sons, Cameron, Gavin and Tony, and three daughters, Susan, Justine and Caroline. Married secondly to Chryss Goulandris. Formerly managing director of the Irish Dairy Board, also worked with the Irish Sugar Company. At present president, chairman and chief executive officer, H.J. Heinz Company, chairman Fitzwilton plc, chairman and controlling stock holder of Independent Newspapers, chairman Atlantic Resources, director Washington Post Company, member of Board of New York Stock Exchange and of the General Electric Company of United Kingdom, and partner in Dublin solicitors Cawley Sheerin Wynne. Chairman The American Ireland Fund, member Institute of Directors, fellow British Institute of Management, fellow Royal Society of the Arts, and council member Irish Management Institute, member Stephen's Green Club, Kildare Street and University Club. Honours include officer in the Order of Australia, life fellow Irish Management Institute, and honorary doctorates from TCD, UCD and Queen's University Belfast. Played rugby football for Ireland twenty-nine times and for the British Lions team ten times.

DESMOND RUSHE
Journalist
Irish Independent, Middle Abbey Street, Dublin 1
(01) 731666

Born to John and Mary Rushe (née Holmes) at Elphin on 12 September 1928. Educated at Summerhill College Sligo. Formerly with *The Roscommon Herald*, *Irish Independent* and contributor of regular column on arts in Ireland to *The New York Times*. At present columnist and theatre critic with *Irish Independent*. Publications include *Edmund Rice — His Life and Times*.

JOSEPH DESMOND SMYTH
Company Director
Havelock House, Ormeau Road, Belfast BT7 1EB
(0232) 328122

Born to Andrew and Annie Smyth (née Scott) at Limavady, Co. Londonderry on 20 April 1950. Educated at Dungiven Primary School, Limavady Grammar School and Queen's University Belfast. Qualified as a Chartered Accountant in 1974. Married to Irene Janette Dale with two children. Formerly with Coopers & Lybrand and financial controller/company secretary Ulster Television plc. At present managing director

Ulster Television plc and president Northern Ireland Chamber of Commerce and Industry. Member Institute of Directors and Royal Television Society.

JOHN SOROHAN
Broadcaster
Donnybrook, Dublin 4
(01) 643111

Born in Co. Leitrim in 1934. Educated in Mohill and at Kevin Street College of Technology. Married to Jenny Brady with three daughters and one son. Formerly with the Civil Service, Department of Posts and Telegraphs, RTE as head of Outside Broadcasts, assistant director general of RTE from 1985 responsible for doubling RTE's studio capacity, extending the regional studio network and developing a new Sound Stage that is among the most modern in the world. At present chairman of the RTE Authority since June 1990 for a five year term. Controlled the largest operations ever undertaken by RTE, the visit of Pope John Paul ll to Ireland, the visit of President Reagan and the 1980 Eurovision Song Contest. Worked on the Olympic Games in 1980 for the European Broadcasting Union in Moscow and in 1984 was a manager for the ABC Corporation in Los Angeles.

Chapter 17
Financial Services

This disposition to admire and almost to worship the rich and the powerful and to despise or to neglect persons of poor and mean condition is, at the same time, the great and most universal cause of the corruption of our model sentiments.

Adam Smith

There is said to have been a revloution in the financial services industry and, while revolution may be too strong a word for it, policies of deregulation and innovation have produced a stimulating excitement in the Republic, following the so called 'Big Bang' in the United Kingdom. Deregulation came about because the authorities realised that many old regulations were no longer beneficial. Old barriers and rigid structures were removed and competition, as a result, increased. The Irish financial sector is small in international terms, and it was burdened with a multiplicity of regulatory agencies. New building society legislation and new companies legislation helped relieve this situation. The process of reform has momentum, and should continue. Shannon was approved as a location for offshore banking services and an international financial services centre was established at the Custom House Docks in Dublin.

The Irish banks responded to consumerism by disbanding the cartel, by having fees displayed and freely available in brochure form in all branches, by adhering to a code for financial advertising, by being members of the deposit protection fund administered by the Central Bank, and by the establishment of a low-cost dispute resolution procedure through a Banking Ombudsman.

The effects of innovation have included the creation of many new products, some offered by old suppliers and some by new. The greater innovations are technology related. Some of these facilitate the rapid transfer of resources, the elimination of cash in many functions and increased liquidity. Sometimes changes in technology have been so great as to allow non-financial institutions enter the financial services market because of their communications capabilities. On stock exchanges the traditional trading floor will become obsolete as screen-based trading systems take over. The Stock Exchange Irish Unit is part of 'THE Stock Exchange', which embraces all the former independent stock exchanges in Britain and Ireland.

The Central Bank licenses and supervises the commercial banks, operates an exchange for the clearance of cheques, and ensures that the Republic's obligations under the European Monetary System are met. The EMS came into operation in March 1979 and two weeks later the system of parity between the Irish pound and the pound sterling was discontinued. Over forty banks are licensed under the terms of the Central Bank Act and, of these, four — AIB Bank, Bank of Ireland, National Irish Bank and Ulster Bank are the main clearing banks.

National Irish Bank trades in Northern Ireland as the Northern Bank. Both are subsidiaries of the National Bank of Australia. Ulster Bank is a subsidiary of National Westminster Bank, while both AIB and Bank of Ireland are independent public limited companies. All four operate Automatic Teller Machines, as do the Trustee Savings Banks. These 24–hour daily sources of cash are extremely popular, and are used also for access to information on cardholders' accounts, and for making certain payments. Both AIB Bank and Bank of Ireland each facilitate about 14 million ATM transactions annually.

Steps have been taken in the Republic to create a so called 'level playing field' for competition between the banks, building societies and other deposit takers. The impending Single European Market scheduled for 1993 implies the creation of such a playing field on a European scale, and Irish banks should not be expected to compete on a European playing field, if they are to be subjected to more onerous supervision and regulation than their European competitors. One of the complaints made by the banks is that the control exercised by the Central Bank over fees and charges results in a situation where the transmission service is unprofitable. Bank customers find this hard to believe as they are constantly complaining not only about the level of Irish bank charges but also about the rate at which they have been allowed to increase.

The negotiation by the Irish Government of a derogation from full competition for the non-life insurance industry, was designed to keep insurance costs down for industry. The derogation, which has no effect on motor or life insurance, is aimed specifically at very large liability industrial business. Besides, many foreign insurers had already established subsidiary companies in the Republic, and Lloyds are major underwriters. Ireland was one of four EC member states found guilty by the European Court of infringing insurance laws designed to liberalise trade in insurance within the community. The other countries were Denmark, France and Germany. Protecting the Irish insurers in this way seems strangely at odds with the speed at which established Irish manufacturing activities were exposed to competition from the beginning of EC membership in 1973.

Leading figures in the insurance industry admit that insurance costs in Ireland are substantially higher than in most other European countries. This is particularly true of motor insurance where many companies are reluctant to insure young drivers. On the other side of the coin, it is also generally accepted that the cost of claims in Ireland is substantially higher than other countries, that there are more accidents, that higher compensation is paid to victims, and that there is a very high level of uninsured driving. The products of the insurance industry are complex and policy holders frequently have difficulty in understanding the language of the policy. In 1974 the insurance companies established an Insurance Information and Complaints Service which provided its services free of charge, but was not seen to be independent. Early in 1991 the members of the Irish Insurance Federation agreed to establish an Ombudsman service.

Watching the developments in this area is the Irish Brokers' Association, formed by the merger of the Corporation of Insurance Brokers with the National Insurance and Investment Brokers. The main companies are the AIB Bank subsidiary, Ark, and Bank of Ireland subsidiary, Lifetime, together with French-owned New Ireland and Insurance Corporation of Ireland, and such internationally well known names as Abbey Life, Celtic Life, Eagle Star, Prudential, Norwich Union, Guardian Royal Exchange who purchased the new PMPA, Royal Life, Standard Life, and Sun Life. Hibernian and its subsidiary, Hibernian Life, are Irish companies quoted on the stock exchange together with Irish Life which obtained a stock exchange quotation when it was privatised in 1991.

Scottish Equity

Scotland, like Switzerland, is a low-profile source of inward foreign investment. NWS Bank, a subsidiary of Bank of Scotland, acquired Equity Bank Limited in June 1989. Pictured outside Equity Bank's Dublin headquarters in Ballsbridge (from right to left) Joseph P. Lyons (General Manager), John McGilligan (Chairman), John Brown (Director) NWS Bank plc.

NORBERT BANNON

Carrisbrook House, Pembroke Road, Dublin 4
(01) 604733
Educated at St Malachy's College Belfast and Queen's University Belfast. Qualified as a Chartered Accountant. Married with four children. Formerly with Hill Vellacott & Baily and worked in a variety of positions and locations with AIB Group including AIIB, the Merchant Banking subsidiary, AIB Brussels, AIB Singapore as general manager, and AIB New York as executive vice president. At present with AIB Venture Capital as managing director. Member Howth Golf Club, Howth Yacht Club and Fitzwilliam Lawn Tennis Club.

JAMES T. BARTON

Chairman
32/34 Harcourt Street, Dublin 2
(01) 720055
Born to Oswald and Eileen Barton (née Cooney) at Dublin in 1924. Educated at Glenstal Abbey, Co. Limerick. Married to Margaret Heywood-Jones with six sons, Bernard, Philip, John, Arthur, Richard and Patrick. At present chairman ICC plc, ICC Corporate Finance, ICC Finance, ICC Fund Management, Shipping Finance Corporation, and Boardroom Centre. Director Cranford Group. Member Royal Irish Yacht Club, fellow Institute of the Motor Industry and trustee Society of Irish Motor Industry.

JAMES EDWARD BOWEN

Chairman
Upper Leeson Street, Dublin 4
(01) 684688
Born to James F. and Eileen Bowen (née Flannery) in Co. Waterford on 26 June 1939. Educated at Christian Brothers College Cork. Married to Mary Whitelaw with two sons, Andrew and Simon, and one daughter, Jennifer. At present executive chairman BCP Asset Management and BCP Stockbrokers, director Premier International Trading House, Walls Trading House and Liazon Trading House. Member Portmarnock and Foxrock Golf Clubs, Royal St George Yacht Club, Carrickmines Lawn Tennis Club, Stephen's Green Club and Killarney Golf/Fishing Club.

PAUL AIDAN CARTY

Chief Executive
87 Merrion Square, Dublin 2
(01) 613061
Born to Patrick and Bridget Carty (née Dargan) at Dublin on 18 July 1935. Married to Bernadette Roche with three children. Formerly tours director Brendan Tours Ltd and national director National Insurance and Investment Brokers' Association. At present chief executive Irish Brokers' Association.

JOHN F. CASEY

Managing Director
11/12 Dawson Street, Dublin 2
(01) 717077

Born to John and Mary Casey (née Murray) at Cork on 1 October 1942. Educated at CBC Cork. Married to Audrey Dillon with one son and two daughters. Formerly managing director Beamish & Crawford (Sales) Ltd, director Beamish & Crawford plc, Rohan Group plc and president Cork Chamber of Commerce. At present managing director New Ireland Assurance Co plc, director New Ireland Holdings plc, Telecom Éireann, Cablelink Ltd, chairman New Ireland Financial Services Ltd and Etos International Ltd. Council member and fellow of the Institute of Chartered Accountants in Ireland and Marketing Institute of Ireland.

LIAM COUGHLAN

Banker
13/16 Fleet Street, Dublin 2
(01) 713311

Born to Thaddeus and Mary Coughlan (née Aherne) at Cork on 12 January 1937. Educated at Presentation Brothers College Cork. Married to Yvonne Kelly with three children. At present chief executive UDT/First Southern Group, chairman Irish Finance Houses Association, chairman TSB Overseas Bank (IOM) Ltd. Member Cork, Monkstown and Portmarnock Golf Clubs and Constitution Rugby Football Club.

RAYMOND MICHAEL CURRAN

Chief Executive
94 St Stephen's Green, Dublin 2
(01) 774573

Born to John James and Ellen Curran (née O'Connor) at Dublin on 13 May 1946. Educated at O'Connell's Schools. Married to Maria Luisa Gomez de Arcuello with two children. Formerly with Craig Gardner, and financial director Smurfit Investment and Financial Services Division. At present chief executive Smurfit Paribas Bank Ltd, director Smurfit Finance Ltd, MacDonald Boland Beech Hill Ltd and Woodfab Ltd. Member Royal Dublin Golf Club, Hibernian United Sevice Club, K Club, Riverview Racquet & Fitness Club and Malahide Tennis Club.

DERMOT FACHTNA DESMOND

Chairman
Ferry House, 48/53 Lower Mount Street, Dublin 2
(01) 614977

Born to Andrew and Sheila Desmond (née Twomey) at Cork on 14 August 1950. Educated at Marino NS and at Good Council College New Ross. Married to Patricia Brett with three sons and one daughter. Formerly worked in Citibank, all departments, IBI Lending executive, project leader for World Bank in Afghanistan and Coopers & Lybrand consultant. At present executive chairman/chief executive National City Brokers, which he formed in 1981, and chairman Irish Futures and Options Exchange (IFOX), director of R & J Emmet plc and Classic Thoroughbreds plc. Board member Michael Smurfit Graduate School of Business, chairman Financial Courseware and Quay Financial Software Systems. Member President's Development Council UCD and board member People in Need.

FREDERICK JOHN DINMORE

Managing Director
1 Adelaide Road, Dublin 2
(01) 751888
Born in London on 22 November 1937. Fellow Institute of Actuaries. Married with three children. Formerly assistant general manager Cornhill Insurance plc. At present managing director Ark Life Assurance Co Ltd.

PATRICK MICHAEL DOWLING

Banker
Bankcentre, Ballsbridge, Dublin 4
(01) 600311
Born to Nicholas and Elizabeth Dowling (née O'Brien) at Tralee, Co. Kerry on 24 September 1932. Educated at CBS Tralee. Fellow of the Institute of Bankers and holds diplomas in General Management, Accountancy and Economics. Married to Ann M. Smith with one daughter and three sons. Formerly general manager Banking Services and International Lending & Trade Services, and chief general manager AIB Finance and Leasing. At present director and deputy chief executive AIB Group, director Allied Combined Trust Ltd and National Concert Hall. Member Delgany Golf Club.

DR DERMOT EGAN

Banker
Ballsbridge, Dublin 4
(01) 600311
Born at Tullow, Co. Carlow on 26 May 1934. Educated at UCD and Columbia University New York and visiting scholar at University of Michigan. Married to Noreen Egan with four children. Formerly head of In-Company Management Development at the Irish Management Institute, and worked with Irish International Airlines for three years. At present deputy chief executive of AIB Group, director First Maryland Bankcorp, USA, vice chairman of Irish Management Institute and chairman Cothú Teoranta. Conferred with Doctor in Laws degree honoris causa by Trinity College Dublin in July 1991.

RONAN JOSEPH FEARON

Insurance Broker
Phoenix House, South Leinster Street, Dublin 2
(01) 616 211
Born to Patrick and Lucy Fearon (née Collier) at Dublin on 14 April 1937. Educated at Catholic University School and UCD. Later admitted fellow Chartered Institute of Management Accountants. Married to Kay McArdle with two sons, Ronan and Conor, and three daughters, Denise, Sandra and Alison. Formerly finance director Brunswick of Ireland, accountant Guinness Engineering Department, president Corporation of Insurance Brokers of Ireland. At present chairman and chief executive Coyle Hamilton Group Ltd. Member Fitzwilliam and Carrickmines Lawn Tennis Clubs, Hibernian United Service Club and Edmonstown Golf Club.

RONALD GRAHAM HEATHER

Insurance Broker
80 Harcourt Street, Dublin 2
(01) 783877
Born to George and Evelyn Heather (née Graham) at Dublin on 9 August 1934. Educated at The High School Dublin. Fellow of the Chartered Insurance Institute. Married to Meriel Fox with three sons, Jonathan, Colin and Alan, and two daughters, Hilary and Lynda. At present chairman/managing director Willis Wrightson (Ireland) Ltd, director Willis Wrightson Management (Dublin) Ltd and Hinton & Higgs Ireland Ltd. Member Hibernian United Service Club, Milltown, Portmarnock and Rathfarnham Golf Clubs, Royal Irish Yacht Club, The Strollers, governor The High School and Mercers Hospital Foundation.

JIM HEGARTY

Insurance Broker
Kildress House, Pembroke Row, Dublin 2
(01) 760357
Born to John Joseph and Elizabeth Hegarty (née Allen) at Cork on 9 August 1950. Educated at Togher NS and at Farranferris College Cork. Married to Maura Beirne with two children. Formerly president National Insurance Brokers' Association. At present director Barrett Hegarty Moloney Ltd Insurance & Pension Brokers, Barrett Hegarty Moloney Mortgage and Finance Brokers Ltd and Seán Barrett Bloodstock Insurances Ltd. Fellow Life Insurance Association and National Insurance Brokers' Association. Editor *Irish Broker Magazine*. Member Grange Golf Club, Civil Service and St Finbarr's Gaelic Football Clubs.

DANIEL THOMAS HICKEY

Venture Capitalist
32/34 Harcourt Street, Dublin 2
(01) 720055
Born to Patrick and Geraldine Hickey (née Walsh) at Dublin on 10 Aug-

ust 1953. Educated at St Mary's College Rathmines, TCD and Chartered Institute of Management Accountants. Married to Valerie Anna-Maria Tyrrell with one child. At present head of Industrial Credit Corporation Equities Division and director Solar Enterprises Ltd, Largo Food (Exports) Ltd, L & P Financial Trustees of Ireland Ltd and of Marine Computation Services Ltd. Member Fitzwilliam and Lansdowne Lawn Tennis Clubs, Business Discussion Group, and chairman Irish Venture Capital Association.

MARK HELY HUTCHINSON
Company Director and Consultant
Larch Hill, Coolock Lane, Dublin 17
(01) 428718
Born to 7th Earl and Countess of Donoughmore at London in 1934. Educated at Eton College and Magdalen College Oxford and at Massachusetts Institute of Technology. Married to Margaret Woods with two sons and one daughter. Fromerly managing director Guinness Ireland Ltd, chairman Irish Management Institute, chairman National Enterprise Agency and chief executive Bank of Ireland. At present director BHP Group Ltd, chairman New City Initiative Ltd and director Dublin Inner City Partnership. Member Turf Club, Irish National Steeplechase Committee and Fitzwilliam Lawn Tennis Club.

HOWARD EDWARD KILROY
Accountant
Beech Hill, Clonskeagh, Dublin 4
(01) 2696622
Born to Percy and Kathleen Kilroy (née Howard) at Dublin on 30 January 1936. Educated at The High School. Married to Meriel McCullagh with five children. Formerly with J.A. Kinnear & Co, Chartered Accountants, CPC Ireland, CPC UK and CPC Europe (Brussels). At present president and chief operations director Jefferson Smurfit Group plc and governor Bank of Ireland Group. Director MacDonagh & Boland Ltd, Aran Energy plc, and president Irish Management Institute.

T. DAVID KINGSTON
Assurance Executive
Lower Abbey Street, Dublin 1
(01) 7042000
Born in 1943. Educated at Portora Royal School Enniskillen and Oxford University. Graduated with MA degree. Admitted FFA. Married to Georgina Ashmore with two daughters. Formerly with Scottish Widows' fund in Scotland. Also held a number of management posts in investments, group pensions, life assurances, marketing and sales departments Irish Life. At present managing director Irish Life Assurance plc and director Church and General Insurance plc, Irish Continental Bank, and

Irish Life Building Society. Publications include *Measuring Investment Performances* and *The Effect of Inflation on Pension Schemes and their Funding*.

JOSEPH PATRICK LYONS

Banker
85 Pembroke Road, Ballsbridge, Dublin 4
(01) 685199
Born to Ignatius and Anne Lyons (née O'Neill) at Dublin on 19 March 1953. Educated at Belgrove NS, St Paul's College Raheny and Institute of Chartered Accountants. Married to Sheila Godfrey with two daughters. Formerly manager Bank of Ireland Corporate Banking and senior lending executive Industrial Credit Corporation. At present general manager Equity Bank Ltd. Fellow of Institute of Chartered Accountants in Ireland.

DÓNAL S. McALEESE

Banker
91 Merrion Square, Dublin 2
(01) 764611
Born to Daniel and Catherine McAleese (née Nolan) at Dublin on 29 August 1926. Educated at CBS Glasnevin, Belvedere College and UCD. Married to Elizabeth McCann with five children. Formerly general manager Irish Life and chief executive Dublin Gas Company. Past president Federation Irish Employers. At present chairman Irish Intercontinental Bank. Member Hibernian United Service Club, Portmarnock, Royal &Ancient and Connemara Golf Clubs.

PEADAR MacCANNA

Managing Director
Hume House, Ballsbridge, Dublin 4
(01) 689777
Born to Leo and Kathleen MacCanna (née O'Kelly) at Dublin on 3 June 1935. Educated at St Patrick's Drumcondra, Coláiste Mhuire, UCD and North Carolina State University. Married with four children. Formerly agricultural adviser Meath, Sligo and Cork, project director World Bank, chief agricultural adviser Bank of Ireland and head of retail marketing Bank of Ireland. At present managing director Bank of Ireland Commercial Finance, Bank of Ireland Export Services Ltd and International Factors (Ireland) Ltd, director Bank of Ireland Finance Ltd and B I Commercial Finance Ltd (UK). Chairman Bank of Ireland GAA Allstars and director Fonnduireach Chlann Lir and member International Association of Business Communicators. Member Binn Eadair GAA Club, Howth Golf Club, Sutton Lawn Tennis Club and Agricultural Science Association. Former president Irish Grassland Association and Agricultural Economics Association.

JOHN DAVID McCARTHY

General Manager and Actuary
60/63 Dawson Street, Dublin 2
(01) 717220
Born to Joseph and Lilian McCarthy (née Maddy) in London on 15 August 1948. Educated at Ayloff Primary School Essex, Royal Liberty Grammar Essex and Southampton University. Fellow of Institute of Actuaries. Married to Mary Elizabeth Cassin with five children. Formerly pensions marketing manager Irish Life Assurance plc, Dublin, and technical services manager Irish Life London. At present general manager and actuary for the Republic of Ireland, Norwich Union Life Insurance Society and vice president Irish Insurance Federation. Member Society of Actuaries in Ireland and Institute of Actuaries, Lahinch and County Louth Golf Clubs.

GERARD W. McCOY

Investment Broker
Clyde House, 15 Clyde Road, Dublin 4
(01) 681499
Born to Noel and Joyce McCoy (née Neary) at Dublin on 20 October 1961. Educated at De La Salle Preparatory School, De La Salle College Churchtown and Rathmines College of Commerce. Single. Formerly sales and marketing director Taylor Investment Group. At present group managing director Taylor Investment Group and director Micropal (Irl). Member Old Wesley RFC and Friarsland Leisure Club. Associate of the Marketing Institute of Ireland.

GERALD C.J. McCRACKEN

Chartered Accountant
88 Lower Leeson Street, Dublin 2
(01) 613499
Born to William and Catherine McCracken (née Blanche) at Dublin on 8 June 1938. Educated at St Andrew's College Dublin and the Institute of Chartered Accountants in Ireland. Married to Ann Bentley with two children. Formerly executive director and secretary Guinness & Mahon Bankers, and president Institute of Bankers in Ireland. At present secretary general Irish Pension Fund Property Unit Trust, and fellow of the Institute of Bankers in Ireland. Member Kildare Street and University Club, Rathfarnham Golf Club and Donnybrook Lawn Tennis Club.

DAVID McCROSSAN

Managing Director
IFSC, Dublin 1
(01) 740222
Born to John and Maureen McCrossan (née Cosgrave) at Dublin on 11 September 1941. Educated at Dundrum NS and De La Salle College

Churchtown. Qualified as a Chartered Accountant. Married to Noreen McGettrick with two daughters. Formerly finance specialist with Stokes Kennedy Crowley Dublin. At present managing director AIB Corporate Finance Ltd.

EAMON F. McELROY
Managing Director
4 Queen's Square, Belfast BT1 3DJ
(0232) 325599
Born to Joseph and Anna-May McElroy (née McEntee) at Belfast on 14 July 1943. Educated at De La Salle Brothers and St Malachy's College, Belfast. Married to Una Adams with one son, Joseph. Formerly manager, regional manager, retail services and general manager, Branch Banking Ireland with AIB plc. At present managing director AIB Group Northern Ireland and director Leisure Holdings plc. Member Portmarnock and Belvoir Park Golf Clubs.

JOHN McGILLIGAN
Banker
Heritage House, 23 St Stephen's Green, Dublin 2
(01) 7663333
Born to Patrick and Ann McGilligan (née Conolly) at Dublin on 24 March 1939. Educated at St Michael's, Belvedere College, UCD and University of California, Los Angeles. Married to Grace O'Driscoll with one daughter, Tanya. Formerly planning executive Aer Lingus, head of management services RTE and joint managing director Trinity Bank Ltd. At present chairman Equity Bank Ltd, managing director Business and Trading House Investment Company Ltd, director Bula Resources plc, Irish American Partnership Ltd and representative in Ireland of Brown Shipley & Co Ltd. Member Portmarnock and Milltown Golf Clubs, Royal Irish Yacht Club, UCD Rugby Club and Glenageary Tennis Club.

KEVIN McGUINNESS
Banker
23 St Stephen's Green, Dublin 2
(01) 766333
Born at Dublin on 2 June 1930. Educated at O'Connell Schools and Dublin University. Married with five children. Formerly held managerial positions in Industrial Credit Corporation and Foir Teo. Managing director of Foir Teo until he retired in April 1991. At present secretary the Irish Building Societies' Association, and financial consultant.

CRAIG McKINNEY
Managing Director
Christchurch Square, Dublin 8
(01) 535570
Born in Scotland on 9 September 1948. Educated at Coatbridge

Secondary School, Lanarkshire. Divorced with two daughters. Formerly sales manager Hamilton Leasing Ltd, Scottish regional manager Hamilton Leasing Ltd UK, managing director Hamilton Leasing (Ireland) Ltd, and managing director Woodchester Investments Ltd. At present chairman and managing director Woodchester Investments plc. Member All Ireland Polo Club Dublin and Joint Master of the South County Hunt and of the Kildare Hunt.

JOHN JOSEPH McNALLY
Bank Director
33 College Green, Dublin 2
(01) 777623
Born to William and Peggy McNally (née Kehoe) at Naas on 1 January 1947. Educated at Clongowes Wood College and UCD. Widower with one son, Hugh, and two daughters, Sandra and Jennifer. Formerly held various positions with the Ulster Bank Group, also chairman of business development committee Dublin Chamber of Commerce. At present director Ulster Bank Ltd and associated companies. Member Hibernian United Service Club, Dún Laoghaire Golf and Royal Irish Yacht Clubs.

BRIAN P. MATHEWS
Executive Chairman
10 South Leinster Street, Dublin 2
(01) 717151
Born to John G. and Nora Mathews (née McHenry) at Dublin on 28 November 1927. Educated at Catholic University School Dublin. Married to Clare Carton with four sons and three daughters. Formerly with London and Lancashire Insurance Co and held a number of positions with Mathews Mulcahy and Sutherland Ltd including director and chief executive. President Corporation of Insurance Brokers of Ireland and of US Chamber of Commerce in Ireland. At present executive chairman Mathews Mulcahy and Sutherland Ltd, managing director Marsh and McLennan Inc. New York, director Bowring UK Ltd London, and director Gypsum Industries plc. Member Stephen's Green Club, Milltown Golf Club, Fitzwilliam Lawn Tennis Club and Royal Irish Yacht Club.

MICHAEL J. MEAGHER
Banker
Lower Baggot Street, Dublin 2
(01) 615933
Born to Michael and Kathleen Meagher (née Murphy) at Templemore, Co. Tipperary on 12 May 1942. Educated at CBS Templemore, UCD and Graduate School of Business, University of Chicago. Married to Pauline Finney with one daughter, Karen. Formerly Head of Corporate Banking, Citibank Dublin, and chief executive Ulster Bank, Dublin. At present executive director of Bank of Ireland, director various Bank of Ireland Group companies and director Development Capital Corporation Ltd.

Member Fitzwilliam Lawn Tennis Club, Portmarnock, Mount Juliet and Blainroe Golf Clubs.

PATRICK JAMES MOLLOY
Banker
Lower Baggot Street, Dublin 2
(01) 615933
Born at Galway on 4 January 1938. Educated at St Joseph's College Ballinasloe, TCD and Harvard University. Married to Ann Lynch with three sons and two daughters. Formerly general manager, Area East, Bank of Ireland, and managing director Retail Division, Bank of Ireland. At present group chief executive Bank of Ireland.

AUGUSTINE GERARD MURPHY
Banker
18/21 St Stephen's Green, Dublin 2
(01) 760141
Born to George and Ellen Murphy (née Colligan) at Dublin on 19 May 1933. Educated at O'Connell Schools, N. Richmond Street, Dublin. Admitted as member Institute of Chartered Accountants in Ireland. Married to Mary Reynolds with two daughters, Anne Marie and Jane. Formerly managing director City of Dublin Bank plc and Anglo Irish Bank Corporation plc, and president European Finance Houses' Association. At present chairman Anglo Irish Bank Corporation plc, and vice president Irish Bankers' Federation. Member Hibernian United Service Club and Howth Yacht Club. Says that today's jobs can be done today.

THOMAS ROBERT (ROY) NEILL
Insurance Broker
Bedford Street, Belfast BT2 7DX
(0232) 243681
Born to William and Margaret Neill (née Chestnutt) at Belfast on 21 September 1935. Educated at Antrim Road PE School and Royal Belfast Academical Institution. Married to Margaret Watters with two sons. Formerly fire superintendent with Norwich Union Insurance Co, director of various Bowring subsidiaries in UK, president Belfast Insurance Institute, and president Northern Ireland Chamber of Commerce and Industry. At present executive director Bowring Marsh & McLennan Ltd, chairman Bowring Marsh & McLennan (IOM) Ltd and Ulster Insurance Services Ltd, and regional director Bowring Financial Services Ltd. Fellow Chartered Insurance Institute and British Institute of Management and member Northern Ireland Partnership, Industrial Court of Northern Ireland and Northern Ireland Chamber of Commerce and Industry. Member Royal Belfast and Helen's Bay Golf Club.

TOMÁS Ó COFAIGH
Institute President
4 Burlington Park, Dublin 4
(01) 760115
Born to James and Sarah Ó Cofaigh at Dublin on 7 October 1921. Educated at St Canice's CBS and O'Connell CBS, Dublin and later at TCD. Married to Joan Kinsella with three sons and one daughter. Formerly governor Central Bank of Ireland, secretary Dept of Finance, alternate governor for Ireland at International Monetary Fund and World Bank, member committee of Governors of the Central Banks of the EC and board of governors European Monetary Co-operation Fund and chairman Government Representative Group, Irish Financial Services Centre. At present director Irish Life plc, and president and member executive committee and council Economic and Social Research Institute of Ireland and member Institute of European Affairs. Member Royal Society of Antiquaries of Ireland, Old Dublin Society, Royal Dublin Society and Royal Zoological Society. Awarded LL.D by NUI. Peace Commissioner.

GERALD ANTHONY O'MAHONY
General Manager
IFSC, Dublin 1
(01) 740222
Born to Gerald and Elizabeth O'Mahony (née McGuinness) at Mullingar on 11 May 1933. Educated at CBS Tramore, Waterpark College Waterford and Harvard Business School. Married to Berna Mehigan with two sons and one daughter. Formerly general manager Britain and general manager South East AIB Bank. At present general manager international, chairman Grofund Currency Fund Ltd, director AIB Capital Markets plc and AIB International Consultants Ltd. Member Killiney Golf Club, Lansdowne Football Club and Hibernian United Service Club and Knight of the Equestrian Order of the Holy Sepulchre (KHS).

PATRICK O'REILLY
Chief Executive
30 Westmoreland Street, Dublin
(01) 775599
Born to Terence and Maureen O'Reilly (née Smith) at Cavan on 13 September 1941. Educated at Tullyvin NS, St Patrick's College Cavan and UCD. Married with four children. Formerly with Ulster Bank, company secretary Irish Merchants Ltd, and general manager, banking, ICC. At present chief executive EBS. Member Castle Golf Club.

FRANCIS BERNARD O'ROURKE
Building Society Chairman
Lower Baggot Street, Dublin 2
(01) 770983
Born to Frank and Teresa O'Rourke (née McGriskin) at New York on 7

August 1931. Educated at National School and St Patrick's College Cavan and Harvard Business School. Married to Rose Browne with five children. Formerly deputy chief executive Bank of Ireland Group, director Lifetime Assurance Co Ltd and of First NH Banks, New Hampshire, USA, and president Institute of Bankers in Ireland. At present chairman ICS Building Society and director National Concert Hall.

PETER BRODERICK PEARSON
Stockbroker
74 South Mall, Cork
(021) 270647
Born to Charles Broderick and Mary Eileen Pearson (née Morrogh) at Cork on 9 March 1924. Educated at Miss Scannell's Private School, St Angela's School and CBC Cork, St John's Beaumont and Beaumont College Old Windsor, Berkshire. Married to Mary Bernadette Roche with six sons, Mark, David, Jeremy, Roger, Peter and Christopher, and five daughters, Rosemary, Jennifer, Fiona, Ruth and Daphne. Formerly president Cork Stock Exchange, vice president Irish Association of Sovereign Military Hospitaller Order of Malta. At present partner W. and R. Morrogh, president Irish Association of Sovereign Hospitaller Order of Malta, member and former chairman Cork & County Club, member and former trustee St Michael's Lawn Tennis Club, member An Taisce and Cork Preservation Society. Knight Grand Cross of Obedience, Order of Malta.

DR WILLIAM GEORGE HENRY QUIGLEY
Banker
47 Donegall Place, Belfast BT1 5AU
(0232) 320222
Born to W.G.C. and Sarah Hanson Quigley (née Martin) in Co Londonderry on 26 November 1929. Educated at Maghera PE School, Ballymena Academy and Queen's University Belfast. Married to Moyra Alice Munn. At present chairman Ulster Bank Ltd, director National Westminster Bank plc, Short Brothers plc, member of Fair Employment Commission for NI, chairman Institute of Directors (NI division), member Executive Committee Economic and Social Research Institute of Dublin, member Management Committee NI Economic Research Institute, member Board of Co-operation North and of Irish-American Partnership.

MICHAEL QUINN
Banker
32/34 Harcourt Street, Dublin 2
(01) 720055
Born to Charles and Kathleen Quinn (née McCormack) at Mullingar on 26 November 1946. Educated at St Mary's CBS Mullingar and UCD. Admitted to Chartered Institute of Management Accountants. Formerly assistant general manager ICC and regional manager ICC Cork. At present chief executive ICC plc. Member Grange Golf Club.

SÉAMUS QUINN
Managing Director
Main Street, Longford
(043) 45280
Born to Liam and Mary Ellen Quinn (née Clarke) at Ballina on 21 May 1936. Educated at Garracloon NS Ballina and at Patrician College, Ballyfinn. Married to Maura Healy (separated) with one son and two daughters. Formerly held a number of senior positions with Ulster Bank before becoming general manager Midland and Western Building Society in 1983. At present managing director Midland and Western Building Society. Member Hermitage Golf Club and Royal Irish Automobile Club.

JAMES J. RUANE
Managing Director
Lower Baggot Street, Dublin 2
(01) 761888
Born to James B. and Linda Ruane (née Gordan) at Dublin on 26 September 1944. Educated at Athenry NS, Belgrove NS, Franciscan College Gormanston, UCD whence he graduated with MAgrSc degree, and Pennsylvania State University, USA (PhD). Married to Frances Virzi with two sons, James and John. Formerly managing director Bank of Ireland Finance, ICS Building Society, general manager Dublin, First National Bank of Chicago, senior consultant Stokes Kennedy Crowley, and economist John Deere and Co, Moline, USA. At present managing director Bank of Ireland Corporate Banking, director Royal Victoria Eye and Ear Hospital and director Foundation for Fiscal Studies. Member Hibernian United Service Club, Fitzwilliam and Donnybrook Lawn Tennis Clubs.

GERALD B. SCANLAN
Banker
Bankcentre, Ballsbridge, Dublin 4
(01)600311
Educated at CBS Carlow, Newbridge College Co. Kildare, and at Harvard Business School. Married with three children. Formerly held various positions within AIB Group. At present deputy chairman and group chief executive AIB Group and director First Maryland Bancorp.

ALEX SPAIN
Business Manager
46 Upper Mount Street, Dublin 2
(01) 762002
Born at Dublin on 1 October 1932. Educated at Blackrock College and UCD, whence he graduated with BComm degree. Admitted to fellowship of Institute of Chartered Accountants in Ireland and to Chartered Institute of Management Accountants. Married to Maureen Murphy with four sons, Alex, John, Brian and Justin, and two daughters, Catherine and Elizabeth. Formerly managing partner Stokes Kennedy Crowley,

president Institute of Chartered Accountants in Ireland and chairman Financial Services Industry Association. At present director National Irish Bank and Murray Group Holdings, chairman Prudential Life of Ireland Ltd, Development Capital Corporation Ltd and B and I Line plc.

ANTHONY TAYLOR
Investment Broker
15 Clyde Road, Ballsbridge, Dublin 4
(01) 681499
Born to Thomas and Bernadette Taylor (née Duffy) at Dublin on 14 May 1947. Educated at St Mary's College Rathmines, Rockwell College Cashel and UCD. Married to Shirley O'Brien with two sons. Formerly insurance broker. At present executive chairman Taylor Investment Group.

SAMUEL HENRY TORRENS
Director and Chief Executive
Donegall Square West, Belfast BT1 6JS
(0232) 245277
Born to William and Mary Isobel Torrens (née Taylor) at Coleraine on 24 August 1934. Educated at Model School Coleraine and Coleraine Academical Institution. Married to Marjorie Ann Gillespie with four children. Formerly regional director Home Counties Midland Bank plc, and deputy chief executive and general manager (Administration) Northern Bank Ltd. At present director and chief executive Northern Bank, and director National Australia Group (UK) Ltd. Council member Royal Ulster Agricultural Society, member Ulster Reform Club and Greenisland Golf Club, governor Coleraine Academical Institution, president Institute of Bankers in Ireland and fellow Institute of Bankers in Ireland (FIB).

KENNETH ROBERT PATRICK WALL
Industrial Banker
54/57 Lower Mount Street, Dublin 2
(01) 615288
Born to Thomas Samuel and Sarah Frances Wall (née Devlin) on 1 January 1929. Educated at CBS Synge Street. Awarded diploma in Social & Economic Studies. Fellow Bankers Institute in Ireland. Married to Nuala Quinlan with two sons and two daughters. Formerly with Irish Shell and American Express. Retired March 1989 chief executive Lombard & Ulster Banking, April 1990 director Ulster Bank. At present chairman Ulster Bank Commercial Services and Software Professionals (Irl), director Clonmel Chemicals and Bizquip Ltd, member Royal Irish Automobile, Fitzwilliam Lawn Tennis and Milltown Golf Clubs, and St Mary's RFC.

DR NOEL WHELAN
Professor
Plassey, Limerick
(061) 333644
Born at Cork on 28 December 1940. Educated at Buttevant NS, Sacred

Heart College Buttevant and at UCD. Married to Joan Gaughan with two sons and two daughters. Formerly executive officer Civil Service, senior administrative officer and head of Research Evaluation An Foras Talúntais (The Agricultural Institute), manager (Research and Development) then assistant general manager CIE, deputy secretary Department of Finance and of the Public Service, secretary Department of the Taoiseach, and vice chairman board of directors, European Investment Bank. At present vice president and dean of College of Business, University of Limerick, honorary vice president European Investment Bank, and Government appointed chairman Sectoral Development Committee.

DAVID WENT
Banker
47 Donegall Place, Belfast
(084) 320222
Born to Arthur E.J. and Phyllis Went (née Howell) at Dublin on 25 March 1947. Educated at Kingstown School, High School, TCD and King's Inns Dublin. Married to Mary Milligan with one son and one daughter. Formerly general manager Citibank Jeddah, and Citibank Dublin, director and chief executive Ulster Investment Bank, and deputy chief executive Ulster Bank. At present chief executive Ulster Bank. Member Kildare Street and University Club, Royal Belfast Golf Club and Royal North of Ireland Yacht Club.

WYNDHAM WILLIAMS
Banker
Bankcentre, Dublin 4
(01) 600311
Born to William and Maureen Williams at Cork on 1 June 1940. Educated at CBC Cork, TCD and New York University. Married to Cecily Butler with six children. Formerly North American representative, senior lending manager and senior vice president International Corporate Banking with AIB. At present chief manager with AIB. Member Royal Dublin Golf Club and Fitzwilliam Lawn Tennis Club.

GEORGE DAVID WOODS
Chief Executive
121 St Stephen's Green, Dublin 2
(01) 717333
Born to George and Sheila Woods (née Crisp) at Dublin on 28 September 1955. Educated at Sandford NS, High School Dublin and Harvard University. Married to Petronella Anna Hoolwerf with one son and one daughter. Formerly credit analyst with American National Bank of Chicago in London, credit analyst and assistant manager loans at RBC Finance BV at Amsterdam, and also held various senior marketing positions with Orion Royal Bank in London, including director Eurocommercial Paper and head of marketing, sales and training. At present chief executive Algemene Bank Nederland (Ireland) Ltd.

Chapter 18
Sport and Recreation

For when the One Great Scorer comes
To write against your name,
He marks — not that you won or lost —
But how you played the game.

Grantland Rice

Diversity
The major sports are:

* Gaelic football for men and women.
* Hurling for men and the female version known as camogie.
* Soccer for both men and women.
* Rugby organised by the Irish Rugby Football Union.
* Track and field athletics organised by BLE, the Irish Athletics Board.
* Equestrian sports, including leisure riding, hunting, pony trekking, show jumping and, above all, horse racing which is hugely popular throughout the island, and
* Golf, a highly popular participator sport for both men and women.

While this list gives some idea of the extent and diversity of Irish sporting life, it should be noted that it is only a selection, and there remain cricket, shooting, angling, boxing, wrestling, badminton, wind surfing, and many others.

Visitors are often amazed to learn that, on a per capita basis, Ireland has more golf courses than any other country in the world and the number is growing as farmers convert farms or parts of farms to more courses. The sport is hugely popular with over 30 clubs having 800 to 1,000 members and 23 clubs having 1,000 members or more. There are a total of 275 clubs affiliated to the governing body, the Golfing Union of Ireland. A small number of clubs charge visitors' green fees of £20 or more for a day's play on a summer weekend, and 4 clubs charge £40 or more. On the other hand, there are still a number of clubs where a game of golf can be enjoyed for £5 or less. For spectators, the Carroll's

Irish Open is a leading event on the international professional golf circuit. The number of horse-racing tracks is also very high, with 26 on the island for a population of 5 million compared with 59 on the neighbouring island for a population of 55 million.

Soccer in recent years has enjoyed an increase of over 40 per cent in the number of players, of whom there are now over 125,000 in over 3,200 clubs in the Republic. The governing body is the Football Association of Ireland which has been enjoying improved performances on the financial front, supported undoubtedly by the continuing success of the international team. FAI also enjoys the sponsorship of some key supporters such as Opel, Addidas, Harp Lager and Mars.

The pity about sport is that people cannot simply get on with it. Like so many other areas of Irish life, politics, religion and the law inevitably tend to raise their ugly heads.

Or not raise his head, in the case of the Taoiseach Mr Charles J. Haughey. It seems that Mr Haughey's view of sport is a narrow one. He rarely misses a hurling or gaelic football all–Ireland final. He has attended an Ireland-Australia compromise Rules Match, and has rushed to Paris to share the limelight of Stephen Roche's win in the Tour de France. However, he has prior engagements when it comes to supporting Irish teams in rugby and soccer internationals. It is certainly to be hoped that this does not reveal any narrowness in his view of Irishness, given that Irish rugby is organised on a thirty-two-county basis, and while that unfortunately cannot be said of soccer, this game was played internationally by no less a figure than the former Tánaiste and Minister for Foreign Affairs, Brian Lenihan. The last Taoiseach to attend an international soccer match during his term of office was the late Éamon de Valera.

The premier sporting organisation in the island is the Gaelic Athletic Association which repealed its ban on 'foreign' games about twenty years ago. It still refuses to make Croke Park available for soccer because of 'ideological differences' with the Football Association of Ireland — differences which are said to have continued for over sixty years. It is high time to forget past differences and emphasise common interests and common problems. All major sporting organisations share common problems, in particular public liability, safety, hygiene, and crowd control.

Hands-On Football
Gaelic football is one of the most popular sports in Ireland. Here Brian
O'Hagan of Dublin makes a determined effort to break away from Colm
O'Rourke of Meath.

In other spheres of Irish life contemporary presidents of organisations inevitably come to know each other quite well, if only because they attend the same dinners and the same festivities! The president of the chartered accountants would inevitably know the president of the certified accountants and of the management accountants, as well as the president of the solicitors and of the bankers. Yet, early in 1988 the President of the Rugby Union, Paddy Madigan, admitted that he would not recognise Dr Michael Loftus, the GAA President, if he met him in the street simply because they had never encountered one another. He added that this situation was 'a sad commentary on life in Ireland in 1988', and all would agree that this lack of ecumenism should soon pass away.

State Aid

The Republic has a Minister of State with responsibility for youth and sport, and State financial support for sport and recreation including the Olympic Council of Ireland, has been increasing.

In addition to the GAA, other organisations have been supported with funds from the National Lottery. For example, ten organisations were supported with a view to enabling them to employ full-time personnel to develop their sports. The ten in question were:

* Irish Women's Squash Racquets Association
* Irish Amateur Swimming Association
* Federation of Irish Cyclists
* Irish Judo Association
* Irish Basketball Asociation
* Irish Yachting Association
* Irish Amateur Gymnastics' Association
* Irish Special Olympics
* Irish Lawn Tennis Association
* The Irish Mini-Sport Movement

The Community Games Movement, a thirty-two-county organisation, has twenty-three years of experience in motivating people, and because of changing lifestyle, providing sport and recreation facilities for their children may not always be on top of the list of priorities of parents, especially if their disposable income is stretched to provide essentials. Community Games Movement provides activities which encourage and allow family participation. It has introduced countless young people to sport and to culture. It provides an antidote to violence, delinquency and vandalism behind the motto 'A healthy mind in a healthy body'. For the Movement, the emphasis is on sportsmanship, with participation more important than victory.

Visitors, who appreciate that Gaelic football is a fairly robust 'physical' game, may be surprised to find it played by women too. This was, of course, foreseen by Oscar Wilde, who said: 'I feel that football is all very well as a game for rough girls, but it is hardly suitable for delicate boys.'

Hurling — The Clash of the Ash
Michael O'Sullivan of Laois reached highest to get the hurling ball, known as the *sliotar*, during a match with Wexford. Challenging him were (left to right) John Bohane, Laois, Billy Byrne, Wexford, Andy Dunne, Laois, O'Sullivan, John O'Connor, Wexford, and Tom Dempsey, Wexford.

NOEL CARROLL
Public Relations Officer
City Hall, Dublin 2
(01) 6796111
Born to Patrick and Bridget Carroll at Annagassan, Co. Louth on 7 December 1941. Educated at Villanova University, PA, whence he graduated with an honours BSc degree. Married to Deirdre O'Callaghan with two sons and two daughters. Formerly with IBM (Ireland) Ltd and Eastern Regional Tourism Organisation. Member Sports Council. At present public relations officer to Dublin Corporation, co-founder Dublin City Marathon, member Business Houses' Athletic Association, and patron of GOAL, a third world relief agency. Author of *Sports in Ireland* and *The Runners' Book*. Represented Ireland in two Olympic Games, 1964 (Tokyo) and 1968 (Mexico). Was Irish record-holder 800 metres and 880 yards and many times Irish champion at 440 yards and 880 yards. Also formerly European indoor and British AAA Champion, and world record-holder for veterans (over 40) 800 metres.

FRED COGLEY
Sports Broadcaster
Donnybrook, Dublin 4
(01) 643111
Born to Mitchel and Muriel Cogley (née Costigan) at Dublin on 27 June 1934. Educated at St Mary's College Rathmines. Married to Madeleine White with two sons and two daughters. Formerly sports sub-editor *The Irish Times*, sports columnist *Evening Herald*, sports organiser RTE and Irish sports correspondent *Sunday Telegraph*. At present head of sport RTE, chairman Libra House Publishers and member of Advisory Board Ansvar Insurance Co. Member Grange Golf Club, Golf Societies — Dublin Journalists and RTE, Pioneer Total Abstinence Association, Rugby Writers of Ireland and English Rugby Writers.

JOSEPH CONNOLLY
22 Store Street, Dublin 1
(01) 788095
Born to John and Esther Connolly (née McNally) at Dublin on 11 March 1922. Studied work study and human relations in modern industry. Married to Josephine Brunton with three sons, Brendan, Leonard and Joseph, and one daughter, Joyce. Formerly clerical officer, work study officer and executive officer with CIE. At present founder and general secretary of Community Games, general secretary Walkinstown Sport and Athletic Federation, chairman Federation of Irish Sport Bodies; member Cospóir; trustee Walkinstown Association for Handicapped. Recipient of People of the Year Award. Peace Commissioner, Councillor, member of Dublin Corporation, Eastern Health Board and Irish Lights Board.

Irish Open Golf Championship
The 1988 winner, Ian Woosnam, is seen here with his caddy leaving the seventeenth green at Portmarnock.

IVAN EDWARD ROBERT DICKSON

General Secretary
81 Eglinton Road, Dublin 4
(01) 2694111
Born to Cecil Robert and Eva Constance Dickson (née Maguire) at Dublin on 14 December 1928. Educated at St Andrew's College, Clyde Road. Married to Alice Sallie Hudson with two daughters, Heather Ann and Suzanne. Formerly managing director C. Jones and Sons Ltd. At present general secretary Golfing Union of Ireland. Honorary secretary Grange Golf Club and honorary secretary Leinster Branch of Golfing Union of Ireland. Member Royal Zoological Society, Association of Golf Club Secretaries and honorary member of most Irish golf clubs.

MICHAEL GERARD DOYLE

Company Director/Veterinary Surgeon
Millbrook, Naas, Co Kildare
(045) 66676
Born to Michael and Ellen Doyle (née Dennehy) in Co. Kerry on 13 October 1940. Educated at Ranalough NS, Dominican College Newbridge, UCD, Veterinary College of Ireland and Cambridge University. Married to Mandy Power-Smith. Four children. Formerly Irish rugby coach, British Lions Coach and chairman of Government Zoo Committee. At present executive member Irish Veterinary Association, managing director MD Marketing International Ltd, Specialist Laboratory Services Ltd, member European Veterinary Discussion Group and sports columnist *Sunday Independent*. Irish Life Manager of the Year Award 1985, Texaco Award 1985, Rupert Cherry Award, Pat Marshall Award — UK 1986 for services to rugby.

NOEL C. DUGGAN

Horse Show Organiser
Green Glens, Millstreet Town
(022) 22666
Born to Cornelius Andrew and Catherine Duggan (née Murphy) at Millstreet on 25 December 1936. The eldest of eleven children, was educated locally to age thirteen, when he left school on the death of this father. Married to Maureen Corkery with two sons and two daughters. Formerly master of Dunhallow Hunt 1975–9 and chairman Cork Hibernian Football Club 1976–9. At present (and since 1951) managing director of Noel C. Duggan Ltd Structural Steel Engineers. Transformed a struggling agricultural show into a prestigious international horse show attracting 40,000 people to Millstreet and warranting six hours live television coverage. Received a People of the Year Award 1987.

EDWARD PETER (EDDIE) KEHER
Bank Manager
Green Street, Callan, Co. Kilkenny
(056) 25224
Born to Stephen and Noreen Keher (née Browne) at Inistioge, Co. Kilkenny on 14 October 1941. Educated at Inistioge NS and at St Kieran's College Kilkenny. Married to Kathleen Phelan with two sons, Eamonn and Colm, and three daughters, Clodagh, Deirdre and Catherine. Formerly assistant manager AIB Capel Street, deputy manager AIB Carlow, development manager Kilkenny region AIB. At present manager AIB Bank Callan. Winner of six All-Ireland medals, three National League medals, ten Leinster championships, nine Railway cups, and recipient of five All-Star awards and one Texaco award. Member Callan Golf Club, No Name Club, numerous GAA committees and of the Council of *Gaisce* (the President's Awards). Patron of GOAL.

LORD KILLANIN
The Rt Hon. Sir Michael Morris, Bt. was born to Lt Col the Hon. George Maurice and Dora Mary Wesley Hall at London on 30 July 1914. Educated at Eton, the Sorbonne Paris and Magdalene College Cambridge (BA 1935, MA 1939). Married to Mary Sheila Dunlop MBE with three sons, Redmond, Michael and John, and one daughter, Deborah. Joined *Daily Express* in 1935 and later *Daily Mail*, where he became assistant political and diplomatic correspondent and wrote the political column in *Sunday Dispatch*. Served through the war in the Queen's Westminsters (King's Royal Rifle Corps), Brigade Major, 30th Armoured Brigade 1942–5, and took part in landing in Normandy, for which he was made a Member of the Order of the British Empire (Military Division) and earned the Territorial Decoration and campaign stars. Formerly associated with the late John Ford in making *The Quiet Man*, subsequently produced a number of films including *The Rising of the Moon*, *The Playboy of the Western World* and *Gideon's Day*. Also formerly president Olympic Council of Ireland and International Olympic Committee. Member Cultural Relations' Committee and National Monuments' Advisory Council, honorary secretary Irish Red Cross Society, and vice president Royal National Lifeboat Institution. Honorary consul general for Monaco. At present chairman National Heritage Council, member Royal Irish Academy, honorary member Royal Dublin Society, fellow Royal Society of Arts and Royal Society of Antiquaries of Ireland, honorary life member NUJ and fellow of Irish Management Institute. Honorary life president International Olympic Committee and Olympic Council of Ireland. Has been decorated by Spain, Yugoslavia, Italy, Tunisia, Greece, Malta, Poland, Monaco, Germany, Congo, Japan, Great Britain, Ivory Coast, France, Dominican Republic, Bulgaria, Czechoslovakia etc. and holds Olympic Order of Merit (gold). Awarded hon-orary degrees LL.D (NUI), D.Litt (NUU) and Chubb Fellowship (Yale).

MICHAEL JOSEPH LOFTUS
Medical Practitioner
Main Street, Crossmolina, Mayo
(096) 31313
Born to Martin and Mary Loftus (née Conmy) at Athlone on 9 August 1929. Educated at Crossmolina NS, St Muredach's College Ballina and UCD. Married to Edie Munnilly with three sons, Michael, Patrick and Joseph, and one daughter, Orla. Formerly chairman National GAA Referees' Association, past president of Gaelic Athletic Association. At present member of RTE Authority, patron Salesian Fathers' Centenary Committee and Connacht Council GAA.

WILLIAM JAMES McBRIDE
Bank Manager
97 Mill Street, Ballymena BT43 5DA
(0266) 46116
Born to William James and Irene McBride (née Patterson) at Toomebridge, Co. Antrim on 6 June 1940. Educated at Duneane PS and Ballymena Academy. Married to Penny Michael with one son and one daughter. Formerly public relations manager and press officer for Northern Bank. At present bank manager Northern Bank, Ballymena and president Ballymena RFC. Member Ballymena Rotary Club and vice president Northern Ireland Region Riding for Disabled. Awarded MBE 1971 for services to sport.

LIAM MULVIHILL
Director General
Croke Park, Dublin 3
(01) 363222
Born to John and Bridie Mulvihill (née Gerety) at Mullingar on 25 May 1946. Educated at Ballymahon NS, St Mel's College Longford, St Patrick's College Drumcondra, UCD and Maynooth. Married to Máire Ní Shiocrú with one son and one daughter. Formerly primary teacher at Ballynacargy and schools' inspector with Department of Education. At present director general GAA, member RTE Authority and member Bord na Gaeilge. Member of a number of historical societies and Kenagh GAA Club.

MICHAEL VINCENT O'BRIEN
Racehorse Trainer
Ballydoyle House, Cashel, Co. Tipperary
(062) 61222
Born to Daniel P. and Kathleen O'Brien (née Twomey) at Churchtown, Co. Cork on 9 April 1917. Educated at Mungret College, Limerick. Married to Jacqueline Wittenoom with two sons and three daughters. A horse trainer since 1944. Has won all major English and Irish

steeplechases. Trained winners of forty-four Classics, trainer of Nijinsky, first triple crown winner since 1935. Principal races won include three successive Grand Nationals, four Cheltenham Gold Cups, three Champion Hurdles, five July cups, six Epsom Derbys, two Epsom Oaks, three St Legers, four 2,000 Guineas, 1,000 Guineas, three King George VI and Queen Elizabeth Stakes, Ascot Gold Cup, five Eclipse Stakes, two Champion Stakes, four Sussex Stakes, two Benson and Hedges Gold Cups, Grand Criterium, seven Dewhurst Stakes, six Irish Derbys, four Irish Oaks, nine Irish St Legers, five Irish 2,000 Guineas, three Irish 1,000 Guineas, Washington DC International, Prix du Jockey Club, three Prix de l'Arc de Triomphe, Breeders' Cup Mile, seven Dewhurst Stakes, three Cheveley Park Stakes, Middle Pork Stakes, and Observer Gold Cup. Conferred with honorary LL.D degree by NUI in 1983.

PÁDRAIG SEOSAIMH Ó NUALLÁIN
Zoo President
(01) 685641
Born to Tomás and Annie Ó Nualláin (née O'Reilly) at Dublin on 27 October 1918. Educated at CBS Synge Street, Terenure College, Blackrock College and UCD. Fellow Institute of Chartered Accountants in Ireland. Married to Máire Ní Mhaoileoin with four children. Formerly managing director New Ireland Assurance plc and chairman Post Office Users' Council. At present president Royal Zoological Society of Ireland, member board of guardians Coombe Lying-in Hospital, and chairman Elbistan Investments Ltd and General Investment Trust Ltd. Member Fitzwilliam Lawn Tennis Club, Military History Society of Ireland and 1916–21 Club.

BRENDAN O'REILLY
Television Sports Presenter
RTE, Donnybrook, Dublin 4
(01) 693111
Born to James P. and Catherine O'Reilly (née Donegan) at Granard on 14 May 1931. Educated at St James CBS and University of Michigan, Awn Arbor. Married to Johanna Lowry with four children, Myles, Kelan, Rossa and Hannah. Formerly in Marine Insurance, professional actor, school teacher and with McConnell's Advertising. At present senior reporter/presenter of RTE sport, songwriter and host of RTE weekly flagship sports programme, 'Sports Stadium'. Former Irish high jump and javelin record-holder and decathalon champion. TV commentator for five Olympics. Poems and short stories published. Summer lecturer in Communication at University of Michigan. Member NUJ and AIPS. First non-political figure to give the Michael Collins oration at Béal na mBláth. Writer/composer of the international Olympic song, 'Let the Nations Play'.

FRANCIS JOSEPH CHARLES O'REILLY
Retired Banker
Born to Lt Col. Charles Joseph and Dorothy O'Reilly (née Martin) at Dublin on 15 November 1922. Educated at St Gerard's Bray, Ampleforth College York and TCD. Married to Teresa Mary Williams with three sons, Charles, Peter and Paul, and seven daughters, Mary, Jane, Olivia, Margaret, Rose, Louise and Julie. Formerly with Royal Engineers, 7th Indian Division, South East Asia Command, chairman John Power and Son Ltd, Irish Distillers Group, Player and Wills Ireland, RDS Executive Committee, pro-chancellor University of Dublin and Association of Irish Racecourses. President Equestrian Federation of Ireland, chairman Ulster Bank, director of National Westminster Bank and member board of governors and guardians National Gallery of Ireland. At present chairman Punchestown Races, Kildare Hunt Club, and of Collège des Irlandais, Paris, and director Fairyhouse Club. Member and trustee of Turf Club and Irish National Hunt Steeplechase Committee. Honours include LL.D from University of Dublin and from NUI, fellowships of Institute of Bankers in Ireland, Marketing Institute of Ireland, Irish Management Institute and Institution of Engineers of Ireland. Honorary Life Delegate — General Assembly Fédération Équestre Internationale.

CAHIR EDWARD O'SULLIVAN
Chief Executive
The Curragh, Co. Kildare
(045) 41599
Born to Edmond and Annette O'Sullivan (née Martin) at Dublin on 12 February 1935. Educated at St Malachy's School and St Mary's College Dundalk and at UCD. Married to Gretta Nicholson with two sons and two daughters. Formerly managing director Scanglo International Ltd. At present Keeper of the Match Book (chief executive) The Turf Club. Associate member Chartered Institute of Secretaries and Administrators and of the Chartered Institute of Management Accountants. Member Curragh Golf Club and Curragh Squash Club.

PETER WILSON
Veterinary Surgeon
Phoenix Park, Dublin 8
(01) 771425
Born to Robert Morton and Muriel Eileen Wilson (née Ganly) at Dublin on 28 August 1943. Educated at Wesley College Dublin and TCD. Married to Jane Burrows with one son and one daughter. Formerly veterinary surgeon in practice and lecturer in Veterinary College and TCD. At present director Dublin Zoo and of the Royal Zoological Society of Ireland. Member Royal Irish Yacht Club, Irish Wildbird Conservancy and Royal Society for the Protection of Birds.

WHERE IRISH PEOPLE WOULD
LIKE TO SPEND HOLIDAYS

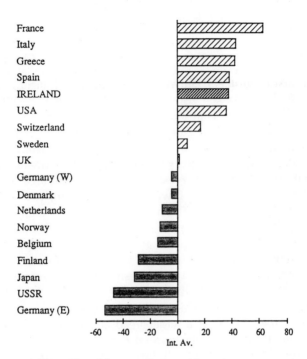

(Reproduced by permission of Lansdowne
Market Research and the *Sunday Press*.)

Chapter 19
Culture and Genealogy

For the great Gaels of Ireland
Are the men that God made mad,
For all their wars are merry,
And all their songs are sad.

Chesterton

In the sixth century, Irish was the sole language throughout the island and was spoken also by Irish Missionaries in Scotland and in the Isle of Man. That language, Old Irish, is the earliest language from north of the Alps in which an extensive literature still exists. Irish remained almost the sole language for ten centuries.

In the sixteenth century there were two Irish-English bilingual areas, South East Wexford and the Fingal area of Dublin. In addition certain major towns, such as Dublin, Waterford and Cork, maintained some fluency in English for their administrative affairs.

The plantations, conquests and settlements of the sixteenth and seventeenth centuries marked the turning point for the Irish language, which gradually diminished to the present state of affairs in which, it is estimated, only about 2 per cent of the population are Irish-speaking. However, a great many people know Irish and there is a widespread affection for the language as an important part of the cultural heritage of the island.

Hiberno-English is only slightly at variance with general English and, similarly, it is only slightly at variance with American English. The gift of 'English as she is spoken in Ireland' is perhaps one of the few gifts for which we should be forever grateful to our British neighbours. Countless visits by innumerable visitors have been facilitated by the people of this island having English.

The Tyrone Guthrie Centre at Newbliss, Co. Monaghan celebrated in 1991 the first 10 years of its existence, during which time nearly 1,000 individuals from all branches of the arts, and from all over Ireland and even from abroad, used Annaghmakerrig, the former Guthrie residence, as a colony for periods of intensive work, making it a great meeting place and melting pot.

Connoisseur

Dr James White, a former Curator of the Municipal Gallery of Modern
Art in Dublin and also a former director of the National Gallery of
Ireland, is seen here viewing 'In a Churchyard' by Clodagh Thornton, at
an exhibition of forty paintings by artists associated with the Kilkenny
area, at the Royal Hospital, Kilmainham, in January 1988.

Visitors should look at obituaries, especially those published in local newspapers, to see how fond we Irish are of using verses. We all recited poetry as children and perhaps because of this there has been a spectacular growth in the popularity of poetry readings in recent years. It seems that the recent popularity of poetry is more to do with the ear than the eye — more readings rather than more publications of slim and expensive volumes.

The development of Irish Literature involved a fusion of the languages, aspirations and cultures of Gaelic Catholic and Anglo-Irish Protestant. The best known deceased Irish authors include Aogán Ó Rathaille, Jonathan Swift, Maria Edgeworth, Somerville and Ross, George Bernard Shaw, Oscar Wilde, James Joyce, Samuel Beckett, and Brendan Behan.

The visitor with a taste for theatre will certainly not be disappointed in Ireland where theatrical talent is to be found in abundance. There is a thriving amateur drama movement throughout the island, and the Amateur Drama Council organises the All-Ireland Drama Festival in April of each year in Athlone.

The National Theatre Movement found a permanent home in the Abbey Theatre in 1904 and nurtured the emergence of a distinguished group of leading dramatists, including Colum, Synge, Yeats and Lady Gregory.

Other well known Irish dramatists are Seán O'Casey, Denis Johnston, Brian Friel and Hugh Leonard, while well known venues include the Olympia Theatre, Andrews Lane, The Gate, and The Gaiety.

Cothú — the business council for the arts is a young organisation actively promoting and encouraging business sponsorship of the arts, and acting as the representative voice of business arts sponsors. The organisation has a full time chief executive and a permanent office at the Irish Management Institute. Cothú does not act as an agent for art organisations or approach members seeking sponsorship on behalf of individual art organisations, but it offers advice to its members on art sponsorship opportunities. In 1991 it organised the first arts sponsor of the year awards. In Northern Ireland, the Association for Business Sponsorship of the Arts (ABSA) was established there in 1987, having been established in Great Britain in 1976

The Royal Hibernian Academy (founded 1823), having been without a permanent home for many years, occupies the new Gallagher Gallery in Ely Place. The annual RHA Exhibition is a feature of the artistic year, as is the GPA sponsored exhibition of work by emerging artists. Recent RHA academicians included Thomas Ryan, James Nolan, Arthur Gibney, Pauline Bewick, Desmond Carrick, Gerry Clarke, Edward Delaney, David Hone, Marshall C. Hudson, Richard Kingston, Tom Nesbitt and Fergus Ryan. Well-known honorary members included Maurice Craig, Terence de Vere White, Derek Hill, Louis Le Brocquy, Patrick Leonard, Homan Potterton and Dr James White.

The Irish Museum of Modern Art was officially opened on 25 May 1991 at the Royal Hospital Kilmainham, which is considered to be the finest seventeenth-century building in Ireland. It was built in 1684 as a home for retired soldiers and is based on Les Invalides in Paris. Its restoration in 1986 cost IR£21 million.

Irish artists whose work reveals an influence of impressionism include John Butler Yeats, Walter Osborne, William Orpen, Roderick O'Conor, Sarah Purcell, John Lavery and Nathaniel Hone. Jack B. Yeats was a leading artist of the twentieth century and a brother of the poet William B. Yeats. One of the best known twentieth-century artists was Paul Henry whose Connemara landscapes are known throughout the island.

Other well known Irish artists include Mainie Jellett, Evie Hone, Louis Le Brocquy and Nora McGuinness. These four founded the Living Art Exhibition which has featured painters and sculptors, such as Oisín Kelly, Hilary Heron, Patrick Scott, Gerard Dillon, Gerda Fromel, Nano Reid, Barrie Cooke, Cecil King, Camille Souter, Patrick Collins, Tony O'Malley, Brian King, Michael O'Sullivan, Tim Goulding, Michael Farrell, Martin Gale and Robert Ballagh.

The best known Irish harpist composer is Turlough O'Carolan and John Field is probably the Irish composer who had most influence abroad as the creator of the nocturne. Better known perhaps are the Irish composers Vincent Wallace and Michael Balfe. Other well-known Irish composers include Seoirse Bodley, John Buckley, Brian Boydell, Hamilton Harty, Victor Herbert, A.J. Potter and Gerard Victory.

Founded in 1848, the Royal Irish Academy of Music is a thirty-two-county institution and, to quote from its prospectus, 'a home of musical excellence and dynamisn, a place of teaching and learning which consistently achieves its objective of transmitting and maintaining the highest standards of performance and appreciation'. The Academy is controlled by a board of governors and a board of studies.

The National Concert Hall was opened on 9 September 1981 by the then President of Ireland, Dr Patrick J. Hillery, and NCH Chairman, Fred O'Donovan. The Hall is now the home of the Radio Telifís Éireann Symphony Orchestra. Bernadette Greevy, Frank Patterson, Michael O'Rourke, Charles Lynch, Theresa Timony, John O'Conor, Hugh Tinney and Ashling Drury-Byrne are among many Irish artists who have appeared on stage at the NCH.

Venues likely to attract the music lover include the Opera Houses at Cork and Belfast, the RDS Concert Hall and the Point Depot.

Many visitors will associate Ireland with traditional, or popular music. The introduction of the Fleadh Cheoil in the 1960s allowed the best traditions of Irish music to permeate the urbane western democracy that was modern Ireland. The Irish discovered their own music. A leading figure in this movement was Seán Ó Riada (1931–77), who not only wrote music but formed a group of traditional musicians to play it. Following in the footsteps of that group are The Chieftains who have won international acclaim from audiences all over the world. Other prominent groups are Clannad, The Dubliners, and the Saw Doctors. Popular music in Ireland today consists mainly of country music and rock. The U2 group has earned a degree of fame which is not always appreciated in Ireland and it is said that U2 are known even in places where Ireland itself is not known.

The Ulster Museum is located at the Botanic Gardens in Belfast and has local history galleries, antiquities galleries, botany and zoology galleries, geology galleries and art galleries which include glass, silver, ceramics, paintings, costume and textiles, sculpture and the Hull Grundy jewellery collection.

From an enormous range of cultural organisations the following may be of particular interest: Cairde Gael-Linn, Comhaltas Ceoltóirí Éireann, Comhaltas Uladh, Comhdhail Náisiúnta na

Gaeilge, Conradh na Gaeilge, Glór na nGael and An tOireachtas to mention but some of the Irish language organisations; Association of Irish Musical Societies, the Library Association of Ireland, Federation of Irish Film Societies, Foras Éireann, the Friends of the National Collections of Ireland, the Heritage Trust, the Irish Architectural Archive, the Irish Association for Cultural Economic and Social Relations, the Irish Film Institute, Irish Georgian Society, the Music Association of Ireland, the National Folk Theatre of Ireland (Siamsa Tíre), Royal Dublin Society, Royal Irish Academy of Music, Royal Society of Antiquaries of Ireland and An Taisce — the National Trust, to mention a few of the many many others. The Arts Council is an independent organisation formed to promote and assist the arts. It reports to the Oireachtas through the office of An Taoiseach, and receives annual grants from the Exchequer, the National Lottery, local authorities and private sources. The Arts Council of Northern Ireland aims to improve the practice and appreciation of the Arts and to increase their accessibility to the people of Northern Ireland. The income of the Council comes mainly from the Arts Council support grant, and in addition the Grand Opera House has in recent years returned a small surplus.

Visitors wishing to dabble in genealogy should prepare well for such an adventure by gathering all possible information before arrival in Ireland. The most important elements are the names and addresses of ancestors as these lead in to the great lists of householders and landholders — the Griffith Valuation and the Tithe Applotment Survey. Obviously, by having even rough addresses, one can establish the relevant parish and from there have access to the appropriate parish registers. For many cities and even some towns, there are commercial directories which are useful sources of information. For the latter part of the nineteenth century onwards, the Register of births, marriages and deaths is invaluable. Other sources include gravestone inscriptions, wills, marriage bonds and newspaper notices. Visitors to Dublin should consider having a general consultation at the Genealogical Office. Other important archives are the National Library of Ireland, National Archive, the Registry of Deeds and the Office of the Registrar General. There are a number of organisations who will perform research on a fee basis and a number of societies well worth contacting — local history societies such as the Old Dublin Society, Old Athlone Society and many others, and specialist societies such as the Irish Palatine Association and the Huguenot Society.

The Irish Heritage Association in Belfast is administered by Don and Kathleen Neill and undertakes genealogical and historical research and organises Clan Gatherings. It is the official office for several Clan societies, and organises for the O'Neill, McCarthy, McGuire and Crawford Clan societies. It publishes newsletters for these Clan societies and a magazine, *Irish Heritage Links*. It has published *How to trace family history in Northern Ireland*, and *O'Neill Commemorative Journal* with a separate work on the O'Neills, entitled *The O'Neills of Leinster*, planned for late 1991.

The Irish Family History Society was formed at Tullamore, Co. Offaly in September 1984 with the object of promoting and encouraging the public study of Irish family history, genealogy, heraldry and local history and promoting the preservation, security and accessibility of archival material. The society takes a particular interest in research activities throughout Ireland on a county by county basis, and membership has grown extremely rapidly since formation.

The Irish Genealogical Research Society was formed in the College of Arms, London on 15 September 1936. The objects of the society are to promote and encourage the study of Irish genealogy, and to collect books and manuscripts of genealogical value, especially copies of records which were destroyed in the Public Record Office Dublin in 1922. The society's journal, *The Irish Genealogist*, first appeared in 1937, and since more recent times, this has been augmented by a newsletter. Membership extends far beyond the British Isles to North and South America, Australia, New Zealand and South Africa. A branch of the society has been established in Dublin since 1986.

MARTYN ANGLESEA

Curator
Ulster Museum, Belfast
(0232) 381251

Born at Mold, Flintshire, North Wales on 7 June 1947. Educated at Alun Grammar School Mold, University of Leeds and University of Edinburgh. Formerly chairman Association of Irish Art Historians, honorary secretary Irish Museums Association, consultant to Royal Hospital Kilmainham, and visiting fellow Yale Centre for British Art. At present curator of watercolours, prints and drawings at Ulster Museum. Publications include a centennial history of the Royal Ulster Academy of Arts.

JAMES LINDSAY ARMSTRONG

Musician
26 Westland Row, Dublin 2
(01) 764412

Born to James and Margaret Armstrong (née Lecker) at Belfast on 13 September 1942. Educated at Brownie's Primary School and Friends School Lisburn, and Royal Academy of Music, London. Married to Gillian Smith with two daughters. Formerly in RTE symphony Orchestra, manager Irish Chamber Orchestra, manager National Concert Hall, organised commercial recordings with James Galway and tours of China, USSR and USA. Life member Royal Dublin Society. At present director Royal Irish Academy of Music. Decorated in 1985 by French Government — Chevalier dans l'Ordre des Arts et des Lettres.

BRUCE ARNOLD

c/o Irish Independent, Middle Abbey Street, Dublin 1
(01) 731666

Born to George and Margaret Arnold (née Shaw) at London on 6 September 1936. Educated at Kingham Hill School Oxfordshire and at TCD. Married to Ysabel Mavis Cleave with two sons, Hugo and Samuel, and one daughter, Polly. Formerly with staff of *Irish Times*, Dublin correspondent of the *Guardian*, editor *The Dubliner* and in the period 1966–72 freelance journalist. Since 1972 with *Irish Independent* for whom he has travelled widely on assignments, in addition to being political commentator, parliamentary correspondent, political features writer and London editor. Chairman and member board of National College of Art and Design. At present literary editor *Irish Independent*. Publications include *A Concise History of Art*, *A Singer at the Wedding*, *The Song of the Nightingale*, *The Muted Swan*, *Running to Paradise* (These four books constitute the group of novels know as *The Coppinger Chronicle*), *William Orpen: Mirror to an Age*, *Margaret Thatcher: A Study in Power*, *What Kind of Country*, *Art Atlas of Britain and Ireland*, *The Scandal of Ulysses*, *William Orpen* (in Lives of the Artists series) and *Mainie Jellett and the Modern Movement in Ireland*.

PAULINE GALE BEWICK
Artist
c/o Taylor Gallery, Kildare Street, Dublin 2
(01) 776089
Born to Corbet and Alice May (Harry) Bewick (née Graham) at Northumberland on 4 September 1935. Educated at Douris NS Kenmare, St Catherine's School Bristol (progressive), and National College of Art, Dublin. Married to Dr Patrick I. Melia with two daughters, Poppy and Holly. Formerly singer, dancer in reviews and set designer at Pike Theatre Dublin, book illustrator and, above all, artist. Her work has been exhibited in London, Paris, Brussels, Italy, Germany, Canada and USA, as well as in Ireland. Member Royal Hibernian Academy, Aosdana and Chelsea and Dublin Arts Clubs.

CLARE BOYLAN
Journalist and Novelist
c/o Roger Coleridge and White, London
(03 071) 221 3717
Born to Patrick and Evelyn Boylan (née Selby) at Dublin on 24 April 1948. Educated at St Louis Rathmines and Rathmines College of Commerce. Married to Alan Wilmes. Formerly freelance journalist, news reporter *Irish Press*, editor *Young Woman*, editor *Woman's Choice*, regular participant as interviewer on TV 'Current Affairs' series and as radio interviewer on 'Here and Now', and later freelance contributor to *Evening Press*, editor *Image Magazine* 1981–4. At present prolific writer and adjudicator; the film version of the story *Making Waves*, was nominated for a Hollywood Oscar in 1988, she has written book reviews for *The Sunday Times*, the *Irish Press*, *Evening Herald*, *The Irish Times*, *Booms Magazine*, *Cosmopolitan*, RTE Radio and TV, *Sunday Tribune* and *Image*, and is a regular contributor to the *Guardian*. Publications include *Holy Pictures*, *Last Resorts*, *Black Baby* and *Concerning Virgins*.

BRIAN CLEEVE
Author
Born to Charles and Josephine Cleeve (née Talbot) at Thorpe Bay, Essex on 22 November 1921. Educated at Selwyn House Broadstairs, Saint Edward's, Oxford, University of South Africa and UCD. Married to Veronica McAdie with two daughters, Berenice and Tanga. Formerly in military service, journalist in South Africa, and journalist and broadcaster in Ireland. Publications include novels and short stories such as *The Far Hills*, *Death of a Painted Lady*, *Horse Thieves of Ballysaggert*, *Cry of Morning*, *Tread Softly in this Place*, *Sarah*, *The House on the Rock*, *The Seven Mansions* and *The Fourth Mary*. In non-fiction: *A Dictionary of Irish Writers* 2nd edition 1985, revised with Anne Brady as co-author/editor. *1938: A World Vanishing* and *A View of the Irish*.

LEWIS CLOHESSY
Consultant
Golden Hill, Manor Kilbride, Co. Wicklow
(01) 582138
Born to Denis and Joan Clohissy (née Quinlan) on 11 March 1939. Educated at Cistercian College Roscrea, Christian Brothers Kilkenny and at UCD. Married to Frances O'Callaghan with two sons and one daughter. Formerly chief executive The Heritage Trust and An Taisce, chairman National Concert Hall Dublin and director Dublin Theatre Festival. At present chief executive Dublin 1991 European City of Culture, board member Dublin Film Festival and trustee Irish Resource Development Trust. Member Strand Players Theatre Company.

PATRICK JOSEPH CORISH
Historian
Born to Peter William and Brigid Mary Corish (née O'Shaughnessy) in Co. Wexford on 20 March 1921. Educated at St Peter's College Wexford and at NUI. Ordained as priest in 1945. Formerly professor of ecclesiastical, and of modern history, and member Royal Irish Academy, secretary Catholic Record Society of Ireland, editor journal *Archivum Hibernicus*, member Irish Manuscripts Commission and Domestic Prelate. At present working on bicentenary history of Maynooth College. Publications include *A History of Irish Catholicism*, *The Catholic Community in the Seventeenth and Eighteenth Centuries* and *The Irish Catholic Experience*.

BRIAN COYLE
Fine Art Auctioneer
26 St Stephen's Green, Dublin 2
(01) 760261
Born to Cornelius and Aileen Coyle (née Kelly) at Dublin on 1 June 1934. Admitted to fellowship Royal Institution of Chartered Surveyors, fellowship Irish Auctioneers' and Valuers' Institute and fellowship of Society of Valuers and Auctioneers. Joined James Adam and Sons in 1952, a firm founded in 1887. At present senior director James Adam and Sons, and lecturer at UCD. Past president Irish Auctioneers' and Valuers' Institute, member Kildare Street and University Club, Royal Dublin Society, Irish Georgian Society, Royal Zoological Society of Ireland, An Taisce, National Trust (UK), William Morris Society, Dún Laoghaire Golf Club, Victorian Societies in England and United States. Board member GPA Dublin International Piano Competition.

SÉAMUS FRANCIS DEANE
University Professor
Belfield, Dublin 4
(01) 2693244
Born to Frank and Winifred Deane (née Doherty) at Derry on 9 February

1940. Educated at CBS and St Columb's School Derry, Queen's University Belfast and Cambridge. Married to Marion Treacy with three sons, Conor, Ciarán and Cormac, and one daughter, Emer. Formerly Fulbright Scholar, Woodrow Wilson Fellow, Reed College USA, visiting professor, University of Notre Dame, Indiana and Walker-Ames professor University of Washington, Seattle. Distinguished Visiting Benedict Professor, Carleton College, Minnesota. At present professor Modern English and American Literature at UCD. Member Royal Irish Academy and director Field Day Theatre Company. Member Aosdana. Publications include *Celtic Revivals*, *A Short History of Irish Literature* and *The French Enlightenment and Revolution in England*, *Gradual Wars*, *Rumours*, *History Lessons*, and *Selected Poems*. General Editor *Field Day Anthology of Irish Writing*.

DR PAT DONLON

Librarian
Kildare Street, Dublin 2
(01) 618811
Born to Patrick Joseph and Marcella McCarthy (née Garr) at Dublin on 28 January 1943. Educated at Holy Faith Convent, the Coombe, UCD and Universidad de Madrid. Married to Phelim Donlon with two daughters, Lorna and Sinéad. Formerly research assistant RTE, library assistant UCD, assistant librarian Royal Irish Academy, reference librarian and curator of Western Collection — Chester Beatty Library. Part-time lecturer department of Library and Information Studies UCD. At present director National Library of Ireland, trustee Chester Beatty Library Dublin, Writers' Museum and patron Irish Children's Book Trust. Member Irish Museums Association, Library Association of Ireland and Rare Books Group of LAI.

DERMOT K. DOOLAN

Born to William and Bridget Doolan (née Parker) at Dublin on 29 October 1926. Educated at Rialto NS, Synge Street CBS, UCD and Dublin Institute of Adult Education. Married to Margaret Balfe with one son and four daughters. Formerly group secretary Irish Actors' Equity Group ITGWU, general secretary Society of Irish Playwrights and Association of Artists in Ireland, president Performing Artists Trust Society, and member board of Royal Hospital Kilmainham. At present writer, lecturer in industrial relations in the DIAE, and member board of DIAE, and shareholder in Abbey Theatre. Life member Irish Actors' Equity Group, member Balbriggan Golf Club and Irish Labour History Society.

VINCENT GERARD DOWLING

Theatre Director
East River Rd, North Chester, Huntingdon, MAO 1050
(413) 667 8818
Born to William and Mai Dowling (née Kelly) at Dublin on 7 September 1929. Educated at St Laurence O'Toole Stillorgan, CBC Dún Laoghaire,

St Mary's College Rathmines, Rathmines School of Commerce and Brendan Smith Academy of Acting. Married to Olwen O'Herlihy with one son, Cian, and four daughters, Bairbre, Louise, Valerie and Rachael. Formerly actor, director and artistic director Abbey Theatre Dublin, artistic producing director Great Lakes Shakespeare Festival Cleveland Ohio, and artistic and producing director Pacific Conservatory of the Performing Arts Calfornia. At present artistic director Miniature Theatre of Chester, and lifetime associate director of Abbey Theatre. Member Irish and American Actors' Equity, Society of Directors and Choreographers, American Federation of Television and Radio Artists and American National Theatre Association. Awarded an honorary doctorate by the John Carroll University.

ALFRED JAMES FAULKNER
Retired Teacher
(0902) 72191
Born to Dr Alfred Joseph and Bridget Faulkner (née Studdert) at Castlebar on 3 January 1913. Educated at De La Salle Brothers Castlebar, and at De La Salle Teacher Training College Waterford. Married to Mary Donnelly with one daughter. Formerly teacher and school principal, chairman Athlone Urban District Council. President Irish National Teachers' Organisation, director An Foras Forbartha and member of Censorship Appeals Board. At present chairman Foras Éireann (C.F. Shaw Trust and Carnegie Trust) and vice president of Old Athlone Society.

BRIAN FERRAN
Art Teacher
18/19 Stranmillis Road, Belfast BT9 5DU
(0232) 381591
Born in Derry in 1940. Educated at Courtauld Institute of London University, Queen's University Belfast and at Brera Academy of Fine Art Milan. Formerly on staff of the Arts Council of Northern Ireland. In 1980 he was a commissioner at the Paris Biennale and in 1985 at the São Paulo Bienal. He has exhibited widely and has won some presitgious awards including a Leverhulme European Fellowship. At present director Arts Council of Northern Ireland.

DESMOND FITZGERALD, KNIGHT OF GLIN
Art Historian
Co. Limerick
(068) 34173
Born in 1937. Studied art history at Harvard Fogg Museum where he was a teaching fellow and received an MA in 1962. Married to Olda with three daughters. Formerly Deputy Keeper of Department of Furniture and Woodwork at Victoria and Albert Museum in London. Representative in Ireland of Christies, the fine art auctioneers. With his wife, he runs an extensive dairy farm at Glin. At present president Irish Georgian

Society and chairman Irish Georgian Foundation, director Historic Irish Tourist Houses Association, Irish Architectural Archive and trustee Castletown Foundation. Books and booklets include *Irish Furniture*, *The Norfolk House Music Room*, *Irish Gardens*, *Vanishing Houses of Ireland*, and with Maurice Craig, *Ireland Observed — a handbook to the buildings and antiquities*, with Edward Mallins *Lost Demesnes*, *Irish Landscape Gardens* and with Professor Ann Crookshank *The Painters of Ireland*.

BRIAN FRIEL
Writer
Born to Patrick and Christina Friel (née McLoone) in Co. Tyrone on 9 January 1929. Educated at St Columba's Boys' School Derry, St Columb's College Derry, St Patrick's College Maynooth and St Joseph's Training College Belfast. Married to Anne Morrison with one son and four daughters. Formerly teacher in various schools in Derry, member Seanad Éireann. At present full-time writer, member Aosdana and Irish Academy of Letters, and honorary life member Royal Dublin Society. Published works include short story collections and plays such as *The Enemy Within*, *Philadelphia Here I Come*, *The Loves of Cass Maguire*, *Lorcas*, *Crystal and Fox*, *The Mundy Scheme*, *The Gentle Island*, *The Freedom of the City*, *Volunteers*, *Faith Healer*, *Aristocrats*, *Translations*, translation of *Three Sisters*, *The Communication Cord*, *Fathers and Sons*, *Making History*, *Dancing at Lughnasa*, translation of *A Month in the Country*, and *The London Vertigo* (after Charles Macken). Editor *The Last of the Name* by Charles McGinley.

MICHAEL GILL
Publisher
Goldenbridge, Dublin 8
(01) 531005
Born to William and Kathleen Gill (née Quigley) at Dublin in 1940. Educated at Belvedere College and UCD. Married to Anne Leonard with three daughters. At present managing director Gill and Macmillan. Member Portmarnock Golf Club.

AIDEN GRENNELL
Actor
c/o RTE, Donnybrook, Dublin 4
Born to Aiden Peter Joseph and Stella Mary Grennell (née O'Donovan) on 19 January 1920. Educated at St Columb's College Derry, Clongowes Wood College and TCD. Married to Iris Lawler with two sons and one daughter. Formerly at Abbey School of Acting, Abbey Theatre, freelanced with Illsley McCabe, Carl Clopet etc, Gate Theatre, Longford Productions, Globe Theatre Productions and member RTE Radio Repertory Company 1962–72, taking early retirement in 1972 to return to stage. At present freelance actor in all the media, appearing regularly in the major Dublin theatres with special emphasis on the Gate Theatre. Does occasional radio work with RTE and BBC Northern Ireland.

SÉAMUS HEANEY
Dublin
Born to Patrick and Margaret Heaney (née McCann) in Northern Ireland on 13 April 1939. Educated at St Columb's College Londonderry and at Queen's University Belfast. Married to Marie Devlin with two sons and one daughter. Formerly lecturer St Joseph's College of Education Belfast, Queen's University Belfast, freelance writer, lecturer Carysfort College, senior visiting lecturer Harvard University, Boylston Professor of Rhetoric and Oratory. At present professor of poetry at Oxford University. Publications include: (poetry) *Death of a Naturalist*, *Door into the Dark*, *Wintering Out*, *North*, *Field Work*, *Sweeney Astray*, *Station Island*, *The Haw Lantern* and *Seeing Things*: (prose) *Preoccupations* and *The Government of the Tongue* and (play) *The Cure at Troy*. Member Aosdana, honorary degrees from Queen's University Belfast, University of Dublin and NUI.

DICK HILL
Opera House General Manager
Emmet Place, Cork
(021) 276357
Born to Richard W. and Olive Hill (née McIlwaine) at Kinsale on 23 August 1938. Educated at St Multose NS Kinsale, Midleton College Cork, Crawford Institute Cork and TCD, whence he graduated with BA(Mod) degree. Married to Susan Buswell with two sons, Richard and Ronan. Formerly director of Television at RTE. At present general manager of Cork Opera House, chairman Coco Television Productions Ltd and proprietor Leeline Media Services.

JOHN B. KEANE
Playwright
Listowel, Co. Kerry
Born to William and Hanna Keane (née Purtill) at Listowel on 21 July 1928. Educated at Listowel Boys' School and St Michael's College Listowel. Married to Mary O'Connor with three sons and one daughter. Formerly in a variety of jobs in England before returning to Ireland in 1953 where he worked as a chemist's assistant in Doneraile before purchasing a public house in Listowel; columnist with *The Limerick Leader*, *Evening Herald* and *The Irish Echo*, New York. Publications include *Sive*, *Sharon's Grave*, *The Highest House on the Mountain*, *No More in Dust*, *The Man from Clare*, *Many Young Men of Twenty*, *The Year of the Hiker*, *The Rain at the End of the Summer*, *The Field*, *Hut 42*, *Big Maggie*, *The Change in Mame Fadden*, *Moll*, *The One-Way Ticket*, *The Chastitute*, *The Buds of Ballybunion*, *The Good Thing* and *The Bodhrán Makers* as well as poems, essays, novels, recordings, albums, a biography and eight books in the Letters series.

RAYMOND KEAVENEY
Gallery Director
Merrion Square, Dublin 2
(01) 615133
Born to James and Margaret Keaveney (née Collins) at Carlanstown, Co. Meath in 1947. Educated at Carlanstown NS, Franciscan College Gormanstown and at UCD, whence he graduated with BA and MA degrees and a Diploma in Librarianship. Separated. Formerly assistant librarian St Patrick's College Maynooth, assistant and assistant director National Gallery of Ireland. At present director National Gallery of Ireland. Specialising in Italian art and old master drawings, he has published internationally on these subjects.

DESMOND JOSEPH BERNARD (DES) KEOGH
Actor
c/o RTE, Donnybrook, Dublin 4
(01) 693111
Born to Stephen and Maura Keogh (née O'Connor) at Birr on 27 February 1937. Educated at Glenstal Abbey, UCD, King's Inns and University of Munich. Graduated BA in French and German from UCD. Admitted barrister-in-law. Married to Geraldine O'Grady with one daughter, Oonagh. Formerly clerk at Guinness', and worked on contract with RTE. At present actor, broadcaster and entertainer, he has appeared in all major theatres in Ireland. Member Milltown Golf Club and Donnybrook Tennis Club.

THOMAS KINSELLA
Co. Wicklow
Born to John Paul and Agnes Casserly Kinsella at Dublin on 4 May 1928. Married to Eleanor Walsh with one son and two daughters. Formerly with Civil Service Department of Finance, Artist in Residence at Southern Illinois University, Professor of English at Temple University Philadelphia, director Dolmen Press Ltd, Cuala Press Ltd Dublin, founded Peppercanister Dublin, member Irish Academy of Letters, Guggenheim Fellowship, Guinness Poetry Award, Irish Arts Council Triennial Book Award, Denis Devlin Memorial Award, Hon D.Litt NUI. Publications include *Another September, Downstream, Nightwalker and other Poems, Notes from the Land of the Dead, New Poems, Selected Poems, Song of the Night and other Poems, The Messenger, Fifteen Dead, One and Other Poems, Peppercannister Poems, One Fond Embrace, The Táin, Selected Poems of Austin Clarke*, Co-ed *Poems of the Dispossessed, Ireland's Musical Heritage: Séan O'Riada's Radio Talks on Irish Traditional Music, Songs of the Psyche* (poems), *Her Vertical Smile, The New Oxford Book of Irish Verse, St Catherine's Clock, Out of Ireland, The Complete Fond Embrace, Blood and Family, Personal Places* and *Poems from Centre City*.

LOUIS LE BROCQUY
Artist
c/o Gimpel Fils, 30 Davies Street, London W1Y 1LG
Born to Albert and Sybil Le Brocquy (née de Lacy Staunton) at Dublin on 10 November 1916. Educated at St Gerard's School Wicklow. Married first to Jean Atkinson Stoney with one daughter and second to Anne Madden Simpson with two sons. Formerly visiting instructor Central School of Arts and Crafts London, visiting tutor RCA London, member Irish Council of Design, director Kilkenny Design Workshops and Irish Museum of Modern Art. Chevalier de la Légion d'honneur.

HUGH LEONARD (JOHN KEYES BYRNE)
Playwright
Dalkey, Co. Dublin
Born in Dublin on 9 November 1926. Educated at Harold Boys' School Dalkey and at Presentation Brothers Glasthule. Married to Paule Jacquet with one child. Formerly a civil servant. Has written 28 plays, three books, much television and journalism. At present working writer. Awarded D.Litt (hon) TCD, Doctor of Humane Letters Rhode Island College, Tony Award and various others.

PROINSIAS MacAONGHUSA
Sráid Fhearchair, Baile Átha Cliath 2
(01) 757401
Born to Críostóir and Máiread MacAonghusa (née de Lappe) at Galway on 23 June 1933. Married to Catherine McGuinness with one daughter and two sons. Formerly programmes editor RTE TV, UN Consultant in Central Africa, member Presidential Committee of World Peace Council and vice chairman of Irish Labour Party. At present president Conradh na Gaeilge, chairman Bord na Gaeilge and member Arts Council of Ireland. Author of political, economic and general books in Irish and English. Authority on African and Latin American political affairs. Member United Arts Club, Conradh na Gaeilge Dublin, Wig and Pen Club London and Ndola Golf Club Zambia.

MÁIRTÍN McCULLOUGH
Company Director
11/13 Suffolk Street, Dublin 2
(01) 773138
Born to Denis and Agnes McCullough (née Ryan) at Dublin on 2 December 1924. Educated at Scoil Colmcille, Marlborough Street, Coláiste Mhuire, CBS Parnell Square and UCD. Married to Mary Frances Little with one son, Aidan, and three daughters, Éilis, Catriona and Margaret. Formerly chairman Arts Council and director National Concert Hall. At present chairman Irish National Insurance Company plc, director New Ireland Holdings plc, chairman McCullough Pigott Ltd, director of Cothú (Irish Business Council for the Arts), chairman Tyrone Guthrie

Centre, vice chairman St Michael's House, director Executive/Advisory Committee Ireland Funds, trustee National Library of Ireland, Member Stephen's Green Club, Fitzwilliam Lawn Tennis Club, Royal Dublin Society, Royal Zoological Society and Friends of the National Collection.

JOHN McGAHERN
Writer
c/o 3 Queen Square, London
Born to Francis and Susan McGahern (née McManus) at Dublin on 12 November 1934. Educated at Presentation College, Carrick-on-Shannon, St Patrick's College Drumcondra and UCD. Married to Madeline Green. Formerly national teacher, O'Connor Professor of Literature at Colgate University, New York, and fellow at Trinity College. At present member of Aosdana, the Irish Academy of Letters, and fellow of the Royal Society of Literature. Recipient of the AE Memorial Award, McAuley Fellowship, British Arts Council Awards and Society of Authors Award. Also Arts Council of Ireland Award, American Irish Foundation Literary Award, Tenth Anniversary Award of the Galway Arts Festival and Society of Authors' Travelling Fellowship. Short listed for the Booker Prize 1990, Aer Lingus Irish Times Literature Award 1990, Hughes & Hughes Award 1990. Chevalier de l'Ordre des Arts et des Lettres 1989, Hon D.Litt TCD 1991. Publications include *The Barracks*, *The Dark*, *Nightlines*, *Sinclair*, *The Leavetaking*, *Getting Through*, *The Pornographer*, *High Ground*, *The Rockingham Shoot*, *Amongst Women* and *The Power of Darkness*.

PAUL McGUINNESS
Manager
30/32 Sir John Rogersons's Quay, Dublin 2
(01) 777330
Born to Philip and Sheila McGuinness (née Lyne) in West Germany on 16 June 1951. Educated at Clongowes Wood College and TCD. Married to Kathy Gilfillan with two children. At present manager U2, member Arts Council and director Principle Management Ltd.

THOMAS PATRICK McKENNA
Actor
535 King's Road, London SW10
(071) 351 3971
Born to Ralph and May McKenna (née O'Reilly) in Co. Cavan on 7 September 1931. Educated at Mullagh National School and at St Patrick's College Cavan. Married to May White with four sons and one daughter. Formerly member Abbey Theatre Dublin. At present honorary life member Abbey Theatre and member Royal National Theatre London. Member United Arts Club Dublin.

AUGUSTINE MARTIN

Professor
Belfield, Dublin 4
(01) 693224

Born to Patrick and Mary Martin (née McHugh) at Ballinamore, Co. Leitrim on 13 November 1935. Educated at Ballinamore, at Cistercian College Roscrea and at UCD. Married to Claire Kennedy with four children. Formerly English teacher at Cistercian College Roscrea. Member of Seanad Éireann, director Yeats' International Summer School, Irish representative at Salzburg Seminar of American Studies, and founder director of James Joyce Annual Summer School at Newman House UCD. At present professor of Anglo-Irish literature and chairman board of Abbey Theatre. Has lectured on Irish literary topics, especially Yeats, Joyce, poetry, the short story, literature and politics and Northern Irish poetry at the Universities of Cologne, Frankfurt, Fordham, Cambridge, Stanford, San Diego, Boston, Magill, Montreal, London, Birkbeck, Tokyo, Kyoto, Caen, Singapore, Delhi and Bombay. Books published include *James Stephens: A Critical Study*, *History of Anglo-Irish Literature*, *Winters' Tales from Ireland* (ed), *Yeats: A Biography* and *The Genius of Irish Prose* (ed).

ADRIAN MUNNELLY

70 Merrion Square, Dublin 2
(01) 611840

Born to Patrick and Eileen Munnelly (née McCaffrey) at Ballina on 31 December 1946. Educated at St Muiredach's College Ballina and UCG whence he graduated with a BA degree and HDipEd. Formerly with Monaghan and Mayo Vocational Education Committees, served as education office on secondment to Dept of Education. Married to Eithne Forbes with one son and one daughter. At present director of Arts Council, and member Cultural Relations' Committee of the Dept of Foreign Affairs, National Distance Education Council, CIRCLE — Centres for information, research liaison in Europe (under the auspices of the Council of Europe) and trustee of the National Self-Portrait Collection.

PATRICK JOSEPH MURPHY

Maltster
Athy, Co. Kildare
(0507) 31716

Born to Patrick and May Ann Murphy (née Furlong) at New Ross, Co. Wexford on 11 March 1939. Educated at St Mary's Convent of Mercy, St Joseph's CBS New Ross, TCD and College of Commerce Rathmines. Married to Antoinette Amelia Cummins with four children. Formerly president Irish Exporters' Association, brewery manager Guinness Ghana Ltd, managing director Irish Malt Exports Ltd and director National College of Art and Design. At present chairman Minch Norton Ltd, ROSC, Irish Shippers Council, National Review Committee on Ports and managing director Irish Malt Products Ltd. Member Contemporary Irish Art Society, World Art Forum, Geneva, Kildare Street and University Club. Winner 1st Sir Charles Harvey Award for Management Studies, IMI 1965 and the Lord Mayor's Millennium Award 1988 for outstanding achievement.

JOHN C. NOLAN
Museum Director
Botanic Gardens, Belfast BT9 5AB
(0232) 381251
Born to Francis and Margaret Nolan (née Leavy) at Ballisodare, Co. Sligo on 31 May 1931. Educated at St Eugene's Boys' Primary School, St Columb's College, St Mary's College of Education, Belfast College of Art, Queen's University Belfast, Open University and Sheffield City Polytechnic. Married to Maureen McAlindon with five children. Formerly deputy principal St Joseph's College of Education, Belfast. At present executive director Ulster Museum, director Museum Training Institute, treasurer Educational Guidance Service for Adults, committee member University Centre for the Arts, Queen's University, member Royal Overseas Club London, Ulster Arts Club, and Belfast Senior Common Room, Queen's University. Fellow of Museums Association, Royal Society of Arts and British Institute of Management.

TONY Ó DÁLAIGH
Festival Director
Nassau Street, Dublin 2
(01) 778439
Born to Daniel and Margaret Ó Dálaigh (née McDonnell) at Mallow on 2 August 1933. Educated at Patrician Brothers Mallow. Married to Margaret O'Callaghan with two sons, Cormac and Ruaidhrí, and two daughters, Eimhear and Aoife. Formerly private secretary to Minister of Education, head of Youth and Sport at Dept of Education, manager Damer Theatre, manager Irish National Opera, administrator Irish Theatre Company and director Royal Hospital Kilmainham. At present director Dublin Theatre Festival, board member Gate Theatre, City Centre Arts, Wexford Festival Opera, and shareholder Abbey Theatre. Member Strand Players and An Taisce. Takes particular pride in bringing the Madden/Arnholz prints to the Royal Hospital Kilmainham, opera to 80 towns in 30 counties and Archaos to Tallaght.

PROINNSIAS Ó DUINN
Conductor
c/o RTE Donnybrook, Dublin 4
(01) 643111
Born to Seosamh and Patricia Ó Duinn (née Langan) at Dublin in October 1941. Educated at St Mary's Marino, St Joseph's Fairview, College

of Commerce Rathmines, Royal Irish Academy of Music, College of Music and privately. Separated. One son and one daughter. Formerly principal conductor Iceland Symphony, principal conductor and music director National Symphony of Ecuador, and conductor of RTE choir. At present and since 1978 permanent principal conductor of RTE Concert Orchestra. Formerly cellist, his compositions include 'Essay for String Quartet', 'String Quartet No. 1', 'Essay for Wind Quintet', 'Symphony No. 1 Torchflame', 'Sonata for three Violins', the musical *Stuff and Nonsense* (Life of Edward Lear), Soundtrack for film/TV, and numerous orchestrations and orchestral suites.

GERALDINE MARY O'GRADY
Violinist
c/o Royal Irish Academy of Music, 36 Westland Row, Dublin 2
(01) 764412
Born to Gerald and Sheila O'Grady (née Cassidy) at Dublin. Educated at Loreto College Crumlin and Conservatoire National Supérieur de Paris. Married to Des Keogh with one daughter, Oonagh. Formerly leader of RTE Symphony Orchestra. At present pursues an international career as solo violinist, particularly in USA where she has been soloist with many major orchestras, and teaches at Royal Irish Academy of Music, Dublin. Awarded Premier Prix and first place at Conservatoire National Supérieur de Paris, also winner of Prix Sarasate, Prix Milanollo and Prix Christine Nillsson. Conducts master classes in the USA and West Indies.

CELIE O'RAHILLY
Archaeologist
Merchant's Quay, Limerick
(061) 415799
Born to Richard MacEllistrim and Elgin O'Rahilly (née Barry) at Dublin on 2 April 1948. Educated at Convent of the Sacred Heart Dublin, UCD and at Sorbonne, Paris. Single with one child. Formerly freelance archaeologist, excavation assistant, supervisor, director on excavation survey work in Counties Kerry and Donegal. Former Secretary of Irish Association of Professional Archaeologists. Has experience working in Sweden, Norway, Faroe Island, Scotland and Ireland. At present senior archaeologist with Limerick Corporation. Member Royal Society of Antiquaries and Thomond Archaeological Society.

JOSEPH ROBINS
Writer
Terenure, Dublin 6W
Born to Eugene and Kitty Robins (née Connell) on 15 April 1923. Educated at Marist College Athlone and at TCD. Married to Maureen O'Regan with two sons and two daughters. Formerly assistant secretary Dept of Health. At present chairman of Council of Barnardos, Republic of

Ireland. Member of Council Barnardos UK, St Michael's House, Dublin Rape Crisis Centre, and Mental Health Association of Ireland. Member Committee of Management, Exchange House Day Care Centre for Travellers and president Adoptive Parents' Association of Ireland. A social historian, his publications include *The Lost Children, A Study of Charity Children in Ireland 1700–1900*, and *Fools and Mad, A History of the Insane in Ireland*. Member Royal Horticultural Society of Ireland.

MICHAEL EDWARD FITZGERALD RYAN
Archaeologist
Kildare Street, Dublin 2
(01) 618811
Born to Thomas FitzGerald and Catherine Ryan (née Carty) at Skerries. Educated at Holy Faith Convent and De La Salle College Skerries, UCD and TCD. Married with three sons. Formerly assistant lecturer Dept of Archaeology UCG and assistant keeper National Museum, chairman National Committee for Archaeology and member Historic Monuments Council Belfast. At present keeper of Irish Antiquities National Museum and chairman Irish Association of Professional Archaeologists. Fellow of Society of Antiquaries of London (FSA), member Royal Irish Academy, Frend Medallist Society of Antiquaries of London 1991 for contribution to Christian Church archaeology. Author of 75 scientific papers and editor of five books.

MICHAEL PETER KENNEDY (KEN) RYAN
Managing Director
18 Old Kilmainham Dublin 8
(01) 777285
Born to Michael Francis and Mary J. Ryan (née Henry) at Dublin on 18 July 1945. Educated at Belgrove NS Clontarf, St Paul's College Raheny and College of Advanced Technology, Bolton Street. Widowed and remarried to widow Muriel Anne Lowry with one stepson and two stepdaughters. Formerly managing director Cullinane Bros and Ryan PVT Ltd, Zimbabwe. At present managing director Abbey Stained Glass Studios.

THOMAS RYAN
Portrait and Landscape Painter
Born to John and Mary Ryan at Limerick City on 16 September 1929. Educated in Limerick at St Philomena's NS, Christian Brothers Sexton Street and School of Art, and also at National College of Art, Dublin. Married to Mary Joyce with six children. At present president Royal Hibernian Academy, Limerick Art Society and United Arts Club Dublin. Honorary member Royal Academy London, Royal Scottish Academy

Edinburgh, governor and guardian of National Gallery of Ireland. Member Stamp Design Committee An Post, and Union of European Academies Madrid. Council member 'The British School at Rome' and the British Institution. Knight of the Order of St Lazarus of Jerusalem. Member United Arts Club and Friendly Brothers of St Patrick.

NICHOLAS JOHN SANDON
Musicologist
University College Cork
(021) 276871
Born to Sydney Herbert and Ivy Gladys Sandon (née Venus) at Faversham, Kent on 16 February 1948. Educated at Eastling County Primary School, Kent College Canterbury and Birmingham University. Married to Virginia Donne with one stepson, Richard and two stepdaughters, Alison and Rosamond. Formerly lecturer in music and head of music department at Exeter University. At present professor and head of music department, UCC. Member Royal Musical Association, Plainsong and Mediaeval Music Society, Henry Bradshaw Society and Touring Club Italiano.

MARIA THERESA SIMONDS-GOODING
Artist
c/o The Taylor Galleries, 6 Dawson Street, Dublin 2
(01) 776089
Born to Hamilton and Dorothy Simonds-Gooding (née Reilly) at Quetta, India on 6 October 1939. Educated at Convent of the Holy Child Killiney, Domestic Science Course Errollston, Dublin College of Art, Centre de Peinture Brussels, and Bath Academy of Art, Corsham. Single. Member of Aosdana, An Taisce, Greenpeace, Earth Watch and International Dolphin Watch. Numerous exhibitions in Ireland and New York, illustrated *An tOileánach* by Tomás Ó Críomhthain, designed two postage stamps on Irish folklore for Europa series and received numerous art awards.

IMOGEN STUART
Sculptor
c/o The Arts Council, 70 Merrion Square, Dublin 2
Born to Bruno and Katharina Werner (née Kluger) at Berlin on 25 May 1927. Educated at a private school and at Bismarck Lyceum in Berlin and afterwards for five years a private pupil of Professor Otto Hitzberger. Awarded a travelling scholarship at the Hochschule für Bildende Künste Berlin (1960). Divorced with three daughters, Aoibheann, Siobhán (deceased 1988) and Aisling. Member of Sculptors' Society of Ireland, Artists' Association of Ireland, Royal Hibernian Academy, toscaire of Aosdana, International Society of Christian Artists, Figurative Image, and Ireland-Israel Friendship League.

WILLIAM TREVOR
Author
c/o Peters, Fraser and Dunlop, Chelsea Harbour, London SW10 OXF
Born to James William and Gertrude Cox. Educated at St Columba's and TCD. Married to Jane Ryan with two sons. Publications include *The Old Boys, The Boarding House, The Love Department, The Day we got Drunk on Cake, Mrs Eckdorf in O'Neills Hotel, Miss Gomez and the Brethren, The Ballroom of Romance, Elizabeth Alone, Angels at the Ritz, The Children of Dynmouth, Lovers of their Time, Other People's Worlds, Beyond the Pale, Fools of Fortune, A Writer's Ireland: Landscape in Literature, The News from Ireland, Nights at the Alexandra, The Silence in the Garden, Family Sins* and *Two Lives*. Awarded CBE, and Honorary Doctorate of Literature by Exeter, Dublin, Belfast and Cork Universities.

GERARD VICTORY
Composer
Stillorgan, Co. Dublin
Born to Thomas and Delia Victory (née Irwin) at Dublin on 24 December 1921. Educated at a private school and later at Belvedere College, UCD and TCD (Degree of D.Mus). Married to Geraldine Herity with two sons, Raymond and Alan, and three daughters, Alma, Fiona and Isolde. Formerly radio producer, television producer, deputy director and director of music at RTE. At present freelance composer and member of Aosdana, Dublin Institute for Advanced Studies), and member of the board of Celtic Studies. Honours include the French Government Order of Arts and Letters, the German Government's Order of Merit, and presidency of UNESCO's Rostrum of Composers (1981–4).

BARBARA MARY FRANCES WALLACE
Public Relations Counsultant
Mulgannon, Wexford
(053) 43467
Born to Francis and Eileen Goodall (née Ronan) at Wexford on 3 December 1935. Educated at Loreto Wexford and at Dublin City University. Separated with four children. Formerly development manager and conference officer with South East Tourism. Also Captain Girl Guides, first lady president Junior Chamber Ireland and president Soroptimists International Wexford and first lady president Public Relations Institute of Ireland. At present runs own public relations business and chairman Wexford Opera Festival.

DR JAMES WHITE
Art Historian and Author
Born to Thomas John and Florence White (née Coffey) on 16 September 1913. Educated at Belvedere College and privately in European Museum

Galleries. Married to Agnes Bowe with three sons and two daughters. Formerly art critic *The Standard*, the *Irish Press*, *The Irish Times*, curator Municipal Gallery of Ireland. Also chairman the Irish Arts Council, International Council of Museums, Ireland, Irish Museums' Association and Irish Art Historians. Honorary Secretary AICA Ireland and Royal Dublin Society, and honorary secretary, council member and late president The Friends of the National Collections of Ireland. At present trustee the Chester Beatty Foundation and Library, and the Alfred Beit Foundation. Council member Royal Dublin Society and member Advisory Commission on Art and Architecture Dublin Diocesan Commission. Professor history of art at Royal Hibernian Academy. Publications include works on Louis Le Brocquy, George Campbell, Brian Bourke, Jack B. Yeats, John Butler Yeats, Pauline Bewick and on the National Gallery of Ireland. Author of *Masterpieces of the National Gallery of Ireland* and *Irish Stained Glass* with Michael Wynne.

Chapter 20
Mining and Energy

Did you ever expect a corporation to have a conscience, when it has no soul to be damned, and no body to be kicked?

Lord Thurlow

Mineral resources in Ireland include industrial minerals, such as baryte, limestone and gypsum, and metals, such as the zinc-lead deposit at Navan. In recent times gold has been discovered near Killary Harbour, Co. Mayo, in the Sperrin Mountains, and near Croagh Patrick.

Bord na Móna (The Turf Board) markets about 5,000,000 tonnes of peat each year and 15 per cent of Ireland's electricity is generated from peat. Machine turf and briquettes are key products in the domestic market and moss peat is used extensively in horticulture, both at home and abroad. In fact, 90 per cent of horticultural peat is marketed worldwide under the Shamrock Irish brand name. The Board developed special harvesting machinery which it has successfully exported and it also engages in developmental work overseas and in consultancy. Its marketing efforts enable it to achieve IR£20 million of moss peat exports to the UK and France. Unfortunately, the financial results of the company have shown losses in recent years which called for management action, consultants' reports and rationalisation. The Peat Research Centre is located 28 miles from Dublin at Newbridge, and is a self-financing body, with the primary objective of undertaking, commissioning and sponsoring research and development activities such as would strengthen the peat industry in Ireland in terms of new products, new processes and new businesses. IPB Global is the International Consultancy arm of the Board and it offers services in the areas of surveying and land recovery, engineering, marketing, product development, transport and information technology services.

A committee on the use of Bord na Móna cutaway bog was set up by the Minister for Energy to examine the best uses to which cutaway bog can be put. Their report was completed in July 1991, and publication was eagerly awaited. In 1982, a group of peatland scientists, who were alarmed at the rate of peatland destruction, set up an organisation which re-emerged in 1985 as the Irish Peatland Conservation Council with the aim of identifying and monitoring peatland sites of conservation value, making the public aware of the need for conservation, lobbying agencies responsible for conservation and exploitation, and raising funds for site purchase, publicity and educational programmes.

Another State company with a large dependence on the Electricity Supply Board is Bord Gáis Éireann (Irish Gas Board), established in 1976 to develop and to maintain a supply of natural gas. To achieve this, it commissioned an onshore pipeline from the Kinsale Head gas field, initially to Cork, and later to Dublin. The Board's dependence on the ESB has been reduced from a peak of 80 per cent in 1983 to 43 per cent in 1990. This was a significant year for the company because the introduction of legislation limiting bituminous fuels in Dublin had the effect, when coupled with promotional campaigns by the Board, of increasing the sale of natural gas appliances by 50 per cent. The Board is committed to keeping natural gas as the most competitive fuel for home heating. Detailed investigations have been carried out into the possibility of putting in place an undersea gas interconnector to the west coast of Britain in order to secure adequate alternative supplies of gas well into the next century. Liquefied petroleum gas is supplied to the Irish market mainly by Calor Teo, which is believed to have a 70 per cent market share and is owned by the Calor Group of the UK. Significant competitors are Flogas, a company quoted on the Irish Stock Exchange, and Blugas set up in 1989 with the Jones Group, R & H Hall, and Richmond Industrial as major shareholders.

The Electricity Supply Board, the key customer of both Bord na Móna and Bord Gáis, was established in 1927 to generate and distribute electricity. It now has over 1.28 million customers, to whom it supplies over 11,700 million units at 220 volts/50 cycles, employing about 10,000 people to do so. The great contribution which the ESB has made to the Irish economy stemmed from 80 per cent of its production being based on domestic sources, such as natural gas, peat, hydro and coal. The mix of fuels used in generation in 1990 was coal: 42 per cent; Kinsale gas: 27 per cent; peat: 16 per cent; hydro: 5 per cent; with oil at 10 per cent. Playing its part in the fight for economic recovery, the ESB promised in 1989 to hold prices stable for a three year period.

ESB International Ltd is well established internationally as a leader in utility engineering and consulting. Its most spectacular success was a 10 year contract for the operation and maintenance of a new 350MW gas-fired power station at Corby in England.

The mission statement is 'We in ESB will provide our customers with quality energy services at competitive prices, with due care for the natural environment. We will also support national economic progress by engaging in profitable ancillary activities'.

Offshore exploration began in 1970 and the third well, drilled by the Marathon Co, discovered the Kinsale Head gas field. No subsequent discovery has been quite as exciting — not even Gulf's discovery of oil in the Celtic Sea. The exploration industry is very dependent on Government policy and the terms and conditions upon which licences are granted. These terms were substantially eased early in 1988 and, probably as a result, deep water drilling programmes were announced for the Porcupine Basin.

Total primary energy requirement is about 9.4 million tonnes of oil equivalent. Dependence on oil has been reducing with reliance on natural gas and coal increasing. The Whitegate oil refinery, purchased in 1982 by the state-owned Irish National Petroleum Corporation, produces about 27,000 barrels per day.

Earthwatch, the environmental awareness organisation based in Bantry, Co. Cork published a comprehensive report in December 1990 on energy alternatives — options for Ireland in the 1990s. The report, which received generous sponsorship from a number of organisations, predicted that the present decade would see the greatest implementation yet of energy conservation and efficiency, together with an unprecedented uptake of renewable energy options. Earthwatch campaigns frequently hit the mark with politicians and the media, although much of their work is done on a voluntary basis. They are concerned with global warming, the use of renewable energy, toxics, ozone, smog, tropical rain forests and other such issues.

The Department of Energy is responsible for policy on the supply and use of energy in all forms, for planning, exploration and forestry. This Department also controls the Geological Survey of Ireland and the Mining Board. In Northern Ireland energy supply and conservation is the responsibility of the Department of Economic Development. Representative organisations include the Irish Mining and Exploration Group, the Irish Mining and Quarrying Society, and the Irish Offshore Service Association.

Peat Production
Bog production machinery from Bord na Móna/Irish Peat Corporation being loaded at Dublin Port and destined for Deblois, Maine, USA. Bord na Móna is currently engaged on a consultancy basis in a bog development project in the region for Down East Peat LP. Down East is on contract to Boston Edison Co to generate electricity from a peat-fired plant in Deblois.

MICHAEL N. CONLON
Company Director
Little Island, Co. Cork
(021) 509199
Born to James and Margaret Conlon (née Poynton) at Athlone on 15 December 1926. Educated at Marist College Athlone. Married to Kitty Mac Donald with two sons, Bryan and Rory, and five daughters, Deirdre, Niamh, Orla, Clodagh and Dara. Formerly town clerk Athlone, secretary Tipperary County Council, Cork county manager, general manager Pigs and Bacon Commission. Member governing body UCC, and Central Development Committee Dept of Finance. At present chairman Bord Gáis Éireann and Alexander Stenhouse Ltd, director Cork and Limerick Savings Bank, Woodchester Investment Bank, and Business and Trading House Investment Co Ltd. Member Irish Management Institute, Institute of Bankers in Ireland, National Economic and Social Council, Douglas Golf Club and Sunday's Well Tennis Club.

RICHARD CONROY
Senator
55 Dawson Street, Dublin 2
(01) 6795833
Born to Richard and Maureen Conroy (née Fitzpatrick) on 12 September 1933. Educated at Willow Park, Blackrock College and Royal College of Surgeons Dublin, and at Manchester University. Married to Pamela Murphy with two daughters, Deirdre and Sorcha. At present member of Seanad Éireann, spokesman on Foreign Affairs and Energy, chairman and chief executive Conroy Petroleum and Natural Resources plc, professor of Physiology Royal College of Surgeons in Ireland, Cathaoirleach of Dún Laoghaire Corporation and member Dublin County Council. Member Royal St George and Howth Yacht Clubs, Kildare Street and University Club and Malahide Golf Club. Joint author with J.N. Mills of first published textbook on Human Circadian Rhythms, and of other medical and scientific papers.

PHILIP CRONIN
Chief Executive
Little Island, Cork
(021) 509199
Born to Patrick and Mary Cronin (née Murphy) at Cork on 9 September 1936. Educated at CBC, North Monastery and Institute of Public Administration. Married to Nora Reynolds with three children. Formerly town clerk, housing officer, county development officer, personnel manager and company secretary. At present chief executive Bord Gáis.

BRENDAN HALLIGAN
Public Affairs Consultant
28 Lower Baggot Street, Dublin 2
(01) 612167
Born to Patrick and Jane Halligan at Dublin on 5 July 1936. Educated at
St James' CBS, College of Technology, UCD and King's Inns Dublin, and
at College of Technology, Battersea, London. Married to Margie Brennan
with one son, Fergal, and two daughters, Gráinne and Aoife. Formerly
economist, analyst, lecturer, TD, Senator, MEP, and general secretary of
the Labour Party, and chairman of the Irish Council of the European
Movement. At present chairman of Bord na Móna, Adjunct Professor of
European Affairs at University of Limerick, and president Institute of
European Affairs, Dublin. Member Royal Dublin Society, Irish Georgian
Society, and Action Committee for Europe.

DAVID M. KENNEDY
46 Upper Mount Street
(01) 762463
Born at Dublin in 1938. Educated at Terenure College and UCD, whence
he graduated in 1961 with MSc degree in experimental physics. Later
studied operations research at the Case Institute of Technology in USA.
Married to Una Barry with three sons and one daughter. Formerly held a
number of posts with Aer Lingus including operations research analyst,
systems manager, senior vice president New York, assistant chief executive of operations, chief executive 1974–88, and a director of the airline
1976–88. Former president International Air Transport Association and
chairman Association of European Airlines. At present chairman Irish
National Petroleum Corporation and Irish Refining Company, director
CRH plc, Jury's Hotel Group plc, Mount Juliet Estates Ltd, Co-operation
North, and member of Court of Bank of Ireland. Professor of Strategic
Marketing at the Michael Smurfit Graduate School of Business UCD.

WILLIAM EDWARD PATRICK MEAGHER
Chief Executive
Hume House, Ballsbridge, Dublin 4
(01) 746591
Born to William Joseph and Kathleen Sabina Meagher (née Gilmartin) at
Dublin on 22 March 1934. Educated at Blackrock College, UCD and
Harvard Business School. Fellow of Institute of Chartered Accountants.
Married to Patricia Daly with one son, Bill, and four daughters, Sonja,
Anna, Rachel and Sarah. Formerly chief accountant and secretary
Burmah-Castrol (Ireland) Ltd, and former chairman of the Blood Trans-
fusion Service Board. At present chief executive and managing director
Burmah-Castrol (Ireland) Ltd and fellow of Institute of Petroleum.

JOE MORAN
Chief Executive
Lower Fitzwilliam Street, Dublin 2
(01) 765831
Born in 1932. Educated at St Gerald's College, Castlebar, Co. Mayo. Fellow of the Chartered Institute of Management Accountants. Married to Cathleen Adams with four children. Formerly served in a variety of senior posts in ESB including regional accountant, audit manager, corporate development manager, finance manager and director finance. At present chief executive Electricity Supply Board, vice president Irish Council of the Chartered Institute of Management Accountants, chairman advisory committee of National Treasury Management Agency, chairman Peamount Hospital, member Government appointed Task Force on Employment. Highly regarded internationally for his expertise in all aspects of financial management.

DR PATRICK JOHN MORIARTY
Chief Executive
27 Lower Fitzwilliam Street, Dublin 2
(01) 765831
Born to Timothy and Catherine Moriarty (née Quinn) at Dingle, Co. Kerry on 18 June 1926. Educated at Christian Brothers Dingle and High School of Commerce Rathmines. Married to Esther O'Sullivan with five children. Formerly personnel director Electricity Supply Board and chairman RTE. At present chairman ESB and Garda Advisory Board and president Irish Quality Control Association. Member Chartered Institute of Secretaries, Irish Management Institute, Institute of Public Administration, and Institute of Personnel Management. Awarded honorary doctorate (LL.D) by NUI, and admitted fellow Institution of Engineers of Ireland and of Irish Management Institute. Member Grange, Co. Louth and Ballybunion Golf Clubs.

EDDIE O'CONNOR
Managing Director
76 Lower Baggot Street, Dublin 2
(01) 688555
Born to Robert and Una O'Connor (née Rushe) at Roscommon on 26 June 1947. Educated at Convent of Mercy Elphin, Blackrock College and UCD. Married to Hildegarde Kirby with two children, Lesley and Robert. Formerly maintenance superintendent at Moneypoint Generating Station and fuel purchasing manager ESB. At present managing director Bord na Móna. Awarded honorary doctorate by International Management Centres Europe in June 1991. Fellow of Institute of Engineers of Ireland, member of Marketing Institute of Ireland, Irish Management Institute council and the board of the Institute of Public Administration. Member Hibernian United Service Club, Lansdowne Rugby Football Club and Elm Park Golf Club.

MICHAEL E.J. O'KELLY
University Professor
University College Galway
(091) 24411
Born to Dr M.J. and Mrs O'Kelly (née Casey) at Charleville on 10 April 1937. Educated at Convent School Charleville, Charleville CBS, Newbridge College, UCC, Columbia University and California Institute of Technology. Married to Ann Walsh with four sons, John, Eamon, Paul and David, and two daughters, Ita and Jane. Formerly managing director Electronic Components Cork and head of Manpower Forecasting Unit, Dept of Labour. At present Professor of Industrial Engineering UCG, director of a number of private companies, deputy chairman ESB.

EOIN RYAN
Senior Counsel
Clanwilliam Court, Dublin 2
(01) 760696
Born to Dr James and Máirín Esther Ryan (née Cregan) at Dublin on 12 June 1920. Educated at Presentation College Bray, Cistercian College Roscrea, at UCD whence he graduated with BA degree, and at King's Inns Dublin (barrister-at-law). Married to Joan Olive Dowd with three sons, James George, Eoin Daithí and Mark Joseph, and one daughter, Dearbhail Máire. Formerly in the Defence Forces, barrister, member Seanad Éireann 1957–87, member Irish delegation to Council of Europe, member Senate of NUI and vice president Fianna Fáil Party and chairman New Ireland Assurance. At present chairman Aran Energy plc and director Jefferson Smurfit Group, Lyons Irish holdings, P.V. Doyle Hotels and Oilbase Ireland Ltd. Member Elm Park Golf Club and Fitzwilliam Lawn Tennis Club.

DENIS J. SHELLY
Company Director
41 Merrion Square, Dublin 2
(01) 612584
Born on 9 October 1922. Educated at O'Connell Schools and afterwards admitted to membership of Institute of Chartered Accountants in Ireland. Married to Marie Jenkinson with two children. Formerly secretary McMullan's Kosangas Ltd, general manager Calor Gas Ltd, president Irish Liquefied Petroleum Gas Association, Dublin Chamber of Commerce and European Liquid Petroleum Gas Association. At present chairman Dublin Business Innovation Centre and Calor Teoranta. Initiated formation of World Liquefied Petroleum Gas Association (World LPG Forum). Member Dublin Port and Docks Board and RDS Council.

Chapter 21
Manufacturing

*We demand that big business give the people a square deal: in return
we must insist that when any one engaged in big business honestly
endeavors to do right he shall himself be given a square deal.*

Roosevelt

Once upon a time, and a very good time it was, the Irish manufacturer calculated his selling price by applying the formula:

English Selling Price + Irish Import Duty + 1p or 1%, in the case of the sophisticated.

The creation of the Anglo-Irish Free Trade Area in 1965 and accession to membership of the European Economic Community in 1973 were two major milestones in the transition from the protection of the past to the dynamic environment of the present.

It has been claimed that Ireland had no real manufacturing culture at all until the 1960s and it has even been suggested that any culture which we now have is attributable to the dominant role of foreign-owned companies, which account for 80,000 out of the Republic's total of 200,000 manufacturing jobs. But such claims must not be allowed to go unchallenged because any consideration of Irish manufacturing which deals with past centuries, as opposed merely to past decades, will show that there was substantial industrial activity in Ireland in the eighteenth and nineteenth centuries. This activity embraced not only the production of food and drink, but also textile and other products. It has been estimated, for example, that by 1770 the textile industry in Dublin provided the main source of support for up to 15,000 families or about half the population.

But to return to the present ... employment in manufacturing today is about 19 per cent of the workforce, quite close to the OECD average of 22 per cent. Industry employs more people than agriculture but much less than services. It is a glamour area and the successful, especially those who are successful overseas, are rightly seen as modern Irish heroes.

The long term survival of Ireland's manufacturing industry depends on our ability to produce quality manufactured goods.

Top Quality
Professor John A. Murphy, Chief Executive Irish Quality Association
(left) with Dr J.M. Juran, the renowned Quality Guru, at the EOQ
Conference.

The exceptional quality of Irish linen, glass, dairy products, beer and pottery is world famous, but now the challenge is to ensure that all Irish products become famous for quality. The Q-Mark or quality mark is granted on the basis of an assessment of the quality control system by questionnaire and by an in-depth factory audit. This study involves areas such as management responsibility, quality system, contract review, document control, purchasing, process control, quality records, quality audits, training and several other headings. The Q-Mark is also available to service industries where it is known as the Service Quality Mark. When a company has earned the Q-Mark it can go on to be approved under the international quality management standard IS/ISO 9000 which is organised in Ireland by the National Standards Authority.

The Irish Quality Association was originally organised in 1969 and formally incorporated in 1980. Its aims were the promotion of modern quality control in industry and in services, the raising of quality standards in Ireland, and the advancement of the exchange of information and ideas on all aspects of quality. The Association is concerned to ensure that manufacturing industry in the Republic which employs almost 300,000 people, and services which employ nearly 625,000, all hear the quality message. The Association has even been co-operating with school book publishers so that the message can get through to those in primary and secondary education. They have also been running courses for Quality Assurance Auditors.

Programmes in advanced technology are aimed to channel skills that exist in higher education into certain priority areas, and in this way help make Ireland internationally competitive in terms of technological development. One of these programmes is known as Optronics Ireland and it draws together the research expertise of five Universities. Another programme is BioResearch Ireland, and Advanced Manufacturing Technology. The National Micro Electronics Research Centre at University College Cork is equipped to undertake all aspects of integrated circuit design and production. Eolas is the state organisation providing a comprehensive range of support services in the science and technology area. It is made up of many departments and divisions, performs many roles, and is funded by a combination of fee earnings and, to the extent of about 60 per cent, subvention paid through the Office of Science and Technology, which in turn is a division of the Department of Industry and Commerce.

Contemporary success stories in the manufacturing area include Jefferson Smurfit, which has grown to be the world's biggest paper and board company, and Waterford Crystal, the cut glass manufacturer which merged its operations with the famous English porcelain manufacturer, Wedgwood. Shares in both Smurfit and Waterford are quoted on the Stock Exchange. Another success story is the privately owned Glen Dimplex which was founded by leading Irish engineer, Martin Naughton, and which is a significant European producer of domestic appliances and heating equipment. Ireland's young educated and skilled workforce and attractive corporate tax incentives appeal to foreign investors, and during 1990 the Industrial Development Authority announced plans for some of the leaders in the world of electronics to invest in greenfield facilities. These included positive decisions for a £30 million investment by Seagate and a £28 million investment plan by Maxtor, both to produce disc-drives, while Intel Corporation commenced construction of a £200 million wafer fabrication plant. Existing overseas companies who were already established in Ireland announced major expansions such as the £62 million for the Schering-Plough Pharmaceutical Plant, the £10 million by Micro Soft Corporation for software and R & D and £14 million by Motorola. Bigger even than the Intel project is Aughinish Alumina which started construction in 1978 and was completed early in 1983 and which absorbed capital investment in excess of IR£630 million. The Alumina is supplied to the shareholders in the company in proportion to their equity — Alcan 65 per cent and Billiton 35 per cent.

The crux of the industrial development scene is that job losses are running at a rate which is higher than job creations. The losses have been particularly noticeable in protected industries, such as textiles and car assembly, and are running at about 20,000 a year compared with job creations of about 18,000. In this regard it should be noted that the numbers employed in manufacturing industry have increased by about 3 per cent in each of the last three years. At the end of June 1991 the number of people unemployed in the Republic was 261,000 which was the highest in the history of the state. With emigration slowing down almost to a standstill it seems that unemployment will continue to rise and the burden on the shrinking number of tax payers will become increasingly intolerable.

Vigorous action is frequently needed to stem these losses. The IDA successfully negotiated with Thermo King the taking over of the redundant Hyster Plant in Blanchardstown, for example, and over 250 jobs are expected to be provided there within three years. The involvement of the British company Coates Viyella in Youghal Carpets preceded the return of that business to profitability. An Irish management consultant, Frank Cruess-Callaghan, with his partner, Owen Conway, and merchant bank Guinness and Mahon acquired Pierce of Wexford in 1980 and later acquired two other ailing companies, Waterford Iron Foundry and Springs of Wexford. Today these three companies employ over 300 workers with combined sales of IR£15 million.

Vincent Coakley is one of many Irish executives who rescued his own company. He was General Manager of the Westport household textiles company owned by the Danish company, Northern Feather. When the parent company became insolvent, he arranged the purchase of the Westport operation and is now a principal shareholder and managing director of Northern Feather Ireland.

Technical innovation is alive and well and Irishmen, often with the benefit of experience gained within high-tech multinationals, have founded many new electronic companies with huge growth potential. This has been recognised by the purchase of the Irish computer software company, CBT Systems, by the British group Hoskyns, and the purchase of an equity stake in another Irish software company, Dillon Technology, by Austria's largest bank.

A comparison of wage costs in manufacturing industry in Ireland with those of the main trading partners (UK, US, Germany, France, Italy, Japan, Netherlands, Belgium and Denmark) expressed in common currency terms (ECUs) and taking 1985 @ 100 reveals the following picture:

	Main Partners	Ireland
1985	100	100
1986	97	101
1987	95	89
1988	98	82
1989	100	83

Expansion by Irish companies outside Ireland has been a feature of Irish business life in recent years. The many manufacturers who have been involved, include P.J. Carroll, Cement Roadstone, Clondalkin Group, Glen Dimplex, Jefferson Smurfit and Waterford Crystal. Overseas acquisitions are frequently financed by overseas borrowings, so that there has been no huge outflow of scarce Irish capital.

The public sector observers of Irish manufacturing include the Department of Industry and Commerce in Dublin and the Department of Economic Development in Belfast. The main private sector organisations are profiled in chapter 28.

In Japan
Champion Cyclist Seán Kelly, wearing a T shirt with the message 'Ireland — The Quality Business Location', helped the Industrial Development Authority promote Ireland in Japan. He is seen here with Mr Kieran McGowan, Managing Director of the Industrial Development Authority.

LESLIE AUCHINCLOSS
Company Director
Carrigaline, Co. Cork
(021) 372541
Born to Angus and Isabella Auchincloss at Glasgow on 12 June 1933. Educated at Allan Glens School and later at Glasgow University. Graduated with honours degree BSc biochemistry. Married with three children. Formerly brewing co-ordinator for Canadian Breweries Ltd and plant manager at Beamish and Crawford. At present chairman of Biocon Group and director of BM Browne.

MATTHEW JOHN BROWNE
Pharmacist
Cookstown, Tallaght, Dublin 24
(01) 511544
Born to Andrew and Mary Browne (née Furlong) at Enniscorthy on 31 May 1942. Educated at Enniscorthy CBS and at UCD whence he graduated with BSc (pharmacy) degree. Married to Joan Bernie with five children, Andrew, Bobby, Siobhán, Maria and Tara. Formerly president Federation of Irish Chemical Industries. At present managing director Hoechst Ireland Ltd, honorary treasurer the Pharmaceutical Society of Ireland, chairman Master Plast Ltd, Master Plast UK Ltd, Banorwell Holdings and director Kenlis Publications. A keen sportsman, he is a former inter-county and inter-provincial hurler with Wexford and Leinster.

RICHARD BURROWS
Company Director
Smithfield, Dublin 7
(01) 715566
Born to George and Daisy Burrows (née Beamish) in Dublin on 16 January 1946. Educated at Wesley College and qualified as a chartered accountant. Married to Sherril Dix with three daughters and one son. Formerly chairman NADCORP (non executive), director CIE (non executive) and managing director the 'Old Bushmills' Distillery Co Ltd. At present chairman and chief executive Irish Distillers Group and chairman Edward Dillon & Co Ltd. Member of Committee of Management of Royal National Lifeboat Institution.

DÓNAL SHEMUS ALLINGHAM CARROLL
Retired
Born to J. Dónal and Sheila Carroll (née Flynn) on 26 December 1927. Educated at Dominican Convent Wicklow, Glenstal Abbey and at TCD. Later admitted to membership of the Institute of Chartered Accountants in Ireland. Married to Monica Moran with one son and one daughter.

Formerly governor Bank of Ireland, director Central Bank of Ireland, director Dunlop Holdings plc, deputy chairman Rothmans International plc, and chairman P.J. Carroll and Company plc. Awarded honorary LL.D by Dublin University. Also honorary life member Royal Dublin Society, Society of Designers in Ireland and honorary life fellow Irish Management Institute. Fellow International Academy of Management. Centenary award Institute of Chartered Accountants in Ireland.

FRANK CRUESS-CALLAGHAN
Company Director
Bilbery, Waterford
(051) 75911
Born to George and Ita Cruess-Callaghan (née Senior) at Dublin on 22 March 1934. Educated at St Conleth's, Glenstal Abbey, UCD and Institute of Chartered Accountants in Ireland. Divorced with six children. At present managing director Waterford Foundry Ltd, manufacturers of solid fuel & oil burning stoves, which he rescued in 1980. Member Stephen's Green Club, Fitzwilliam Tennis Club and Connemara Golf Club.

JOHN D.S. DAVIES
Managing Director
St James' Gate, Dublin 8
(01) 536700
Born in Cardiff, Wales in 1935. Educated at Howard Gardens, Cardiff. Married to Angela Begnet with two sons. Formerly chief accountant Beecham Products Intl Division, commercial director Beecham Products Intl Division, managing director Beecham Products Far East and of Guinness Brewing Worldwide International Division. At present managing director Guinness Ireland. Member Chartered Institute of Management Accounants and of the Chartered Institute of Secretaries. Member Killiney Golf Club and RIAC.

JOHN HEALY DONOVAN
Company Director
Born to Daniel and Margaret Donovan (née Healy) at Cork on 2 February 1920. Educated at CBC Cork, UCC MIT and College of Industrial Relations. Married to Eleanor Mary Fitzgerald with one son and two daughters. Formerly chairman and chief executive of Esso Ireland, chairman Industrial Development Authority, Dublin Port and Docks Board and Public Service Advisory Council and president Federation of Irish Industry and Institution of Engineers of Ireland. At present chairman Cornel Electronics Ltd, Irish Industrial Glass Ltd, Reynolds Tankers Ltd, SMC Ltd; and director Irish Tar and Bitumen Suppliers, Ryan Hotels plc and Chas Tennant & Co (Eire) Ltd. Member Dublin Port and Docks Board and Review Body for Higher Remuneration in the Public Service.

MICHAEL J.S. EGAN
Chemical Engineering Consultant
St James' Gate, Dublin 8
(01) 536700
Born to James Joseph and Kate Egan (née Kelly) at Dublin on 26 December 1942. Educated at O'Connell Schools and UCD whence he graduated as a chemical engineer with an MEngSc degree and where he was later awarded PhD. Married to Teresa Mary Vaughan with two sons, Cormac and Kevin, and three daughters, Katrina, Michelle and Lorraine. Formerly process engineer Du Pont Canada, project engineer Hiram Walker Canada, chief engineer Irish Distillers, manager and director Jacobs International. At present director of brewery redevelopment Arthur Guinness Son and Co (Dublin) Ltd, and owner and managing director MJSE Ltd. Fellow of Institute of Chemical Engineers and Institution of Engineers in Ireland, member Irish Family History Foundation, chairman Irish Family History Society and chairman Irish Genealogical Research Society (Ireland Branch).

MICHAEL FOLEY
Managing Director
Leitrim Street, Cork
(021) 503371
Born to John and Anne Foley (née Stafford) at Enniscorthy, Co. Wexford. Educated at CBS Enniscorthy, UCD and Institute of Chartered Accountants in Ireland. Married with three children. At present managing director Murphy's Brewery Ireland Ltd. Member Cork Golf Club, Royal Cork Yacht Club and president Wexford Supporters Club.

ANTHONY GERARD GROGAN
Chief Executive
South Circular Road, Dublin 8
(01) 537900
Born to Francis M. and Teresa Grogan (née Potter) at Waterford on 22 January 1936. Educated at St Declan's Primary and De La Salle College Waterford. Married to Vivienne Keeling with two children, Suzanne and Garret. Formerly managing director Brooks Thomas Ltd, and other positions with Henry Denny & Sons, Beecham of Ireland Ltd, Irish Sugar Co, and Chesebrough Ponds Ltd and Marketing Partners Ltd. At present chairman and managing director John Player & Sons Ltd and Player Wills (Ireland) Ltd and director Irish Carton Printers Ltd and Irish Tobacco Exports Ltd. President Federation of Irish Employers 1988–90.

HENRY HANNON
Association Director
Confederation House, Kildare Street, Dublin 2
(01) 779801
Born to Reginald (Rex) and Grace Hannon (née Telford) at Athy, Co.

Kildare on 6 January 1924. Educated at Model School Athy, Kilkenny College and Mountjoy School. Married to Margaret Rachel Wilson with one child. Formerly director Guinness Ireland Ltd, A. Guinness Son & Co Ltd, Irish Ale Breweries Ltd, Guinness Group Sales Ltd and other subsidiaries. Director Irish Marketing Surveys and chairman Tank Trans. At present director Irish Brewers' Association. Member Stephen's Green Club, Fitzwilliam Lawn Tennis Club and Rathfarnham Golf Club.

THOMAS PATRICK HOGAN
Company Chairman
Mallow, Co. Cork
(022) 21345
Born on 4 August 1908. Educated at Cistercian College Roscrea and UCD. Married to Mary Joan Bourke with five children. Formerly chairman CIE, Plessey Ireland Ltd, Blackwood Hodge and Triplex Ireland. At present chairman Mica & Micanite (Ireland) plc, and director Irish Tam. Member Royal Alfred, Royal St George and Royal Irish Yacht Clubs, Portmarnock Golf Club and Fitzwilliam Lawn Tennis Club. Honorary Consul General of Iceland. Order of the Falcon (Iceland).

TERENCE ALPHONSUS LARKIN
Company Director
Charlotte Quay, Ringsend Road, Dublin 4
(01) 683571
Born to Felix and Ellen Larkin (née Quinn) at Newry on 1 February 1924. Educated at the Abbey CBS Newry, UCD and Sheffield University. Married to Eileen McGeown with three sons, Felix, Arthur and Terence, and one daughter, Yvonne. Formerly chief executive Irish Glass plc, council member Irish Management Institute and UNICE, president European Federation of Glass Packaging, and Confederation of Irish Industry. Member board of College of Industrial Relations, board member Council of AnCo, member Dublin Diocesan Finance Committee. At present chairman governing body Dublin City University, director Ardagh plc, member national executive and national council Confederation of Irish Industry, fellow of Institution of Engineers of Ireland, member Institute of Directors, Dublin Chamber of Commerce and Royal Dublin Golf Club.

RONALD W.A. LE BAS
Assay Master
Dublin Castle, Dublin 2
(01) 751286
Born to Ronald and Alice Le Bas (née Counihan) on 3 June 1955. Educated at St Mary's College Rathmines. Married to Adrienne McCarthy with one son, Samuel. At present Assay Master for Ireland. Member of Company of Goldsmiths of Dublin. Technical advisor on precious metals to Dept of Industry and Commerce. Technical expert to the Vienna Inter-

national Hallmarking Convention. Chairman Irish Jewellery Trade 1992 Committee. Member of UILI (Union Internationale des Laboratoires Indépendants). Member of the European Assay Offices' Association. Represents National Standards Authority of Ireland in International Standards Organisation. TC/174 precious metals. Represents in CEN (Comité Européen de Normalisation). TC/283 precious metals. Organiser and chairman of the International Conference Precious Metals and the European Consumer After 1992. Member of the Irish Management Institute and the Federation of Irish Employers.

MICHAEL FRANCIS LUCITT
Managing Director
Athlone, Co. Westmeath
(0902) 75001
Born to Michael and Theresa Lucitt (née Murray) at Galway on 19 April 1948. Educated at Peterswell NS, St Mary's College Galway and UCG, and Chartered Institute of Management Accountants. Married with two children. At present managing director Irish Cable & Wire Ltd, director ICW Cable Ltd, Irish Cable Distributors Ltd, Plascon Cables Ltd, Strathclyde Cables Ltd and Power Cables & Accessories Ltd. Member Athlone Golf Club, Rotary Club of Athlone and Athlone Rugby Club.

DR JULIAN MacAIRT
Senior University Lecturer
Trinity College, Dublin 2
(01) 772941
Born to Captain and Mrs Vincent Hart (née MacNamee) at Hull, Yorkshire. Educated at Model National, CBC, PBC and UCC and Oxford University. Married to Nora Hogan with two daughters, Bláthnaid and Eileen. Formerly market research analyst Aer Lingus and Irish Dunlop. Fellow in Economics UCC. At present senior lecturer in Statistics TCD. Editor *Operations Research in Ireland*, published by Mercier in 1988. Honorary secretary Operations Research and Management Society of Ireland.

DOMHNALL McCULLOUGH
Company Director
2 Wellington Road, Dublin 4
(01) 606277
Born to Denis and Agnes McCullough (née Ryan) at Belfast on 17 January 1921. Educated at Scoil Colmcille and Coláiste Mhuire Dublin and at UCD. Married to Sarah Elizabeth Ryan with three sons, Denis, Hugh and John and two daughters, Sarah and Una. Formerly Irish Army captain, executive chairman Weartex Ltd and director Packaging Sales Ltd. At present chairman James Crean plc and Clondalkin Group plc and director McCullough Pigott Ltd. Member Milltown Golf Club, Fitzwilliam Lawn Tennis Club, Royal Dublin Society, Royal Zoological Society and Military History Society of Ireland.

SEÁN MacHALE
Businessman
Woods House, Blackrock, Co. Dublin
(01) 2832766
Born to John and Una MacHale (née Durcan) at Ballina on 6 April 1936. Educated at Clongowes Wood College, College of Pharmacy Dublin, and Harvard Business School. Married to Rosemary Barry with one son, Seán, and two daughters, Lisa Maria and Rachel Mary. Formerly managing director Warner Lambert, director Irish Press and chairman Nitrigin Éireann Teo/Irish Fertilizer Industries. At present managing director and principal Inbucon/Seán MacHale and Associates business consultants, director Algemene Bank Nederland (Ireland) Ltd, Arklow Pottery, Calor Teo, Noritake Ireland, Semperit Ireland, IRD North Mayo/West Sligo Ltd and Top Secretaries and Personnel Consultants Ltd. Member Lansdowne RFC, Fitzwilliam LTC, and Hibernian United Service Club. Played rugby for Ireland 1965–7.

JOHN FRANCIS (SEÁN) McHENRY
Kinsale Road, Cork
(021) 964377
Born to John J. and Nan McHenry (née Rice) at Cork on 11 October 1933. Educated at CBC Cork. Married to Patricia Agnes Shaw with two sons, John and Kevin, and four daughters, Margaret, Deirdre, Patricia and Niamh. Formerly director Central Bank of Ireland and president Cork Chamber of Commerce. At present chairman Vita Cortex Holdings, chairman Plant Bio-Technology (UCC). Director GTE Ireland Ltd and Russo-Burns Corporation. Member Hibernian United Service Club and Douglas Golf Club. Admires the many Irish men and women emigrants who have brought great credit to the reputation of Ireland by their work in business, in the professions and in the missions.

BARRY McSWEENEY
Biochemist
Eolas, Glasnevin, Dublin 9
(01) 370177
Born at Cork on 8 May 1959. Educated at UCC and TCD. Married to Beatrice Hoch with three sons. Formerly clinical biochemist Our Lady's Hospital Crumlin, analytical services supervisor Warner Lambert, research fellow Birmingham University, European marketing and applications manager American Hospital Supply Corp, Switzerland, head of biotechnology NBST and director of medical business Biocon Cork. At present director of Bioresearch Ireland.

JOSEPH GERARD MASTERSON
Company Chairman
High Street, Dublin 8
(01) 718491
Born to Laurence and Violet Masterson (née Hayes) at Dublin on 19 August 1930. Educated at Belvedere and Castleknock Colleges, UCD and University of Uppsala, Sweden. Married to Lotti Baumgartner with four sons, Eric, Raoul, Laurence and Philip. Formerly professor of medical genetics UCD and corporate president and managing director Elan Corporation. At present chairman & ceo of Drug Research Corporation plc.

LAURENCE MURTAGH
Managing Director
Ballivor, Co. Meath
(0405) 46159
Born to James and Ann Murtagh (née Cunningham) at Dundalk, Co. Louth on 13 June 1943. Educated at CBS Dundalk and at UCG. Married to Helen O'Connell with three children. Formerly production director NEC. At present managing director NEC Semiconductors Ireland Ltd.

JOHN J. O'FLAHERTY
Managing Director
Plassey Technological Park, Limerick
(061) 334699
Born to Matthew and Catherine O'Flaherty (née Mahony) at Tralee, Co. Kerry on 14 December 1953. Educated at CBS Tralee and UCD. Married to Máiréad Hughes with four children. Formerly managing director Automated Circuit Layouts Ltd, development director Intelligence Ireland and senior engineer RTE. At present managing director MAC The National Microelectronics Applications Centre Ltd and adjunct associate Plassey Technological Park and of Information Systems & Services Centre of Plassey Technological Park. Chartered Engineer, Institute of Electrical Engineers and Institute of Engineers of Ireland and technical auditor and evaluator on EC Drive Programme. Member MBA Association

JOHN THOMAS O'HALLORAN
Managing Director
Aughrim, Co. Wicklow
Born to James and Susan O'Halloran (née Griffin) at Co. Clare on 16 January 1942. Educated at Clohanes NS and Ennistymon CBS. Married to Maeve Siggins with three sons and three daughters. Formerly in construction industry and timber trade. Past president Arklow Chamber of Commerce and Grand Knight of St Columbanus. At present founder and managing director Woodfab Ltd, president Irish Timber Council, chairman Arklow Enterprise Centre and director Coillte Teo. Member Woodenbridge and Arklow Golf Clubs.

COLM O'NEILL
Managing Director
Westport, Co. Mayo
(098) 26284
Born to Séamus and Caitlín O'Neill (née O'Keefe) at Dublin on 29 July 1950. Educated at Scoil Lorcan Dublin, Presentation Brothers Glasthule and at UCD. Married with five children. Formerly plant manager Allergan Pharmaceuticals. At present managing director Allergan Pharmaceuticals. Member Westport Golf Club and Westport Trout Fishing Club.

DONALD MONTAGU PRATT
Joint Managing Director
Kilmacanogue, Bray, Co. Wicklow
(01) 2867466
Born to Charles Y. and Stella M. Pratt (née McVeagh) at Dublin on 9 July 1935. Educated at Castle Park Dalkey, College of St Columba, TCD and Incorporated Law Society. Married with five children. Formerly partner T.G. McVeagh & Co Solicitors. At present joint managing director Avoca Handweavers, director and joint owner of Fragrances of Ireland. Member Carrickmines and Woodenbridge Golf Clubs. Captain Irish Cricket and Squash Teams. Ten times Irish Squash Champion. Three times captain Three Rock Rovers Hockey Team. Played hockey for Leinster.

RICHARD W. SCULLY
Managing Director
South Main Street, Cork
(021) 276841
Born to Richard and Alene Scully (née Montgomery) in Ohio in August 1946. Educated at St Dominic's Elder High School, Harvard University and at Ohio University. Married to Pamela Smith with two daughters. Formerly president Carling O'Keeffe Breweries, Ontario, Canada. At present managing director Beamish & Crawford plc and director of European Operations Courage Ltd, England. Member Young Presidents' Organisation International. Awarded Marketing Executive of the year 1990 from the Marketing Institute of Ireland.

BRIAN AODH SLOWEY
Company Chairman
St James' Gate, Dublin
(01) 533645
Born to Henry and Nora Slowey (née Beggan) at Clones, Co. Monaghan on 22 November 1933. Educated at Castleknock College and UCD. Married to Marie Pobjoy with three daughters and one son. Formerly managing director Cantrell & Cochrane Group Ltd and Guinness Ireland Ltd and chairman Aer Lingus/Aerlínte Éireann plc. At present chairman Guinness Ireland Ltd and vice chairman Guinness Brewing Worldwide

Ltd (London). Member Milltown and Woodbrook Golf Clubs and Royal St George Yacht Club.

DR MICHAEL W.J. SMURFIT
Company Chairman
Beech Hill, Clonskeagh, Dublin 4
(01) 696622
Born at St Helen's, Lancashire on 7 August 1936. Educated at St Mary's College Rathmines and Clongowes Wood College. Management training with Continental Corporation USA. Married first to Norma Treisman with two sons and two daughters, second to Brigitta Bejmark with one son. Joined Jefferson Smurfit and Sons in 1955, leaving in 1961 to form Jefferson Smurfit Packaging Ltd, Lancashire. Rejoined Jefferson Smurfit Group in 1964, appointed director in 1967, deputy chairman in 1969. Formerly chairman Telecom Éireann (until September 1991). At present chairman Jefferson Smurfit Corporation, Container Corporation of America, Beech Hill Life and Pensions Ltd and the Racing Board, chief executive (since 1977) Jefferson Smurfit Group Ltd. Conferred with honorary LL.D degrees by TCD, NUI and University of Scranton, Pennsylvania. Fellow of International Academy of Management. Honorary Consul of Ireland in Monaco. Has made Smurfit Group the largest paper packaging company in the world.

CHRISTOPHER HENRY TAYLOR
Chief Executive
Shannon Industrial Estate, Shannon, Co. Clare
(061) 61655
Born in UK in 1940. Educated at Lindisfarne College Wales and Institute of Chartered Accountants in England and Wales. Married to Patricia McAuley with one son and one daughter. Formerly chartered accountant G. Cummins & Co, London. At present chief executive Northern Hemisphere and resident director (Ireland) De Beers Industrial Diamond Division.

JOHN J. TEELING
Company Chairman
Riverstown, Dundalk, Co. Louth
(042) 76102
Born to James and Emily Teeling (née Kinsella) at Dublin. Educated at St Joseph's CBS Fairview, UCD, Wharton School and at Harvard Business School. Married to Deirdre Shaw with two sons and one daughter. Formerly lecturer in Business Administration at UCD. At present executive chairman and founder African Gold plc, Pan Andean Resources plc, deputy chairman Kenmare Resources plc, executive chairman and founder Cooley Distillery plc, executive chairman County Glen, and founder director Cambridge Group plc.

HOWARD LYNN TEMPLE
Company Chairman
Donegal
(073) 21100
Born to Robert and Ellen Sarah Temple (née Hill) at Donegal on 9 June 1913. Educated at Donegal NS, Methodist College Belfast and at TCD. Married to Frances Mary Woods with three children. Formerly managing director Magee & Co Ltd Donegal, and Magee Clothing Ltd Ballymena. At present chairman Magee & Co Ltd Donegal, and Magee Clothing Ltd. Director W & J Leight Ltd. Member National Council of CII, Kildare Street and University Club and Friendly Brothers of St Patrick.

CHARLES A. WALSHE
Managing Director
Ninth Lock Road, Dublin 22
(01) 572000
Born to Stephen and Maud Walshe (née Geraghty) at Westport on 4 February 1943. Educated at CBS Westport, St Jarlath's College Tuam and UCD whence he graduated with a BComm degree. Married to Patricia Marrinan with two sons, Stephen and Robert, and one daughter, Caroline. Formerly sales director Alfred Bird and Sons Ireland Ltd, sales and marketing manager Glaxo Farley Foods, catering sales manager Hanlon Group and regional sales manager CPC Ireland Ltd. At present managing director Kraft General Foods Ireland Ltd. Member Riverview Sports Club and Irish Grocers' Benevolent Fund. President Grocers' Benevolent Fund, 1987, and member Philatelic Advisory Committee, An Post.

DR DERMOT P. WHELAN
Managing Director
Raheen, Limerick
(061) 27711
Born to Comdt P.J. and Mrs B. Whelan (née O'Connor) at Dublin on 15 September 1932. Educated at Coláiste Mhuire and UCD and at Technische Hochschule Brunswick, Germany. Graduated with BE and DPA degrees. Chartered engineer. Married to Eithne Hession with six children. Formerly chief engineer Irish Sugar Company/Erin Foods, director of training at AnCo, director/general manager Waterford Iron Founders, managing director SPS International and president of CII. At present managing director Howmedia International Inc., director Sfadco, member national council Irish Management Institute, member Limerick Harbour Commissioners, chairman Plassey Management and Technology Centre, director National Technological Park Plassey Ltd, and trustee Cork and Limerick Savings Bank. Honorary Doctorate (LL.D) NCEA, fellow Irish Management Institute and fellow Institution of Engineers in Ireland.

PÁDRAIC ANTHONY WHITE

Managing Director
Heritage House, Dublin
(01) 766333

Born to Batt and May White (née Loughlin) at Kinlough, Co. Leitrim on 25 June 1942. Educated at Four Masters' School Kinlough, Uragh NS, De La Salle Secondary School Ballyshannon and UCD. Married to Mary M. Casey with one daughter, Clionadh. Formerly executive officer Dept of Defence and administrative officer Dept of Health, and managing director Industrial Development Authority of Ireland. At present member of board of Industrial Credit Corporation plc, and Custom House Dock Development Authority. Chairman Northside Partnership local area company set up under the Programme for Economic and Social Progress. Group chairman BRN Insurance and Financial Services Group. Director Dresdner International Finance plc, Cornel Electronics Ltd, and Berry's Printing Group, Westport. Executive committee member ESRI and IMI and Irish Hungarian Economic Association. Trustee Eisenhower Exchange Fellowships, USA. International advisory board member of National Economic Alliance Foundation, USA. Director Irish American Partnership Inc. Boston.

JOHN MORRISON WHYTE

Managing Director
Athlone, Co. Westmeath
(0902) 74615

Born to John and Agnes Whyte (née Allison) in Scotland on 7 October 1943. Educated at Carnoustie PS, Arbroath High School, Dundee University and TCD. Married to Naomi Beveridge with two children. Formerly production manager NCR Scotland, director quality General Electric, managing director Bose Corp and managing director Ericsson. At present managing director Omnitron. Member Athlone Golf Club, St Stephen's Green Club and Marketing Institute of Ireland.

Chapter 22
Selling Goods and Services

What need you, being come to sense
But fumble in a greasy till
And add the halfpence to the pence
And prayer to shivering prayer, until
You have dried the marrow from the bone?

Yeats

Satisfying the demands, needs and whims of the 944,000 house-wives in the Republic has come a long way from the days of the 'greasy till'. The bad old days of Irish retailing were perhaps epitomised by the crossroads or street-corner grocer who was, as likely as not, also the local publican, hardware merchant, wool buyer, funeral undertaker, and money lender. Today's 944,000 housewives are each understood to spend more than an average IR£57 on food each week, which makes the Republic of Ireland food market worth IR£2,800 million.

There are over 7,000 grocers in the State, including grocers with off-licences, so that much of the food business is in the hands of Irish-owned companies, like Dunne's Stores, Roches Stores and Superquinn, to name three retailers, and Musgrave's and Keen Cost, to name two wholesalers. A significant market share has, however, been acquired by overseas-owned companies, such as Quinnsworth. All multiple retailers sell for immediate payment in cash or by credit card and sell on the basis of display only. There is little or no service and customers are left to select the merchandise they require from well-stocked shelves. The success of this method of doing business has been such as to raise irrevocably the multiples' market share, which has been steadily increasing at the expense of the independents, who have been forced to make major changes in their operating methods in order to survive on their declining market share. This very often takes the form of late opening and, in the bigger centres of population, sixteen hours a day trading seven days a week is not unusual, and even in some instances, stores never close at all.

Extended trading is typical of stores which are much smaller than supermarkets, but which carry a much wider range of merchandise than the conventional grocer. In other words, in addition to popular branded grocery products, there are also popular branded products in health and beauty, hardware, stationery, snacks, beverages and take-away fast foods.

Away from the major centres of population other competitive volleys are fired at the multiples, and the eight D.H. Burke Supermarkets delivery service is a particularly interesting one. The multiples are simply not organised to match this. Unfortunately, this service is only available in the west of Ireland.

Publicity-Shy

Secrecy is a trait shared by almost all the big names in Irish retailing. If there is an exception to prove the rule, it might be Feargal Quinn of Superquinn, who is coy when it comes to disclosing personal information, but who in February 1989 voluntarily published extracts from the accounts of Superquinn Limited for the year to 30 April 1988. When private companies go to the stock market, or when they are acquired by companies whose shares are already quoted on the stock exchange, the lid is lifted and interesting information can be revealed. This occurred in the case of Atlantic Homecare which, having commenced trading in Dublin in 1981, had five stores operating in Dublin by 1989 through a private company. Some confidential information was revealed however, when three of the stores owned by the Hollington Group were acquired by Heiton Holdings plc at the end of 1989.

Future historians will, no doubt, find it odd that the people in our society who are closest to the public at large and to the 944,000 housewives in particular, find it necessary to be secretive. Is this caused by over-familiarity with the Irish public? Do they secretly loathe the public? Are they filled with revulsion at the sight of queues at their own cash registers? This is hardly the case, but on the other hand, the impact of new company law will inevitably result in more information being revealed, about their corporate lives at any rate.

The Local

After the grocer's shop, the pub is, perhaps, the retail outlet with which the Irish are most familiar. Like the grocery shops of old, pubs have been changing rapidly, away from the saw-dust and the cosy snug to the bright lounges where not only drink but also food is available, and, as often as not, a few pool tables, a darts board, a conversation-inhibiting television set and the prospect of live entertainment at the weekend.

There are nearly 10,000 fully-licensed premises in the Republic or one for every 350 citizens. This calculation includes, of course, those who are too young ever to want to use the facilities, those who are too old, and those who choose never to do so.

The pattern of life in the pub trade was quite different in Northern Ireland, at least until early 1988. Prior to then only premises selling food, and private clubs, were allowed to sell drink on Sundays when pubs were forced to close. There has been a major shift in trade, from the time of this change in legislation, away from the club to the pub. The situation in Northern Ireland is an interesting example of how law and religion become involved in what is, after all, a very basic form of economic activity.

The Republic has not been without a similar involvement and legislation to abolish what was traditionally known as the 'Holy Hour' in Dublin and Cork was only introduced in 1988. The same legislation allows restaurants to apply for licences to sell spirits. There was a considerable anomaly for many people who were 'Introducing Ireland' to find that having entertained a visitor to a first class dinner in a first class restaurant, it was quite out of the question to round off the proceedings with a ball of malt!

Factory Shops

Direct selling to the customer is a curious phenomenon. It has been a source of particular irritation to Irish retailers. Competition is the life of trade, and, however much people may dislike it, they rarely admit to disliking it, and their dislike of it is very often deliberately confused with pleas for fair competition, fair trade and level playing fields.

The factory shop in the Republic presents a particularly interesting question for study and research especially where the factory has been grant-aided. This is perhaps best highlighted by taking an extreme example — a situation where the grant-aided factory is situated not only within a built-up area but also close to the main shopping street. Add in a further ingredient — the production by the factory of an item suitable for sale in a department store on the main street. The owner of the store buys similar products from a wholesale distributor whose services are rewarded by a margin, to which the department store must, of course, add its cut. The premises in which the store carries on its business are not grant-aided in any way nor is the cost of construction allowed as a deduction against profits, which are taxed at 40 per cent. On the other hand the factory, which may be foreign-owned, will probably have received a State grant towards the cost of construction, and will, in any event, have been entitled to deduct the net cost of the building from its profits, which are then taxed at 10 per cent of whatever remains to be taxed after deduction of the cost of the premises.

Needless to say, such a factory was never intended to sell any significant portion of its production in Ireland and certainly not to sell by retail. Hence the righteous indignation of the department store owner who sees his taxes being used by Government to subsidise the cost of construction of a factory which then engages in retail activity in competiton with the store owner! The 10 per cent tax rate concession would not of course apply to the retail sales in this extreme example.

Department Stores
Visitors are most likely to encounter our retailing skills and traditions in the big department stores, such as Cash's in Cork, Moons in Galway, Arnotts, Brown Thomas and Switzers in Dublin. These city centre show pieces are often under severe pressure to earn a reasonable return on the capital employed. Certainly taking contemporary property valuations into account, it is doubtful if any of them really makes an adequate return for their shareholders.

Behind the elegant facade of Cash's, on Patrick Street in Cork, however, there is an extensive mail order business and while other companies, such as Emerald and Shannon, also carry on extensive mail order trades, Cash's is perhaps the leading exponent among department stores. Brown Thomas, which used to claim in its radio advertising that there was 'no place quite like it', revealed early in 1988 that it needed eighty redundancies from its 250 employees in order to remain open. This show-piece store had been expanding its retail area in previous years, and the announcement was a major surprise. It is controlled by Mr Galen Weston of Associated British Foods, the company which also controls Quinnsworth and Penneys. Cash's, Moons and Switzers were part of the House of Fraser Group until acquired by Brown Thomas early in 1991.

These department stores suffer very often from huge over-heads, unwieldy floor space and sometimes from over-staffing. They face strong competition from multiples such as Marks and Spencer, British Home Stores, Penneys, Dunnes, Next and Laura Ashley. Marks and Spencer opened their first Irish store in 1979 in Mary Street, Dublin, and subsequently decided, in 1986, not only to expand this store but to open a further one on Merchants' Quay in Cork. A third Dublin store has been opened in Grafton Street. These three stores give the company over 100,000 square feet of selling space and provide over 500 jobs.

While this is only a fraction of the scale of operations of the Irish family-owned Roches Stores, the really stark comparison lies in their rate of expansion. The Roches Stores shops are at Cork, Dublin, Limerick, Galway, Wilton (Cork) and Blackrock (Dublin) and are understood to provide over 1,900 jobs on over 570,000 sq. ft floor space. But this wonderful company has been building up its business steadily over a period of seventy years, or more, since the founder, William Roche (1874–1939), established his first major store in Cork when he purchased 'The London House' in 1919. Marks and Spencer achieved their stake in nine years.

The late Ben Dunne was a buyer for Roches Stores before leaving to establish what has become one of the biggest Irish companies today with over forty stores and an estimated 3,000 employees. Unlike Roches Stores, Dunnes Stores have expanded outside the country with outlets in Northern Ireland, in England and even in Spain. The Dunnes' foray into the UK is said to have been met with fierce opposition from Marks and Spencer, Sainsbury and others. About 8 stores are operated there, and turnover has been reported to be about £80 million. Both Dunnes Stores and Roches Stores, having been founded in Cork, expanded to Dublin before expanding elsewhere. Nowadays, both families live in Dublin.

Retail Razzmatazz

When Mitchelstown Co-operative Agricultural Society relaunched their chain of retail stores in May 1988, they enlisted the help of Gay Byrne and a helicopter, and in this way had seven of their ten stores relaunched by the TV personality during one busy Saturday. Mr Byrne is seen here accompanied by Mitchelstown's William Fox (left) and Liam Gamble (right).

The solid achievements of these firms and many others would certainly cause any reasonable-minded visitor to wonder why the Irish State sector is involved in retailing. Kilkenny Design Workshops were established in 1963 to foster good design in Irish industry and its original shop in Kilkenny had for a long time been a tourist attraction and, indeed, its second shop in Nassau Street, Dublin, had been a show-piece for Irish products. In 1986 a third shop was opened in Bond Street, London, only to be closed two years later due to heavy losses, which lead to a decision to sell the Kilkenny and Dublin shops too. The company was understood to have sales of IR£5 million in 1987 and it received a State grant of IR£714,000. However praiseworthy the design activities of the company were, their need to be involved in retailing was suspect. This activity is best left to private enterprise and to companies, such as Blarney Woollen Mills, House of Ireland, and other vendors of Irish quality products.

Ethic

Moral and ethic considerations come to the fore when questions such as Sunday Trading are debated. One retail company, the Body Shop, has maintained a strong focus on environmental awareness and made this a feature of its whole ethos. It has organised High Street campaigns such as Stop the Burning (which called for a halt to the unscrupulous burning of the Brazilian rain forest), Against Animal Testing, and Reuse Refill Recycle, a campaign designed to celebrate Earth Day 1990 and to show customers that bringing back their bottles to be refilled would help save the resources of the world — and the customers' money. The regard for and confidence in the high standards of the pharmaceutical profession undoubtedly played a part in bringing pharmacies to the top of the chart as the most favoured location suitable for the sale of condoms, according to a *Sunday Press/* Lansdowne Market Research poll. The key organisations are RGDATA and IADT, or the Retail Grocery, Dairy and Allied Trades Association and the Irish Association of Distributive Trades. These organisations merged in 1984 bringing wholesalers together in IADT linked to the retail organisation RGDATA.

SALE OF CONDOMS

SUITABLE PLACES

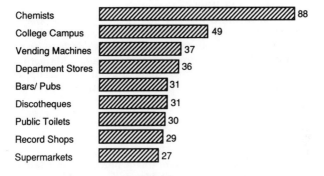

Chemists	88
College Campus	49
Vending Machines	37
Department Stores	36
Bars/ Pubs	31
Discotheques	31
Public Toilets	30
Record Shops	29
Supermarkets	27

Q: There has been a lot of talk about places where condoms may be bought - in your opinion, which of the places on this card are suitable and which are not suitable for the sale of condoms ?

(Reproduced by permission of Lansdowne Market Research and the *Sunday Press*.)

MINIMUM LEGAL AGE TO PURCHASE CONDOMS

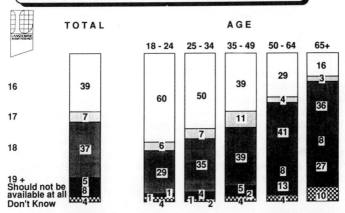

Q: In your opinion what should be the minimum legal age at which condoms can be purchased - should it be 16, 17, or 18 ?

(Reproduced by permission of Lansdowne Market Research and the *Sunday Press*.)

ROBIN JAMES ADDIS
Group Managing Director
12 Hatch Street, Dublin 2
(01) 613483
Born to Ronald and Nina Addis (née James) at Gloucestershire on 13 April 1939. Educated at St White's School Gloucestershire, Monmouth School Wales and at Bristol University. Married to Jane Margaret Evans with four children. Formerly market researcher Reckitt & Colman UK, held management positions Irish Marketing Surveys and Hunter Advertising. At present chairman Lansdowne Market Research, Marketing Institute, group managing director Irish Marketing Surveys Group. Member Royal St George Yacht and Riverview and Glenageary Tennis Clubs.

MARY BENNETT
Retailer
William Street, Galway
(091) 63862
Born to Thomas and Marie O'Donohue (née Conroy)in Co. Clare on 28 April 1938. Educated at Boston NS, St Mary's College New Ross, and Convent of Mercy Gort. Married to Eddie Bennett with three children, Ultan, Melita and Adeline. Formerly chairman Ireland West Tourism, director Bord Fáilte, national president Skal Clubs of Ireland, president Galway Chamber of Commerce and Industry, president the Chambers of Commerce of Ireland. Proprietor Treasure Chest Galway. At present director Ireland West Tourism, Corrib Airport Ltd and Aer Lingus. Admires entrepreneurs who are prepared to work hard and use initiative.

PATRICK J. CAMPBELL
Caterer
19/20 Fleet Street, Dublin 2
(01) 776761
Born to Michael and Brigid Campbell (née Kelly) at Dublin on 14 November 1942. Educated at Scoil Colmcille Marlborough Street and at Belvedere College Dublin. Also at Dublin College of Catering. Married to Veronica Dolan with three sons and two daughters. Formerly chairman Irish Offshore Services Association, chief executive Campbell Catering Ltd and chief executive Bewley's Cafés Ltd. At present chairman Campbell Bewley Group Ltd. Founder of Campbell Catering, he successfully rescued Bewley's in 1986. Received Irish Distillers/ *Irish Press* Business Person of the Year Award 1989/90. Member Old Belvedere RFC. Hobbies include running. Completed New York Marathon in 1983.

JOHN D.CARROLL
Caterer
3 Eustace Street, Dublin 2
(01) 712700/717536
Born to Thomas Gerard and Mary Carroll (née D'Arcy) at Dublin on 6

February 1931. Educated at Terenure College Dublin. Married to Bosco Kerrigan with one son, Kenneth. Formerly managing director Ireland, Northern Ireland and Wales of Bateman Catering. At present chairman and managing director John D. Carroll Group. Fellow of Campanion of Bordeaux, Irish Restaurant Owners' Association in Ireland and England, Marketing Institute of Ireland, and of the Irish Management Institute. Past president Rotary Club of Dublin and past district governor Rotary International — District 1160. Fellow of Royal Society of Health and of Institute of Management Accountants. Member Fitzwilliam Lawn Tennis Club, National Yacht Club and Grange Golf Club.

TOM CAVANAGH
Managing Director
Monahan Road, Cork
(021) 963222
Born to Thomas and Bridget Cavanagh (née O'Connor) at Fermoy, Co. Cork on 6 September 1931. Educated at Fermoy CBS and UCC whence he graduated with a BComm degree and HDipEd. Married to Marie O'Neill with four children. Formerly director Dunloe House. At present managing director Cavanagh Motor Group, director AIB Bank, chairman Conrad International Hotel, and member governing body UCC.

MICHAEL JAMES DONNELLY
Advertising Executive
3 Christchurch Square, Dublin
(01) 545111
Born to Michael and Kathleen Donnelly (née Daly) at Drogheda on 31 October 1950. Educated at CBS Wexford and at College of Marketing. Married to Geraldine O'Loughlin with three children. Formerly accounts director Arrow Advertising, account executive Wilson Hartnell and media executive McConnell's Advertising. At present managing director DDFH&B Advertising and council member Insititute of Advertising Practitioners. Member Mountpleasant Lawn Tennis Club, Shamrock Rovers, Marketing Society and of the Marketing Institute.

BASIL DUFFY
Retailer
Orwell Shopping Centre, Templeogue, Dublin 12
(01) 500688
Born to Gerard and Mary Duffy (née Murphy) at Dublin on 1 November 1949. Educated at Terenure BNS, De La Salle Churchtown and Marketing College Dublin. Married to Máiréad Dempsey with one son, Steven, and two daughters, Joanne and Gillian. Formerly with L'Oreal, ADM Londis and Unigroup N. Ireland. At present chairman Excel Group and managing director Duffy Group, has built up Newsextra chain of retail newsagents. Won a major EC law case against Fisher Price

Toys in December 1987. Formed Duffy Group Old Bawn Ltd in June 1990 and built Old Bawn Shopping Centre in Tallaght. Involved in building another Centre and hopes to continue to develop in this way.

BERNARD MARTIN DUNNE
Retailer
South Great George's Street, Dublin 2
(01) 543666
Born to Bernard and Nora Dunne (née Moloney) at Cork on 11 March 1949. Educated at Presentation Brothers College Cork. Married with four children. Chairman and managing director Dunnes Stores Group.

MARY FINAN
Managing Director
14 Leeson Park, Dublin 6
(01) 960244
Born to John and Mary Finan (née Fitzmaurice) at Roscommon on 2 August 1944. Educated at Loughglynn NS Roscommon, St Louis High School Dublin and at UCD. Married to Geoffrey MacKechnie with one daughter, Victoria. Formerly PR assistant Kenny's Advertising and PR executive Peter Owens Advertising. At present managing director Wilson Hartnell Public Relations, chairman Gate Theatre, director Irish Life Building Society and of the Automobile Association of Ireland.

AUBREY N. FOGARTY
Company Director
72 Haddington Road, Ballsbridge, Dublin 4
(01) 681455
Born to Edward and Winifred Fogarty (née Hunt) at Dublin on 6 January 1927. Married to Anne Gill with two children. Formerly managing director Aubrey Associates Ltd, AF Associates Ltd, AF Display Ltd and AF Communication Ltd, chairman Marketing Institute of Ireland and of Publicity Club of Ireland. At present chairman Aubrey Fogarty Associates Ltd. Member Hibernian United Service Club, Rotary Club of Dublin and Culwick Choral Society.

ALFRED HUGH THOMAS FOSTER
Grocer
Marino, Dublin 13
(01) 337166
Born to Alfred and Margaret Foster (née Killackey) at London on 1 August 1922. Educated at Eton House School, Southend on Sea and at Highfield College, Leigh on Sea. Married to Mary (née Burgess) with five sons. Formerly and at present grocery owner and operator. Founder member and currently president National Association of Independent Retailers. Member Balbriggan Golf Club.

RICHARD ANTHONY (TONY) HALPIN
Algonquin House, Glanmire, Co. Cork
(021) 353535
Born to Tom and Lena Halpin (née Dalton) at Cork on 23 January 1940. Educated at St Patrick's NS and Presentation College Cork and City of London College, Moorgate. Married to Noelle (née Bates). Formerly managing director Beamish and Crawford plc, chairman and managing director Beamish and Crawford Sales Ltd, Beamish and Crawford (UK) Ltd, managing director Seagram Ireland Ltd, sales manager Seagram UK Ltd, worked in the watch business for both US Time Corporation and Smiths Insustries, with Huntley and Palmers Ltd in sales, as a management trainee for the J. Lyons Group UK and as a management trainee with Harrods. At present managing director Protecol Ltd and chairman Concept Group. President Irish Management Institute, Ringaskiddy Freeport Advisory Board, director An Post and chairman Irish Brewers' Association. Member board of Cork Harbour Commissioners and of University College/Industry Liaison Board

CATHERINE FREDA HAYES
Chief Executive
Blarney, Co. Cork
(021) 385280
Born to John Christopher and Maureen Kelleher (née O'Regan) at Cork on 11 September 1951. Educated at Blarney NS, Blarney Secondary School and at the Catholic Institute in Paris. Married to Colin Hayes. Has son, Ronan Quinlan, from previous marriage. At present chief executive Blarney Woollen Mills Group, director An Bord Tráchtála, member management committee Cork/Kerry Tourism, executive committee Cork Chamber of Commerce and regional executive Federation of Irish Employers. Fellow of Irish Management Institute. Member Irish Hotels Federation and secretary Blarney Tourism. Member Royal Cork Yacht Club, St Michael's and Sunday's Well Tennis Clubs, SKAL Club and Network.

J. RICHARD F. HILLIARD
Company Director
6/7 Main Street, Kilkenny
(064) 31888
Born to R.M. and E.M. Hilliard (née Dunnell) at Killarney on 5 June 1930. Educated at St Mary's School Killarney, Midleton College and at Leicester College of Art and Technology. Married to the late Pearl Shine with three children. Managing director Hilliard's of Killarney Ltd and company secretary Squadron Shoes Ltd Tralee.

JOSEPH P. LANE
Consultant
Born to Matthew and Mary Lane (née Maher) at Mullingar on 12 March

1936. Educated at CBS Mullingar and afterwards at College of Distribution and College of Music. Married to Lucy MacCarthy with two sons and five daughters. Formerly retail manager Henshaw's and managing director Londis for twenty-five years. Retired in March 1991. At present general secretary Rathmines & Rathgar Musical Society and consultant to all distributive trades.

JAMES A. LENEHAN
Managing Director
124 Capel Street, Dublin 1
(01) 730466
Born to Thomas and Mary Frances Lenehan (née Nugent) at Dublin on 6 February 1940. Educated at St Michael's Ballsbridge, Clongowes Wood College and UCD whence he graduated with BComm and MBA degrees. Married to Dara MacEllin with two sons and three daughters. Formerly president Dublin Chamber of Commerce and Irish Hardware Association and chairman Dublin Port. At present managing director Thomas Lenehan & Co Ltd and Cargo Equipment Ltd. Board member Dublin Port, Temple Street Hospital, and council member CCII.

JERRY V. LISTON
Managing Director
32 Upper Fitzwilliam Street, Dublin 2
(01) 762721
Born to T.K. and Peggy Liston (née Slattery) at Dublin on 19 September 1940. Educated at St Michael's, Gonzaga College, UCD and King's Inns. Graduated with BL and MBA degrees. Married to Noreen Wall with three daughters, Karen, Julie and Zoë. Formerly product manager P.J. Carroll, marketing manager Urney Chocolates and general manager Warner Lambert (Irl). At present managing director United Drug plc and executive council member IMI. Member Milltown Golf Club, Fitzwilliam Lawn Tennis Club and Royal St George Yacht Club.

HUGH NEIL MacKEOWN
Company Chairman
Airport Road, Cork
(021) 963700
Born to John Ainslie and Vivenne Rosalie MacKeown (née Musgrave) at Delhi on 14 December 1941. Educated at Gloucester House, Portora, Radley College and TCD whence he graduated with BA in history. Married to Heather Thompson with four sons, Philip, Keith, Scott and David. At present chairman and managing director Musgrave Ltd, IMD Ltd and IADT Ltd and director Shield Insurance and Ulster Investment Bank. Member Cork, Douglas and Portmarnock Golf Clubs and Royal Cork Yacht Club. British Sailing Champion (national 18' class), 1982. Selected to play golf for Ireland in 1973.

NOEL McMAHON
Chief Executive
IPC House, 35/39 Shelbourne Road, Dublin 4
(01) 608766
Born to Bryan and Frances McMahon (née Hynes) at Mullingar, Co. Westmeath on 21 December 1929. Educated at St Patrick's NS Drumcondra, O'Connell School Dublin and at TCD. Married to Maura Lynch with four children. Formerly secretary Depts of Transport and Power, Communications, and Tourism and Transport, and president European Civil Aviation Conference. At present chief executive Advertising Standards Authority. Commander Order of Leopold (Belgian Decoration).

MATHEW MICHAEL MAUGHAN
12/15 Leeson Park, Dublin 6
(01) 960244
Born to Kevin and Avice Maughan (née Hearn) at Dublin on 19 May 1938. Educated at Clongowes Wood College and College of Commerce Rathmines. Married to Gemma Smith (née Faccenda) with four daughters, Fiona, Christiana, Maria and Alba Smith-Maughan. Formerly accounts director Domas Advertising, advertising representative Cahill and Co. At present chairman and managing director Wilson Hartnell Group, chairman Wilson Hartnell Advertising, Bell Advertising, Wilson Hartnell Public Relations, and Ogilvy and Mather (Ire) Ltd. Member Institute of Directors, Public Relations Institute, Institute of Advertising Practitioners of Ireland, IMI, Marketing Institute and president Publicity Club of Ireland. Member Stephen's Green Club, Royal Irish Yacht Club, Fitzwilliam Lawn Tennis Club and Milltown Golf Club.

JAMES MILTON
Public Relations Consultant
35 Upper Mount Street, Dublin 2
(01) 614666
Born to Thomas and Philomena Milton (née O'Neill) at Dublin on 21 September 1945. Educated at St Michael's and St James' CBSs. Married with four children. Formerly editor *Business & Finance*, property correspondent *Irish Press*, business correspondent *Cork Examiner*. Founding chairman Public Relations Consultants' Association. At present director Murray Consulatants. Member Baldonnel Squash Club and Dublin Gliding Club, and committee member Friends of St Luke's Hospital .

MICHAEL RONALD NESBITT
Managing Director
Henry Street, Dublin 1
(01) 721111
Born to Ronald and Eleanor Nesbitt (née Houston) at Dublin on 16 January 1941. Educated at Castle Park Dalkey, Uppingham School

Rutland and TCD. Married to Marie Daphne (Jacko) Bushe with one son, William, and one daughter, Penny. Gained business experience in England before joining Arnotts plc. At present managing director Arnotts plc. Member Royal Irish Yacht Club, Powerscourt Flying Club and Society of Amateur Aircraft Constructors.

WILLIAM NEWMAN (BILL) O'HERLIHY

Public Relations Consultant
7 Lower Fitzwilliam Street, Dublin 2
(01) 768455
Born to David and Mary Frances O'Herlihy (née Horgan) at Cork on 27 September 1938. Educated at Glasheen NS and at St Finbarr's College Cork. Married to Hilary Joan Patterson with two daughters. Formerly staff writer *Cork Examiner* Group, presenter RTE current affairs, director Royal Hospital Kilmainham and council member Public Relations Institute. At present managing director Public Relations of Ireland and chairman Mediawise Productions. Member Hibernian United Service Club, Foxrock and Elm Park Golf Clubs and Carrickmines Lawn Tennis Club. Presenter RTE Television Sport. Independent producer/presenter 'The Distant Drum', the TV series on Irish expatriates.

ROBERT MICHAEL OSBOURNE

General Manager
Mary Street, Dublin
(01) 728833
Born to Raymond Alex and Joyce Osbourne (née Williams) at Surrey on 26 March 1954. Educated at Lovelace Junior School Chessington, Tiffin Boys' School Kingston-on-Thames and Manchester University. At present general manager and company secretary Marks & Spencer (Ireland) Ltd. Member Seapoint Rugby Club.

CONOR QUINN

Managing Director
43 Lower Leeson Street, Dublin 1
(01) 608088
Born to Malachy and Julia Quinn (née Hoey) at Dublin in June 1943. Educated at St Michael's, Blackrock College and UCD. Married with four children. At present joint managing director Quinn McDonnell Pattison Ltd, director Holden Communications and Park Travel. Member Elm Park Golf Club, Blackrock Anglers' Club and Carrickmines Tennis Club.

FEARGAL QUINN

Grocer
Sutton Cross, Dublin 13
(01) 325700
Born to Eamonn and Maureen Quinn (née Donnelly) at Dublin on 27

November 1936. Educated at Monkstown NS, Koska College Clontarf, Newbridge Dominican College and UCD. Married to Denise Prendergast with five children. Formerly founder member of Irish Grocers' Benevolent Fund, chairman An Post, president and chairman Irish Management Institute and chairman Irish Quality Control Association. At present managing director Superquinn, board member of French-based Centre Internationale des Entreprises du Secteur Alimentaire. Member Portmarnock Golf Club. Awarded honorary doctorate by the National Council for Educational Awards and by University of Dublin, and winner of a 'People of the Year' award in 1984.

MERVYN V. SHAW

Retailer
Centrepoint, Portlaoise
(0502) 21316
Born to Samuel B. and Ann Shaw (née McCaig) at Dublin in 1930. Educated at Athy Model School and Wesley College. Married to Rosemary Jeffers with two sons. Formerly held a number of positions with the Shaw Group. At present joint managing director Shaw Group.

DON TIDEY

Retailer
Graham House, Marine Road, Dún Laoghaire
(01) 808441
Born in London in 1935. Formerly in management with Marks & Spencer, Greater London and four years with Dunnes Stores, Ireland. At present company chairman and chief executive Powers Group incorporating Quinnsworth, Crazy Prices, Lifestyle Sports & Leisure, Stewarts Group (NI), incorporating Stewarts, Crazy Prices (NI). Director Penneys/Primark, Associated British Foods plc, and various other international companies. Member national council of Confederation of Irish Industry. Fellow of Irish Management Institute, member Portmarnock and Castle Golf Clubs, Fitzwilliam and Donnybrook Tennis Clubs and Hibernian United Service Club.

THOMAS C. TONER

Company Director
Henry Street, Dublin 1
(01) 721111
Born to Thomas and Susan Toner (née Monaghan) at Curragh Camp on 2 June 1932. Educated at Curragh Camp, St Joseph's Academy Kildare and UCD. Widower with three sons, Kevin, David and Alan, and one daughter, Oonagh. Formerly area manager Dublin CIE, executive director Allied Irish Investment Bank, and chief executive Brooks Watson Group. At present chairman Arnotts, ICG, Inishtech plc and Tullow Oil. Director Bank of Ireland, Shell Ireland and ICL. Member

Royal St George Yacht Club, Royal Dublin Society and Carrickmines Lawn Tennis Club.

ARTHUR J. WALLS
Company Director
O'Connell Street, Dublin 1
(01) 786000
Born to Arthur C. and Mabel Walls (née Murray) at Dublin on 25 May 1926. Educated at O'Connell Schools, CBS and UCD. Married to Margaret Fahey with one son, David, and three daughters, Anne, Sheila and Brenda. Formerly general manager Aer Lingus and managing director of RTD Ltd. At present chief executive and deputy chairman Clery & Co, chairman Ryanair, Air Tara and Dublin Crystal.

ROGER STUART WORNELL
9 Appian Way, Dublin 6
(01) 609300
Born to Reginald and Grace Wornell (née Taylor) at London on 3 May 1938. Educated at Archdeacon Cambridge's School Twickenham, Christ's Hospital Hersham and Jesus College Cambridge University. Married to Jean Marie Freeman with three children. Formerly director Kenny's Advertising, marketing manager Chesebrugh-Ponds, chairman Marketing Society of Ireland, Advertising Press Club and member Performing Rights Society. At present board member Bell Advertising Ltd. Member Marketing Society and honorary life member Advertising Press Club.

Chapter 23
Imports and Importers

If a man write a better book, preach a better sermon, or make a better mouse-trap than his neighbour, tho' he build his house in the woods, the world will make a beaten path to his door.

Emerson

The most unglamorous function to fulfil in the Irish economy is that of the importer. If the exporter is a hero, it would not be fair to say that the importer is quite a villain, but it could certainly be argued that, where the exporter is loved and appreciated, the importer receives benign, if not total, neglect. Yet, the importer is like any other merchant — his function is to provide the right goods at the right price. In fulfilling this function the importer runs considerable risks which can arise from such diverse causes as foreign exchange rate fluctuations, strikes, delays in transit, and even Government interference.

Ireland's most important supplier country is undoubtedly Great Britain which accounts for about 39 per cent of imports by value, well ahead of the second biggest supplier, the USA at about 15 per cent. The next most significant countries are Germany, Japan, France and Belgium and Luxembourg. Irish businesses often find it difficult to buy from long-distance sources because of the high minimum quantities which are required. To some extent this difficulty is overcome by the use of buying groups such as National Hardware, Amalgamated Hardware and Associated Hardware who operate in the hardware and construction materials sectors.

Sanctions
In Ireland, as indeed elsewhere, nothing follows fashion more predictably and more illogically than public opinion. It has been highly fashionable to call for trade sanctions against South Africa. Early in 1986 the fashion was Libya. At the time of the Solidarity crisis it was Poland's turn.

A great many businessmen, trade associations and chambers of commerce are opposed to sanctions which present them with a public relations dilemma. If they speak on the subject when it is

335

not in fashion their utterances are, of course, ignored. (Journalists will not write what their editors do not wish to review, and editors will not release what readers are not expecting to read.) On the other hand, if they condemn calls for sanctions against a particular country, they run the risk of having their opposition to sanctions interpreted as support for the Government in question.

The most basic reason for not invoking trade sanctions, against whatever particular government is considered to be misbehaving, is that they do not work. That is a simple and a pragmatic fact and, for that reason alone, sanctions should be avoided at all costs. Any consideration of the question, however, has to assume that they will work because that is the intention of the parties who cry out for them.

Competitiveness is vital. Goverments look to business to provide jobs but, all too often, these jobs depend on foreign trade, on exports of finished products, and imports of raw materials. Foreign trade provides millions of jobs and livelihoods for people all over the world. Yet, foreign trade is a fragile thing, and should not become an instrument whereby the people of one country try to force change on the people of another one. Disapproval of a situation in another country can very easily be expressed without interfering with foreign trade.

Of course, in a situation where one country imports, in value terms, the bulk of the exports of another country, it is in a position to exert pressure, but where there is inter-dependence, there is inevitably the possibility of counter-sanctions. In relation to EC/South African trade, for example, we have to consider the havoc which would be caused in Europe by a ban on the export of chromium.

With such a ban it has been claimed that a million Americans would be put out of work and that the Western European car industry would be brought to a standstill. What effect such a disaster would have on the parent companies of foreign-owned Irish manufacturing companies is unclear. Several hundred jobs in Shannon would, of course, be directly vulnerable to a South African ban on the export of diamonds.

In the late 1980s, the issue of trade sanctions against South Africa came closer than any other issue to fooling all of the Irish people all of the time. Politicians of every hue espoused this cause which had the ready endorsement of trade unionists and clerics. But the reforms introduced by President de Klerk have led to a new enlightenment and the fading away of the threat of interference with foreign trade.

Northern Ireland

Ireland should have banned imports from Northern Ireland, if it genuinely believed that the Nationalist minority was unfairly treated by the Unionist majority, but, of course, Northern Ireland is geographically so near as to make this unthinkable! So much for the distance law which works in direct proportion — passion increases as the distance from the enemy increases. There is also another law — 'passion increases as the impact of the proposed sanction decreases'.

Imports from Northern Ireland in 1990 increased to IR£499 million from IR£489 million in 1989. This is a very significant figure in terms of Irish foreign trade and close, for example, to the total imports from the Netherlands in 1990 at IR£515 million.

Crucial to the development of trade between Northern Ireland and the Republic is the question of VAT harmonisation. There has been and there will continue to be much speculation on the effects of this in the Republic and preliminary guesses suggested that there was a distinct prospect of cheaper drink and petrol with more expensive electricity and gas. It is probably too early to guess, as the European Commission which originally sought a common VAT rate somewhere between 14 and 20 per cent, now seems to aim for a minimum VAT rate of 15 per cent with no fixed maximum. This is particularly relevant to the Republic which has a 21 per cent rate.

In considering any measures which effect North-South trade, it must also be borne in mind that in recent years there has been an extremely healthy surplus in favour of the Republic which, if the statistics tell the whole story, exported IR£816 million in 1990 against imports of IR£499 million.

Long Term Credit

Meeting of the Club of Institutions in the European Community specialising in long term credit, hosted by Industrial Credit Corporation in July
1991. Seen above are (left to right) Mr Olav Grue, managing director Fin-
ansieringsintitutte for Industri og Handvaerk A/S, Denmark, Mrs Ruth
Grue and Mr Michael Quinn, chief executive Industrial Credit Corporation plc.

BRENDAN DERMOT COAKLEY

Managing Director
Bracetown, Clonee, Co. Meath
(01) 251566

Born to Denis and Margaret Coakley (née O'Reilly) at Dublin on 27
January 1953. Educated at Gonzaga College, Castleknock College and
NUI where he obtained an Hons BA degree. Fellow of Institute of
Chartered Accountants in Ireland. Married to Lisa Mullen with three
daughters. Formerly worked with Stokes Kennedy Crowley and with
BASF AG in Germany. At present managing director of Denis Coakley
Ltd, director Gillespie & Co Ltd and Walls (Trading House) Ltd. Mem-
ber Milltown Golf Club, Fitzwilliam and Lansdowne Tennis Clubs.

RYNAL COEN
Managing Director
Oranmore, Galway
(091) 61161
Born to Bernard and Eileen Coen (née McInerney) at Gort, Co. Galway on 18 May 1934. Educated at Gort NS and Blackrock College. Married to Dairin Matthews with six children. At present managing director Bernard Coen and Sons (Galway) Ltd.

SEAN O. GARVEY
Managing Director
Castle Street, Roscommon
(0903) 26293
Born to P.M. and Maura C. Garvey (née Cunningham) at Glenamaddy, Co. Galway on 23 October 1940. Educated at Glenamaddy NS and Mount St Joseph's College Roscrea. Married to Catherine C. Murray with seven children. Formerly managing director Garvey (Ballyhard) Ltd. At present managing director Garvey (Roscommon) Ltd and Garvey (Tuam) Ltd and chairman National Hardware Ltd.

JOHN EDWARD GILLOOLEY
Chief Executive
Ballymount Cross, Tallaght, Dublin 24
(01) 500155
Born to Timothy and Mary Gillooley (née Jennings) at Cork on 4 May 1941. Educated at CBC Cork. Married to Paula Kennedy with three sons, Timothy, William and John. Formerly managing director McCarthy Dockrell Ltd and executive director Thomas Dockrell Sons and Co Ltd. At present chairman and chief executive Dockrell Glass Distribution Ltd and director Dockrell Double Glazing Ltd, Dockrell Toughened Glass Ltd, Dockrell Glass (UK) Ltd, Rathmon Investments Ltd, Franford Services Ltd and Rathsallagh House Ltd. Member Hibernian United Service Club, Sutton Golf Club and Royal Dublin Society.

J. RICHARD B. HEWAT
Company Director
Ashfield, Naas Road, Clondalkin, Dublin 22
(01) 591000
Born at Dublin in 1940. Educated at Aravon School Bray, at Oundle Northamptonshire and at TCD. Qualified as a chartered accountant. Married with one son and one daughter. Chairman Heiton Holdings plc.

IAN HARRY HUTCHINSON
Managing Director
College Park House, 20 Nassau Street, Dublin 2
(01) 6795799
Born to John and Marion Hutchinson (née Skeet) at Sheffield on 9 June 1934. Educated at Alwoodley Elementary School Leeds, Leeds Grammar School and Magdalene College Cambridge. Married to Hazel D. Maddox with two daughters and one son. Formerly worked with Investment Department of Prudential Assurance London before joining ICI, manager Salt Business ICI plc and chairman Hilton Products Ltd, Dublin. At present chairman and managing director ICI Ireland Ltd, director Associated Irish Gases Ltd and member national council Confederation of Irish Industry. Member Kildare Street and University Club and liveryman of Worshipful Company of Feltmakers of London.

LEO KEOGH
Chief Executive
5 Upper Pembroke Street, Dublin 2
(01) 761690
Born to Ignatius and Josephine Keogh (née Ennis) at Dublin on 11 July 1927. Educated at O'Connell Schools Dublin and at TCD where he was awarded a Diploma in Public Administration. Married to Kay McCullagh with three sons and one daughter. Formerly general secretary RGDATA and secretary Federation of Trade Associations. At present chief executive Society of the Irish Motor Industry (SIMI). Founder member and former president Howth/Sutton Lions Club.

JOSEPH PATRICK LYSTER
Company Director
Pearse Street, Athlone
(0902) 94433
Born to Lionel and Alice Lyster (née Begley) at Dublin on 20 March 1937. Educated at St Gerard's Bray and Glenstal Abbey Limerick. Married to Lola Walshe with two sons, Lionel and Nigel and two daughters, Rosemary and Vanessa. Formerly director National Hardware Ltd. At present chairman and managing director P. Lyster and Sons Ltd, Lyster Lawnmowers Ltd and Mercury Finance Ltd. Member and past president Co. Galway Cricket Club, member Phoenix Club, life member Athlone Rugby Club, president Midland Cricket Union and member Irish Danish Business Association.

JAMES PATRICK AUGUSTINE McHUGH
Chief Executive
Broombridge Road
Dublin 11
Born to Patrick and Kathleen McHugh (née Clancy) at Sligo on 24 April

1929. Educated at Sisters of Mercy, Marist Brothers and Summerhill, Sligo. Married to Geraldine Underwood with two daughters and one son. Formerly director Abbey Building & Civil Engineering, Abbey Homesteads, Abbey Manufacturers, Abbsy Properties, Associated Manufacturers & Sales Organisation, Basta, M & J Plant Hire, Milton Ireland, Patrick Kelly & Co, P.J.Matthews & Co Tool & Gauge Co and Torc Manufacturing. At present chief executive National Hardware Ltd. Member Kildare Street and University Club, Royal Dublin Society and life member Dublin Zoo.

MICHAEL JOSEPH MURPHY
Lord Edward Street, Ballina, Co. Mayo
(096) 21344
Born to Joseph and Delia Murphy (née Hurst) at Ballina on 10 December 1919. Educated at CBC Dún Laoghaire. Married to Joan Huggard (deceased) with two sons and four daughters (one deceased). Formerly director Ulster Bank Ltd, president Golfing Union of Ireland, chairman Council of National Golf Unions. At present chairman and managing director Joseph Murphy (Ballina) Ltd. Member Royal and Ancient Golf Club of St Andrew's, Portmarnock, and Ballina Golf Clubs, Fitzwilliam Lawn Tennis Club, Hibernian United Service Club, Rotary and Killarney Golf and Fishing Club. A past president of Ballina Golf Club, he has been awarded the Paul Harris Fellowship of Rotary.

EDWIN J. NOLAN
Company Director
Elm Court, Boreenmana Road, Cork
(021) 329277
Born to George F. and Ethel Nolan (née Caverly) at Cork on 1 December 1940. Educated at Presentation Brothers College Cork. Married to Cintra Courtney with three sons, Michael, John and Peter, and one daughter, Helen. Formerly held a number of senior positions with the Ford organisation in Ireland and in Europe. At present chairman and managing director of Henry Ford and Son Ltd. Member of Marketing Institute of Ireland.

ARNOLD JOSEPH O'BYRNE
Managing Director
Belgard Road, Tallaght, Dublin 24
(01) 514033
Born to Joseph and Bridget O'Byrne (née Memery) at Dublin on 14 May 1939. Educated at O'Connell Schools Dublin. Married to Monica Harris with two sons, Colin and Kevin, and three daughters, Audrey, Sandra and Karen. Formerly general accountant, credit manager and chief auditor at General Motors UK, and president of Society of the Irish Motor Industry. At present managing director General Motors Distribution Ireland Ltd and director US Chamber of Commerce in Ireland. Admitted fellow of the Institute of Motor Industry.

KENNETH O'REILLY-HYLAND

Company Director
Hume House, Ballsbridge, Dublin 4
(01) 686422
born to Lt Col. Hugh Joseph Anthony and Anna Hyland (née O'Reilly) at Dublin on 12 November 1925. Educated at Xavier School and Dublin University. Admitted to fellowship of the Chartered Institute of Secretaries. Married to Marie Howard-Williams with five children. Formerly director Central Bank of Ireland, Aer Lingus, Irish Spinners, Greenmount Oil, Hill Samuel (Ireland), and Fastnet Finance. Chairman Hospital Joint Services Board, governor Central Remedial Clinic, trustee Cheshire Foundation in Ireland, member Eastern Health Board, member Committee on Court Practice and Procedure, and joint master of Meath Foxhounds. At present chairman Burmah-Castrol (Ireland), MacDonagh and Boland Group, Friends Provident, governor Royal Hospital Donnybrook and City of Dublin Skin and Cancer Hospital. President Institute of Directors in Ireland. Member City of London, Naval and Military, and St Stephen's Green Clubs, Royal St George Yacht Club, Royal Overseas league, Royal Dublin Society, Royal Zoological Society of Ireland and Irish Master of Foxhounds Association.

JOHN PHILIP REIHILL

Company Director
Dunleary House, Dún Laoghaire
(01) 2808461
Born to John Philip and Elsie Reihill at Dublin on 28 June 1933. Educated at Castleknock College. Married to the late Emer Collins with three sons, John, Mark and Raymond, and three daughters, Zita, Christina and Karen. Following death of first wife in 1973, married Ann Dillon-Malone with two stepsons, Hugo and Patrick and, one stepdaughter, Louise. At present chairman Tedcastle McCormack and Company Ltd. Member Milltown Golf Club, Stephen's Green Club, Fitzwilliam Lawn Tennis Club and Royal St George Yacht Club.

BRYAN STUART RYAN

Company Director
Main Road, Tallaght, Co. Dublin
(01) 524499
Born to Joseph Albert and Mary Josephine Ryan (née Rock) at Dublin on 20 February 1928. Educated at Blackrock College, UCD, College of Commerce and Wharton. Married to Rosemary Daly with one son and two daughters. Formerly chairman Bryan S. Ryan Group Ltd. At present chairman Woodstream Estates. Member Royal St George Yacht Club and Fitzwilliam Lawn Tennis Club.

Chapter 24
Exports and Exporters

Breathes there the man, with soul so dead,
Who never to himself hath said,
This is my own, my native land!
Whose heart hath ne'er within him burn'd,
As home his footsteps he hath turn'd,
From wandering on a foreign strand!

Scott

Exports and industrial output have increased many times since the late 1950s. This multiplication has not been in value only but also in volume, in quality and in variety. Expansion of the industrial base added many hundreds of new products to the list of Irish exports while, at the same time, traditional Irish export products continued their overseas successes — products, like processed foods, drinks, fabrics and clothing, footwear and carpets, glasswear, handcrafts, and so on. To these must be added the more recent sports goods, computers and other office equipment, freezers and cookers and a whole range of technical and professional services. The greatest boost came from industrial goods, such as chemicals, electronics and machinery. 'Natural' products, like beef, butter, tweed, whiskey and stout, are now found leaving Ireland in the company of digital integrators, radar protection apparatus, industrial sealants, telecommunications equipment and man-made fibres.

Destinations
For all the Irish-Americans in the United States (up to forty million are said to claim Irish ancestry) this market accounts for only 8 per cent of Irish exports, compared with Great Britain which takes 28 per cent. While 8 per cent is not to be sneezed at, the United Kingdom remains the main market, although it has been declining in importance since accession to full membership of the European Community in 1973.

Recent performances in IR£ million were:

	1990	1989
Great Britain	4,020	4,119
Northern Ireland	816	776
Other EC	5,882	5,936
USA and Canada	1,286	1,250

When we try to see how trade balanced with the above groups of countries in 1990 we get the following picture in IR£ million:

	Imports	Exports
Great Britain	4,764	4,020
Other EC	3,048	5,882
USA and Canada	1,904	1,286

This shows that we had a positive balance of IR£2,834 million with the other EC member states compared with a deficit of IR£618 million with USA and Canada.

The United Kingdom as a whole was the only country in the EC with whom the Republic had a trade deficit in 1990. At IR£427 million, this was only a small percentage of the value of total Irish/UK trade of IR£10,099 million — about 4 per cent in fact.

When we look at figures for trade between Portugal and Ireland we find no growth at all in total value of trade measured in IR£ million immediately after EC membership as follows:

	Imports	Exports	Total
1985	45	25	70
1986	40	26	66
1987	41	31	72

The significance of these figures is that Portugal became our fellow-full-member of the EC on 1 January 1986, and, while one might not have expected a significant growth in the first year, it should certainly have come in the second year, whereas, in fact, it merely returned in the second year of membership to the level which it had achieved in the year prior to that. The growth came later, however —

	Imports	Exports	Total
1989	57	53	110
1990	64	69	133

The delay in growth between the smaller member states is interesting, and suggests that exporters in these states are more attracted by the larger member states, where competition is probably much keener. Similarly, State export boards may prefer to concentrate on major markets, and it is significant that for over 3 years after January 1986 the Export Board of neither of these countries made any substantial effort to develop trade between the two countries.

English-speaking visitors find it easier to pronounce Irish Trade Board than Córas Tráchtála, the name by which the Board is still known to most citizens. Following the merger of Córas Tráchtála and the Irish Goods Council, An Bord Tráchtála — the Irish Trade Board was officially inaugurated on 2 September 1991, and will provide marketing services to Irish companies both on the home and on export markets. From its head office in Dublin, regional offices in Cork, Limerick, Sligo and Waterford, and twenty-two overseas offices, the Board promotes and develops the Republic's exports. The promotion of UK exports is entrusted to BOTB, the British Overseas Trade Board, which is represented in Northern Irleand by IDB, the Industrial Development Board.

In April 1988 the first new special trading house licences were issued to Premier International Trading House and Technology Trading House. The Trading House is an innovative concept in so far as it extends the Republic's 10 per cent Corporation Tax rate from manufacturing to exporting, provided the exports are of Irish manufactured products bought from companies which qualify for the 10 per cent rate, and which have less than 200 employees. Several further trading-house licences have been issued since this first brace.

ROBIN BURY
Export Director
Belgard Road, Tallaght, Dublin 24
(01) 511111
Born to Phineas and Lucy Robinson Bury (née Pitcher) at Nagpur, India on 12 November 1940. Educated at Midleton College, St Columba's and TCD. Married to Mary Geraldine Reidy with three children. Formerly president Irish Exporters' Association. At present export director Irish Biscuits Ltd, council member Arab/Irish Chamber of Commerce, CADBISCO Trade Committee Brussels and of the Irish Exporters' Association. Member Royal Dublin Society.

ANTHONY C. CUNNINGHAM
Professor
Born to Matthew and Kathleen Cunningham (née Mansfield) at Waterford. Educated at Kinsalebeg NS, CBS Youghal, UCC and Cornell University New York, with honorary doctorates from University of Ulster and International Management Centre for Buckingham (IMCB) — in the UK. Married to Eibhlín Máiréad McKenna with one son, Mark Anthony and one daughter, Maeve. Head of Commerce at UCD. Past council member Irish Marketing Society. At present holder of P.J. Carroll Chair of Marketing at UCD, and former member of Governing Body. Director of Market Research Bureau of Ireland, member advisory board *European Journal of Marketing*, editorial board *Journal of Marketing Management*, and *International Journal of Advertising*. Member National Marketing Group established to advise the Minister for Trade and Marketing, and member Advisory Committee on Management Training. Advisor to UN International Trade Centre UNCTAD/GATT Geneva, and director Irish Technical Co-operation Programme in International Marketing.

GERALD PATRICK DEMPSEY
Chartered Accountant
46 Upper Mount Street, Dublin 2
(01) 762475
Born to Patrick and Nora Dempsey (née Murphy) at Dublin on 29 November 1928. Educated at Glenstal Abbey and UCD whence he graduated with BA degree in economics. Later admitted to membership and fellowship of Institute of Chartered Accountants in Ireland. Married to Patricia McNally with two sons and two daughters. Formerly held a number of senior positions with Aer Lingus, including assistant chief executive (finance), deputy chief executive, and chief executive of ancillary activities. At present chairman Waterford Crystal Ltd, and Atlantic Magnetics Ltd, director Waterford Wedgwood plc, Gilbey's of Ireland Group, Abbey Life (Ireland), and Chartered Institute of Transport and IMI. Member Dún Laoghaire and Portmarnock Golf Clubs, Fitzwilliam Lawn Tennis Club and Royal Irish Yacht Club. Was the first chartered accountant from industry to be elected president of the institute.

346

Waterford

One of the best-established Irish luxury export products, Waterford Glass, is becoming ever more famous in more and more distant markets following the merger of Waterford with Wedgwood.

PAUL PATRICK HOGAN

Company Chairman
138 Lower Baggot Street, Dublin 2
(01) 611903

Born to Sarsfield and Sheila Hogan (née Boland) at Dublin on 30 October 1934. Educated at St Mary's Haddington Road, Catholic University School, St Mary's College Dundalk, National College of Art and Royal Danish Academy at Copenhagen. Married to Virginia Connolly with three sons and one daughter. Formerly director technical assistant programme Córas Tráchtála, and consultant to United Nations, World Bank and various governments. At present chairman Trade Development Institute of Ireland, vice chairman Multiple Sclerosis Society of Ireland, director Rural Development International Ltd and of MS Care Centre. Fellow Chartered Society of Designers and Royal Society of Arts, and member Society of Designers in Ireland.

TERRY LEYDEN

Public Representative
Kildare Street, Dublin 2
(01) 614444

Born in Roscommon on 1 October 1945. Educated at CBS Roscommon, Roscommon Vocational School, and UCG (extra-mural, Diploma in politics, sociology and economics). Fellow of Irish Architects' Society. Formerly Minister of State at Dept of Health, Dept of Transport and Dept of Posts and Telegraphs. Former member Dáil Committees on Public Accounts, on Procedures and Privileges and on Small Businesses. At present Minister for Trade and Marketing and TD for Roscommon. Member Roscommon Agricultural and Industrial Show Society, founder member Roscommon Enterprise Development Society Ltd and member Comhaltas Ceoltóirí Éireann.

ALAN McCARTHY

Chief Executive
Merrion Hall, Strand Road, Dublin 4
(01) 2695011

Born at Dublin on 11 July 1938. Educated at Blackrock College Dublin and Stanford University USA. Married to Carolyn Browne with two daughters. Having worked in banking and export marketing in industry, joined Córas Tráchtála in 1963. Appointed general manager UK, assistant chief executive/development, assistant chief executive/overseas, and chief executive. In September 1991 Córas Tráchtála was merged with the Irish Goods Council. Appointed chief executive of merged organisation, An Bord Tráchtála/The Irish Trade Board. Council Member of Irish Management Institute and of Dublin Chamber of Commerce. Member of Industrial Committee of the RDS. Former chairman of the Marketing Society.

To Tokyo
Specially designed for display at the EXPO 90 International Cultural and
Trade Exhibition in Osaka, Japan, this unique and magnificent bridal
dress of Belfast linen and Clones lace was made by the Clones Lace
Workers to the design of Brídín Twist, National Hon. Secretary ICA.

PETER McCARTHY

Ballinasloe, Co. Galway

Born at Cork in 1934. Educated at Western New England College, St John's University New York, Cork School of Commerce and at Sullivan's Quay Cork. Married to Carol Barry with four children. Formerly with Michael Roche Jewellers Cork, cargo handler/budget analyst TWA New York, financial analyst Pratt & Whitnet USA and managing director A.T. Cross Ltd. At present vice president European manufacturing A.T. Cross Ltd, director An Post, American International Insurance Company of Ireland, A.T. Cross Subsidiaries in UK, France, Spain. Member CII executive council, trustee Protiuncula Hospital and executive council member CII.

JOHN A. MURRAY

Chief Executive
Strand Road, Sandymount, Dublin 4
(01) 2695255

Born to Austin and Agnes Murphy (née Feeney) at Dublin on 9 December 1948. Educated at Derrylea NS, St Patrick's College Ballyhaunis, UCC (dairy science degree) and TCD (MSc degree). Married to Eleanor Greene with two sons, Niall and John Gerard, and one daughter, Maria. Formerly manager Clare Dairies and technical executive An Bord Bainne. At present chief executive Irish Quality Association, director EOLAS, and the National Standards Authority of Ireland and member National Council for Education Awards. Member Rotary Club of Dublin and Leopardstown Tennis Club. Fellow of Institute of Quality Assurance, Royal Institute of Public Health and Hygiene and Royal Society of Health. Member American Society for Quality Control and Marketing Institute of Ireland. Author *Quality in Practice*, *Hygiene in Practice* and *A National Strategy for Quality*.

MARTIN L. NAUGHTON

Executive Chairman
Dunleer, Co. Louth
(041) 51700

Born to Martin and Mary Naughton (née Ryan) at Dublin on 2 May 1939. Educated at De La Salle Dundalk and Southampton College of Technology. Married to Carmel McCarthy with two sons and one daughter. At present group executive chairman Glen Dimplex Ltd. Honorary Doctor of Laws (UCD).

WILLIAM PATRICK O'GRADY

Company Director
11 Richview Office Park, Dublin 14
(01) 2837860
Born to William and Annie O'Grady (née O'Reilly) at Mallow on 1 July
1940. Educated at Patrician Primary and Patrician Academy Mallow,
UCC and Cambridge University. Married to Anthea Heagney with three
sons, Tony, John and Paul, and one daughter, Ann Marie. Formerly
commercial director, An Bord Bainne, managing director Adams Foods
and chief executive Minch Norton. At present chief executive Premier
International Trading House, the first company to be awarded a special
trading house licence. Member Milltown Golf Club.

BRIAN PATTERSON

Kilbarry, Waterford
(051) 73311
Born to Cyril and Madge Patterson (née Otter) at Cork on 4 August 1944.
Educated at Newtown School Waterford, St Andrew's College and UCD.
Married to Jennifer Beaven with two sons, Garrath and Ross. Formerly
personnel director A. Guinness Son and Co. (Dublin) and director
general Irish Management Institute. At present assistant chief executive
Waterford Crystal. Fellow of Irish Management Institute, and Institute of
Industrial Engineers. Board member An Post and St James' Hospital.
President European Domestic Glass Federation. Chairman International
Crystal Federation.

GEOFFREY DEAN READ

Company Director
4 Marine Road, Dún Laoghaire, Co. Dublin
(01) 284400
Born to Gerald and Margaret Read (née Oxer) at Dublin on 31 December
1954. Educated at Kill-o-the-Grange, Deansgrange, Sandford Park, High
School and Kevin Street College of Technology, Dublin. Married to
Wendy Wolfe with two sons, Alexander and Christopher. Founder and
managing director, Ballygowan Group Ltd and director of the University
of Limerick Foundation. Member of Riverview Club.

Chapter 25
Tourism

Beauty is altogether in the eye of the beholder.

Lew Wallace

Arriving in a country for the first time arouses the curiosity and gets the adrenalin flowing in most visitors. The first human contacts are especially important — the ground staff at the airport, the immigration officers, the staff at the car-hire desk, and at the hotel reception. The Irish take pride in Ireland, in the wonderful scenery, and in the friendly people. For the older and more widely-travelled visitor, at any rate, the friendliness of the people will be the more important of these. One can tire of landscape, but never of the warm greeting, which makes one feel welcome, appreciated and just a little bit special.

Peace

Speaking at the 1990 peace through tourism conference, Mr Niall Reddy of Bord Fáilte (Irish Tourist Board) highlighted the possibility that some types of 'mass tourism' do not succeed in fostering goodwill. He cited Northern European tourists who flock to Mediterranean resorts where they have little or no contact with the host population and very often have no desire to have it. These invasions may in fact build up resentment by insensitive behaviour. Mr Reddy pointed out therefore that one could not generalise about tourism and its beneficial effects but suggested that the independent traveller usually had 'a better opportunity to be a good ambassador than the package-tour visitor'.

Subject to this reservation of course, tourism in general must be a basic force for the elimination of potential causes of conflict, through the creation of better understanding.

As each part of the island through tourism gains a better understanding of the other, a better basis for peace is being laid down. Tourism gives people an exposure to the ideas and ideals of a variety of people, some of which are bound to open closed minds. Visitors from multi-racial tolerant and democratic societies bring to the island their experiences and thought processes which are beneficial and influential, provided some contact with the indigenous population takes place.

As Robert Schuman explained in 1956, the founding of the European Coal and Steel community would: 'create that fusion of interests which is indispensable to the establishment of an economic community and that will be the leaven from which grow a wider and deeper community between countries long opposed to one another by bloody conflicts', and he argued that his proposal would 'build the first concrete foundation of a European Federation which is indispensable to the preservation of peace'.

Recent History

Since the mid-1980s tourism, one of the oldest businesses in this country, has been 'discovered' by all sorts of political and economic commentators, to the mild surprise of the great many tourist-industry leaders, who had been working away for years to improve the industry. It seemed that tourism was an 'overnight' success.

After the Chambers of Commerce of Ireland conference 'Tourism 2000' in May 1986, the Department of Tourism and Transport commissioned a major study of Irish Tourism. In addition, the Irish Hotels' Federation commissioned an independent study to show the benefits which would result from a doubling of income from tourism in real terms over a five-year period, and to identify the measures which might be taken to achieve this.

In October 1986 ITIC published a major study on the importance of the environment to tourism. ITIC — the Irish Tourist Industry Confederation — represents all the major segments of the tourism industry, including carriers, providers of accommodation and other tourist services.

The death of Paschal Vincent Doyle, for many years chairman both of Doyle Hotels and of Bord Fáilte, coincided with the resignation of Michael MacNulty as Director General, and both posts were then filled by Mr Martin Dully, formerly Chief Executive of Aer Rianta (Irish Airports Authority), who had previously been an executive with Aer Lingus.

Such an intense period of change was not without controversy and a recommendation, during this period by the Irish Hotels' Federation that Bord Fáilte should be confined to marketing abroad, was condemned by the chairman of the six regional tourism organisations. In spite of any controversy that may have arisen, the Taoiseach told the members of Galway Chamber of Commerce and Industry at their 1988 annual dinner in March that tourism offered the 'best and most immediate opportunity of a major economic advance in the west of Ireland'.

All this was against a background of a record IR£700 million earnings from two million visitors in 1987. Credit for these record figures was attributed by Bord Fáilte to the package of tourism initiatives introduced by the Government which had reduced access, travel and accommodation costs.

The dynamism which has been injected into tourism by the Task Force and by the combination of the two roles of Chairman and Director General at Bord Fáilte in the highly capable hands of Martin Dully, gave reason to hope for better things to come. Tough policy decisions had to be taken and the role of the State defined. The most important functions of the Department should be the development of policies and their co-ordination. Public expenditure on advertising should be critically examined, as should the marketing support services. The 1989 results for tourism in the Republic featured foreign earnings at £991 million an increase of nearly 18 per cent. Looking at the principal markets, Britain accounted for £306 million of this, North America £177 million and Germany £43 million, France £35 million, other European markets £72 million and other areas (including Australia, New Zealand and Japan) £45 million. Revenue from Northern Ireland tourists grew to £56 million.

Environment and Hygiene

1987 was designated by the European Commission as European Year of the Environment with a view to getting common action for a clean Europe. This is still a highly desirable aim. There is a great awareness throughout the island of the damage which has been done to the environment by pollution of rivers and lakes, indiscriminate dumping, crumbling historic buildings, unsuitable housing developments, litter and so on.

For many visitors coming to Ireland from polluted industrialised and pressurised areas of the world, environment-friendly local communities which show pride in conserving their physical and natural characteristics will be great sources of pleasure. Hotels, restaurants and bars should not merely be clean — they should be spotless. Public toilets should be coin operated and supervised by caretakers to eliminate what has been a persistent source of complaint by visitors.

Prices

A few international comparisons expressed in US$ are available by courtesy of the Union Bank of Switzerland Spring 1991 survey of fifty-two cities around the world (Belfast was not included, unfortunately):

	Dinner in a good restaurant	Bed & Breakfast for 2	Gross pay for cook p.a.
Dublin	36	178	13,000
London	28	365	11,800
New York	30	285	31,000
Tokyo	95	237	28,100

Organisations

In 1939 the Irish Tourist Board was set up by the Government and it began its work in earnest in 1945. Bord Fáilte was established in 1955 and has representation in Northern Ireland, Britain, United States, Canada, Germany, France, Holland, Belgium, Italy, Japan, Scandinavia, Australia and New Zealand. It coordinates the activities of the regional tourism organisations who engage in tourism activities that can be more easily organised at regional and local level. The Northern Ireland Tourist Board has seen a steady increase in tourist figures, and is the public agency responsible for tourism in Northern Ireland. Joint activities are undertaken frequently and an example is the Ireland Desk jointly operated by Bord Fáilte and the Northern Ireland Tourist Board in the BTA Travel Centre in London. The Board attaches great importance to the Republic of Ireland market, and, in 1990 opened an office in Dublin's Nassau Street which it publicised with the slogan 'North by Nassau'.

The Board also promotes heavily in Great Britain, France, Germany, the US and Canada.

The International Fund for Ireland has in fact funded NITB and Bord Fáilte to undertake joint marketing campaigns around the world, which has enabled risks to be taken in promoting on an all-Ireland basis, so that test marketing can overcome worries about the image of Northern Ireland. CERT is the Republic's tourism training agency dealing with recruitment and training of personnel at all levels of hotel, catering and tourism. It aims to ensure high operational standards in the Industry. There are seven Regional Tourism Organisations in the Republic with leadership roles in overseas marketing and promotion by various interests, providing visitors with a countrywide network of tourist offices and information services, encouraging environmental awareness and promoting tourism development and investment.

The Restaurants' Association of Ireland is the representative body for the sector, and the producer for the first time in 1990 of the guide, *Eating the Best of Irish*.

Holiday World
Seen promoting Camping, Caravan and Holiday Home Parks at the annual holiday Fair in Dublin were TV presenter Bibi Baskin, Angela Dillon Managing Director Irish Caravan and Camping Holidays and Maureen Ledwith, Director Holiday World.

Leaders
Mr William Davis, Chairman of the British Tourist Authority, seen here
with Mr Martin Dully, Executive Chairman of Bord Fáilte.

FRANCIS BRENNAN
Hotelier
Kenmare, Co. Kerry
(064) 41200
Born at Dublin on 25 September 1935. Educated at Christian Brothers Westland Row, Catholic University School Leeson Street and afterwards at Dublin College of Catering whence he graduated after a four-year hotel management course with a BSc (man.) degree from TCD. Single. Formerly duty manager at Great Southern Hotel Parknasilla, assistant general manager at Victoria Hotel Cork and managing director of Park Hotel Kenmare. At present proprietor of Park Hotel Kenmare, recipient of Egon Ronay Hotel of the Year and many other awards.

DAVID PAUL DOYLE
Hotelier
Lansdowne Road, Ballsbridge, Dublin 4
(01) 601711
Born to Paschal Vincent and Margaret Doyle (née Briody) at Dublin on 21 April 1958. Educated at Willow Park, Blackrock and Cathal Brugha Street Colleges. Married to Christina Kelly. Formerly operations manager Doyle Hotel Group. At present managing director Doyle Hotel Group and director Bord Fáilte. Member Fitzwilliam Lawn Tennis Club.

MARTIN DULLY
Executive Chairman
Baggot Street Bridge, Dublin 2
(01) 765871
Born to Patrick and Catherine Dully (née Brien) at Athlone in 1932. Educated at Marist College Athlone. Married to Edith Mary Golden with one son, Martin, and two daughters, Majella and Hilary Ann. Formerly chief executive Aer Rianta, general sales manager Aer Lingus, chairman Youghal Carpets and Shannon Hotel Management School, and board member Airport Operators Council International. At present full-time chairman and director general Bord Fáilte.

PATRICK J. FITZPATRICK
Hotelier
Killiney, Co. Dublin
(01) 2897021
Born to John J. and May Fitzpatrick (née Crimmons) at Dublin on 11 January 1930. Educated at Willow Park and Blackrock College Dublin. Trained in hotel management at Gresham Hotel. Married to Eithne Dunne with four sons, John, Paul, Patrick Jnr, and Tony, and one daughter, Eithne. Formerly trainee manager graduating to assistant manager Gresham Hotel, under Toddy O'Sullivan, manager Old Ground Hotel Ennis, under Brendan O'Regan, general manager/director Talbot Hotel

Wexford and general manager/director Doyle Hotels. President Wexford Chamber of Commerce, Blackrock PPU and Irish Hotel and Restaurant Managers' Association. At present owner/managing director Fitzpatrick Hotels (including Castle Hotel Killiney, Shannon Shamrock Hotel Bunratty, Silver Springs Hotel Cork, and Fitzpatrick Manhattan, in New York). Member Woodbrook and Killiney Golf Clubs.

BRIAN FLYNN
Tourism Manager
Bord Fáilte, Galway
(091) 63081
Born to Daniel and Elizabeth Flynn (née Clogher) at Ballygar, Co. Galway on 17 December 1940. Educated at Ballyforan NS, CBS Roscommon, College of Commerce Cork and UCG. Married to Patricia Curtin with one son and one daughter. Regional tourism manager with Western Regional Tourism Organisation Ltd.

JOHN HORAN
Chief Executive
13 Northbrook Road, Dublin 6
(01) 976459
Born to Joe and Brigid Horan (née Strain) at Milford, Co. Donegal in 1948. Educated at Carmelite College Moate and TCD whence he graduated with MSc management degree. Married to Ann Dillon with one son, Raymond, and one daughter, Ann-Marie. Formerly with Aer Lingus and Airmotive Ireland. At present chief executive Irish Hotels Federation.

MADELAINE JAY
Managing Director
Ashford, Co. Wicklow
(0404) 40138
Born to Ernest and Marian Roentgen (née McHarg) in Switzerland on 14 September 1921. Holds Diploma for Medical Laboratory Assistants. Widowed with one son. Formerly managing director of 200–acre farm. At present managing director of Mount Usher Gardens. Member Irish Peatland Conservation Council, Compassion in World Farming, An Taisce, RIHS, RAC, IWBC, RSPB, WWF, WSPCA, WSPA, Save the Redwoods USA, Badgerwatch Ireland, Dublin Bat Group, RSPCA, IFAW, Jane Goodwall Institute UK, International League for Protection of Horses, Woodland Trust and Hawk & Owl Trust.

CHRISTOPHER J. KANE
Tourism Director
Baggot Street Bridge, Dublin 2
(01) 765871
Born to Joseph and Mary Kane (née Roe) at Dublin. Educated at Westland Row CBS, College of Commerce Rathmines and at Strathclyde

Business School. Married to Geraldine O'Toole with five children. Formerly president Association of Travel Trade Clubs UK and Ireland. At present director — Europe, Irish Tourist Board, president Republic of Ireland Region and chairman Dublin Branch of Institute of Chartered Secretaries and Accountants. Member Greystones Golf Club.

TOM MacCARTHY O'HEA
Hotelier
Ardilaun House Hotel, Galway
(091) 21433
Born to John and Gladys MacCarthy O'Hea (née Dorgan) at Cork on 24 April 1940. Educated at Shannon School of Hotel Management. Trained in London at Claridges. Married to Eilish McCoy with four sons. Formerly senior assistant and personnel manager at Gresham Hotel. At present general manager Ardilaun House Hotel. (He is the longest serving manager in any hotel in Ireland.) Council member Galway Chamber of Commerce and Industry, director Western Regional Tourism Organisation. Member County Club, Golf Club, Tennis Club, Galway Bay Sailing Club, Skal Club of Ireland and Irish Hotels Federation and served as chairman Galway International Oyster Festival.

MATT McNULTY
Tourism Manager
Baggot Street Bridge, Dublin 2
(01) 765871
Born to Joseph and Margaret McNulty (née Connolly) at Ballyshannon, Co. Donegal. Married to Margaret Sharkey with one son, Killian, and three daughters, Suzanne, Linda and Sandra. Formerly chairman Dublin Metropolitan Streets' Commission, director Heritage Advisory Council, manager Dublin and East Tourism, and managing director Dublin Millennium. At present deputy director general Bord Fáilte, director Castletown Foundation, Convention Bureau of Ireland and Temple Bar Development. Member Tourism Task Force, Genealogical Task Force and Urban Renewal committee. Member Skal, Junior Chamber, Royal Dublin Society, An Taisce, Old Malahide Society and City Centre Business Association. Trustee of Tara's Palace Project and Drimnagh Castle Project. Founder and director People In Need charity. Senator of Junior Chamber International. Gold Shamrock Award for services in directing the Dublin St Patrick's Day parade for 21 years. Lord Mayor's Special Millennium Award for contribution to tourism development in Dublin. Admires people who get things done.

The Wild Beauty of Slea Head
The ruined cottages tell their own sad story.

MICHAEL J. MacNULTY

Marketing Consultant
32 Fitzwilliam Place, Dublin 2
(01) 610993
Born on 31 October 1935. Educated at Belvedere College and as Merchant Navy Cadet and studied also with Irish Management Institute, British Institute of Management, Cranfield School of Management and Harvard Business School. Married to Phylis Treacy with four sons. Formerly director and general manager Advance Tyre Company, director of marketing and development Irish Dunlop Company Ltd and board member Irish Dunlop, director general Bord Fáilte 1982-8, chairman Irish Marketing Society, chairman Marrowbone Lane Fund, president Belvedere College Union, vice chairman European Travel Commission. At present principal of Tourism Development International and board member Irish American Cultural Institute.

FRANK MAGEE

Regional Tourism Manager
1 Clarinda Park North, Dún Laoghaire, Co. Dublin
(01) 2808571
Born to Frank and Katherine Magee (née O'Reilly) at Enniskillen on 7 February 1952. Educated at Creevy NS Ballyshannon, St Macargan's Monaghan, De La Salle Ballyshannon and Institute of Public Administration. Married to Clare O'Brien with four children. Formerly president Skal Club Lakelands, chairman Midlands Branch Irish Hotels Federation, founder president Rotary Club of Mullingar, investment adviser and hotel adviser to Bord Fáilte and manager Greville Arms Hotel Mullingar. At present director Dublin Promotions Ltd, Dublin Tourism Enterprises Ltd, Convention Bureau of Ireland and secretary Dublin City & County RTO. Member Rotary Club Dún Laoghaire, Skal Club of Dublin, Hibernian United Service Club and Irish Hotel & Catering Institute.

JAMES NUGENT

Business Consultant
25 Merrion Square, Dublin 2
(01) 618866
Born to Patrick and Joan Nugent (née Owens) at Dublin in 1947. Educated at Oblate Fathers, Belcamp College, UCD, Irish Management Institute and TCD. Married to Mai Monaghan. Formerly trade union official, personnel director and senior specialist at IMI. At present chairman CERT (Council for Education Recruitment and Training), chairman International Tourism Marketing plc and Woodgrange Consultants Ltd, director W. Malone & Sons Ltd and Mag Result Ltd.

Morning Reflections
Glanmire Lake, Co. Kerry

PYERS O'CONOR NASH
Historic House Owner
Castlerea, Co. Roscommon
(0907) 20014
Born to Rupert Richard and Gertrude Mary Nash (née O'Conor) at Limerick on 6 January 1951. Educated at St Conleth's Dublin, Clongowes Wood College, TCD and King's Inns. Married to Marguerite Helen Egan with one son and two daughters. Formerly chairman Historic Houses & Gardens Association and governor European Union of Historic Houses. At present director HITHA, Irish Georgian Foundation and of Warcham Investments Ltd. Member Steering Committee of National Heritage Council, and Castlerea Golf Club.

TIMOTHY J. O'DRISCOLL
Born in Cork in 1908. Educated at Presentation College Cork and at TCD. Formerly chairman Algemene Bank Nederland (Ireland) Ltd, board member Irish International Airlines, first director general Irish Tourist Board (BFE), Irish Ambassador to the Netherlands, first chairman and chief executive Irish Export Promotion Board (CTT), president of ROSC, Marketing Institute of Ireland and president and chairman An Taisce and chairman Dublin International Theatre Festival. At present chairman Trustees Edward de Bono Foundation and member executive committee Europa Nostra. Honoured by five countries, Doctor of Laws conferred by Dublin University, Honorary Life Member Royal Dublin Society and of An Taisce — The Irish National Trust.

EILEEN O'MARA WALSH
Managing Director
37 Main Street, Donnybrook, Dublin 4
(01) 2696944
Born to Power and Joan O'Mara (née Folwell) at Limerick on 15 January 1941. Educated at FCJ Convent Limerick, Muckross Dominican College Dublin and Institut Catholique Paris. Single. One son. Formerly chairman Irish Tourist Industry Confederation and Great Southern Hotels Ltd, director Aer Lingus plc and council member Confederation of Irish Industry. At present managing director O'Mara Travel, director Great Southern Hotels, the executive council Irish Tourist Industry Confederation and president Incoming Tour Operators' Association. Member Dublin Chamber of Commerce, Ireland-France Chamber of Commerce and Marketing Institute.

AIDAN C. PRIOR
Company Director
Castleknock, Dublin 15
(01) 387822
Born to Francis and Margaret Prior (née Conlon) at Ballinamore, Co.

Leitrim on 21 November 1931. Educated at Mercy NS Ballinamore, Blackrock College and School of Commerce Rathmines. Married to Geraldine Sullivan with two daughters, Sharon and Aisling, and one son, Aidan Desmond. Formerly vice chairman St Michael's Hospital Dún Laoghaire, Castleknock Tennis Club, chairman Dawson St Association and treasurer Royal Zoological Society of Ireland. At present managing director Prior Interiors, director and secretary Newpark House Hotel Ltd and chairman Newpark Trust Co. Chairman Hibernian United Service Club and member Society of Designers in Ireland.

EARL OF ROSSE
Birr Castle, Co. Offaly
(0509) 20056
Born to the Rt Hon. sixth Earl of Rosse and Anne, Dowager Countess of Rosse (née Messel) on 21 October 1936. Educated at Aiglou College Switzerland, University of Grenoble France, and at Oxford whence he graduated with an MA degree. Married to Alison Cooke-Hurle with two sons, Patrick Lord Oxmantown and the Hon. Michael Parsons, and one daughter, Lady Alicia Parsons. Formerly principal officer with the UN Development Programme in Ghana, Benin, Algeria, Iran and Bangladesh. Chairman International Co-ordinating Committee on Disaster Relief. Director Agency for Personal Service Overseas, and member Advisory Council on Development Co-operation. At present director Irish Heritage Properties and Birr Scientific and Heritage Foundation.

EGERTON RICHARD GEOFFREY SHELSWELL-WHITE
Director
Bantry, Co. Cork
Born to Geoffrey and Clodagh Shelswell (née Leigh-White) at London on 3 December 1933. Educated at Castle Park Dalkey, Winchester College and at Oxford University. Married to Brigitte Kleihs with four children, with two from a previous marriage. Formerly deckhand on trawler out of Hull, 3rd assistant director MGM Film Studios, interpreter with British European Airways, history teacher in USA and chairman Bantry Brass & Reed Band. At present director Bantry Estates Company and chairman Bantry Church Vestry.

JOE WALSH
Tour Operator
8/11 Lower Baggot Street, Dublin 2
(01) 789555
Born at Bangor on 7 December 1931. Educated at St Patrick's College Armagh. Married to Margaret Sheeran with three sons and two daughters. Formerly with Thomas Cook Ltd London and the Ulster Transport Authority. President Irish Travel Agents' Association. At present chairman and managing director Joe Walsh Tours Ltd. Member Milltown Golf Club. Decorated Cavalier of the Italian Republic.

Chapter 26
Transport

Remember, that time is money.

Benjamin Franklin

By Road

The low population density in Ireland contributes to high distribution costs for products and services marketed throughout the island, where inter-linking national, regional, and county roads provide a high level of access. The more important roads are the national primary routes which connect the principal centres of population. National secondary routes are important links between the primaries, which are best in terms of quality and attract the heaviest utilisation. Roads in the regional network serve as feeder routes into the national roads. The county and urban roads serve the transport needs of local communities.

Responsibility for maintaining and improving existing roads rests with local authorities. The State, however, reimburses about 50 per cent of their expenditure. Local authorities are also responsible for the licensing of vehicles and drivers, road safety and traffic management, and have an important role in the development of new roads under the overall control of the National Roads Authority. This was to be established on a statutory basis by the Roads Bill 1991 introduced at the end of April with a view also to updating, strengthening and modernising the law on public roads.

Under the terms, the NRA is to have overall responsibility for planning and supervising the construction, improvement and maintenance of the network of national roads, including access roads to the main ports and airports. It is to promote the provision of private funding for national roads and will have power subject to the usual ministerial consents, to borrow up to £500 million. It will also have power to direct road authorities to carry out works, but it can carry out these functions itself where the road authority fails or refuses to comply. Again, road authorities are to be relied upon to prepare road design and maintenance programmes and grant road works contracts, but the Authority will have the power to do these things itself, where it decides that this would be more convenient, expeditious, effective or economical.

Road transport is extremely important for the economic development of the country because over 90 per cent of inland passenger and freight traffic depends on it. Late in 1988, the Minister for the Environment, Mr Flynn, revealed that a review carried out by his Department concluded that IR£8.5 billion would need to be spent on all roads over the next twenty years.

Public road-transport is organised by the National Transport Company, CIE, which has been divided into Dublin Bus, Provincial Bus and Irish Rail Subsidiaries. In addition to CIE over 1,000 private bus-owners operate a fleet of over 4,000 private buses. These are involved in school transport, coach tours and even scheduled services on a club or charter basis.

Road haulage is a regulated business and the proposals for a unified European market by 1993 encompass the idea of abandoning the existing national quota system. Wide differences exist in the taxes payable by hauliers in the different EC member states and, in addition, some member states impose road tolls, while others do not. It is expected that progress will be made towards harmonisation of this situation by 1993.

A comparison of prices and wages in public transport is provided by the results of the spring 1991 Union Bank of Switzerland Survey which encompassed fifty-two cities. The public transport comparison was based on a six-mile journey by bus, street car or subway. The taxi comparison was based on three miles within city limits during daytime, inclusive of tip.

	Dublin	London	New York	Tokyo
6 miles by public	1.18	1.85	1.15	1.32
3 miles by taxi	8.02	7.58	7.00	8.67
busdriver's earnings	15,700	18,500	34,000	34,200

All figures in US$

In Northern Ireland, Ulster Bus emphasises the importance of road transport by highlighting in its 1990/91 annual review, that 93 per cent of all public transport trips are made by bus and 40 per cent of shoppers in Belfast city centre arrive by bus. The company is one of the largest businesses in the province, with 2,900 employees, over 1,300 vehicles carrying over 78 million passengers annually.

By Rail
The CIE company, Iarnród Éireann, provides passenger and freight services between the principal towns and cities. In the Dublin area there is a rapid transit system, known as DART, which is an electrified system, unlike the rest of the rail network which uses diesel power. The transport of bulk materials and containers is heavily dependent on rail freight. The Dublin/ Belfast rail service is popular and heavily utilised despite many terrorist disruptions. There is excellent co-operation between the road and rail operators in both parts of the island.

By Sea
Sea links are the lifeline of any island and this is true not only for Ireland and the services which connect it to the outside world, but it applies equally to the services which connect Ireland to the small islands around the coast. The ports handle the bulk of international trade and much of the traffic is in the form of unit loads, either load on/load off or roll on/roll off. The most significant exceptions to this development are oil, coal and ores. The major ports are Belfast, Cork, Dublin, Dún Laoghaire, Foynes, Rosslare and Waterford.

The principal companies providing passenger car-ferries are the State-owned B & I Line, Cork/Swansea, Sealink, Irish Ferries, Irish Continental Line and Brittany Ferries. These services include Dún Laoghaire/Holyhead, Rosslare/Pembroke, Rosslare/ Fishguard, Rosslare/Le Havre, Rosslare/Cherbourg, Cork/Roscoff, Larne/Stranraer, Larne/Cairnryan and Belfast/Liverpool. Fares tumbled in recent years to enable the ferry services to compete with falling airfares.

Airfares
High airfares had been a cause of concern for many years, and were the subject of many 'Letters to the Editor' in 1981 when the Irish Air Travellers' Association was formed with the Freudian initials IATA, as in International Air Transport Association. The

founders included Desmond O'Kennedy, Chairman of OKB Limited, who afterwards became advertising agent for British Airways and Colm McCarthy of Davy Kelleher and McCarthy, Economists. They were joined on the first committee by well-known transport economist, Dr Seán Barrett. In spite of the support of frequent business travellers, such as Don Tidey of Quinnsworth, Edmund Williams of D.E. Williams, solicitor Max Abrahamson, Tom Toner of BWG, Alan Buttanshaw of Maguire and Patterson and David Dand of Gilbey's, the Association languished and was taken over by the Chambers of Commerce of Ireland in April 1984.

Less than three months later the Government introduced the Air Transport Bill 1984 to close off a loophole which had resulted in fares being sold below 'approved levels'. In 1983 the High Court had granted a temporary injunction restraining Transamerica from selling unapproved fares but this was lifted by the Supreme Court. The Bill was Government's response.

Seven years later, it is hard to believe that Government introduced legislation to make it an offence for a travel agent to give a 1 per cent discount to a good customer. Penalties proposed included a year in jail and fines of up to IR£100,000. By early October the Air Transport Users' Committee had publicly expressed its opposition to the Bill and called for its progress to be halted. Thus, the Chambers of Commerce of Ireland found themselves in bed with the Consumers' Association, Bord Fáilte and the Irish Hotels Federation, but without the Confederation of Irish Industry who maintained a low profile throughout the controversy, meekly advocating the merits for Ireland of waiting for a European solution to an Irish problem. Although the Bill was to allow the Minister to control for the first time the level of commissions paid to travel agents, the Irish Travel Agents' Association joined Aer Lingus in supporting the Bill.

The opposition forces were strong enough to delay the passing of the Bill and interest eventually waned. Interest in the fares issue did not wane and, when the Air Transport Users' Committee realised that the cost of London Flights was up to 30 per cent cheaper from Belfast than from Dublin, they felt obliged (in the public interest) to place advertisements in daily newspapers drawing the attention of the public to this situation.

Dublin Chamber protested and Aer Lingus, who had enjoyed pooling arrangements with British Airways for many years, said in a ten-page letter to the Committee that it oddly befitted them to suggest to businessmen that they buy British!

Liberalisation was well and truly on the way when Ryanair introduced their Dublin/London service in May 1986. By 1987 fares had fallen by as much as 54 per cent and 1.65 million passengers were carried on the Dublin/London route, an increase of 65 per cent on 1985, the last full year of the pre-liberalisation era. This 1987 level was greatly exceeded again in 1988 when an estimated 2.13 million passengers were carried, and in 1990 when the number rose to 2.36 million.

By Air

The main international airports are at Belfast, Cork, Dublin, Knock and Shannon, with Dublin the busiest. Belfast has two airports in fact: Aldergrove for International Flights and Harbour for UK destinations. Transatlantic services are routed through Shannon, a feature of the transatlantic routes for many years, although several operators aspire to fly directly to Dublin. There is a network of local airports, and freight and passenger services are provided by plane and by helicopter. The principal Irish companies providing these services are Aer Lingus, Celtic Helicopters, Irish Helicopters and Ryanair.

The state-owned Aer Rianta operates the airports at Cork, Dublin and Shannon, and the Great Southern Hotel Group. Aer Rianta has an enviable reputation as being one of the most successful state-owned enterprises. How successful it really is, of course, should depend on an international comparison of its costs and of the landing charges. Its successes include contracts to provide and maintain ground service vehicles for Moscow International Airport, the operation by Aerofirst, an Aer Rianta-Aeroflot joint company, of the Moscow and Leningrad Airport Duty Free Shops, the land border duty free shop at Torfionovka on the Soviet/Finnish border, and several city-centre shops. Aeroflot has made extensive use of Shannon Airport for many years and regularly flies from there to Washington DC, Cuba and Peru.

From Canada
The Canadian Prime Minister, Mr Brian Mulrooney being welcomed to Ireland on his arrival at Dublin Airport in July 1991, by
the then Aer Rianta chairman, Mr Dermot Desmond.

MICHAEL S. ENNIS
Managing Director
East Wall Road, Dublin 3
(01) 741221
Born to Laurence Stanislaus and Ellen Mary Ennis (née Dalton) at Dublin on 11 May 1929. Educated at Synge Street CBC Dublin. Married to Christine Mary Mullen with three sons and one daughter. Joined staff of Henry Gowan & Co Shipbrokers in 1946, appointed director in 1953 and managing director in 1966. Appointed Conway Shipping Group Chairman 1984. Entire business career of 45 years has been in Dublin Port. Fellow Institute of Freight Forwarders, member Institute of Chartered Shipbrokers, Irish Ships Agents' Association and Dublin Chamber of Commerce. Member Royal Dublin Golf Club (captain 1981), Catholic Young Men's Society Rugby Football Club, Terenure, Courtown Golf Club and life member Wanderers Football Club.

NIALL GREENE
Chief Executive
GPA House, Shannon
(061) 360000
Born to Robin and Alice Greene (née Kelly) in Yorkshire on 17 April 1943. Married to Nuala Farrell with two sons, Colm and Ciarán. Formerly chairman and chief executive Youth Employment Agency, and chairman AnCo, the Industrial Training Authority. At present chief executive GPA Technologies. Member the Labour Party, Anti-Apartheid Movement, Campaign for Separation of Church and State and Irish United Nations Association. Member council and executive committee of Institute of European Affairs.

ROBERT N. HAYES
Engineer
Alexandra Road, Dublin 1
(01) 722777
Born to Maj. Gen. Liam and Kathleen Hayes (née Walsh) at Cork in 1926. Educated at Belvedere College and UCD whence he graduated with BE (civil) degree, and later at Ohio State University (MSc). Married to Alice J. McMenamin with one son, Liam, and two daughters, Catherine and Barbara. Formerly county manager Tipperary SR Co. Council, county engineer Cavan Co. Council, chief executive Dublin Port and director McCarthy & Partner Consultants Ltd, director Oppenheim International Finance, and chairman An Post: Pension Trust. Member Dún Laoghaire Golf Club and Royal Dublin Society, and past president Institution of Engineers of Ireland and Institute of Transport in Ireland.

Cruising Continentals
No longer used for commercial purposes, the rivers and canals are now a mecca for European boat hirers.

TED HESKITH

Managing Director
Milewater Road, Belfast BT3 9BG
(0232) 351201
Educated at Queen's University Belfast whence he graduated with a BSc degree. Fellow Chartered Institute of Management Accountants. Married with one son, Michael. At present managing director Ulsterbus Ltd and Citybus Ltd, council member Confederation British Industry, board member Road Transport Industry Training Board, member NI Local Government Officers' Superannuation Committee and Industrial Tribunals.

BRIAN W. KERR

Shipbroker
5 Clanwilliam Square, Dublin 2
(01) 618211
Born to Frederick and Dorothy Kerr (née Petrie) at Dublin on 4 October 1938. Educated at St Andrew's College Dublin and later admitted to fellowship of Chartered Institute of Transport. Married to Gladys Florence Wilson with one son and two daughters. Formerly managing director George Bell (Chartering) Community Shipowners' Association, the Irish Chamber of Shipping and the Chartered Institute of Transport in Ireland. At present managing director Brian Kerr Shipping Ltd and Ashford Marine Ltd, board member Dublin Port & Docks Board, Chamber of Shipping, Rehabilitation Institute and St Andrew's College. Member Hibernian United Service Club, Wanderers Football Club and YMCA Cricket Club.

THOMAS McDONAGH

Company Director
Merchants Road, Galway
(091) 66111
Born to Michael and Agnes McDonagh (née Burke) at Galway on 4 June 1935. Educated at St Ignatius' School Galway, Clongowes Wood College Kildare and UCD whence he graduated with a BSc degree. Married to Patrizia Giachin with one son. Formerly president Galway Chamber of Commerce and Industry and Junior Chamber Galway, and national president of Junior Chamber Ireland. At present chairman McDonagh Group of companies and director of about twenty companies. Chairman of Air Transport Users' Committee of the Chambers of Commerce of Ireland. Member Galway Harbour Commissioners, Institute of Directors and Farmers' Club. Past president Galway Rotary Club and vice chairman Galway Race Commiteee. His company is one of the largest private companies in Ireland.

MICHAEL W.S. MACLAREN
Company Chairman
10 Victoria Street, Belfast
(0232) 230581
Born to Bryan and Elizabeth Maclaren (née Edmenson) at Belfast on 14 July 1948. Educated at Mourne Grange Preparatory School Kilkeel, Marlborough College Wiltshire and TCD. Married to Pauline Farr with one son, Frank, and one daughter, Kate. Formerly president Northern Ireland Chamber of Commerce and Industry. Member General Committee Lloyds' Register of Shipping and Fair Employment Agency, Northern Ireland. At present chairman and managing director G. Heyn and Sons Ltd, Commissioner of Irish Lights, deputy lieutenant of Belfast and honorary consul in Belfast for Denmark and Sweden.

PETER GERARD MALONE
Hotelier
Ballsbridge, Dublin 4
(01) 605000
Born to Frank and Mary Malone (née Sweeney) at Dundalk on 12 April 1944. Educated at St Malachy's NS and St Mary's College Dundalk and Shannon College of Hotel Management. Married to Mary Brassil with three daughters, Chanel, Aislinn and Clara. Formerly manager Hillgrove Hotel Monaghan, catering manager Shelbourne Hotel Dublin, and manager Pat Quinn's Club, general manager Jury's Cork and general manager Jury's Dublin. Eisenhower Exchange Fellow 1989 and past president Irish Hotels Federation. At present managing director Jury's Hotel Group plc. Member board Shannon College of Hotel Management and fellow Irish Hotel and Catering Institute.

CATHAL MULLAN
Airline Executive
Dublin Airport, Dublin
(01) 370011
Born at Kildare in 1939. Educated at De La Salle College Kildare and later graduated in commerce and public administration from UCD and admitted to fellowship of Institute of Transport and to membership of Marketing Institute. Married to Margery Dowling with one son and three daughters. Formerly held a wide variety of executive positions in Aer Lingus, including terms in the UK sales region and in the North American region. At present, and since December 1988, group chief executive Aer Lingus, member executive council Irish Management Institute and of the council of the Confederation of Irish Industry. Director Irish-American Cultural Institute. Member Royal Dublin Golf Club and Sutton Tennis Club.

DENIS JOHN MURPHY
Company Director
Douglas, Co. Cork
(021) 894851
Born to Cornelius and Anna Murphy (née Forrest) at Cork on 18 August 1933. Educated at Presentation Brothers Cork, Glenstal Abbey and Leeds University. Married to Anne Upton with one son, Denis, and one daughter, Jennifer. Formerly president Junior Chamber of Commerce, Cork and Ireland, president Cork Chamber of Commerce and Chambers of Commerce of Ireland and chairman Cork Harbour Commissioners. At present chairman Swansea Cork Ferries, Munster Agricultural Shows and Securicor Ireland, and group director AIB Bank plc. Joint master South Union Hunt, chairman Cork Game Conservancy and Gun Club.

PATRICK F. MURPHY
Managing Director
2/4 Merrion Row, Dublin 2
(01) 610714
Born at Dublin on 3 January 1941. Educated at Catholic University School Dublin and at UCD whence he graduated with BComm and MBA degrees. Married to Elizabeth McGorlick with two sons, Gordon and David. Formerly sales manager Ireland and Continent, marketing manager and general manager strategic development with Aer Lingus, and chairman Irish Tourism Industry Confederation. At present managing director Irish Continental Group plc. Member Marketing Society, Skal, and Institute of Directors. Fellow of Chartered Institute of Transport. Received international marketing award 1973.

NOEL SHANLEY
Chief Executive
Port Centre, Alexandra Road, Dublin 1
(01) 722777
Born to Bernard and Kate Shanley (née O'Regan) in Co. Roscommon on 25 December 1930. Educated at Croghan NS Co. Roscommon, Rosary High School Carrick-on-Shannon, UCD and Transport Tutorial Committee London. Married to Philomena Howard with four sons and one daughter. Formerly clerical office with CIE, joined Dublin Port 1954, secretary to the Board, deputy general manager, and chief executive. At present group chief executive Dublin Port/Dublin Cargo Handling Ltd, chairman Dublin Cargo Handling Ltd and director East Link Ltd. Member Donabate Golf Club and Institute of Directors.

C. DAVID WATERS
Managing Director
Connolly Station, Dublin 1
(01) 363333
Born to Charles and Ann Waters (née Courel) in Ballina on 11 February 1936. Educated at St Muredach's, O'Connell Schools, UCD and at Harvard Business School. Married to Betty Flannery with three children. Formerly project director DART, assistant chief engineer man operations Iarnród Éireann. At present managing director Iarnród Éireann. Chairman O'Dwyer Forestry Foundation, Bachelor of Engineering, fellow Institute of Engineers of Ireland, Chartered Institute of Transport and member Institution of Civil Engineers (London).

BRIAN JOSEPH WHELAN
Chartered Accountant
20 Rostrevor Road, Dublin 6
(01) 979932
Born to Col. Joseph and Estelle Whelan (née Fegan) at Dublin on 23 March 1934. Educated at St Mary's College Rathmines and UCD. Admitted to membership and later fellowship of the Institute of Chartered Accountants in Ireland. Married to Eithne Thérèse O'Connor with two sons and four daughters. Formerly with Forsyth and Co, joint general manager Irish Industrial Bank, deputy director Irish Management Institute, chairman Irish Welcome Hotels, past president European Association Training Centres, chief consultant to Allied Irish Banks plc, and council member of the Institute of Chartered Accountants in Ireland. At present principal of corporate and management development, and vice chairman Aidlink — Third World Agency.

Chapter 27
Postal and Telecommunications

Come up and see me sometime.

Mae West

On the basis of a survey by Union Bank of Switzerland of prices in fifty-two cities in spring 1991, a five-minute local telephone call cost on average 19 cents compared with 17 cents in the Republic and 46 cents peak/31 cents off-peak in the North. The large North/South discrepancy results from local calls in the Republic being charged at a flat rate, whereas the Northern price is time-related. A letter weighing up to 20g cost an average of 24 cents to post to a domestic address, compared with 43 cents in the Republic, and 35 cents in the North.

Northern Ireland postal communications services are fully integrated with those of the rest of the United Kingdom. There is a Northern Ireland Postal Board and a Post Office Users' Council for Northern Ireland. British Telecom there is headed by a chief executive who is assisted by a Northern Ireland Advisory Committee on telecommunications. Since 1983 postal and tele-communications services in the Republic have been operated by two separate state companies: An Post and Telecom Éireann.

An Post
Over one million items of mail are carried each day in the Republic and independent surveys show that over 90 per cent of all letters are delivered the following day. This wonderful service is provided through more than 2,000 local post offices throughout the State by about 7,800 direct employees and 3,000 sub-office employees. An Post made a loss of IR£9.8 million in 1990 compared with IR£3.6 million in 1989. The basic business of An Post has been sluggish in recent years while the economy has been in recession. Sales of postage stamps rose by 4 per cent in 1986 but volume growth has stabilised at around 2 per cent since then.

Against this background it is interesting to note that An Post took on the management of the National Lottery which had instead sales of IR£168 million in 1990. The directors are keenly interested in developments in areas such as business reply services, express mail, free post and direct mail. An Post also runs the Post Office Savings Bank on behalf of the Minister for Finance and had savings services funds at end 1990 of IR£1,932 million. Its postal monopoly position was formerly under the scrutiny of a Post Office Users' Council which was abolished by the present Government.

Telecom Éireann

The bigger of the two state-owned communications companies, Telecom Éireann, assumed responsibility for operating tele-communication services including telephone, telex, data trans-mission and telefacsimile services also from 1983. It is by far the bigger of the two companies, with 15,000 staff servicing, amongst other things, about 850,000 automatic exchange lines. Telecom Éireann operates international services through a network of submarine cables, radio links and for North America a satellite earth station which is located at Midleton.

Telecom invested IR£20 million for a share in a direct fibre optic cable link to North America in 1989. A similar fibre optic link between Portmarnock, Co. Dublin, and Holyhead in Wales was inaugurated in Autumn 1988, at a cost of IR£8 million.

The cost of communications services frequently led to criti-cism of Telecom Éireann, who reduced prices in 1988. These were very significant reductions of up to 25 per cent in the case of calls to Europe and North America, 16 per cent to Britain and 30 per cent to Australia and the Far East.

Like An Post, the activities of Telecom Éireann were observed by a Telecommunications Users' Council, which was abolished by the present Government.

Visitors might be surprised to find that Telecom Éireann sells consultancy services abroad, holds a stake in Broadcom Éireann Research Limited, a company set up with other telecommuni-cations interests to secure major EC projects in research for ad-vanced communications for Europe, has a wholly-owned subsid-iary, TEIS, which markets a range of telecommunication systems for business and finally a 49 per cent shareholding in Golden Pages Limited, which publishes the alphabetical and classified directories. In 1990 Telecom purchased half the RTE 80 per cent shareholding in Cablelink Limited.

Telecom Hungary

In June 1990 the Telecom Éireann subsidiary, Irish Telecommunications Investments plc, announced a joint venture with the Hungarian telecommunications company, MATAV, and three of Hungary's largest domestic banks to finance the accelerated development of Hungary's telephone system estimated to cost US$ 5 billion over the next ten years. Seen above are HE Dr Istvan Pataki, first ever Hungarian Ambassador to Ireland (right), with Mr A.J. Flynn, Managing Director of ITI.

DAVID ALAN D'ESTERRE BLAKE KNOX
Television Producer
Donnybrook, Dublin 4
(01) 643111
Born to Ernest and Phyllis Blake Knox (née May) at Belfast on 4 November 1951. Educated at Brackenber House, Campbell College Belfast, Jesus College Cambridge University, University of Ulster and TCD. Married to Deborah Spillane with three children. Formerly Irish delegate to Standing Conference of Young People's Theatre, trainee producer/ director and senior producer with RTE. At present group head Entertainment with responsibility for RTE's television drama, variety and Young People's departments. Also Irish delegate to International Music Centre in Vienna and RTE's representative to European Broadcasting Standing Conference on Television Variety Programming. Member General Committee of National Entertainments Awards and sponsor of the Peace Train Movement.

DAVID CABOT
Film Producer and Environmental Advisor
Born to Philippe Sidney and Isabel Cabot (née Boyd) on 13 July 1938. Educated at Shady Hill School Cambridge, Mass, Dartington Hall School Devon, University College Oxford, TCD and UCG. Married to Penelope Ann Gibbon with three sons. Formerly assistant film editor BBC, assistant lecturer in zoology UCG, freelance TV/radio broadcaster BBC, head of conservation and amenity research An Foras Forbartha. At present managing director Wildgoose Films Ltd and Environmental Consultancy Services. Special advisor to the Taoiseach on environmental affairs since January 1990. Member National Heritage Council. Fellow Royal Geographical Society, Friendly Federation of Wildlife Film Makers, executive committee TCD Association and Trust. Publications include a first report on *The State of the Environment*, and *Handbook for Irish Local Authorities on EEC Environmental Legislation*.

BRIAN FARRELL
Associate Professor
University College, Belfield, Dublin 4
(01) 2693244
Born to Francis and Teresa Farrell (née McDonagh) at Manchester on 9 January 1929. Educated at Coláiste Mhuire, UCD and Harvard University. Married to Marie-Thérèse Dillon with three daughters and four sons. Formerly appointments officer and director extra-mural studies UCD, assistant to registrar and secretary UCD and radio and TV broadcaster. At present associate professor Department of Politics UCD, vice president Institute of Public Administration, patron British Association for Irish Studies, and member Advisory Council of Economic and Social Studies. Presenter for every current affairs series on Irish national

television and anchorman for all general election coverage. Author of *The Founding of Dáil Éireann, Chairman of Chief? The Role of Taoiseach in Irish Government* and *Seán Lemass.* Contributing editor to *The Irish Parliamentary Tradition, Communications and Community in Ireland, Ireland at the Polls, 1981, 1982, 1987* and *De Valera's Constitution and Ours.*

JOHN P. FITZPATRICK

Chief Executive
Merrion House, Merrion Road, Dublin 4
(01) 6837300
Born to Timothy and Marjorie Fitzpatrick (née Clarke) at Dublin on 7 March 1945. Educated at CBC Monkstown, St Vincent's College Castleknock and at UCD. Married to Klayre Mortell with one son and one daughter. Formerly director Ancillary Business, An Post, National Lottery director, assistant chief executive Marketing An Post, president Association of Advertisers in Ireland, president World Federation of Advertisers and member Management Committee of European Advertising. At present chief executive Minitel Communications Limited, director An Post National Lottery Company and member Fellows' Committee Marketing Institute of Ireland. Member Hibernian United Service Club and Dún Laoghaire Golf Club.

NOEL MARTIN GILMORE

Company Director
27 Sydney Parade Avenue, Dublin 4
(01) 2830088
Born to Peter and Anne Gilmore (née Furlong) at Bray on 8 January 1941. Educated at St James' CBS, College of Technology Kevin Street, College of Commerce and at Harvard. Married to Pauline O'Toole with one son and two daughters. Formerly chief executive National Dairy Council and director Government Information Service. At present managing director Gilmore Communictions Ltd and Total Communications Ltd. Board member People in Need, Guild of Agricultural Journalists, member Hermitage Golf Club, Public Relations Consultants' Association and Public Relations Institute and Marketing Institute.

MICHAEL GERARD HOGAN

Radio Station Consultant
O'Connell Bridge, Dublin 2
(01) 777111
Born to Michael and Breda Hogan (née O'Neill) at Athy, Co. Kildare on 3 April 1960. Educated at CBS Athy, St Mary's College Carlow and VEC Athy. Single. Formerly lighting technician RTE, general manager Radio Nova and Q102 and chief executive officer Rock 104 Dublin until August 1991 when he resigned to establish a private media consultancy and

advertising sales bureau for provincial radio stations. Member Riverview Sports Complex.

NICHOLAS PAUL KOUMARIANOS
Company Director
Airton Road, Tallaght, Dublin 24
(01) 598333
Born to Captain D.I. and Mrs Z.M. Koumarianos (née Merrick) at Kensington, London on 12 June 1943. Educated at Anselm's College Cheshire and Sandford Park School Dublin. Widower of Susan Edwina Jones. Formerly managing director Irish Time Systems and president Sandford Park Old Boys' Union. At present managing director Cable & Wireless (Ireland) Ltd, director Irish Time Systems Ltd, and Kevin Broderick Ltd and governor Northbrook Home. Member and past chairman Kildare Street and University Club, member Royal St George Yacht Club and The Strollers.

JOSEPH CLAYTON LOVE, Jnr
Company Director
55/60 South Main Street, Cork
(021) 276841
Born to Joseph Clayton and Nancy Love (née O'Brien) at Cork on 27 April 1929. Educated at CBC Cork. Married to Elizabeth McCann with two sons, Neil and Clayton, and one daughter, Sarah. Formerly managing director of family firm, a post from which he resigned in 1974 to develop property and other business interests. At present chairman Cork Communications, Beamish & Crawford, Ivernia West plc, director Clayton Love Group. Member and past president Cork Chamber of Commerce and Irish Yachting Association, and member and past admiral Royal Cork Yacht Club, member Royal Ocean Racing Club, Cobh Sailing Club, Kinsale Yacht Club, Royal Yachting Association, Irish Cruising Club, Baltimore Sailing Club, and Royal Yacht Squadron. Deputy chairman RNLI and chairman Committee of Management for Ireland.

FERGUS McGOVERN
Chief Executive
St Stephen's Green West, Dublin 2
(01) 714444
Born at County Cavan. Graduated from university with BSc degree. Chartered engineer, fellow Institute of Engineers of Ireland. Married to Angela Staunton with four sons. Formerly with Dept of Posts and Telegraphs, Radio Éireann, and Waterford Telecommunications District. Studied switching systems in Sweden, 1965. Appointed executive director Operations, Telecom Éireann, 1984. At present chief executive Telecom Éireann, chairman Cablelink Ltd and Irish Telecommunications

Investments Ltd, chairman and member of executive committee and of council of Irish Management Institute. Member of council of Economic and Social Research Institute, and trustee of International Institute of Communications. Member Dún Laoghaire and Woodbrook Golf Clubs.

MICHAEL V. MURPHY
Chief Executive
St Martin's House, Waterloo Road, Dublin 4
(01) 608488
Born to Michael and Christina Murphy (née Walsh) at Drogheda on 21 January 1934. Educated at North Brunswick CBS Dublin, Redemptorist College Limerick and UCD. Married with two sons, Michael Gerard and Niall Anthony. Formerly business advisor to Agricultural Co-operative Movement, consultant to Inbucon AIC, and deputy director general UK Newspaper Publishers. At present chairman and chief executive Golden Pages Ltd and ITT Corporation, chairman Grubb Institute of Behavioural Studies (London) and Hazelden Educational Materials International, and president Children at Risk in Ireland. Member RAC Town and Country Club London, Greystones Golf Club, Courtown Golf Club and Riverview Leisure Centre. Fellow Institute of Directors and fellow of Irish Marketing Institute.

RAYMOND JOSEPH O'KEEFFE
Chairman and Managing Director
49 Fitzwilliam Square, Dublin 2
(01) 765901
Born to William Edward and Mary O'Keeffe (née Spadaccini) at Dublin on 28 March 1929. Educated at Catholic University School. Married to Deirdre McNamara with three sons and four daughters. Formerly held a number of positions with O'Keeffes Ltd. At present chairman and managing director O'Keeffes Ltd, chairman Irish Permanent Building Society and chairman Ferrydale Investment Company. Member Marketing Institute of Ireland, Bective Rangers RFC, Fitzwilliam Lawn Tennis Club and Royal Dublin Society.

MYLES TIERNEY
Public Relations Consultant
Grange Road, Dublin 16
(01) 943465
Born to Michael and Eibhlín Tierney (née MacNeill) at Dublin in 1935. Educated at Presentation Brothers Bray and Glenstal Abbey. Married to Brenda O'Connor with five daughters, Orla, Claire, Niamh, Brenda and Clodagh. Formerly with Irish Industrial Supplies Ltd, Kevin C. Breslin and Associates, Myles Tierney Lighting Ltd. At present managing director PASS PR Ltd and director Irish Federation of Self-Employed.

ROBERT WELCH
University Professor
University of Ulster, Coleraine
(0265) 44141
Born to Patrick and Kathleen Welch (née Kearney) at Cork on 25 November 1947. Educated at Scoil Chríost Rí and UCC and at University of Leeds. Married to Angela O'Riordan with three sons, Killian, Eltan and Tiernan, and one daughter, Rachel. Formerly university lecturer. At present professor of English and head of Department of English Media and Theatre Studies at University of Ulster, Coleraine.

Chapter 28
Business Organisations

Members of the new left do not 'control' the Media. In many instances, they are the media.

Dr Ivor Kenny

Irish businessmen associate, federate and confederate for the same basic reasons as their counterparts in other countries — to tackle problems which they find they have in common with one another, to search for new markets and new opportunities, to make submissions to Government on matters of concern to business or to Government, and above all to ensure that business participates in public debate on matters of importance to the society in which it makes its living. This has become increasingly necessary in recent years and the leading business organisations see the task of communicating the views of business to the wider public as part of their function.

Businessmen in their business organisations are inevitably earnest and anxious to impress. They deal effectively with matters of common interest and crave the trappings of power, trusting that these will help gain influence, or as it is frequently known, clout. The pursuit of influence is dangerous and frequently leads to organisations losing touch with their constituencies. One could argue, for example, that there is little 'manufacturing industry' in the Confederation of Irish Industry — only high level economics and politics.

Similarly, it could be argued that there is little 'commerce' in the Chambers of Commerce, only macro-economics and politics. The Federation of Trade Associations is probably closer to commerce nowadays, city centre business associations closer to retail activity, and foreign trade, for so long the hallmark of the Chambers, has been slipping away to the Irish Exporters' Association, the Institute for Foreign Trade, and the Irish Trade Board.

The question which must be asked is, in the event of five Irish businessmen occupying a desert island, how many business organisations would they form? Certainly, at present there is a multiplicity of representative bodies which mirrors the multiplicity of trades unions. In spite of this, however, CCI, CII and

FIE carry out most of the vital task of representing the views of Irish business to Government and keeping Government in touch with economic reality.

CCI — The Chambers of Commerce of Ireland

Visitors from Continental European countries are likely to be surprised at the voluntary private law status of the Irish Chambers. In France, Germany, Greece, Italy, Luxembourg, the Netherlands and Spain, Chambers are institutions established by public authorities with the right to raise levies on companies registered in their particular areas. Visitors are also likely to be surprised at the number of Irish Chambers. For the Republic's population of three and a half million there are over 50 Chambers compared to Portugal with a population of ten million and only two Chambers.

The national organisation, CCI, was not formed until 1922, which is comparatively recent in Chamber terms, as both Dublin and Waterford Chambers are over 200 years old. The objects of CCI are the promotion, development and protection of the common interests of member Chambers and Irish industry and commerce generally, and also communicating to the public, to Government and to others, the views of the Chambers of Commerce and Industry on matters of importance.

CCI is in regular contact with Government departments, such as the Departments of Finance, Foreign Affairs and Industry and Commerce, and is a nominating body for elections to Seanad Éireann, the upper house of the Irish parliament. All business organisations are prone to being regarded as 'mere talking shops' by certain businessmen, and it is inevitable that by their very nature direct involvement in economic activity remains the exception rather than the rule. CCI supported the economic development of the country in February 1989 when, jointly with Merchant Banker John McGilligan, it established Business and Trading House Investment Co Ltd with a view to managing Business Expansion Scheme funds.

CCI has four honorary members: former Taoiseach Dr Garret FitzGerald TD, former Dublin Chamber President Mr Niall Crowley, former Galway Chamber President and Honorary Life President of the International Olympics Committee, Lord Killanin, and the current Taoiseach, Mr Charles Haughey.

In Washington DC
Mr Dónal P. Flinn, president United States Chamber of Commerce
in Ireland with Mr John Philipsborn, chairman of the European
Council of American Chambers of Commerce at their April 1991
meeting in Washington.

CII — The Confederation of Irish Industry

The CII is an association of organisations. Membership is corporate, the organisations are the members, not the individuals nominated to represent them. All firms operating in Ireland which manufacture products or provide commercially traded services are eligible for membership. Members are drawn from both the private and state-sponsored commercial sectors, thus reflecting the mixed economy of Ireland. Members currently comprise over 2,000 firms, of which approximately 50 per cent are direct and the balance are members of affiliated associations.

Members are grouped according to common interests into one or more of twelve major divisions and about 65 associations or groups of firms. Each of the main divisions — agri-business, building materials, clothing, electronics and informatics, engineering, financial services, marine and offshore, mining, plastics and packaging, textiles, small firms — embraces a series of industrial groupings. Through these federations and associations, the CII provides a service for dealing with specific problems. Individual federations and associations have autonomy in relation to sectoral issues.

The CII's major objective is to ensure that a climate for enterprise exists in Ireland; its job is to ensure that business identifies areas of common interest, to translate its members' views into sound, well-researched policies and then to get them across to the widest possible audience. The primary focus of all the representations of the Confederation relates to business confidence, the encouragement of enterprise, the creation of an environment conducive to increased investment in productive assets and the expansion of output which alone will support better living standards and more jobs in the economy.

The President is elected by the CII National Council and serves for two years. In addition to chairing the monthly National Council meeting, the President leads major CII delegations to meet Government Ministers. The CII's Director General heads the permanent staff of around 60 who carry out the day-to-day work of running the CII, preparing policy and negotiating with Ministers and Civil Servants.

FIE — The Federation of Irish Employers

The Federation of Irish Employers was formed in 1941, and is an independent organisation dedicated to furthering and protecting employer interests in industrial relations, social affairs and people at work issues. It changed its name from the Federated Union of Employers in October 1989. The promotion of sound employer-employee relations is the foundation on which the FIE has been built. Over the past fifty years, the Federation has represented the interests of Irish employers in discussions and negotiations with Government and other national interest groups. In that time, FIE has built up a special relationship with its members through the provision of a range of employee relations' services which has expanded to anticipate and reflect the growing complexity and importance of good human resource management.

The Federation is the largest employers' organisation in the country. Membership is composed equally of large and small employers and is drawn from all sectors of commercial activity. Services are provided by executive and professional staff, through a divisional and regional network which includes five permanent regional offices and a headquarters in Dublin. FIE participates in the work of over 80 organisations, institutions, and committees, including the Labour Court, Employment Appeals Tribunal, Employer Labour Conference, National Economic and Social Council, FÁS (The Training and Employment Authority), the Employment Equality Agency, and the National Authority for Occupational Safety and Health. In conjunction with the Irish Congress of Trade Unions, it controls the Irish Productivity Centre.

Irish Business Overseas

The three organisations outlined above co-operate in organising the Irish Business Bureau in Brussels, which serves as a representative office for each of them. Both Germany and the United States had bilateral Chambers of Commerce in Ireland for many years prior to the formation of a German Irish Business Association in Bonn in November 1988. One month earlier in New York, the Ireland Chamber of Commerce in the United States of America was launched, with the stated aims of broadening and enhancing Irish-American trade, actively complementing the efforts of the Irish Government and its promotional agencies and furthering educational, ethnic and cultural exchange.

NICCI — The Northern Ireland Chamber of Commerce and Industry

Belfast Chamber of Commerce was formed in 1783, incorporated in 1869, and reconstituted and renamed NICCI in 1966. As part of the 1966 reorganisation, an Association of Northern Ireland Chambers of Commerce, which had been formed after the First World War to link the Belfast Chamber with the other Chambers in Northern Ireland, was merged with the reconstituted Belfast Chamber. This reorganisation undoubtedly gave the Chamber Movement in Northern Ireland an enviable cohesion, but the strategy adopted to bring this about could not, of course, be applied in the Republic, because the geographical area is greater, and the characters and traditions of the Chambers more diverse.

NICCI is a member of the Association of British Chambers of Commerce, which in turn, like CCI, is a member of Euro-chambres — the Association of European Chambers of Commerce and Industry.

The theory and practice of management is the concern of the Irish Management Institute, and marketing is the bailiwick of the Marketing Institute. Their mission is 'to position the marketing profession as the crucial factor for business success'. The Advertising Standards Authority for Ireland aims to promote and enforce throughout Ireland the highest standards of advertising in all media of communication. The Boardroom Centre was founded in 1984 to promote the role of the independent non-executive company director and to help companies find appropriate candidates.

The German Irish Chamber of Commerce is eleven years old and in 1990 took on the 'happy task' of looking after the interests of business people trading with the former GDR.

The United States Chamber of Commerce in Ireland is a much older organisation, having been established in 1961. The members who are American owned or American connected companies, are serviced by the Executive Director of the Chamber from the Chamber office in Dublin.

There are numerous other bilateral trade organisations, and in fact the Republic seems to have one for every major trading partner, other than the biggest trading partner of all, the United Kingdom. There are so many close ties between the two countries, however, that it may not be absolutely necessary and both CCI and CII, for example, maintain close links with their opposite numbers in the UK. There are even bilateral business organisations for countries where there is no significant trade — but where there is vast potential for growth in economic relations. The Portuguese Irish Chamber of Commerce and the Irish Hungarian Economic Association are examples of such organisations.

DENIS JOHN BERNON
Company Director
Sandyford Road, Dublin 16
(01) 956911
Born to Francis and Monica Bernon (née Keogh) in England on 6 August 1928. Educated at St Benedict's School Ealing, St George's College Weybridge and London Polytechnic. Married to Teresa O'Keeffe with three sons. Formerly chief executive UDT Bank Ltd. Past president Irish Finance Houses Ltd and president Irish Trade Protection Association Ltd. At present director The Boardroom Centre, chairman board St Gerard's School Bray, member Audit Registration Committee, Institute of Chartered Accountants in Ireland, panel of assessors for Unemployment Assistance and non-executive director Institute of Credit Control in Ireland. Member Milltown Golf Club.

PETER BRENNAN
Director
66 Av. Cortenberg, 1040 Brussels
Born to Joe and Patricia Brennan (née Hans) at Dublin on 3 March 1953. Educated at Chanel College, TCD and at the Institute of Public Administration. Married to Ursula O'Dwyer with two sons, Simon and Damian. Formerly principal Dept of Industry and Commerce, and director Irish Steel Ltd and Ceimicí Teo. At present director Irish Business Bureau, Irish Belgian Business Association, and secretary Irish German Business Association.

ROBERT P. CHALKER
Chamber of Commerce Director
20 College Green, Dublin 2
(01) 793733
Born to Isaac Watts and Harriet Marshall Chalker (née Phelps) at Linden, Alabama. Educated at public, primary and secondary schools in Alabama and West Florida, MA, Duke University, Durham, NC, graduate from studies Sorbonne, Chicago University, Columbia University and Naval War College, Newport, Rhode Island. Married first to Edna Wood (deceased 1985) with one son, Jeffrey Phelps, and one daughter, Janet Wood Chalker, second to Louise Studley, 1990. Formerly with US consular and diplomatic service in Berlin, Lisbon, Birmingham, London, Madras, Bremen, Düsseldorf, Washington, New York, Kobe-Osaka, Amsterdam and Dublin. At present and since 1969 executive director US Chamber of Commerce in Ireland (member of the Chamber of Commerce of the United States of America and of the European Council of American Chambers of Commerce). Member Stephen's Green Club, Dublin Rotary, Milltown and Woodbrook Golf Clubs, Zinfandel Club, Royal Irish Automobile Club and Dublin Grand Opera Society.

JOHN COLGAN

Engineer and Economist
Old Finglas Road, Dublin 9
(01) 370101

Born to John and Josephine Colgan (née McCann) at Dublin on 11 November 1939. Educated at Holy Faith Convent Glasnevin, Coláiste Mhuire and St Vincent's CBS Dublin, UCD, Manchester University, College of Technology Kevin Street Dublin and at Brunel, London. Married to Janet C. Needs with one son, Justin, and one daughter, Niamh. Formerly college lecturer, industrial engineer with General Electric (USA), Lucas (UK) and Irish delegate OECD and EEC committees, chairman Leixlip Community Council, secretary Dublin City Association of An Taisce, member Co. Kildare VEC and chairman Central Branch and Dublin West constituency executive of Fine Gael. At present chairman Campaign to Separate Church and State, chairman Consumers' Association of Ireland, and vice president Salmon Leap Canoe Club.

LIAM CONNELLAN

Engineer
Confederation House, Kildare Street, Dublin 2
(01) 779801

Born to James Austin and Annie Frances Connellan (née Hughes) at Longford on 19 May 1936. Educated at Marist Brothers Strokestown, Roscommon CBS, Garbally Park Ballinasloe and at UCD whence he graduated with a BE degree in mechanical and electrical engineering CEng and FIEI. Married to Marie Celine Crehan with four sons and one daughter. After post graduate training at STAL, Finspong, Sweden, and Associated Electrical Industries, Rugby, England, he was divisional engineer at ACEC Waterford and head of small business division at Irish Management Institute. At present director general Confederation of Irish Industries. Member European Foundation for Management Development and honorary member German-Irish Chamber of Industry and Commerce. Decorated by Federal Republic of Germany (Bundesverdienstkreuz). Admires chief executives who have guided their companies to profitable international expansion from Irish bases.

BRIAN JAMES CREGAN

Policy Director
Confederation House, Kildare Street, Dublin 2
(01) 779801

Born to Joe and Mary Cregan (née O'Brien) at Dublin on 14 May 1961. Educated at Gonzaga College, UCD, St John's College Oxford and King's Inns Dublin. Single. Formerly director Financial Services Industry Association. At present director of Business Law and Competition Policy, Confederation of Irish Industry.

CHARLES HANCOCK
Executive Director
87/89 Pembroke Road, Ballsbridge, Dublin 4
(01) 680400
Born at Wintersfield on 13 January 1920. Educated at Church School Horsheath, Perse School Cambridge and at Clare College Cambridge. Married to Elizabeth Faichney (née Austin) with one daughter and one son. Formerly plant chemist Royal Ordnance Factories (explosives), senior chemist Shell Petroleum Co, managing director P.A. Management Consultants (Ireland) Ltd, president Institute of Management Consultants in Ireland and chairman Kildare Street and University Club. At present executive director Institute of Management Consultants in Ireland, chairman Regional Activities Committee Institute of Management Consultants UK and Ireland. Member Kildare Street and University Club and Royal Zoological Society of Ireland, and fellow Institute of Management Consultants.

JAMES DEVANE KENNEDY
Manager
Industrial Estate, Waterford
(051) 55001
Born to George and Marjory Kennedy (née McDonald) at Limerick on 9 August 1951. Educated at Ballynacarraige NS, Salesian Secondary School, Pallaskenry and at UCC (BSc degree in chemistry). Holds certificate in management from Cranfield Business School. Married to Mary Lucey with three sons, George, James and Jerome. At present general manager Bausch and Lomb Ireland, president Chambers of Commerce of Ireland, and president Euromcontact, a federation of national associations for the contact lens industry, and chairman of the European Bar Coding Association for the Contact Lens Industry. Founder director of Irish Fight for Sight, a national charity for the prevention of blindness. Director and former president of Waterford Chamber of Commerce.

DR AIDAN O'BOYLE
Industry Federation Director
Confederation House, Kildare Street, Dublin 2
(01) 779801
Born to Edward Joseph and Kathleen O'Boyle (née Quigley) at Downpatrick on 11 January 1946. Educated at Newcastle NS, Monkstown Park CBC, UCD and later at TCD. Married to Deirdre Gray with three sons. Formerly assistant lecturer in pharmacology at UCD, marketing officer IDA, Paris, and director Irish Business Bureau, Brussels. At present director of industrial policy at Confederation of Irish Industry.

DR CON POWER

Industry Federation Director
Confederation House, Kildare Street, Dublin 2
(01) 779801
Born to Henry and Catherine Maud Power (née O'Sullivan) at Waterford City on 29 January 1939. Educated at De La Salle Waterford, St Canice's and O'Connell Schools Dublin, and at UCD whence he graduated with honours BComm and MEconSc degrees. Later admitted as certified accountant, cost and management accountant and chartered secretary. Conferred with an earned PhD in October 1988 and a DBA in 1990, both from Pacific University, Los Angeles. Married to Maria Christina Barrett with one son, David, and three daughters, Aideen, Ruth and Audrey. Formerly inspector of taxes, lecturer College of Technology Bolton Street, research officer An Foras Forbartha and principal Sligo Regional Technical College. At present director of economic policy at the Confederation of Irish Industry (since 1979), and chairman National Roads Authority, member of many committees, including the Central Review Committee for the Programme for Economic and Social Progress (PESP), the board of the Institute of European Affairs, and the Garda Síochána Advisory Group. Non-executive director Kompass Ireland and associated companies and member of Academic Board of Accountancy and Business College, Dublin. Member Royal Dublin Society, Irish Economic Association and UCD Association.

PAUL SKEHAN

Business Executive
22 Merrion Square, Dublin 2
(01) 612888
Born to John Charles and Winnie Skehan (née Butler) at Dublin on 3 May 1961. Educated at St Conleth's College and UCD, and later at Alliance Française and the Irish Management Institute. Married to Lourda Sheppard with one daughter, Bozena. Formerly project executive (company development) with Industrial Development Authority. At present Director of the Chambers of Commerce of Ireland. Council member of the Irish national committee of the International Chamber of Commerce and alternate member of the EC Economic and Social Committee. Member and instructor with Glenans Irish Sailing Centre, member Alliance Française and Bective Rangers RFC.

Chapter 29
Industrial Relations

Sack the lot!
Lord Fisher

There have been a great many amalgamations between trade unions in recent years, the biggest of which was the merger of the Irish Transport and General Workers' Union with the Federated Workers' Union of Ireland. The merged union, known as SIPTU (Services/Industrial/Professional/Technical/Union) is the giant on the Irish industrial relations scene. The mergers came about against a background of falling union membership. In 1981, for example, the total in the Republic was 524,000 which by 1987 had fallen to 457,000.

Strikes
A strike is generally regarded as being an expression by a free man of his fundamental right to withdraw his labour. In itself that is all very well, but does the right to strike not also suggest nowadays that the strikers own their jobs and, while they refuse to work them themselves, they deny the right of other workers to seek whatever jobs are being unworked, and leave the employer without the right to hire substitute labour? Thus, while claiming liberty for themselves, strikers deny liberty to their fellow workers and to employers. This denial can be accompanied by violence or the threat of violence. This situation has evolved in Ireland and in other countries without sufficient examination and without legal justification. It prevents trade unions from taking a more responsible and thoughtful approach to labour problems. Workers have a perfectly free right to withdraw their labour but this is self-dismissal. They do not have the right to claim ownership of the jobs which they have vacated. If unions were to accept this principle it would make them a very different and positive body for reform and productivity, and acceptance would be followed by a free labour-market which would bring with it benefits for Irish industry and for the Irish economy. Improved labour-market information and worker-mobility would go hand in hand with this. Thankfully, the vast majority of disputes are

settled amicably and at an early stage. The system of industrial relations is voluntary, but it is doubtful if a totally voluntary mechanism can be relied upon in so far as essential services are concerned. Strikes in organisations like the Electricity Supply Board seem like nothing short of self-destruction.

The number of strikes has been declining each year and, in terms of the number of days lost, only about 10 per cent were lost due to unofficial strikes in 1987. The decline in strike activity must be attributable to the recession in the economy and the effect this has had on public opinion which favours a climate of realism in the face of more intense competition. At the same time, communications between management and employees have probably been improving slowly but surely and the fact that trade union membership has been falling since 1981, may also be relevant.

The Law

The Republic's Industrial Relations Act 1990 was well received and the introduction of compulsory secret ballots, limitations on secondary and one-person pickets and the outlawing of secondary action in life preserving services have all been considered to be beneficial. The right of workers to decide freely to join or not to join a union should be protected with certain specific exceptions. Unions should be bodies giving true service to the worker in a free labour-market.

Employers should be free to make membership of a union a condition of employment (the 'closed shop') but equally they should be free to make non-membership a condition of employment or to impose neither condition.

Picketing in support of political beliefs should not be allowed at any time under any circumstances. Dunnes Stores, Barclays Bank, Irish Shell and Standard Chartered Bank are companies established in Ireland who have had this form of picketing inflicted on them. Picket-line violence is rare but it should be made a criminal offence and should be subjected to severe penalty. The scale of picketing should be confined to a small number of persons at the place of work of the strikers, each member of the picket to be nominated by the union. Unauthorised picketing, acts of violence and attempts to hinder the free movement of people or vehicles to or from the picketed premises should be an offence subject to severe penalties on the unions.

Employers should and do inform, involve and motivate their employees by profit-sharing or other means of reward for their part in the success of an organisation. The courts should and, indeed do, try to balance the requirements that employers behave fairly towards their employees and vice versa, with a need for industry and business to be efficient if the nation is to prosper.

Over half of all employees are nowadays paid by cheque or by some other non-cash method. The Irish Congress of Trade Unions agreed that the laws which provided entitlement to payment in cash should be repealed, but suggested that employers should be required to make arrangements with local banks to accept and cash wage cheques, regardless of whether or not the employees concerned had accounts with the bank concerned. There is no doubt that non-cash methods of payment are highly desirable both from security and efficiency points of view. Again, where security is improved, insurance costs are reduced, and this is another reason why the move to non-cash payment continues. A Payment of Wages Bill was published by the Minister for Labour in the Republic early in Summer 1991. The new legislation was designed to cover all employees and to legalise specific non-cash methods of payment such as payment by cheque, money order and credit transfer.

Trade Unions
The Irish Congress of Trade Unions is the main representative organisation for the trade union movement. Considering the size of the country, the number of unions affiliated to Congress is staggering at over eighty and the two largest general unions represent only about 40 per cent of the total affiliated membership. Half of the affiliated unions have members in the Republic only, some have members in Northern Ireland only, and some have members in both jurisdictions. The two big unions mentioned are the Amalgamated Transport and General Workers' Union and SIPTU.

There are significant organisations also for the civil service, for local government, and for teachers, but the police organisation cannot affiliate to Congress. Significant Unions affiliated to Congress include the Nurses' Union of Ireland, the Marine, Port, and General Workers' Union and the Irish Distributive and Administrative Trade Union. A new trade union MSF (Manufacturing Science Finance) was launched in February 1988. Almost half of its 30,000 members are in banking and insurance, and about two-thirds are in the Republic.

Other groups to merge and amalgamate in recent years included tax officials who combined with customs people and other public servants, while postal workers combined with telecommunications engineers. Sometimes the attraction of making a greater impact on the national scene is enough to give birth to the amalgamation idea. One teachers' union leader was quoted in early 1990 as saying that a merger of the three teacher organisations would lead to a united teachers' union which would 'effectively replace the Department of Education as the policy making body in the area of Irish education'. Another significant merger was that between the union of professional and technical civil servants and the local government and public services union which formed the Irish Municipal and Civil Trade Union known as IMPACT.

Non-Pay Questions

The Republic's Advisory Committee on Worker Participation recommended in June 1986 that there should be enabling legislation for all private companies, employing more than 100, to have worker-directors. This was a majority recommendation and the employer representatives on the Committee dissented. Worker-directors claim that they help boards of directors to know the views of workers and how workers would be affected by proposed policies. Co-operation between management and workers is, of course, essential to survival but the worker-director is truly a concept with a built-in conflict of interest, and it is normal for worker-directors to oppose reductions in staff members, however necessary these may be. In spite of this, one third of the membership of the boards of directors of several key state companies is elected by the workers. The list includes the Electricity Supply Board, Aer Lingus, Telecom Éireann and An Post. The handling of redundancy calls for great delicacy in view of the human tragedy that redundancy brings in its train. Where the employer is solvent, of course the negotiations are vigorous and the settlements are significantly generous. On the other hand, if the employer is insolvent, the State effectively steps into the breach. The management buy-out of the L M Ericsson plant in Athlone in late 1989 was unusual in so far as 180 unionised employees participated and received 43 per cent of the shares in the MBO company, Erictron. It was reported at the time that the workers would have shared IR£1.5 million in redundancy, but voted 2:1 to accept the shares and the participation in the company. 15 members of management were to share another 17 per cent, with 40 per cent being divided between 4 directors.

The Planned Sharing Research Association was formed in 1978 to study profit sharing world wide with a view to applying this to Irish conditions. The Irish Profit Sharing Association was formed in 1987 to cater for the special needs of members operating approved profit sharing schemes under Irish legislation.

On the political front, the unions work to have more labour members elected to the Dáil and Seanad. In addition to a healthy interest in politics, the modern trade union has significant research support backed up with professional advice. Unions may also have legal departments and health and safety departments.

Rates of Pay

An international comparison of earnings was provided by the Union Bank of Switzerland spring 1991 survey of forty-eight cities, all figures expressed in US$ per annum:

	Machinists	Automobile Mechanics	Female Textile Workers	Saleswomen
Dublin	19,400	13,900	11,200	13,800
London	18,500	17,700	10,100	10,100
New York	33,300	31,200	14,600	14,600
Tokyo	31,000	24,700	14,700	16,700

As can be seen, gross pay in Dublin is lower than in London in only one of the four categories. A Belfast/London comparison would probably have shown a similar picture, had Belfast been included in the survey.

DAVID ALLEN

Trade Union General Secretary
94 Malone Road, Belfast BT9 5HP
(0232) 662216

Born to Robert and Martha Allen (née McCullough) at Ballymena on 24 October 1937. Educated at Harryville Primary School Ballymena, Ballymena Academy and Stranmillis College Belfast. Married to Iris Mehaffey with one daughter, Lynsay. Formerly member Constitutional Convention at Stormont, member Ballymena Borough Council, North Eastern Education and Library Board, and president Students' Representative Council at Stranmillis. At present general secretary Ulster Teachers' Union, member Court of University of Ulster and other positions associated with trade union general secretaryship, including chairman Teachers' Panel, Secondary Standing Conference, chairman Primary Teachers' Council, vice chairman Northern Ireland Teachers' Council and spokesman for Teachers Side on Salaries and Conditions of Service Negotiating Committee.

REV. JOHN BRADY

Lecturer
Sandford Road, Dublin 6
(01) 972917

Born to John J. and Elisabeth Brady (née Tuite) at Dublin on 3 September 1935. Educated at Kostka College Clontarf, UCD and Jesuit House of Studies, Milltown Park. Formerly director National College of Industrial Relations, and currently senior lecturer. At present member of Society of Jesus, chairman society for Co-Operative Studies in Ireland, honorary president Planned Sharing Research Association, board member Greendale Community School and Irish School of Ecumenics, and executive committee member Irish Association for Cultural Economic and Social Relations. Founder member of Glenans in Ireland. Author of numerous articles on economic, social and political questions.

TERRY CARLIN

Trade Union Official
3 Wellington Park, Belfast BT9 6DJ
(0232) 681726

Born to Neil and Elizabeth Carlin (née McFadden) at Derry on 25 January 1946. Educated at CBS Derry, St Columb's College and NUI. Married with one daughter. Formerly training officer ICTU, assistant Northern Ireland Officer, teacher St Columbanus Secondary School Bangor, member Standing Advisory Commission on Human Rights and of Manpower Council. At present Northern Ireland Officer Irish Congress of Trade Unions, member N.I. Economic Council, N.I. Economic Research Centre and board of Charabanc Theatre Company. Member Ulster Arts Club. Awarded Eisenhower Exchange Fellowship 1989.

PETER CASSELLS
Trade Union Official
19 Raglan Road, Dublin 4
(01) 680641
Born at Navan, Co. Meath in 1949. Formerly with education and training service of Irish Congress of Trade Unions, he later became legislation officer, economic and social affairs officer, and assistant secretary. Has represented ICTU on several agencies including Employment Equality Agency, Commission on Social Welfare, Government-ICTU Working Party on Taxation and currently represents ICTU on the National Economic and Social Council, the Sectoral Development Committee, the Employer Labour Conference and the European Trade Union Confederation. At present general secretary Irish Congress of Trade Unions, having succeeded Dónal Nevin on 1 January 1989. Vice president and member of central committee of the People's College. Trustee and executive committee member Irish Labour History Society.

FREDERICK BASIL CHUBB
Professor
Trinity College, Dublin 2
(01) 772941
Born to Frederick John Bailey and Gertrude May Chubb (née McArdle) on 8 December 1921. Educated at Ludgershall Junior School, Bishop Wordsworth's School Salisbury, and Merton College Oxford. Married to Orla Mary Sheehan. Widower of Margaret Gertrude Rafter. Formerly bursar TCD, chairman Comhairle na nOspidéal and professor of political science at TCD. At present chairman Employer-Labour Conference and Irish Banks Joint Industrial Council.

MARY CLARK GLASS
Chief Executive
22 Great Victoria Street, Belfast BT2 2BA
(0232) 242752
Born to Elwin and Marian Chubb (née Burnell) in South Wales in 1940. Educated at Howell's School, Llandaff. Later undertook five-year external degree in English history and law with London University. Married to Basil Glass with four stepsons and two sons from an earlier marriage. Formerly lecturer in law at College of Business Studies Belfast, for seven years broadcaster on legal and consumer topics. Member National Consumer Council, economic and social committee of EC, Consumers in the European Community Group, Women's Law and Research Group, and Northern Ireland Rent Assessment Panel, in addition to being chairman of Lisburn Social Security and Northern Ireland Local Appeals Tribunal to 1984. Member Probation Board for Northern Ireland and an unpaid volunteer with the Northern Ireland Victim Support Scheme. At present chairman and chief executive Equal Opportunities

Commission for Northern Ireland, fellow Royal Society of Arts and fellow Institute of Personnel Management. Chairman Extern Organistion since 1989.

JAMES DORNEY
General Secretary
73 Orwell Road, Rathgar, Dublin 6
(01) 961588
Born to James and Maura Dorney (née Moroney) at Limerick on 1 April 1947. Educated at Synge Street CBS and at UCD. Married with two children. Formerly assistant general secretary (TUI) and vocational teacher. At present general secretary TUI, governor Thomond College of Education, member executive council ICTU and of the European Committee for Education.

PHIL FLYNN
General Secretary
9 Gardiner Place, Dublin 1
(01) 728899
Born to James and Margaret Flynn (née Corrigan) at Dublin on 1 June 1940. Educated at Christian Brothers Dundalk, St Mary's College Dundalk and at London School of Economics. Married to Christian Carney with two sons and one daughter. Formerly London health service officer National Union of Public Employees and vice president Sinn Féin. At present general secretary IMPACT, vice president ICTU, council NESC, board Labour Relations Commission, Institute of Public Administration, and Irish Productivity Centre. Member Central Review Committee Programme for Economic and Social Progress, and Efficiency Audit Group, Council Institute of European Affairs.

CHRIS KIRWAN
Trade Union Official
Liberty Hall, Dublin 1
(01) 749731
Born to Christopher and Ann Kirwan (née Kiernan). Educated at Meath Street NS and Crumlin Boys' Secondary School (Scoil Éanna). Holds a higher diploma in social economics from UCD and a diploma in social economics from the College of Industrial Relations. Married to Bernadette Lawlor with two sons, Ciarán and Shane, and one daughter, Nóirín Áine. Formerly branch secretary, head office official, national group secretary, and vice president and general secretary Irish Transport and General Workers' Union, a member of the human sciences committee of the Irish National Productivity Centre, chairman, vice chairman and member of the Dublin Port and Docks' Board, director of NET and Dublin Cargo Handling Company, member Seanad Éireann 1982-7, and president, vice president, treasurer and executive council member Irish

Congress of Trade Unions. At present joint general secretary SIPTU, chairman board of FÁS, and of Irish Labour Training Services, member board of Aer Rianta, of the Unfair Dismissals Tribunal, EC Coal and Steel Consultative Committee, Luxembourg, and of the Irish Amateur Boxing Association.

PATRICIA O'DONOVAN
Trade Union Official
19 Raglan Road, Dublin 4
(01) 680641
Born to Patrick and Margaret O'Donovan (née Wilson) at Cork on 12 November 1953. Educated at Glasheen NS Cork, Convent of Mercy Carrick-on-Suir, UCC and King's Inns Dublin. Single. Formerly EC Information Officer (ICTU), Legislative and Equality Officer (ICTU), member Whitaker Committee of Inquiry into Penal System, and of board of Employment Equality Agency. At present assistant general secretary (ICTU), member National Economic & Social Council, National Pensions Board and Economic Committee European Trade Union Confederation. Member Irish Labour History Society and of board of Irish Centre for European Law, and member of Council of State.

EDMOND GERARD QUIGLEY
General Secretary
35 Parnell Square, Dublin 1
Born to John J. and Margaret Quigley (née O'Connor) at Belfast on 3 November 1928. Educated at St Mary's CBS, St Joseph's College of Education and at Queen's University Belfast. Married with five children. Formerly Northern secretary Irish National Teachers' Organisation and chairman Northern Committee Irish Congress of Trade Unions. At present general secretary Irish National Teachers' Organisation, chairman European Studies Project, president European Committee and member world executive of World Confederation of Organisations of Teaching Profession, board of FÁS, and University of Limerick board of governors. Member Leopardstown Racing Club and Teachers' Club. Awarded honorary MA Queen's University Belfast and honorary fellowship Educational Institute of Scotland.

PATRICK MARY RABBITTE
Trade Union Official
Liberty Hall, Dublin 1
(01) 749731
Born to James and Margaret Rabbitte (née Kirrane) at Claremorris, Co. Mayo on 18 May 1949. Educated at Coilean NS, St Colman's Claremorris and UCG. Married to Derry McDermott with three daughters, Kate, Maev-Anne and Lucy. Formerly held a number of senior positions in the Irish Transport and General Workers' Union, member of the governing

body of UCG, president UCG Students' Union and president Union of Students in Ireland. At present national secretary Irish Transport and General Workers' Union, member central executive committee of the Workers Party and member Dublin County Council. Member Irish CND and Anti-Apartheid Movement.

CIARÁN G. RYAN

General Secretary
93 St Stephen's Green, Dublin 2
(01) 722255
Born to Thomas and Catherine Ryan (née Condon) at Dublin on 9 June 1939. Educated at Belvedere College Dublin and National College of Industrial Relations. Married to Deirdre O'Brien with three children. Formerly director Federation of Irish Employers, national officer in IDATU and head of personnel at Quinnsworth. At present general secretary Irish Bank Officials' Association.

Chapter 30
Education and Training

A little learning is a dang'rous thing;
Drink deep, or taste not the Pierian spring.

Alexander Pope

The right to education is enshrined in the Republic's Constitution and school attendance is compulsory. Almost all primary schools are state-aided, although a small number are privately run and do not receive State aid. The funding includes teacher salaries. Secondary schools are also heavily funded by the State, although they are usually privately owned, in many instances by religious communities.

The first phase of secondary education in the Republic continues for three years leading to the Intermediate Examination and the Intermediate Certificate (which is to be replaced by the Junior Certificate). This is followed by a second phase of two or three years leading to the Leaving Certificate, which is the basic qualification for admission to third level institutions. Irish is a compulsory study subject in both phases with English, geography, history and mathematics as additional compulsory subjects in the first phase only. In addition, most students take at least one modern language, history and/or geography, and physics and/or chemistry. Business organisation, economics and accounting have been growing in popularity.

The structure in Northern Ireland is similar — primary schools followed by secondary schools which are known either as grammar schools, where there is an academic orientation, or intermediate schools, where the curriculum includes both practical and general subjects. 'O' Levels and 'A' Levels are roughly equivalent to Intermediate and Leaving Certificates.

Third level education is also heavily funded by the State. There are four universities in the Republic: the National University of Ireland with constituent colleges at Dublin, Cork and Galway and a recognised College at Maynooth; University of Dublin or Trinity College (founded in 1591); Dublin City University, and University of Limerick. In Northern Ireland there are two further universities, Queen's University in Belfast and the University of

Ulster with campuses at Coleraine, Jordanstown and Derry. The Republic has also the National College of Art and Design in Dublin and Thomond College of Education in Limerick.

There are also colleges of technology and regional technical colleges which provide courses in business subjects, science and technology. Micro-electronics research is carried out at University College Cork and at Plassey in Limerick. Six colleges of education provide courses for primary teachers. The Incorporated Law Society and the Honourable Society of King's Inns train lawyers, the Royal College of Surgeons provides medical qualifications and the Irish Management Institute trains managers.

Student Numbers
The student population of the Island is extremely large. There are about 950,000 students in full-time education in the Republic and about 350,000 in Northern Ireland to make a grand total of 1.3 million students. Third level education is more expensive in the Republic than in the United Kingdom and, in recent years, there has been a sharp rise in the number of students from the Republic applying for places in colleges in England, Wales and Northern Ireland. The European Community disposes that students from one member state may study in another one under the same conditions as residents. The numbers applying for places in England and Wales increased from under 200 in 1986 to nearly 700 in 1987 — a figure which reached almost 3,000 in 1988. Parents can covenant small portions of their income to children aged over 18 and this results in a tax rebate at the highest rate at which the covenantor pays tax. Covenants can also be made out in favour of schools and colleges to support the teaching of natural sciences. The cost to the exchequer in the Republic of these tax rebates rose steadily from IR£7 million in 1986/7 to IR£20 million in 1989/90.

Multi-Denominational Schools
One of the great needs in Irish society, is the need to break down barriers between members of different tribal groups, and this is certainly being achieved in the Republic, where citizens mix freely without needing to know the denominational loyalties of their friends and acquaintances. This is far from being the case in

Northern Ireland and it has been suggested that there is a need for more mixing between middle- and working-classes, as well as between Protestants and Catholics. It is widely believed that third level Institutions are enriched by having an international mix of students, and many countries take steps to ensure that such an international mix is a feature of the third level system. It is surely not difficult to extend this thinking to having a tribal mix of students at secondary and at primary levels.

There is so much in common between the peoples of these neighbouring islands, there are so many ties and so much good-will, that when an Ulster Unionist stridently proclaims his wish to remain British, he is not really asking for a second head or a third arm, but merely to be distinguished from being Irish, which in European terms is, more or less, the same thing. It seems particularly strange then, that with the corresponding differences in beliefs between Roman Catholics and other Christians so mini-scule, church leaders consistently oppose calls for more multi-denominational schools. Their argument is that the roots of religious intolerance are not in schools but in homes. It cannot surely be argued that increased trans-denominational contacts would result in anything but good. It also seems obvious that children should learn the same version of history, just as they should learn the same version of mathematics. In spite of church leaders' direct opposition, it is likely that multi-denominational schools will increase in number in both parts of the island. At May 1991 the following inter-denominational schools were affiliated to the Educate Together Organisation — Dalkey, Bray, North Dublin, Sligo, Kilkenny, Cork, Ranelagh, Limerick, South City, North Bay, Dublin and North Kildare. Educate Together is committed to the support of schools which are multi-denominational, co-educational, child-centred in their approach, and democratically run with the active participation of parents tempered by due regard for the professional role of teachers. The Portuguese based Calouste Gulbenkian Foundation has given some financial aid to Educate Together.

Beltie (or the Belfast charitable trust for integrated education) reported in early 1989 that eight integrated schools had been established in Northern Ireland against enormous political and religious opposition. These schools operate on an equal allocation of places to children of the two main community groups with an equal allocation also of teaching posts and governorships. One Beltie officer predicted that by the early years of the twenty-first century, integrated schools would cater for one-third of the school going population with the remainder divided equally between Catholic and Protestant schools.

Training

FÁS, the Training and Employment Authority, came into being in the Republic on 1 January 1988. It is charged with the responsibility of operating training and employment programmes, as well as placement and guidance services. FÁS has a staff of about 2,000 and a budget to the order of IR£180 million. It was formed by amalgamating three organisations, one of which was AnCO, the Industrial Training Authority, established in 1967 with a view to raising the skills of Irish workers to higher standards.

Naturally, the primary responsibility for training remains with the individual firm, and, indeed, the individual employee has his or her own responsibility to attend to the development of skills and experience. Unemployed and redundant workers are offered facilities at centres throughout the country. A similar situation prevails in Northern Ireland.

Management Development

Again, members of management have an obligation to look to their own needs, to develop skills and to enhance experience. It is evident that many business enterprises have little or no commitment to METD (Management Education Training and Development). In the Republic, the principal providers of educational services in this area are FÁS, the Institute of Public Administration, and the Irish Management Institute. To look at where METD in Ireland was going and where it ought to go, the then Minister for Labour, Mr Bertie Ahern, established in 1987 an Advisory Committee on Management Training. In the course of a comprehensive report, the Committee emphasised the need to develop highly skilled managers, in order to retain and to attract further inward foreign investment, to develop the economy, and to increase the efficiency and productivity of the public sector.

It seems certain that in the years ahead Irish-owned

companies will spend more on METD than in the past, when their level was much less than that of foreign-owned firms. Similarly, while distribution companies may have different needs from manufacturing and service companies, are they so different that these latter companies should spend almost twice as much on METD? And older companies spend more than younger companies — presumably because appreciation of the importance of METD comes with age.

As in many other countries there is a growing interest in distance learning and open learning systems. Although Ireland cannot compare with the classic situations suitable for distance learning, such as the Canadian Northern Territory, the Australian Outback and the USSR, nevertheless, the facts remain that many small businesses in Ireland are owner-operated, and find distance learning facilities attractive. In open learning, knowledge is presented in a material form without the traditional trainer/trainee relationship. It is important, however, that there be a communications system available to listen to trainees cries for help. The National Distance Education Centre began its work in 1982 at NIHE Dublin (now Dublin City University).

Observers of the education and training scene include the Departments of Education in both parts of the island, the Department of Labour in the Republic and the Department of Economic Development in Northern Ireland, FÁS, the Institute of Public Administration and the Irish Management Institute in the Republic and the Northern Ireland Training Authority and Industrial Training Boards in Northern Ireland and a great many other organisations, such as Educate Together, the National Council for Educational Awards, the Higher Education Authority, the National Parents' Council and the teaching organisations. There is also the Irish Council for Overseas Students which is an independent organisation established in 1970 to look after the needs and promote the interests of overseas students and trainees in Ireland.

Milk Fun Day
The former Tánaiste and Minister for Defence Mr Brian Lenihan who, like six-year-old Karen Jackson from Mullingar, received a liver transplant, seen here promoting Milk Fun Day at Leinster House in March 1990.

DR GORDON S.G. BEVERIDGE

Born in St Andrew's, Fife in 1933. Married with three children. Educated at Inverness Royal Academy, University of Glasgow, Royal College of Science and Technology in Glasgow, University of Edinburgh and at University of Minnesota. Formerly assistant lecturer at University of Edinburgh, Harkness Fellow of the Commonwealth Fund of New York at University of Minnesota, visiting professor at University of Texas, lecturer at University of Edinburgh, senior lecturer and reader at Heriot-Watt University, professor of Chemical Engineering and head of department of Chemical and Process Engineering at Strathclyde. At present president and vice chancellor of Queen's University Belfast. Fellow of the Fellowship of Engineering, of the Royal Society of Edinburgh, of the Institution of Chemical Engineers and of the Royal Society of Arts. Companion of the British Institute of Management, member of the Smeatonian Society of Civil Engineers and of the Royal Irish Academy.

VANI KANT BOROOAH

Professor
Shore Road, Newtownabbey, Co. Antrim BT37 0QB
(0232) 365131
Born to Dev Kant and Priyalata Borooah (née Das) at Bombay, India on 27 December 1947. Educated at St Edmund's College Assam, University of Bombay and at University of Southampton. Married to Vedya Palsokar with one son. Formerly senior research officer Department of Applied Economics University of Cambridge, fellow Queen's University Cambridge and professor of applied economics University of Ulster at Jordanstown. At present head of Department of Applied Economics and Human Resource Management, University of Ulster at Jordanstown

CHARLES CARROLL

Programme Manager
Sandyford Road, Dublin 14
(01) 956911
Born to Michael and Sara Carroll (née McKay) at Cork on 2 March 1944. Educated at CBC Cork, UCC and TCD. Married to Helen Twomey with four children. Formerly marketing service manager Green Shield Trading Stamp Co UK and general manager Barry's Tea Co Cork. At present head of Management Development Irish Management Institute responsible for the strategic and operational direction of the IMI Management Development Programmes. Member of the Marketing Society.

AIDAN CLARKE

University Teacher
Arts Building, Trinity College, Dublin
(01) 772941
Born to Austin and Nora Clarke (née Walker) at Hartfordshire on 2 May

1933. Educated at Rathgar Junior School, Sandford Park, Dalton Tutorial, the High School and TCD. Married to Mary Hughes with four children. Formerly vice provost TCD. At present Erasmus Smith's Professor of Modern History TCD and president Royal Irish Academy. Author of numerous works on the history of early modern Ireland.

LESLIE ALBERT CLARKSON
Professor
Queen's University Belfast
(0232) 24513
Born to Leonard and Rosina Clarkson (née Downes) at London on 27 January 1933. Educated at Hornchurch Essex, S.E. Essex Technical School and University of Nottingham. Married with three daughters and two sons. Formerly lecturer in economic history, Melbourne University, University of Western Australia and Queen's University Belfast. At present professor of social history Queen's University Belfast. At some time president Irish Economic and Social History Society, council member British Economic History Society and general editor *Studies in Economic and Social History*. Member Royal Irish Academy.

CATHERINE M. COXHEAD
Chief Executive
Stranmillis College, Stranmillis Road, Belfast BT9
(0232) 3814114
Born to Stanley and Mary Worrall (née Marshall) in England in 1943. Educated at Birkenhead High School, Denmark Road High School Gloucester and Methodist College Belfast and at Girton College Cambridge. Married. Formerly held teaching posts in Methodist College Belfast, Kenya High School Nairobi, Solihill Sixth Form College, Hitts Road Sixth Form College Cambridge and at West London Institute of Higher Education. At present member of inspectorate Department of Education for Northern Ireland on secondment to Northern Ireland Curriculum Council. Associate Fellow of the Institute of Mathematics and its Applications.

ANNRAOI de PAOR
Professor
University College, Belfield, Dublin 4
(01) 693244
Born to Henry Joseph and Kathleen Maud de Paor (née O'Sullivan) at Waterford on 5 August 1940. Educated at De La Salle Waterford, St Canice's CBS, O'Connell CBS and UCD (BE, PhD and DSc degrees) and at University of California, Berkeley (MS degree). Married to Mary Karen Schnorenberg with two sons, Liam Ruan and Niall Eoin, and one daughter Eilín Niamh. Formerly assistant engineer RTE, lecturer University of Salford, lecturer at UCD, and professor of control engineering

University of Salford. At present professor of electrical engineering UCD. Member Clonliffe Harriers, Royal Irish Academy, fellow Institution of Engineers of Ireland and Institution of Electrical Engineers.

JOHN DAVID GEMMILL EVANS
University Professor
Queen's University Belfast
(0232) 245133
Born to Desmond and Babette Evans (née Gemill) at London on 27 August 1942. Educated at Orley Farm School, Harrow, St Edward's School Oxford and Queen's University Cambridge. Married to Rosemary Ellis. Formerly fellow of Sidney Sussex College Cambridge, and visiting professor, Duke University USA. At present dean of Faculty of Arts Queen's University Belfast, and chairman School of Philosophical and Anthropological Studies. Member Royal Irish Academy, Aristotelian Society, Cambridge Philological Society, Irish Astronomical Association, British Society for the History of Philosophy, Southern Association for Ancient Philosophy and American Society for Ancient Greek Philosophy. Author *Aristotle and Aristotle's Concept of Dialectic*, *Moral Philosophy and Contemporary Problems* (ed).

PATRICK GALVIN
Chief Executive
Kilbarry, Waterford
(051) 73311
Born to Patrick and Ann Galvin (née Callanan) at Cork on 24 February 1933. Educated at CBS Sullivan's Quay Cork and at Harvard Business School. Admitted to membership of Institution of Mechanical Engineers, Institute of Production Engineers and to fellowship of Institution of Engineers in Ireland. Fellow of the IMI. Honorary doctorate from UCD. Married to Mary Grant with one son and three daughters. Formerly operations director Guinness Ireland and chairman Guinness Dublin, Harp Ireland and Irish Ale Breweries. Project engineer, personnel director, executive director, managing director with Guinness. Appointed by Minister for Labour to board of management of University Industry Centre at UCD and president Federated Union of Employers. At present director Waterford Wedgwood plc and chief executive Waterford Crystal Ltd with responsibilities for crystal division worldwide. Director Hibernian Life Association and Gallaher (Dublin) Ltd.

DAVID WILLIAM HARKNESS
Historian
Queen's University Belfast BT7 1NN
(0232) 245133
Born to William Frederick Samuel and Rita Alice Harkness (née Barrett) on 30 October 1937. Educated at Campbell College Belfast, Corpus

Christi College Cambridge and at TCD. Widower of Hilary Katherine Margaret Land with one son and two daughters. Formerly lecturer University of Kent, professor Queen's University Belfast, member Irish Committee of Historical Sciences, board of trustees Ulster Folk and Transport Museum, and BBC General Advisory Council. At present professor of modern history at Queen's University Belfast.

JOHN HEYWOOD
Educationalist
Trinity College, Dublin 2
(01) 772941

Born at Catherham, England on 5 February 1930. Educated at Lancaster University (M.Litt) and at TCD (MA Litt.D). Also LCP, FCP, FRAS, FBIM and Sen.MIEE. Married to Pauline Cook with three sons and two daughters. Formerly Merchant Navy radio officer, radio engineer in industry, assistant lecturer on radio, senior research fellow in technical education Birmingham College of Advanced Technology, senior lecturer in education Enfield College of Technology, Leverhulme senior research fellow and lecturer in higher education University of Lancaster, lecturer industrial studies University of Liverpool, director of research unit for Government Committee on Secondary Examinations in Ireland and research associate professor TCD. At present professor and head of Department of Teacher Education TCD. Awarded Premium of the education science and technology division of the IEE in 1982. Editor *International Journal of Technology & Design Education*.

BRENDAN KENNELLY
Professor
Trinity College, Dublin 2
(01) 772941

Born to Timothy and Bridget Kennelly (née Ahern) at Ballylongford on 17 April 1936. Educated at TCD and at Leeds University. Separated. One daughter. Formerly held a number of posts at TCD and Columbia University, New York. At present professor of modern literature at TCD. Publications include poetry and novels. Fellow of TCD.

ARTHUR EDWARD KINGSTON
Dean of Faculty
University Road, Belfast BT7 1NN
(0232) 245133

Born to Arthur and Henrietta Kingston (née Duff) at Armagh on 18 February 1936. Educated at Armstrong School and Royal School Armagh and at Queen's University Belfast. Married to Helen McCann with one son and one daughter. Formerly lecturer University of Liverpool and visiting fellow University of Colorado, Boulder, USA. At present dean of Faculty of Science, director of School of Mathematics and Physics, and professor of Theoretical Atomic Physics, all at Queen's University

Belfast. Fellow of the Institute of Physics, Royal Astronomical Society and member Royal Irish Academy.

MSGR MÍCEÁL LEDWITH
College President
Maynooth, Co. Kildare
(01) 6285236
Born to Gerald and Margaret Ledwith (née Rossiter) at Taghmon, Wexford in 1942. Educated at Taghmon and Traceystown Wexford, St Peter's College Wexford, Maynooth College, NUI, and on various short term courses at European universities. Formerly chairman Committee of Heads of Irish Universities and editor *Irish Theological Quarterly*. At present president Maynooth College, pro-vice-chancellor NUI, member International Theological Commission and secretary Irish Inter-Church Conference. Member National Library of Ireland Society.

JOHN JOSEPH LEE
Professor
University College Cork
(021) 276871
Born to Thomas and Catherine Lee (née Burke) at Tralee on 9 July 1942. Educated at NS Castlegregory and Ballinasloe, Franciscan College Gormanstown, UCD, Peterhouse Cambridge and Institute for European History, Mainz. Married to Anne Mitchell with three children. Formerly Fellow of Peterhouse Cambridge, dean of arts and vice president UCC. At present professor of Modern History UCC and chairman of Irish Fulbright Commission. Visiting Mellon Professor University of Pittsburgh, visiting professor European University Florence, distinguished visiting professor University of Texas at Austin and Eisenhower Fellow. Member Royal Irish Academy. Awarded James S. Donnelly Sr Prize of American Conference for Irish Studies and Irish Life/ *Sunday Independent* Arts Award.

DONALDSON McCLOY
Professor
Shore Road, Newtownabbey, Co. Antrim
(0232) 365131
Born to Donaldson and Jane McCloy (née Kane) at Belfast on 12 August 1934. Educated at Belfast Model, Belfast Royal Academy, Queen's University Belfast and Imperial College of Science and Technology. Married to Johanna Logan (née Fletcher) with three sons. Formerly visiting professor Georgia Institute of Technology, head of department of Aeronautical Engineering Queen's University, head of School of Mechanical and Industrial Engineering Ulster Polytechnic, dean of Faculty of Technology Ulster Polytechnic, chairman Northern Ireland Low Cost Automation Centre, chairman Polytechnic Innovation and Resource

Centre, member steering group on merger of the new University of Ulster and Ulster Polytechnic, chairman university computer policy/planning committee, and member of Butler committee on research selectivity, chairman Northern Ireland Science and Technology Regional Organisation, chairman 'O' level technology GCE panel, head of British delegation to Soviet Union to study vocational training, chairman Northern Ireland Open Learning Centre, member of council for National Academic Awards, member Northern Ireland Technology Board and member Engineering Board of Studies, NCEA. At present director of Belfast Institute of Further and Higher Education and chairman of Northern Ireland Curriculum Council.

PATRICK MASTERSON
University President
Belfield, Dublin 4
(01) 693244
Born to Laurence and Violet Masterson (née Hayes) at Dublin on 19 October 1936. Educated at Belvedere College, Castleknock College and UCD and at University of Louvain. Married to Frances Lenehan with one son and three daughters. Formerly with Department of Metaphysics UCD, professor in Faculties of Arts, Philosophy and Sociology UCD, Dean of Faculty of Philosophy and Sociology UCD, and registrar UCD. Also visiting lecturer St Patrick's Training College Dublin, St Patrick's College Maynooth, external examiner Queen's University Belfast, University of Bristol and University of Lancaster. Directed PhD research at European University Institute, Florence. Member Higher Education Authority, board of Mater Hospital and St Vincent's Hospital, and member of Academic Council of Irish School of Ecumenics. At present president UCD, member of governing body and Senate of NUI, member high council of European University Institute, Florence and member Royal Irish Academy. Has had a number of books and contributions to books published.

THOMAS NOEL MITCHELL
University Professor
Trinity College, Dublin 2
(01) 772941
Born to Patrick and Margaret Mitchell (née O'Reilly) at Castlebar on 7 December 1939. Educated at Errew Monastery Castlebar, St Nathy's College Ballaghadereen, UCG and at Cornell University. Married to Lynn Susan Hunter with three sons and one daughter. Formerly associate professor and professor of classics Swarthmore College and professor of Latin TCD. At present Provost TCD. Author of three books, *Cicero, The Ascending Years*, *Cicero, Verrines 11.1* and *Cicero, the Senior Statesman*. Awarded research fellowship by American Council of Learned Societies. Elected fellow of TCD and senior vice president Royal Irish Academy.

Training Summit

Photograph shows (left to right) Mr Raymond O'Connor, director CERT, Ms Ann Williams, chief executive Training and Employment Agency, N. Ireland and Mr Duncan Rutter, chief executive of the Hotel and Catering Company, London (Britain) at the Tripartite Meeting on 3 October 1990.

MÁIRE F. MULCAHY
Professor
University College Cork
(021) 276871
Born to John J. and Nan McHenry (née Rice) at Cork on 10 May 1937. Educated at Glasheen NS, St Angela's and Scoil Mhuire Cork, UCC and University of Manchester. Married to Noel Mulcahy with one daughter. Formerly held various academic posts in Zoology, assistant, lecturer, statutory lecturer, associate professor and board member IIRS. At present professor of Zoology, vice president UCC, member of governing body UCC and of the senate NUI. Member Institute of Biology, and Higher Education Authority. Associate member Sunday's Well Tennis Club, member An Taisce, Widows' Association, Cork Arts, Cork Civic Trust, UCC Graduates' Association and Cork Orchestral Society. Awarded Person of Year 1978.

DR COLM Ó hEOCHA
University President
University College Galway
(091) 24411
Born to Séamus and Máiréad Ó hEocha (née Drohan) at Dungarvan on 19 September 1926. Educated at Coláiste na Rinne, CBS Dungarvan, Coláiste Íosagán Baile Mhúirne, UCG, University of California (Scripps Institution of Oceanography). Married to Daiden Fahy with two sons, Séamus and Colm MacDara, and four daughters, Nessa, Orla, Aedin and Aislinn. Formerly lecturer in chemistry UCG, research associate University of Minnesota, and professor of biochemistry at UCG. Chairman New Ireland Forum. At present president UCG, vice chancellor NUI, member administrative board of International Association of Universities, and chairman Arts Council. Decorated by French Government and by the President of Italy, and conferred with honorary LL.D degrees by Queen's University Belfast and by TCD. Honorary fellow of Institution of Engineers of Ireland and of Institute of Chemistry of Ireland.

MAURICE O'GRADY
Institute Director
Sandyford Road, Dublin 16
(01) 956911
Born to James and Sheila O'Grady (née McDowell) at Dublin on 9 January 1937. Educated at Enfield NS, CBS Dún Laoghaire, CBC Monkstown, St Mary's College Dundalk, Mount St Mary's Dublin and TCD/Irish Management Institute whence he graduated with MSc (Mgmt) degree. Married to Gobnait Nic Aongusa with two sons and two daughters. Formerly general manager Nixdorf Computers Ltd. At present director general Irish Management Institute. Member Fitzwilliam Lawn Tennis Club.

DANIEL O'HARE
University President
Dublin City University, Dublin 9
(01) 7045000
Born to Nicholas and Roseanne O'Hare (née Ward) at Dundalk on 5 September 1942. Educated at CBS Dundalk, at UCG (BSc and MSc) and at St Andrew's University Scotland (PhD). Married to Sheelagh Kenny with three sons, Michael, Nicholas and Domhnall, and one daughter, Fiona. Formerly research associate and assistant professor at Michigan State University, research fellow at University of Southampton, principal Letterkenny Regional Technical College, and principal Waterford Regional Technical College. At present president Dublin City University. Chairman National Distance Education Council and Engineering Industry Training Committee, fellow Irish Management Institute, member of board of EOLAS (Irish Science and Technology Agency), Royal Dublin Society, Association for Institutional Research, Society for College and University Planning, International Association of University Presidents, Conference of Rectors, Presidents and Vice Chancellors of European Universities (CRE). Member Kildare Street and University Club and Castleknock Lawn Tennis Club.

J. AIDAN O'REILLY
University Professor
Shore Road, Newtownabbey, Co. Antrim
(0232) 365131
Born to Michael and Josephine O'Reilly (née Benson) at Dublin on 13 April 1937. Educated at Keelogues, Ballyvarry, St Jarlath's College Tuam, UCD, and Graduate School of Business, University of Chicago. Married to Rita Walsh with one son, Barry, and three daughters, Fiona, Jan-Claire and Gráinne. Formerly senior lecturer in Polytechnic of North London and dean of Faculty of Business and Management at the University of Ulster, director of the Labour Relations Agency and member of the board of the Local Enterprise Development Unit and consultant International Trade Centre, United Nations, Geneva. At present pro-vice-chancellor and provost, Coleraine Campus, University of Ulster, director of Coleraine Enterprise Agency and some Northern Ireland companies.

PROFESSOR TREVOR ARTHUR SMITH
University Vice Chancellor
Coleraine, Co. Londonderry BT 52 1SA
(0265) 44141
Born to Arthur James and Vera Gladys Smith (née Cross) in London on 14 June 1937. Educated at Rutland House Preparatory School, Hounslow College/Chiswick Polytechnic and at London School of Economics. Married to Julia Donnithorne (née Bullock) with two sons and one daughter. Formerly professor of Political Studies in University of

London, senior vice principal Queen Mary and Westfield College and vice chairman Tower Hamlets District Health Authority. At present vice chancellor University of Ulster, chairman Joseph Rowntree Reform Trust Ltd, president Political Studies Association of UK, vice president Patients' Association of UK, director Gerald Duckworth and Co Ltd and of Bell Educational Trust. Fellow Royal Historical Society and member Reform Club.

THOMAS DAVID SPEARMAN
University Professor
Trinity College, Dublin 2
(01) 772941
Born to Thomas and Elizabeth Alexandra Spearman (née Leadbeater) at Dublin on 25 March 1937. Educated at Greenlawns NS, Mountjoy School and TCD, and at St John's College, Cambridge University. Married to Juanita Roberta (née Smale) with one son, Patrick, and two daughters, Kate and Anna. Formerly lecturer in theoretical physics at the University of Durham, bursar of TCD, chairman of the Applied Research and Consultancy Group, treasurer Royal Irish Academy, chairman Mount Temple Comprehensive School, board member St Patrick's Hospital, Tallaght Hospital, and School of Theoretical Physics of the Dublin Institute of Advanced Studies, governor Church of Ireland College of Education, and council member European Physical Society. At present professor of natural philosophy and head of department of Applied Mathematics TCD, member Royal Irish Academy, fellow of TCD, chairman board of Douglas Hyde Gallery, member representative body Church of Ireland, trustee of Trustee Savings Bank Dublin, trustee Dalkey School Project, vice president European Science Foundation and member European Space Science Committee.

JOHN TURPIN
College Director
100 Thomas Street, Dublin 8
(01) 711377
Born to Thomas and Mary Turpin at Dublin on 23 August 1945. Educated at Willow Park, Blackrock College, UCD and the Courtauld Institute of Art of London University where he received masters and doctors degrees. Married to Anne Patricia Tuck with one son and two daughters. Formerly tutor for several colleges of Cambridge University, for the Open University and lecturer at schools of art in Cambridge and Cheltenham. Professor of History of Art at the National College of Art and Design. At present director of the National College of Art and Design. Former chairman Association of Irish Art Historians, currently member National Council for Educational Awards, executive member of the European League of the Institutes of the Arts, membre titulaire for Ireland on the Comité International d'Histoire de l'Art. Has published extensively on the history of Irish art and art education.

DR EDWARD M. WALSH

University President
Plassey Park, Limerick
Born to Michael and Ita Walsh (née Leonard) at Cork on 3 December 1939. Studied electrical engineering at UCC, and nuclear engineering and electrical engineering at Iowa State University. Married to Stephanie Barrett with three sons and one daughter. Formerly associate professor and assistant professor Iowa State University, research associate US Atomic Energy Commission Laboratory, Ames Iowa, founding director Energy Research Group Programme and associate professor, both at Virginia National Microelectronics Applications Centre Ltd, senate member of NUI and consultant with Advanced Technology Consultants Corporation US and with American Power Company. At present founding president of University of Limerick, chairman Committee of Heads of Irish Universities, vice president Europe of the International Association of University Presidents, founding director University of Limerick Foundation, founding member Japan-Europe, partnership, founding chairman National Self-Portrait Collection of Ireland, founding director Irish American Partnership, Irish Peace Institute and Craggaunowen Project, director Shannon Development Co Ltd, council member Institute of European Affairs, representative of the International Association of University Presidents to the United Nations, Geneva. Fellow of Royal Society of the Arts, Institution of Electrical Engineers, Institute of Electrical and Electronic Engineers, American Nuclear Society, and Association for Institutional Research.

WILLIAM EDWARD WATTS

University Professor
University of Ulster, Coleraine
(0265) 44141
Born to William and Marion Watts (née Millar) at Stonehouse, Scotland on 23 June 1936. Educated at University of Strathclyde. Married to Janet McLeod. Formerly lecturer in chemistry at University of Strathclyde. At present professor of chemistry and acting dean of Faculty of Science and Technology at University of Ulster. Holds BSc, PhD and DSc degrees. Fellow of the Royal Society of Arts, the Royal Society of Chemistry, the Royal Society of Edinburgh and member of the Royal Irish Academy.

JOHN BRIAN WEIR

Headmaster
St Patrick's Close, Dublin 8
(01) 543388
Born to Horace and Dorothy Weir (née Wright) at Tinahely, Co. Wicklow on 3 December 1928. Educated at Kilcommon School Tinahely, Wesley College and TCD. Married to Mabel Carnew. Formerly vice principal St Patrick's Cathedral Grammar School, honorary treasurer

Irish Schoolmasters' Association, first honorary treasurer Association of Geography Teachers in Ireland, and president Irish School Masters' Association. At present headmaster St Patrick's Cathedral Grammar School. Member Wesley College OBU, Old Wesley RFC, Association of Geography Teachers of Ireland and Irish School Masters' Association.

FRANZ CARL WINKELMANN
Chartered Accountant
Trinity College, Dublin 2
(01) 772941

Born to Franz and Anna Winkelmann at Aussig Czechoslovakia on 12 February 1927. Educated at Sandford Park School and TCD. Admitted to membership and later fellowship of Institute of Chartered Accountants in Ireland. Married to Carmel Aldritt with two sons and one daughter. At present treasurer TCD, and director Ardagh plc, Consolidated Insurance Brokers Ltd, Anglo-Irish Bank Corporation plc, GAM Fund Management Ltd, and member committee of management of Irish Pension Fund Property Unit Trust. Member National, Royal Irish, Royal St George and Howth Yacht Clubs, Irish Cruising Club, Rotary Club of Dublin, and Kildare Street and University Club.

Academic Enterprise
Seen at the presentation of the Academic Enterprise Awards were John McNally, director Ulster Bank, Jim McBride, chief executive Eolas, Kieran McGowan, chief executive IDA and Mrs Mary O'Rourke, then Minister for Education.

Index